SAUL BELLOW

IN THE 1980s

SAUL BELLOW
IN THE 1980ˢ

A COLLECTION OF CRITICAL ESSAYS

Edited By
Gloria L. Cronin and L.H. Goldman

Michigan State University Press
East Lansing, Michigan
1989

All Michigan State University Press books are produced on paper which meets the requirements of American National Standard of Information Sciences—Permanence of paper
for printed materials ANSI 239.48-1984

Michigan State University Press
East Lansing, Michigan 48823-5202

Printed in the United States of America

Library of Congress Cataloging-in-Publication Data

Saul Bellow in the 1980s: a collection of critical essays/editors, Gloria L. Cronin, L. H.
Goldman.
    p.   cm.
  Includes bibliographies and index.
  ISBN 0-87013-270-9
  1. Bellow, Saul—Criticism and interpretation. I. Cronin, Gloria L., 1947–   .
II. Goldman, L. H. (Liela H.)
PS3503.E4488Z8475   1989
813′.52—dc20   89-42698
                                                            CIP

Contents

Permissions

Acknowledgement is hereby made to publishers, periodicals, and authors for permissions to reprint the following:

"Bellow's Sixth Sense: The Sense of History," by Judie Newman. Reprinted with permission from *Canadian Review of American Studies* 13, 1 (1982). Copyright 1982 by *Canadian Review of American Studies.*

"Bellow and Freud," by Daniel Fuchs. Reprinted with permission from *Studies in the Literary Imagination* 17, 2 (1984), edited by Eugene Hollahan. Copyright 1984, Department of English, Georgia State University.

"Saul Bellow and the Philosophy of Judaism," by L. H. Goldman. Reprinted with permission from *Studies in the Literary Imagination* 17, 2 (1984), edited by Eugene Hollahan. Copyright 1984, Department of English, Georgia State University.

"Bellow and English Romanticism," by Allan Chavkin. Reprinted with permission from *Studies in the Literary Imagination* 17, 2 (1984), edited by Eugene Hollahan. Copyright 1984, Department of English, Georgia State University.

"The Symbolic Function of the Pastoral in Saul Bellow's Novels," by Molly Stark Wieting. Reprinted by permission from *The Southern Quarterly* 16 (1977–78).

"Women in Saul Bellow's Novels," by Ada Aharoni. Reprinted with permission from *Studies in American Jewish Literature* 3 (1983). Copyright 1983, Kent State University Press. Updated by the author.

"Saul Bellow and the Lost Cause of Character," by H. Porter Abbott. Reprinted with permission from *Novel: A Forum on Fiction* 13, 3 (Spring 1980). Copyright 1980 by Novel Corp.

"Saul Bellow and the University as Villain," by Ben Siegel. Reprinted by permission of Associated University Presses.

"The Dialectic of Hero and Anti-Hero in *Rameau's Nephew and Dangling Man*," by Jo Brans. Reprinted with permission from *Studies in the Novel* 16, 4 (Winter 1984).

"Bellow's More-or-Less Human Bestiaries: *Augie March* and *Henderson the Rain King*," by Michael O. Bellamy. Reprinted with permission from *The Ball State University Forum* 23, 1 (1982).

"*Henderson the Rain King:* A Parodic Exposé of the Modern Novel," by Gloria L. Cronin. Reprinted with permission from *Arizona Quarterly* 39, 2 (Autumn 1983). Copyright 1983 by *Arizona Quarterly*.

"White Man's Black Man: Three Views," by Mariann Russell. Reprinted from *CLA Journal* 17 (1973) by permission of the College Language Association.

"The World as Will and Idea: A Comparative Study of *An American Dream* and *Mr. Sammler's Planet*," by Susan Glickman. Reprinted with permission from *Modern Fiction Studies* 28, 4 (Winter 1982–83). Copyright 1983 by Purdue Research Foundation, West Lafayette, Indiana 47907.

"Two Different Speeches: Mystery and Knowledge in *Mr. Sammler's Planet*," by Ellen Pifer. Reprinted with permission from *Mosaic* 18, 2 (Spring 1985).

"A *Cri de Coeur:* The Inner Reality of Saul Bellow's *The Dean's December*," by Matthew C. Roudané. Reprinted with permission from *Studies in the Humanities* 11, 2 (December 1984). Copyright 1984 by Indiana University of Pennsylvania.

"Toward a Language Irresistible: Saul Bellow and the Romance of Poetry," by Michael G. Yetman. Reprinted with permission from *Papers on Language and Literature* 22, 4 (1986). Copyright 1986 by Southern Illinois University.

"The Religious Vision of *More Die of Heartbreak*," by Stephen L. Tanner. Reprinted with author's permission.

"The Dean Who Came In from the Cold: Saul Bellow's America of the 1980's," by Gerhard Bach. Reprinted with permission of *Studies in American Jewish Literature*, 8, 1 (Spring 1989), 104–114. Copyright 1989 by the Kent State University Press.

Acknowledgments

The editors wish to give thanks and appreciation to the following: the contributors and the scholarly journals who granted us permission to reprint these essays; editorial assistants Joni Clark and Jill Terry for their valuable help; computer specialist Barbara Carlson who generously helped prepare the manuscript; and the Michigan State University Press for their expertise in publishing it.

Introduction

Saul Bellow's stature in postwar American letters can only be compared to that of Hemingway or Faulkner earlier in this century. A Nobel Laureate and winner of numerous prestigious fiction awards, Bellow has commanded serious attention from a large range of reviewers and critics at home and abroad for the last forty years.

The first major wave of scholarly interest in Bellow occurred approximately between 1966–74 approximately, producing major books by Brigitte Scheer-Schäzler (1965), Keith Opdahl (1967), Pierre Dommerges (1967), Irving Malin (1967, 1969), Robert Detweiler (1968), John J. Clayton (1968), David D. Galloway (1970), Nathan Scott (1973), Sarah Blacher Cohen (1974), M. Gilbert Porter (1974), and Earl Rovit (1974, 1975). Though each study is focused differently, all share in common a celebration of Saul Bellow as humanist and contemporary neo-transcendentalist. These writers performed the extremely valuable function of placing Bellow in the contemporary scene and broadly distinguishing the nature of his thematic concerns, stylistic techniques, and peculiarly affirmative *menschlichkeit* values. Most of these studies represent sophisticated and useful approaches to the Bellow text, and many hint at an array of sources and structures which would have to be unraveled by later critics.

Not surprisingly then, critics like Peter Bischoff (1975), Robert Kegan (1976), Tony Tanner (1978), Yuzaburo Shibuya (1978), Chirantan Kulshrestha (1978), Edmund Schraepen (1978), and Stanley Trachtenberg (1979), developed many of the avenues of inquiry hinted at in these works, yet though they all amplified the earlier works they only slightly modified the "orthodox" vision of Bellow as humanist and contemporary "yea-sayer."

With the advent of the 1980's, a third wave of critical interest produced a spate of new books on Bellow which opened many new avenues of

1

approach. Joseph McCadden (1980), an American graduate student, reproduced his dissertation to provide the first book-length study of Bellow's treatment of women; Mark Harris (1980), a noted American biographer, published the results of his abortive attempt to produce a Bellow biography; Malcolm Bradbury (1982), a British scholar, located Bellow within the historiography of modernism; Frenchman Claude Levy (1983) wrote a structuralist analysis of Bellow's narrative strategies; while L. H. Goldman (1983), an Orthodox American Jew, produced a thorough treatment of Bellow's philosophical debt to Judaism; Jan Bakker, the Dutch critic, produced an exhaustive comparative study of Hemingway and Bellow; Jeanne Braham (1984), American scholar, traced the nineteenth-century American influences on Bellow; Judie Newman (1984), a British scholar, documented his responses to twentieth-century history and historiography; while Dan Fuchs (1984), another American scholar, produced the first full-length textual study of the novels, being one of the few scholars with access to Bellow's manuscripts; and most recently Jonathan Wilson (1985), also an American scholar, expressed his frustration with the orthodox image of Bellow the humanist, by trying to construe Bellow as a thorough-going nihilist.

What we notice in these books is that they all move beyond Bellow's humanism to the particulars that go into making Bellow the kind of author he is. It is this interest in specific areas of concentration, as well as the courage to be distinctive, that make this second wave so much more interesting.

This present volume of essays, coming as it does at the end of the 1980's, rounds out the picture of the new topics of investigation undertaken by critics during this decade of renewed critical interest in Bellow. The topics are even more distinctive, more provocative, and more exciting. We have arranged this book in two sections, (1) General Essays and (2) Specialized Essays providing a novel by novel analysis. This should aid students and researchers who wish to gain a general overview, as well as those hoping for enlightenment with a specific work. What follows will be a series of descriptions of the articles, designed both to place each author's essay in the context of Bellow criticism and to illuminate its particular contribution. Comments appear in the order in which the articles appear in the Table of Contents.

General Essays

Previous critics like John J. Clayton, Brigitte Scheer-Schäzler, Gilbert Porter, Keith Opdahl, and Tony Tanner have all resisted the idea that a sense of history is central to Bellow's novels. In their critical view it is the sense of the transcendent that is imminent, with literal detail merely being employed in its service. British critics Malcom Bradbury and Judie Newman differ sharply with this largely American critical tradition. In "Bellow's Sixth Sense of History," Newman provides a novel-by-novel treatment which describes the two polar entities posited by the Bellow novel as "chaos" and "chronos." Each of the novels, and even the very first of the short stories, echo the "tension[s] between the timeless and the timebound." This essay, therefore, seeks to establish a historical interpretation of the fiction showing how the historical content of Bellow's work, far from being ancillary, does enter the novels function- ally, organizing their structure, and informing their thematic concerns. Newman's major contribution to Bellow criticism is the assertion that Bellow's novels systematically explore different approaches to history, and different retreats from it—"history as nightmare, as tragedy, as farce, as black comedy; the retreat into myth or into the heightened presence of the crisis mentality." The novels also explore the dangers of "pop" or instant history, and those dangers of history governed by stereotypi- cal moral responses.

Fuchs' essay "Bellow and Freud" bears a parallel relationship to Newman's work since he, too, is discussing the subject of Modernism in the Bellow novel, albeit from a philosophical and historiographical perspective. Fuchs' article is the first of several mappings of Bellow's cri- tique of modernism. This subject has been dealt with only tangentially by earlier critics. Though not an exhaustive treatment of Bellow and Modernism, this article provides the definitive treatment of Bellow's rela- tionship to Freudian thought, which system, Fuchs' argues persuasively, represents "a prime instance of modernism" against which Bellow has mounted a life-long sustained critique. Fuchs' study illustrates Bellow's ongoing quarrel with a host of Freudian constructs. He draws convinc- ing evidence from biography, the essays and the fiction, as well as his personal acquaintance with Bellow, to document Bellow's systematic "deconstruction" of Freudian modes of thought.

Also definitive is Goldman's informed treatment of the undergird- ing influence of the philosophy of Judaism in the Bellow canon. There has been undisputed agreement for several decades concerning Bellow's debt to and championing of Western humanism, but, ironically, the ef- forts of previous critics have documented only the Greek, European, and Christian sources of his humanistic outlook. Goldman corrects this par- tial view by providing the missing, and perhaps prior, source in a specifically Jewish cultural and religious tradition. She also suggests that for Bellow writing is a way of coming closer to God, that in his later works there are many overt expressions of covenant Judaism, thus making these works a form of survivor literature.

Tracing yet another source of Bellow's thinking, Allan Chavkin documents Bellow's debt to the English romantics, characterizing Bellow as a prodigious reader and the foremost intellectual among twentieth-century writers. Chavkin first acknowledges the multitude of modern philosophical sources Bellow has drawn upon, and then traces his allegiance to the older tradition of early nineteenth-century English romanticism. Critical formulations written before the mid-seventies concentrated on Bellow's preoccupation with transcendence, affirmations of human potential, humanism, belief in intuition and the realm of enlightenment which lies beyond the rational intellect. Major early critics like Clayton, Opdahl, Tanner, Scheer-Schäzler, Porter, and others, while being perfectly aware of Bellow's connection with the English romantics, mainly described its general translation into the value structure of the fiction, and left it for someone like Chavkin to make the connection explicit. In this study Chavkin asserts that though Bellow so thoroughly assimilates and makes his own whatever sources he uses, his romantic sensibility is largely the result of deliberate borrowing from early nineteenth-century English Romantics.

Related in treatment to Chavkin's essay is Weiting's identification of Bellow's use of the pastoral mode in the novels. While previously critics have focused quite exhaustively on Bellow's metaphorical and literal uses of a Jewish-urban milieu—usually that of New York or Chicago—Weiting points out that in each of the novels "one finds also a corresponding pastoral element, an excursion, either physical or mental, to an environment that is free from the clutter and chaos of the protagonist's urban environment. Whereas their flights to nature have attracted attention in individual novels, they have been virtually ignored as a pervasive pattern that informs a cohesive motif in Bellow's fiction."

The application of feminist theory and methods to the Bellow canon surprisingly begins as late as 1979 and 1980 with the appearance of dissertations and articles by such people as Louana L. Peontek, Nantana Buranaron, Esther Marie Mackintosh, Joseph McCadden, Sherry Levy Reiner, and Judith Scheffler. Of these only McCadden's study, photo-reproduced from his dissertation, appears in book form. With the appearance of the new gender study, Aharoni departs [from the generation of 1980's early feminist critics] who almost exclusively pursued the "images of women" approach, and nearly all of whom failed to distinguish between Bellow's misogyny and that of his protagonists. In the 1960's critics like Leslie Fiedler and John J. Clayton had both lamented

that Bellow's work was singularly lacking in real or vivid female characters. Irving Malin had also chastised both Bellow and his critics: "I am
troubled by the absence of any lengthy discussion of Bellow's women.
Critics assert they are stylized and unreal. But these adjectives are not
enough to explain the complexity of recurring stereotyped roles . . . . It
is time for someone to write an entire essay on all the women."

Aharoni seems to have taken seriously Malin's injunction—particularly
with regard to his hint of the complexity of the women characters in
the novel. She undertakes to reexamine and recover the range of female
characters from a less ideologically radical perspective and discovers:
"Bellow's artistic technique imposes some limitations on his portrayal
of women characters, as we perceive them through the minds of his male
protagonists who often overshadow them; and that because narrators
are men generally going through various existential crises, the female
characters in comparison often do not have the same depth of emotional, moral, and intellectual complexity as the heroes or anti-heroes. Furthermore, we sometimes get the impression that Bellow is more interested
in illuminating certain societal attitudes to women rather than in fully
delineating their characters. However, having said that, the fact remains
that Bellow through his 45 years of writing . . . has given us a vast and
rich gallery of convincing and vivid women of all kinds."

Aharoni accumulates evidence for this thesis by limiting her analysis
to a few representative female characters who appear at different periods of his writing, and who reveal not only Bellow's treatment of the
characterization of women, but the growth and development in his depiction of the female situation as it appears in Bellow's works.

While Aharoni deals with Bellow's attempts to depict women characters in the novels, Abbott deals more broadly with Bellow's commitment
to "character," male and female, in the context of the twentieth-century
critical debate concerning the questionable viability of the "novel of
characters" (Alain Robbe-Grillet). Whereas Abbott argues that for Bellow
"character" is very much a live issue, not a strategy to be dropped, he
agrees with Bellow that the passing of the apogee of the individual has
removed easy assumptions about the power and centrality of the "individual" in our age and, subsequently, in the novel. "Character has become a subject for discussion among humanists," he asserts. "One can
no longer take the existence of character for granted." Abbott's most
important point is that Bellow's novelistic philosophy of character takes
a backwards turn after the very modern treatment of the problematics
of character in his first novel.

An entirely new thematic topic of interest in Bellow criticism appeared
in the 1980's with the advent of Ben Siegel's intensive treatment of

Bellow's attitudes about and relationship to modern academe. Siegel observes that like many other American novelists and poets, Bellow blames it for much of what is wrong with this nation's culture, especially its literary culture. Siegel begins with the assertion that almost no other subject stirs Bellow with as much rancor and resentment as the subject of the modern university. His article is an exhaustive analysis of Bellow's numerous fictional and other recorded statements about the state of the modern university, the American education system, the state of modern culture, and the state of the arts. It takes on particular relevance with the publication of Bellow's "Introduction" to Bloom's *The Closing of the American Mind* in 1987.

Specialized Essays

The essays on individual works presented herein deal mostly with issues that are in some way unique: either they consider areas that have been neglected heretofore, or they deal with a particular subject in an innovative fashion.

Bellow's early novels, specifically *Dangling Man* and *The Victim,* have received very little critical attention in the first twenty five years after their appearance. It is only in the 1970's and 1980's that scholars have begun to take these works seriously and have viewed them as an integral part of the Bellow canon rather than dismissing them as a "Master's" or "Ph.D. thesis" (as Bellow would have it). These later critics search for early influences on Bellow in order to discern the shape his philosophical world view was taking. While previous scholars have recognized the Conradian influence on Bellow's early works—an influence Bellow himself acknowledges in his Nobel Prize speech—Jo Brans' contribution in "The Dialectic of Hero and Anti-Hero in *Rameau's Nephew* and *Dangling Man,*" is in locating a much earlier source—that of the eighteenth century French writer Diderot. Brans claims that Diderot's work had great impact on Bellow's initial novel, the device of the dialectic of hero and anti-hero suggesting alternate modes of thought processes and behavior created by Diderot and recreated by Bellow in *Dangling Man,* but with the refinement of a single character. For both Diderot and Bellow both aspects are necessary. They are both visible in the world and appear in the individual psyche as well. The individual, ultimately, has to choose his way of life.

Critics have recognized that the concern for what it is to be human is the central preoccupation of Bellow's novels. Michael Bellamy's contribution to this discussion in "Bellow's More-Or-Less Human Bestiaries: *Augie March* and *Henderson the Rain King,*" is in pointing out that the animal kingdom in these two works function as a locus for man's humanity. He is more than a beast yet a member of the animal kingdom "in terms of the way he interacts with his fellow creatures." When man seeks to transcend his nature, the animals he comes in contact with remind him of his own "creaturehood" and his place in the scheme of things. For Bellamy, the inordinate use of animals in these two novels indicates Bellow's belief in "man's immanence within nature."

Henderson the Rain King has always been a favorite of students and scholars alike. It is humorous; it is different (with its obnoxious-yet-ultimately-endearing Gentile protagonist); and it lends itself to a variety of literary, theological, and metaphysical interpretations. Recent criticism, as already stated, concerns itself with Bellow's anti-Modernist stance. Gloria L. Cronin, in a vigorously written article entitled, *"Henderson the Rain King:* a Parodic Exposé of the Modern Novel," traces Bellow's critical posture to ideas formulated in his essays and then indicates how these ideas work in *Henderson the Rain King.* Through the use of parody, Bellow exposes the "absurdities of absurdism, the banalities of historicist thinking, and the ignominy of post-modern sewer searching." Bellow's burlesque, however, is functional: "to restore moderation and good sense to the twentieth-century novel which . . . has lost its ability to assess truthfully the possibilities of life."

Although there are not many black characters in Bellow's works, the few that there are have received little meaningful attention by Bellow critics. An excellent early essay is Mariann Russell's "White Man's Black Man: Three Views." She deals with the black figure in *Mr. Sammler's Planet,* but since her approach is a comparative study of three American authors, she doesn't go into the depth that is really needed. Her essay is significant, nevertheless, and makes an important statement: the black man is not seen as an individual but is used by the three authors, Bellow included, in the Conradian sense, as an aspect of the protagonist. He becomes "a convenient metaphor for the disturbing elements in white society and is, in the last analysis, not an image of black culture, but a mirror image of the prevailing white culture." Russell's essay also points to the need for further examination of this subject.

Mr. Sammler's Planet is Bellow's only novel that deals directly with the Holocaust, and critics have recognized that its major concern is human survival in light of this most horrendous crime. Susan Glickman, in "The World as Will and Idea: A Comparative Study of *An American Dream* and *Mr. Sammler's Planet,"* examines this problem but focuses on survival in America since that is the locus of Artur Sammler's present residence. She perceives a similarity in thematic and narrative strategies to Norman Mailer's novel and suggests that Bellow, who has a penchant for parodying and flaying contemporary novelists, "deliberately raided Mailer's novel (*Mr. Sammler's Planet* came out in 1970, *An American Dream* in 1965) in order to make his critique of his rival's viewpoint more witty and more comprehensive." Glickman notes that both authors take radical stances on the "issues of man's place in nature and society, the character of the religious quest, the function of evil, and the roles of will and intellect."

Most critics are not too fond of Artur Sammler, viewing him as a static character devoid of psychological conflict. Ellen Pifer, in her essay, "'Two Different Speeches': Mystery and Knowledge in *Mr. Sammler's Planet*," argues against this reading of Sammler. She claims that it is his Holocaust experience that marks the way he observes phenomena. And Sammler's psyche, not just his mind, is divided on most issues. The "unfolding of his internal self-argument, is profoundly psychological in the root sense of the term." She views Sammler as embodying the "epitome of the 'passionate, conflicted, modern self.'" Bellow uses the device of Sammler's physical infirmity—his "two different-looking eyes"—to communicate this fractured psyche: the "blind side" denotes an uncommunicative or inward process while the operative right eye, representing the intellect, is alert to the phenomena it registers.

The Dean's December, is similar to *Mr. Sammler's Planet* in that it, too, is a "novel of ideas," and also has not fared well with early critics. In fact, its detractors use the same disparaging phrases in their negative critique of the work: it is tedious and its characters lack vitality. Matthew Roudané, however, in his article "A *Cri de Coeur:* The Inner Reality of Saul Bellow's *The Dean's December*," finds that a careful examination of this late novel will reveal a "successful fusion . . . of ideas and image." Roudané claims that *The Dean's December* indeed "embodies an engaging tale, one as complex and multivalent as any Bellow fiction to date." Bellow's technique, as in *Mr. Sammler's Planet*, is to filter the world through the consciousness of the protagonist, Albert Corde, and it is Corde's meditative perceptions which shape the novel. Michael Yetman, on the other hand, uses this work to relate the importance of Bellow's prose in providing the key to an understanding of Bellow's fiction. "Words reflect and at the same time interpret, humanize, even 'save' through imagination the stuff of literal experience." Yetman claims that Bellow, an "old-fashioned, conservative thinker," believes that words "properly used . . . capture and preserve the truth or reality of human experience, including its moral dimension." And in *The Dean's December*, Bellow thematizes poetic language thereby demonstrating how many of the wrongs of society can be attributed to "our having foresworn the poetic and individual for the conceptual, mass media-induced trendy thinking of the day."

While Bellow's religious proclivity has been noted by many critics, few critics have taken the trouble to delineate just how this interest is manifest in his works. Whereas L. H. Goldman traces specific Jewish roots, Stephen L. Tanner, in "The Religious Vision of *More Die of Heartbreak*," uses Bellow's latest book to show how Bellow's religious concerns qualify and define the humanism in his novels. They are encompassed in his preoccupation with the transcendent, that is, with the aspects of human experience and the qualities of the human personality that lie beyond the purview of positivistic science, psychology, and the rationalistic philosophy. He suggests that a statement from the foreword to Allan Bloom's *The Closing of the American Mind,* published the same year, echoes the major theme of *More Die of Heartbreak.* Bellow states therein: "The soul has to find and hold its ground against hostile forces, sometimes embodied in ideas which frequently deny its very existence and which indeed often seem to be trying to annul it altogether." Tanner claims that this is a "religious preoccupation, if a broad definition of religion is allowed." He maintains that in this novel Bellow brings to us a sense of religion by "intimation rather than assertion . . . , by preaching, by a comic mixture of the profound and preposterous rather than a sober polemic."

Gerhard Bach's article, "The Dean Who Came in From the Cold," studies both elements: language and ideas. Bach believes that in *The Dean's December* Bellow presents "a view of the American 1980s which force-fully addresses (masked) 'realities' and (unmasked) 'appearances,' and which brings into focus the artist's struggle to find a language appropriate for describing their origins, their enactments, and their underlying mechanisms." And although *The Dean's December* does provide conclusive insights into America's problems, more importantly, however, is its concentration on those processes—"mental, sensual, and spiritual"—necessary in procuring such insights. Bach further states that "the novel establishes two prerogatives for the protagonist to contend with: in the mental-spiritual realm the refinement of thought into crystal-clear images, and in the pragmatic realm the search for a common language with which to express" them. Consequently, Bellow assigns Albert Corde, protagonist of *The Dean's December*, the soul-searching task of "recover[ing] the world that is buried under the debris of false description or non-experience."

As this collection of essays emerges at the end of the 1980s, it is possible to discern both gaps and future trends in Bellow criticism. Clearly, post-structuralist criticism will have a major impact on the shape of things to come in the 1990s.

GENERAL
ESSAYS

Saul Bellow's Sixth Sense:
The Sense of History

Judie Newman

For Nietzsche, the historical sense in our time forms a sixth sense, pervading the philosophy, history, and culture of the modern era.[1] For most critics, however, the notion of a "sixth sense" operating in the novels of Saul Bellow more readily suggests a sense of transcendent realities, Platonic home-worlds, Steineresque meditations, and intimations of immortality. Overwhelmingly, critical orthodoxy sees Bellow as a writer more concerned with the universal than with the contingent and the particular.[2]

At the International Symposium on Saul Bellow the question of the historical content of Bellow's work was raised. Malcolm Bradbury argued that Bellow's novels encounter the chaos and contingency of the historical world remaining within the historical and experiential continuum, rather than express an urge to transcendence. Bradbury's voice rang out alone on this side of the argument as other critics weighed in on the side of transcendence. John Clayton argued that *Humboldt's Gift* concerned "Transcendence and the Flight from Death"; Gilbert Porter discussed Bellow's "Transcendental Vision"; Keith Opdahl, while describing Bellow's style as "realistic" nonetheless argued that he used radiant "literal detail to portray a transcendental reality"; and Brigitte Scheer-Schäzler affirmed that "Bellow in trying to discover the universal in the particular echoes the Transcendental epistemological quest."

In his comment in the proceedings of the Symposium,[3] Tony Tanner credited Bellow with a sense of history, but argued that this was merely ancillary to his fiction. Tanner begins by arguing against the "Transcendent" interpretation. "To be sure," he said, "by adroit and legitimate quotation one can find 'transcendental-type' statements in Bellow's work, but then whom has he not read, whom does he not quote?"

First printed in *Canadian Review of American Studies* 13 (Spring 1982): 39–52.

"It is my own sense," he continued, "that in Bellow's writing the pained, hyperactive, omnivorous, all-remembering habit of perceiving the given world is more powerful and more convincing than the yearning ... to assert the existence of some Transcendental reality." Tanner, however, also objects to the "historical" interpretation. For Tanner, Bellow's novels fail to incorporate an analytic sense of the dynamics of history. Transcendent glimpses are offered as a reprieve saving the protagonists from trying to comprehend history. The protagonists become, in Tanner's analysis, either "victims," suffering history passively, or "survivors," evading history, but in no sense do they comprehend it. Though Tanner sees Bellow as aware of the problems of history, he argues that such problems "do not functionally enter his fiction."

It is the function of the present article to argue for a "historical" interpretation of Bellow's writing, and to establish that the historical content of his work does enter the novels functionally, organizing their structure, rather than, in Tanner's view, in quotation marks.

Bellow's work presents an increasingly overt tension between the timeless and the timebound, with a consequent modification of his form, from the spatially ordered forms of *Dangling Man* and *The Victim* to "loose and baggy monsters" which express the contingency of the historical process. Bellow's concern with history begins as early as his second published story, "The Mexican General,"[4] an account of the death of a great man (Trotsky) as it impinges on the mean and limited awareness of a petty Mexican police chief. It comes to the fore in *The Adventures of Augie March*, entailing, as Bellow recognized, a new, freer style. Without going into detail, it seems interesting to dwell briefly on its status as a literary manifesto, setting out the problems of history and the manner in which these problems govern the form of the novels. *The Adventures of Augie March* centers on Ortega y Gasset's dictum that "Man has not a nature but a history," testing this statement in the sphere of historical existence (Chicago), in the natural world (Mexico), and finally in the European world of art. The novel falls into three distinct blocks. The Chicago section has a detailed historic time scheme relating Augie's adventures to the events of the Depression. The Mexican adventures initially move out of time into a realm of plumed serpents and nature deities, where Augie reads Utopian writers and historians. And the final parts of the novel steadily introduce the question of Art as timebound or timefree, through a succession of paintings referred to, and a thinner, more formal narrative texture.

Is Augie a validation of Ortega's view or a parodic enactment of it? Ortega's concept of "historical reason" implies that we have no resource but to "tell a story," to re-experience. Man is not an Adamic figure but a member of a society with a past. This "pastness" of society is established

in the early pages of *The Adventures* where each character is delineated
as representative of certain historical periods. For Ortega all truth is relative and historical, every idea is inscribed in a situation. Ortega shares
with Heraclitus the "pure happening" of all existences: the ego is only
activity, pure happening. Man constructs himself whether he will or no,
in various "versions" of himself so that, in Ortega's terms, we are all
"novelists of ourselves." Ortega makes these assumptions, however, on a
metaphysical, nonethical ground. Bellow shifts onto the moral. He accepts
the primacy of historical existence but refuses any acceptance of either
a deterministic or a relativist view of history, the view in which man is
either victimized by history or "survives" at the cost of exploiting others.

The major assertion of Bellow's message comes toward the end of the
novel when Augie observes the doors of the Baptistery in Florence, doors
which tell the entire history of mankind. At this point Bellow links the
question of history versus nature to the problem of form in the novel. These
doors are not selected at random by Bellow. In *Notes on the Novel*[5] Ortega
introduces the doors as an analogy to the importance of formal, timefree
esthetics in art. Contrasting an "art of figures" to an "art of adventures,"
Ortega argues that "in our time the novel of high style must turn from
the latter to the former" (74), a movement which is entirely negated in
the picaresque "adventures" of Augie March. Ortega argues that "the
material never saves a work of art, the gold it is made of does not hallow
a statue. A work of art lives on its form not on its material" (75). This view
is also negated when the argument is put in the mouth of the sinister
Basteshaw who discourses on the goldsmith whose statues were melted
down. Ortega sees culture as a mere "lifeboat" offered to shipwrecked man.
Basteshaw's biological culture is used to attack this non-ethical view of the
creative act. For Ortega, the historical, material quality of art must be
reduced to a minimum, so that the artist's aim is to work within a tiny
circumscribed sphere. It is this necessity which according to him complicates the writing of historical novels involving the clash of two horizons,
the imaginary and the historically correct—precisely the clash in *The
Adventures*. Ortega concludes:

> Let all novelists look at the doors of the Florentine Baptistery, wrought
> by Lorenzo Ghiberti. In a series of small squares they show the whole
> creation. . . . The sculptor was concerned with nothing but to model
> all these forms one after another. We still seem to feel the trembling
> delight with which the hand set down the arched brow of the ram
> Abraham espied in the thicket and the plump form of the apple. . . .
> Similarly a novelist must be inspired above all by a wonderful en-
> thusiasm to tell a tale and to invent. . . . In simpler words a novelist,

while he writes his novel, must care more about his imaginary world
than about any other possible world. (95)

Augie, we remember, is writing his own story for us. His concern with
his own inner world is seen here as indefensible. When an old lady appears to "explain" the doors to him and to recount her own woeful history, Augie brushes her off.

"This is happening to me," she says.
"There always is a me it happens to," says Augie. (597)[6]

This is ambiguous. On the one hand all historical narrative rests on
one postulate—that of the eternal identity of human nature—so that there
always is a "me" it happens to. On the other hand it is Augie's "me," the
pure happening of his ego, which is the one which concerns him. Ortega's
philosophy of history implies an implicit moral relativism. Augie, while
asserting that his story will be the "truth," that he'll be telling it like it was
without selection or suppression of detail (such is the opening statement
of the novel), is first seen by us busily lying to the Charity officers, sup-
pressing the existence of a lodger, constructing not a true history but a
plausible tale. The novel introduces a succession of tales and versions which
become more and more overtly constructions free of truth. Paslavitch tells
the tale of his uncle, Clem describes the children smelling flowers,
Basteshaw tells of his aunt's sleeping sickness, Mintouchian treats Augie
to a series of cautionary tales on the general theme of marriage, and the
entire ship's company of the *Sam McManus* pour out anecdotes, troubles,
personal histories, and even poems to the receptive Augie.

Where Ortega argues that men must construct "versions," that history
is narration, Bellow questions the morality of the process. History is deterministic, powerful, only in so far as the individual collaborates with it.
We remember that Augie visits the doors to kill time before meeting a
black marketeer, collaborating in war profiteering, and, most sinisterly,
buying dental supplies from a person who used to be in Dachau. For
Bellow, then, man cannot escape history, yet need not be entirely conditioned by it. Augie's opening statement that "a man's character is his fate"
is ambiguous. The essential nature of the individual does not govern his
destiny. Yet the individual need not necessarily become the victim of the
self-conscious creation of the self-as-character, of history as narration. History is neither the objective record of "facts" nor entirely interpretive. The
artist need not be swamped by the historical material—nor isolated in the
formal ivory tower of art. In "How I Wrote Augie March's Story" Bellow
said, "We are called upon to preserve our humanity in circumstances of

rapid change and movement. I do not see what else we can do but refuse to be condemned with a time and place."[7]

Bellow's later works continue this examination of historical existence. *Seize the Day* signals a return to the formal poetic novel as its title suggests, and to a present unthreatened by the extension of past or future. Tommy Wilhelm attempts to live for and in the present, to begin again, only to discover that this is the creed of financial America. His "day" becomes a day of atonement subsuming his entire history, and reasserting its importance. Henderson attempts to move out of time into a world of prehistory only to be forced back into the timebound. Herzog, the history scholar, examines his own past and that of Western man and attempts to relate the personal to the public. He attempts to take on his entire historical situation, and his inherited house at Ludeyville represents the chaos which is the result of taking on such a massive task. Herzog's nostalgia for his family's past corresponds to a negative Calvinist view of history—decline from a golden age. His belief in progress, his orientation to the future, corresponds to a positive, Romantic creed (see Mosher; hence the title of his first book—*Romanticism and Christianity*). The two creeds are questioned by an accident which disrupts his historical schemes, and they coalesce in his relation to his daughter, June, the future and the month in which the novel ends. In a reverse development, Mr. Sammler is caught between a nightmare past (the concentration camp) and a Utopian future (the Apollo moonshot), and is consciously established, by reference to Wells, as a time traveler. He is forced out of both horror and Utopia into the recognition that existence in living relation to time is one of the conditions of his being. Finally in *Humboldt's Gift* Bellow explores an encyclopedic assortment of different approaches to history. In order to demonstrate that history does enter the fiction functionally and not merely in quotation marks this argument concentrates on two novels—*Henderson the Rain King*, the most fantastic, and least overtly concerned with history, and *Humboldt's Gift*, the most obviously historical.

At the beginning of *Henderson the Rain King* the narrator emphasizes the problem of dealing with time. Henderson is seen grappling with the problems of organizing his memories, unable to cope with their simultaneity in the present. "A disorderly rush begins—my parents, my wives, my girls, my children, my farm, my animals, my habits, my money, my music lessons, my drunkenness, my prejudices, my brutality.... And they pile into me from all sides. It turns into chaos" (7). The alternative to chaos is, of course, chronos. Yet Henderson strenuously continues to undermine any easy acceptance of the structures within which he is forced to construct his tale. Wandering from one event to another, uncertain where to begin his story, he places a distance between himself and events, expressive of his alienated stance and of its roots in his uncertain relation to time. He says things like, "To go by the ages of the kids we were married for about 20 years" and, "Frances and I were divorced. This happened after V.E. day. Or was it so soon? No, it must have been in 1948" (8).

Henderson is alienated because he is living in an eternal present in which the past does not exist and everyone is always a stranger. This alienation, in part a personal psychological disturbance, is also that of a culture alienated from its origins, living in the expectation of immediate salvation in a new world. The first four chapters of the novel form an extended meditation on the question of an inherited past. Henderson fears mortality and therefore refuses to acknowledge time passing, or, within a family context, to acknowledge the parental generation—the past or his children—the future. By ignoring the claims of passion he attempts to avoid any connection with the generations and thus with time. His passionate encounters with Lily are always checked by images of death.

This psychological theme is linked to a larger cultural context. Henderson's flight from passion and death involves him in the desecration of religious and cultural inheritances. At Monte Cassino, scene of the destruction by U.S. troops of a monument of the European past, Henderson decides to breed pigs in the ancestral home, allowing them to root up statues from Florence and Salzburg. His choice of pigs is motivated by a desire to outrage his friend Goldstein's religious taboos.

Henderson rejects the European past, and that of his WASP ancestors, refusing to take his place in their portrait gallery. He typifies the American belief in the ability to wipe out the past and begin again in a new world where salvation from inherited guilt is a product of salvation from inherited tradition and history.

Such a belief is impossible, however, in psychological terms. Bellow implies a deep rooted schizophrenia here in American society. Although the African experiences operate in the realm of timeless fantasy or dream, Bellow begins by carefully embedding them in a psychological and social reality. The African experiences work as an exaggeration and refraction of elements already alluded to in the prologue. The tenant's cat and Miss Lennox's cat become avenging lions. The misery inflicted on Ricey conjures up a weeping African maiden. Literary allusions to ritual and romance become two full blown episodes. Minor "guilts" are punished by massive retributions in the "dream" experiences which distort scale and proportion in terms of absolute degrees of guilt and innocence. Aware of his own violence and amorality, Henderson is transported to a land where these are the norm. He rejects Ricey's child to find himself surrounded by Africans who hold him in their power. He desecrates his ancestors and the inheritance of the past only to become part of a society where reverence for ancestors and observance of taboo almost prove fatal to him. The past avenges itself in no uncertain terms.

Henderson's journey into Africa is presented as a journey into prehistory. Africa is described as if it had only just emerged from the solar "big bang." The Arnewi, as their name suggests, are presented in terms of radiant newness, light, and harmony, in a golden age of esthetic beauty. They "would have satisfied the standards of Michelangelo himself" (55) we are told. They have no oppositions in their language and appear to possess in the person of Willatale a wisdom outside time. The timeless quality of their life has its counterpart, however, in their paralyzed inertia and the stagnant water of their cistern. It is significant that frogs, with their associations with the primal slime, should be their taboo animal. They are described in terms that suggest the life in time, and the regeneration inherent in it. They are "at all stages of development, with full tails like giant sperm" (58). In typical American fashion Henderson pins his faith on the annihilation of custom and taboo, and a new beginning. Though Henderson gets his technological timing right—the fuse works, the bomb explodes—it is his attitude to time which explains his overall failure. Wedded to an ideal of secular progress, Henderson proclaims that "this is the day and this is the hour," keen to deliver on his Messianic promise of salvation. The explosion ends in disaster, however, with the final image that of the Arnewi culture at war with nature, as the cows drink: "the cows, of course, obeying nature and the natives begging them and weeping" (103)—an image akin to the Freudian repressions of Henderson's America. In Arnewiland two attempts to escape from history are defeated—the esthetic timeless and the technological progressive. The problem of cultural change cannot be resolved either by ignoring it or by its elevation to a supreme value. Nature and culture remain locked in conflict with Henderson as the battleground.

Where the Arnewi experiences involve cultural attitudes toward change, those in Waririland move into the individual psyche. Waririland is established as a timebound fallen world. Romilayu falls at Henderson's approach to it and arises older and greyer. The associations are with darkness, evil, and crime. Wariri kings inherit only by the murder of the father, and live in terror of being denounced for lack of virility by their women. Henderson's own fears are magnified here. The Wariri religion of cyclic recurrence depends upon the belief that man is fallen, doomed to a pointless repetition of passion and violence. Dahfu describes it in terms of a primal crime, "In the beginning of time there was a hand raised which struck" (200). Dahfu, however, involves Henderson in Reichian psychotherapy.[8] If Freudian psychotherapy may be seen as a psychological version of inherited sin, Reichian therapy is the psychological equivalent of

the American transcendental belief in the possibility of instinctual innocence, of harmony between nature and culture. As opposed to the Freudian
view of the necessity of cultural repression to protect against the amoral
urgings of the instincts, Reich suggests that a total freedom from repression would result in an idyllic harmonious society. In the words of Philip
Rieff, "Reich never bothered to argue against the probability that sex suppression functioned to hold societies together against the pressure of nature. It was a dogma to him that nature and culture could not be in tension. . . . He never confronts the horrible possibility which obsesses all
of modern art that the reality behind the appearance may be even more
unpleasant than the appearance."

To some extent Reichian therapy works for Henderson. In learning to
express his rage and face his fears he learns to stop "avoiding" and to dance
in time with Atti, Dahfu's tame lioness, who forces the present moment
upon him. He has to learn to move in time despite his fear that "as I was
in motion I was fair game" (246). The various dances of the tribe and the
skull-throwing ceremony establish a new dynamic of esthetics, moving beyond the stasis of the Arnewi to a musical form in which time is a necessary element. The surroundings of the final lion hunt in the hopo are
described in terms which reveal a delighted sensitivity to temporal processes as if change had been speeded up so that it were visible, as if the
rhythm of life were audible. Rhythm pervades the episode from the sway-
ing of the hammock to the music of cicadas. Yet though this recognition
of change is hopeful to Henderson, his individual regeneration is placed
in a cultural context which is less optimistic. The appearance of a real
savage lion leads Henderson to recognize the possibility precisely outlined
by Rieff—that animal nature is more terrifying than we think, that Melville
may be closer to the truth than Emerson. Henderson's terror of Atti pales
once he sees a real lion and learns what his role as Sungo is. Though Dahfu
supposedly teaches a Reichian ethic in which a new beginning is possible, free from taint or repression, he hands on, in fact, a social role which
can be seen only as a curse. On coming around in the tomb, Henderson's
first thought is of time: "Maybe time was invented so that misery might
have an end. So that it shouldn't last forever?" (293). For man, change and
morality are consolations. Back in Baventai, Henderson is able to reconcile himself to the cyclic recurrence of nature: "You can't get away from
rhythm. . . . The left hand shakes with the right hand, the inhale follows
the exhale. . . . And the seasons. And the stars. . . . You've got to live in peace
with it" (307).

The ending of the novel integrates the two ways of approaching time
and culture—the Old World cyclic view and the American prophetic and
progressive view, each represented emblematically by the lion cub and the

orphan child. Henderson admits that he had "lost count of time," tells the stewardess that he now sees something of value in the past, and faces up to the reason for his estrangement from his father—the latter's grief over the dead brother. Personal and cultural problems are resolved together. In the final dance around the plane Henderson celebrates not the frozen moment but the cyclic dance of human life. The novel moves from an initial refutation of time to a loving acceptance of it and willingness to exist within it. Even in this, the most fantastic and least naturalistic of Bellow's novels, then, the hero's attitude to his individual and social history governs the action. The supposedly "mythic" or "romance" setting is merely a pretext to an exploration of the bases of the historical sense.

This critical relation with myth forms the starting point of *Humboldt's Gift*.[10] To comprehend Bellow's view of history in this novel we need to refer back to the committed criticism of the forties and in particular to Philip Rahv. Writing in 1953, in his essay *The Myth and the Powerhouse*, Rahv argued that the concern with myth in modernist writing resulted from fear of engagement with history. History terrifies because

> modern life is above all a historical life producing changes with vertiginous speed, changes difficult to understand and even more difficult to control. And to some people it appears as though the past were being ground to pieces in the powerhouse of change, senselessly used up as so much raw material in the fabrication of an uncertain future. One way intellectuals have found of coping with their fear is to deny historical time and induce in themselves through esthetics and ideological means a sensation of mythic time ... confounding past, present and future in an undifferentiated unity, as against historical time which is unrepeatable.[11]

Identifying the mythicism of Pound and Eliot with a retreat from the hazards of freedom, Rahv argues that art achieves independence only as it frees itself from myth. The mind needs to recognize its own creations as creations. It is my contention that Bellow is occupied with this freeing of the mind by confronting its own creations. Rahv characterizes the retreat into myth as follows: "To [the myth makers] as to Stephen Dedalus in *Ulysses* history is a nightmare from which they are trying to awaken. But to awake from history into myth is like escaping from a nightmare into a state of permanent insomnia" (208). *Humboldt's Gift* practically opens with Humboldt's quip that "History was a nightmare during which he was trying to get a good night's rest" (4). Insomniac Humboldt is contrasted with Citrine, a sleeper through the events of history, in flight from involvement. In a recent essay Bellow discussed the modern faith in progress by technological innovation and lamented the cultural amnesia which is its byproduct. "The new era will produce men who are no longer attached to the past by any habit of mind. For them history will be nothing but strange incomprehensible tales."[12] Citrine's brother, Julius, for example, suffers from an amnesia extending even to his personal past. As the novel progresses, the initial presentation of the forties and fifties as richly textured historical periods yields to a series of strange incomprehensible tales—the film scenarios, the Thaxter kidnapping, the Cantabile plot. Parody becomes the dominant mode of the novel as Bellow explores ossified "fictions" both historical and literary to free the past as experience. Bellow is concerned with two alternative problems: the danger of avoiding history and the danger of embracing it too fondly.

Humboldt's character is marked by a relentless desire for status in history, a desire Bellow has described, in the same essay, as follows: "Intellectuals try hard to be what Hegel called World Historical Individuals. They may denounce the nightmare past but they have also an immortal craving to be in the line of succession and prove themselves historically necessary" (11).

Humboldt, discoursing on Julien Sorel, Napoleon, and Balzac's *jeune ambitieux* in a car in New Jersey is "especially attached to the World Historical Individual." The Napoleonic myth of intelligence in action controlling events in the thick of battle is satirized here as the two great men pass through an industrial battlefield and rural ghetto. Humboldt as a poet inclines toward a belief in his Orphic role. As a World Historical Individual, however, he fails to remain an instrument of any larger purpose but sets out to wage his own war. In his need to escape from being a victim of history he becomes an aggressor. The cost to Humboldt's poetry is demonstrated through a second series of parallels to Tolstoy. Bellow's novel restates what Isaiah Berlin has described as the central opposition in Tolstoy's work, between the hedgehog and the fox, the opposition between the craving for one absolute idea and the multiplicity of individual events which constitutes life. Humboldt lives in the realm of large abstractions. His conversation is peppered with references to historical events in a way which levels all it touches. No distinctions are made between the Age of Gold and the Gilded Age, the gold death mask of Agamemnon and the golden scandals of yesteryear. Historical events are just so much raw material from which literary capital can be made. The decline of Humboldt's poetic gift is demonstrated in "the recurrent jingle" rhythms associated with him. He is "poet, thinker, problem drinker, pill-taker, man of genius, manic depressive" (25), a tinker-tailor rhythm in which social and historical roles, a succession of categories, eliminate poetry. Citrine notes that Humboldt was "pondering what to do between *then* and *now*, between birth and death, to satisfy certain great questions" (6). In Humboldt's poetic grammar, however, then *has* become now. The idea that he can make history implies a self-conscious casting of himself in a historical character and a consequent transformation of the present moment into a historical moment. The present then becomes an abstract idea, and the individual life is foreshortened, almost erased.

The novel is structured in two ways: first, the horizontal time scheme along which Citrine moves forward into the present and the Cantabile plot, backward into the past and memories of Humboldt, and secondly, a vertical structuring in which the pretensions of "high" and "low" cultures are exposed. Humboldt, in a long monologue in New Jersey, reveals an overpolarization in his view of history. His monologue deals with the reverse of the World Historical Individual, what D. H. Fischer has called "the furtive fallacy."[13] Humboldt dwells on such topics as the secret sex lives of great men, the secret police, the perversions of the military. Either history is made by great men with great motives or it is created out of secret conspiracies, wicked plots, dire psychological needs. Nothing, however, is the result of chance. It all forms part of a pattern. If the "high" plot exposes the pretensions of man as maker of history, to heroic status, the Cantabile plot reveals identical pretensions in low life. The poker game takes place amidst discussion of the territorial imperative and sheds new light on the attraction exercised by abstract categories, suggesting that the attraction of closed philosophical systems is only a refinement of a basic biological drive.

When Citrine needs advice in dealing with Cantabile, he goes to the Russian Bath, deliberately set up as a mythic environment, with antique denizens, eating epic meals and reclining on hot planks as if in Hades. Two senses of the term "underworld" are juxtaposed here: the mythic and the criminal. With a shock Citrine realizes that the Bath may be owned by the Mafia. Bellow suggests here that the attempt to idolize the elemental nature of man, to enthrone the biological imperatives or natural forces as mythic beings is as dangerous as trying to isolate man from them as hero or saint. The "vertical" structuring of the novel therefore works against easy moral dichotomizing in the reading of history.

The horizontal dimension poses a similar question. At the end of a long meditation on Humboldt, Citrine complains of his action in cashing a blank check immediately upon the death of Demmie Vonghel. Citrine complains that "he reads the papers, he knows she's gone" (168). The meditation follows the events of the Cantabile plot in terms of narrative time, but of course precedes them in terms of the supposed historical order of events. When Citrine accuses Humboldt, we, as readers, remember a preceding scene where Cantabile accused Citrine of knowing from the papers about the death of Bill's brother. In both cases the individual is unaware of the public version of events he is living through. The reader's judgment of Citrine depends upon the presentation of the time scheme. Citrine used his involvement in public affairs, his historical role, to justify abandoning down-and-out Humboldt, but the imaginative narrative counters and reverses this justification by positioning Citrine's betrayal first before we learn of Humboldt's cashing the check. The timing of Humboldt's action is morally culpable in terms of the public record of events, but this is not the only temporal perspective. The personal relation to the past becomes as important as the cultural overview. The construction of the novel up to this point may be said to respect A. N. Whitehead's dictum that history may be read in two directions, forward and backward, but that the thinking man must do both.

From this point on, the novel becomes increasingly comic. Events are summed up in oblique fashion by the Caldofreddo filmscript, which Humboldt envisages as "vaudeville and farce but with elements of *Oedipus at Colonus* in it" (182). The novel deliberately tests Hegel's view of the historical process, as described by Marx: "Hegel remarks somewhere that all acts and personages of great importance in world history occur as it were twice. He forgot to add, the first time as tragedy, the second as farce."[14] The double reading of history is then extended in terms of style. The form of the novel avoids the danger of offering the reader simplistic moral judgments on events because similar events occur within very different stylistic modes. In a second deflation of myth Myron Swiebel meets Gaylord Koffritz in the Russian Bath, but the scene is comic as Gaylord launches into a sales pitch for tombs—tombs ranging in style from Etruscan to art nouveau, fitting monuments to those like Myron who live their lives according to a ready-made style. Citrine's first encounter with Renata is seen as a reenactment of established roles of good and evil—but again comically. Citrine refers to the "middle class endeavour . . . to preserve a certain darling innocence—the innocence of Clarissa defending herself against the lewdness of Lovelace" (209).

In the seduction scene, Citrine is cast by his own guilt in the role of Lovelace, with Renata, drugged by martini, an insensible Clarissa. The scene culminates in the reappearance at this of all moments of Citrine's childhood sweetheart—alone at a bar, and taken by Charlie for a hooker. Were he really a Lovelace, of course, this confrontation with the sweetheart now sunk in shameful depths would not be so unlikely! Charlie turns the tables, however, accusing Naomi of ruining him: "I lost my character altogether because I couldn't spend my life with you" (213).

In the court scenes the same stereotyping of roles of good and evil is explored. Although supposedly deployed in his support, Charlie's lawyers will not hear criticism of the opposition because of a code of professional ethics. Since Charlie is also paying both sets of lawyers, the supposed legal battle is merely an empty ritual. Although Charlie is fighting mad he restrains the impulse to burst out in impassioned speech, like Shylock telling off the Christians. The intuitive sense of right and wrong, meaningful appeals on behalf of the human bond, are out of place in a court where everyone is entitled to his pound of flesh. Charlie keeps quiet out of "Respect for the real thing" (232), real suffering and persecution. His own "bleeding" at the hands of Cannibal Pinsker is after all only a metaphor, and by now Charlie is alert to the dangers of allowing a metaphor to govern reality. Strong manly silence is, however, also immediately attacked, first in a tragic mythic sense in the account of the death of Tigler, the hard-boiled Western cowboy, and secondly in comic terms in the variant hard-boiled role, when Charlie is cast by Cantabile in the role of silent hit-man in Stronson's office. When he is arrested, the fact that Charlie is an internationally known historian cuts no ice with the Chicago cops. He is saved by his sweetheart's daughter, Maggie, who is quite unimpressed by his books—"I understand they're history books and history has never been my bag" (290). What motivates her is the memory of her mother's love for Charlie. Charlie is rescued, then, not by rational historical analysis, but by the real force of remembered emotion.

Charlie's attempts to buck out of history, to flee into the transcendent, are also treated ironically. He argues that he has to abandon his children in order to do them any real good. He must first seek a transcendent truth. The tables are turned by Renata, however, whose quest for what Charlie always calls "the riddle of your birth" parodies Charlie's own more ethereal quest. If Charlie can abandon his children for the supposed good of his soul (actually to engage in sexual shenanigans with Renata), so Renata can abandon Roger, supposedly to go in quest of Biferno (actually to engage in similar activities with Flonzaley). Although Charlie does finally propose to Renata, the Senora's comment says it all: "I congratulate you on finally making sense. . . . She didn't say, mind you that I had done this in time" (419). Charlie cannot renegotiate the terms of his existence from scratch, making sense of them with an abstract solution. He has to remain within the contingent.

Given this immersion in history, then, is life therefore reduced to a mere cycle of pointless repetitions? This is the question faced by Charlie when he meets the missionary Vonghels, a second group (the first having been eaten by cannibals) and all exactly alike. Wearily Citrine comments that "the whole thing is disintegrating and reintegrating all the time, and you have to guess whether it's always the same cast of characters or a lot of different characters" (301). The repetitive and parallel structures within the novel pose the same problem. Does the individual merely repeat past

mistakes or does he gain wisdom from a broader time perspective? Is the
pattern of history merely "bleed or be bled," Toynbee's vision of history
as "rout-rally-rout"? Is the reader to finish the novel in a spirit of cynicism, parody, wicked laughter? Bellow's ability to avoid the pitfalls offered
by black comedy and parody is demonstrated by the film *Caldofreddo* which
Citrine watches in Paris. Two points are emphasized here—the historical
nature of the film with its old newsreel style and "Time Marches On" manner, and the audience's reaction to it. For the audience the film is primarily comic: "The plane sank. Thousands of people were laughing" (161).
Only Citrine, who is aware of Humboldt's personal tragedy behind events,
weeps uncontrollably. History is comic only when presented, like the film,
in stylized, oversimplified and over rapid terms, without the awareness of
human suffering within it. Humboldt has taught him to not be a "sleeper"
through history, but this does not mean that he is overwhelmed by a nightmare experience.

The novel therefore explores different approaches to history, and different retreats from it—history as nightmare, as tragedy, as farce, as black
comedy; the retreat into myth or into the heightened present of the "crisis" mentality (Charlie's wife, Denise) or into transcendence; the dangers
of "pop" or instant history (the film scenario, Thaxter's book about his
own kidnapping) or of history governed by stereotyped moral responses.
By the novel's various structurings of time Bellow succeeds in avoiding
any one mode of approach and thereby liberates the event to be judged
in its total context—as it affects participants, as it is recorded publicly,
and as it is inherited, translated and transformed by succeeding generations. The concern with history reveals, then, both an analytic sense of
its dynamics and at the same time an ability to allow it to function for-
mally in the text.

Notes

1. Friedrich Nietzsche, "Beyond Good and Evil," in *The Complete Works of Friedrich
   Nietzsche,* ed. Oscar Levy, vol. 12 (Edinburgh, 1923), 167.
2. Prominent exceptions to the critical consensus are: Malcolm Bradbury, "The
   Nightmare in Which I'm Trying to Get a Good Night's Rest: Saul Bellow and
   Changing History," in *Saul Bellow and His Work,* ed. Edmond Schraepen
   (Brussels, 1978); C. J. Bullock, "On the Marxist Criticism of the Contemporary
   Novel in the United States: A Re-evaluation of Saul Bellow," *Praxis* 1, no. 2
   (1976); 189–98; Harold M. Mosher, "Synthesis of Past and Present in Saul
   Bellow's *Herzog," Wascana Review* 6, no. 1 (1971): 28–38.
3. Tony Tanner, "Afterword," to *Saul Bellow and His Work,* (London: Oliver and
   Boyd), 131–38.
4. Saul Bellow, "The Mexican General," *Partisan Review* (9 May–June 1942):
   178–94.

5. Jose Ortega Y Gasset, *The Dehumanization of Art* (Princeton, 1968); first translated 1948.

6. Page references to Bellow's novels are to the following editions: *The Adventures of Augie March* (London, 1954); *Henderson the Rain King* (London, 1966); *Humboldt's Gift* (London, 1975).

7. Saul Bellow, "How I Wrote Augie March's Story," *New York Times Book Review* (31 January 1954): 3, 17.

8. Reichian overtones in the novel have been detailed by Eusebio L. Rodrigues, "Reichianism in *Henderson the Rain King*," *Criticism* 15, no. 3 (Summer 1973): 212–34.

9. Philip Rieff, "The World of Wilhelm Reich," *Commentary* 38, no. 3 (September 1964): 53.

10. I have developed the following argument in greater detail in "Saul Bellow: *Humboldt's Gift*—The Comedy of History," *Durham University Journal* 72 (December 1979): 79–87.

11. Philip Rahv, "The Myth and the Powerhouse," in his *Literature and the Sixth Sense* (Boston: Houghton Mifflin, 1969), 210.

12. Saul Bellow, "Literature in the Age of Technology," in *Technology and the Frontiers of Knowledge: The Frank Nelson Doubleday Lectures* (Garden City: Doubleday, 1975), 9–10.

13. David H. Fisher, *Historians' Fallacies* (New York: Harper, 1970).

14. Karl Marx, "The Eighteenth Brumaire of Louis Napoleon," in Karl Marx and Friedrich Engels, *Selected Works* (New York: International Publishers, 1968), 96.

Bellow and Freud

Daniel Fuchs

Like many writers and intellectuals of his generation, Bellow was genuinely involved with psychoanalysis. "Off the couch by Christmas" was a common hope or familiar joke in literary circles. Bellow himself tried a variety of approaches stemming from Freud and Reich. "I've had all the psychiatry I can use," Moses Herzog tells Dr. Emmerich.[1] Though much has been made of his switch from Freud to Reich, Bellow's connection with the utopian Reich was short-lived. Freud was the more enduring presence, the genius of psychoanalysis, the therapeutic and ideational father for whom Bellow expressed the inevitable love-hate. He has learned from Freud but essentially opposes him. To say that Bellow knows Freud very well is no exaggeration. There was a period when Freud was his nightly bedtime reading, and Bellow's frequent references to Freud in his fictive works, his notebooks, and his essays reveal an easy intimacy not only with major works but also with minor ones. As for the legitimacy of comparing an artist with a thinker, few thinkers have had more to do with "vision" than Freud, few novelists more to do with the meaning and emotional content of ideas than Bellow. Freud saw all systems of thought, including his own, as mythology. And the Bellow protagonist often breathes in what Bellow, in his spoof of Freud, has called "an environment of Ideas" (*LA,* viii).

Moreover, Bellow does not encounter in Freud an arcane scientist or offbeat mind. Freudian perceptions are at the heart of twentieth-century life. Freud gives us a view of man which is new, denuding, disillusioned, which is radically subjective and iconoclastic, which is, in short, modern. Bellow's resistance to Freud begins in opposition to the terms with which these views are given. Freud is a prime instance of modernism, against which Bellow has mounted a sustained critique.

First printed in *Studies in the Literary Imagination* 17, no. 2 (1984): 59–80.

"I didn't want to be what he called determined," says Augie March (*AM,* 117). He is thinking here of the environmental determinism warned against by Einhorn and extending it to a defense of personal autonomy, a goal that he or anyone else can only partially achieve. Though fully aware of the forces that oppose it, he insists on the reality of autonomy. There is always a margin of self-definition. Rather than determinism there are the irrepressible Bellovian asserters (Augie, Henderson, Herzog, Bummidge). But Freud introduces a determinism deeper than any Augie could imagine, the determinism of the unconscious mind. "What a man thinks he is doing counts for nothing," writes Bellow in a draft of Herzog. "All his work in the world is done by impulses he will never understand— sinful to the priest, sexual to the psychiatrist."[2] Freud said that character was essentially fixed by the age of six, that everything in character was essentially determined by that time. "In most cases," as Philip Rieff says, "Freud insists that character does not change deliberately, through taking thought or through decision; our character is, so to speak, changed for us, by returns from oblivion."[3] This applies to genius as well. So when a Leonardo abandons art for science, it is because his infantile past has gained control over him. The biblical Moses may be considered an heroic exception of conscious self-determination in Freud, and this is a reason why *Moses and Monotheism* has not been influential with the orthodox Freudians. Needless to say, the discovery that childhood experiences are of the greatest importance and that their effects are unconscious is momentous. Yet Freud's emphasis on these truths almost precludes autonomy. Thus the Freudian revisionists withdraw from his determinism. "Freud did not envision people in terms of developing powers and as total personalities," says Clara Thompson. "He thought of them much more mechanistically—as victims of the search for the release of tension."[4] In their critique of determinism and victimization, the revisionists are expressing a humanist concern, one similar to Bellow's, and they do so with an ambivalence not unlike his. For the revisionists, Freud often mistakes cultural phenomena for instinctual ones. Bellow, as we shall see, does not regard the matter with such anthropological detachment, which substitutes a cultural for a biological determinism. But for him, as for the revisionists, the root of the problem is the nature of the Freudian unconscious.

By *unconscious* Bellow means the place first indicated by Freud in the final chapter of *The Interpretation of Dreams* and made more emphatic in *The Ego and the Id* and *New Introductory Lectures*; in other words, the dynamic unconscious which implies a function, not merely the descriptive which implies a quality. If it is a place, it is not an especially pleasant one. "The desire to murder is actually present in the unconscious," says

Freud.[5] The Bellow protagonist is not unfamiliar with that desire. A central theme in Bellow is the overcoming of that impulse, an impulse which is for him indicative of nihilism. In *Totem and Taboo,* murder (the Oedipal killing of the father, the primal crime) does take place, followed by a complex reaction expressing the primal ambivalence and thereby the beginnings of civilization. Professor Herzog addresses himself to just this issue as he waits in his dreary cell after his traffic accident: *"If a primal crime is the origin of social order, as Freud, Roheim et cetera believe, the bond of brothers attacking and murdering the primal father, eating his body, gaining their freedom by a murder and united by a blood wrong, then there is some reason why jail should have these dark tones."* But the perception is fleeting: *"All that is nothing but metaphor. I can't truly feel I can attribute my blundering to this thick unconscious cloud. This primitive blood-daze."* Indeed, his actions, superior to violence and murder, suggest that he should not. This is why he writes in "cheerful eagerness." Herzog sees something other than murderous egotism in the deepest recesses of the unconscious, something which refuses to disappear. *"The dream of man's heart, however much we may distrust and resent it, is that life may complete itself in significant pattern."* Freud may agree with this in the last analysis, but not in the first, and therein lies a great difference. The congenital optimist, Herzog knows that *"you got one last chance to know justice. Truth"* (*H*, 303). Characteristically, he puts things in traditional, moralistic terms. He does not deny the existence of an unconscious, only its Freudian character.

Bellow has said, "the unconscious is anything that human beings don't know. Is there any reason why we have to accept Freud's account of what it is that we don't know? ... Is it possible that what we don't know has a metaphysical character and not a Freudian, naturalistic character? I think that the unconscious is a concept that begs the question and simply returns us to our ignorance with an arrogant attitude of confidence, and that is why I am against it."[6] Bellow is not giving us a positivist unconscious. In this view the unconscious is that of which we are *ex hypothesi* unaware; therefore nothing can be said about it; it is, then, effectively nonexistent. Bellow's metaphysical unconscious is taken on what Santayana calls animal faith. This faith assumes a First Cause which may be called God. Rieff rightly calls Freud's unconscious a "god-term" (Kenneth Burke's words) or "Freud's conceptual ultimate, a First Cause, to be believed in precisely because it is both fundamental to and inaccessible to experience."[7] In effect, Freud attempts "to eliminate religious experience by paralleling it."[8]

Bellow reverses the primary burden of the unknown, choosing to make upward rather than downward comparisons, outward, not just inward comparisons. He wants feeling without symbols, where Freud could not do without symbols. Dreams are, for Freud, the language of determinism, the truth of a totally symbolic, amoral chaos of an unconscious. Freud saw the drama of sleep but not so clearly the drama of being awake. If, as Rieff suggests, free association proves that we are never free, the primacy of dream symbolism implies a stereotyped psychological incarceration, a permanent state of house arrest. Kafka is the great novelist of this mood. Bellow suspects that symbolic interpretation may be an abrogation of free will, a way the unconscious can tyrannize over consciousness, the obscure motive over spontaneity. The result can be a scholasticism which infects not only the Freudian world but the literary world as well. "Deep readers of the world beware," Bellow once warned. "You may never again see common daylight."[9] Freud tells us that though the ego appears autonomous and unitary, marked off distinctly from anything else, it really is "continued inward, without any sharp delimitation into an unconscious mental entity which we designate as the id and for which it serves as a facade."[10] The downward and the inward movement is honorific in Freud, the true source, but the upward and outward is on a tight leash of sublimation. The metaphysical, the religious—these are, for Freud, ways of wrapping the self in a batting of excelsior.

Herzog's resistance to the Freudian unconscious issues into an engaging insight. In a letter to Spinoza, he agrees with the philosopher that thoughts not causally connected may cause pain. *"It may interest you to know,"* he writes, *"that in the twentieth century random association is believed to yield up the deepest secrets of the psyche"* (*H,* 181). While free association may be the ultimate insult to rational purposiveness, the process itself can yield some of the mysteries of the deep. One can argue that Spinoza overvalued reason; in any case, Freud surely knew something that Spinoza did not. Whether, or to what extent, the unconscious is Freudian, it is certainly there. Free association, like the psychopathology of everyday life, is, much more than chaos, a triumph over it. Herzog knows the rules but does not want to play the game, *"believing that reason can make steady progress from disorder to harmony and that the conquest of chaos need not be begun anew every day"* (*H,* 181f.). But isn't there such "progress" in psychoanalysis? Herzog is saved from smugness here by the precariousness of his claim: "How I wish it! How I wish it were so! How Moses prayed for this" (*H,* 182). The yearning for moral clarity even more than the clarity itself is the characteristic Herzog note. His prayer for reason is humanism in the defensive position.

A draft of Herzog's letter to Spinoza undermines the foundation of Freud's unconscious by dismissing its current neo-Freudian expression. Freud holds that "what decides the purpose of life is simply the

programme of the pleasure principle. This principle dominates the operation of the mental apparatus from the start." Rather than happiness,
however, this brings unhappiness through an elaborate sequence of
repression and renunciation. "One feels inclined to say that the intention that men should be happy is not included in the plan of 'Creation,'"
says Freud.[11] Adhering to a different view of the pleasure principle, the
neo-Freudians have given us Freud without pain. Bellow rejects the biological determinism of both by denying the cardinality of pleasure. That
he has to complain to Spinoza may be ominous. But is there anyone better around to talk to? Herzog writes, *"I subscribed at one time to the theory
that it was pleasure and pleasure only that gave one the strength to be moral,
that pleasure was fundamentally a question of health, and that the only possible
source of goodness and happiness was instinctual gratification. I no longer believe
this to be true."* He communicates with Spinoza as he and Ramona embrace. She bites his lip in ecstasy. *"This theory did me a lot of harm,"* he
continues. The comedy of contemporary life does not keep his moral-
ism down: "I think that John Stuart Mill was absolutely right: happiness
cannot be a direct object. Must be a by-product" (*B*, 20.40, 180). Marriage to Ramona would be an ideological misalliance. Not the pleasure
principle but self-directed purpose ought to determine. Something close
to this opposition was made some time ago by Aristotle, who distinguished between pleasure as sensation and pleasure as activity. The latter in Bellow's humanistic view has more to do with happiness.

Freud's conception of the eternal recurrence of the Oedipal drama
reduces religion to psychology and history to nature. History becomes
a sort of secular predestination, with the unconscious as a weedy Garden
of Eden, the primal crime as original sin. For Bellow, Freud minimizes
and perhaps destroys pure motive[12] in a way that victimizes the Christian
as well as the natural man. *"Charity,"* Herzog writes to Edvig, *"as if it didn't
have enough trouble in this day and age, will always be suspected of morbidity—
sado-masochism, perversity of some sort. All higher or moral tendencies lie under
suspicion of being rackets"* (*H*, 56). Herzog is angry at Edvig's indifference
to his attempted *agape* in dealing with Mady, an indifference which
destroys an aspect of the Judeo-Christian tradition he believes is real.
*"If my soul, out of Season, out of place, experienced these higher emotions, I could
get no credit for them anyway. Not from you with your attitude toward good intentions. I've read your stuff about the psychological realism of Calvin. I hope you
don't mind my saying that it reveals a lousy, cringing, grudging conception of human
nature. This is how I see your Protestant Freudianism"* (*H*, 57f.).

The friction between humanism and the Freudian unconscious surfaces again in Freud's view of history. Since history is nature and the
unconscious determines, pre-history is more important than history in

the conventional sense. Though psychoanalysis is an historical process for the individual patient, it also aims to uncover the individual equiva- lent of pre-history. Accordingly, Freud's writings on culture are more concerned with myth than history. "For the very reason that Hegel thought Africa no proper subject for the historian, Freud thought it most proper," Rieff says.[13] Bellow's Africa, on the other hand, is really an af- firmation of traditional morality. And in much of his work Bellow is in- volved with historical reality as such. His time is chronological, not mythological. The momentous event has not occurred in an archetypal past but is unfolding before our contemporaneous eyes. We know what the momentous event is for Freud.

Anyone reading Freud with a clear eye will see that the Oedipus com- plex cannot be explained away in mollifying cultural terms. Freud really means it. However tentative and delicate his rhetorical poses, he never comes up with anything more suited to his purpose, and suggestion soon becomes fact. He sees nothing in history to cause him to change his mind. *"Homo homini lupus,"* says Freud in *Civilization and Its Discontents* (a senti- ment uttered in manuscript by Bellow's Winkelman of *The Last Analysis* as he thinks about contemporary reality in Balzacian terms). "Who in the face of all his experience of life and of history, will have the courage to dispute this assertion?"[14] Bellow longs to accord to human nature the value that Freud grants to civilization. Renunciation is Freud's heroism. Bellow sees its importance, but he resents the parsimony implied by its prevalence in the Freudian system.

II

Comparing Bellow and Freud as thinkers points up perhaps more clearly than anything else can the religious tendency of Bellow's human- ism. Bellow's hostility to Freud may be seen as the obverse of Freud's hostility to the religious temperament. He explicitly attacks Freud's "A Religious Experience" for displaying systematic rigidity comparable to that of Marx: "Once you've given yourself over to one of these systems, you've lost your freedom in a very significant degree." Here then is Freudianism-as-ideology criticized from the point of view of humanist independence. Bellow recognizes that Freud was "a great genius" and recalls what "my feelings were quite early in life when I began to read Freud. It was hard not to see the world in terms of instinct and repres- sion, not to see it in terms of concavity and convexity, not to see it in terms of the struggle of the child with his parents, and so on." Ever the writer, he sees these as "metaphors," as he sees all philosophy from the point of view of imagination. The individual must be moved, and Freud has moved him. "A Religious Experience" has crystallized his contempt. An American doctor had read *The Future of an Illusion* and writes to Freud saying, "I too at one time lost my faith" when as a medical student the body of a "very beautiful old woman" was brought into the dissecting room. He "could no longer believe in a god" who would do such a thing. But the doctor thinks about it and recovers his faith, recommending that Freud too "postpone a final decision on the existence of God for a time." Bellow is outraged by Freud's response, which equates the cadaver with the doctor's mother. "At this moment," he says, "I experienced a violent reaction against Freud. Was it not possible to experience beauty or pity without thinking of your mother, or without the Oedipus complex? The rigidity of this repels me. I felt that it was coarse and cruel. It's this sort of thing that I think of when I think of Freud."[15]

There is more to Freud's piece than Bellow's recollection of it, and what is left out, to be analytic about it, may be as much the reason for Bellow's having selected this minor essay from among many more obvious illustrations. The piece is more explicitly Oedipal than Bellow seems to remember. "Why was it," Freud asks, "that his indignation against God broke out precisely when he received this particular impression in the dissecting room?" Freud equates "his desire to destroy his father" with "doubt in the existence of God." Bellow speaks of the purity of human motive, but, given his own preferences, he might almost as well have spoken of the purity of belief. Freud concludes with just the sort of certitude that repels him:

> The new impulse, which was displaced into the sphere of religion, was only a repetition of the Oedipal situation and consequently soon met with a similar fate. It succumbed to a powerful opposing current. . . . The conflict seems to have been unfolded in the form of hallucinatory psychosis: inner voices were heard which uttered warnings against resistance to God. . . . The outcome . . . was a kind predetermined by the fate of the Oedipus complex: complete submission to the will of God the Father.[16]

Lying supine is a posture which invites the devil, warns the beleaguered Monsignor Sheen in his book on psychoanalysis. Freud's explanation rivals that of his sometime explanation of love, remembered by Herzog as "a psychosis, usually brief" (*B.* 16.1). Is belief psychosis? Bellow thinks not. Yet it is significant that the humanistic rather than the religious content of the piece most sharply elicits Bellow's ire.

"Is it not true," asks Freud in *The Future of an Illusion,* "that the two main points in the modern educational programme are the retardation

of sexual development and the early application of religious influence?"
Freud laments this Victorian asymmetry and wonders how people "dominated by thought prohibitions" will "attain the psychological ideal, the
primacy of the intelligence."[17] But what if the situation is reversed? What
if the spiritual is more repressed than the sexual? The id triumphant
and the superego underground? Body open and soul furtive? This may
be said to have been the situation in America at least from the mid-sixties
through the seventies. The consequences for psychoanalysis were great.
A Freudian analyst speaks of this topsy-turvy swing of history. Virginity
was once a value, notes Henry Lowenfeld; now perhaps it is a taboo.[18]
He cites the case of a patient who broke her hymen with a shampoo bot-
tle. As for the psychoanalytic ethic of honesty, there is the young woman
who invites her four-year old son to watch her sexual performance with
different lovers. Lowenfeld believes that children do not introject parents anymore but parents introject children. The decline of the superego is the root of the problem, signifying the weakened role of the father
and the eclipse of religion. The Oedipus complex is not resolved. Rather
than hysteria or obsessional neurosis, the neurotic constellations of sexual liberation are depression, emptiness, inability to love. There is a
problem for libido theory. You can cure frigidity but what can you do
for promiscuity? Much of Bellow's writing since *Herzog*—the sexual
grotesquerie might almost have come out of *Mr. Sammler's Planet*—
responds to this second reversed reality.

To speak of religion in Bellow, then, is to speak of it in a cultural
predicament quite different from Freud's. Freud was slaying a dragon;
Bellow is preserving a dinosaur. Though he has little sympathy for ritual
orthodoxy, he has far less for Freud's description of religion as universal obsessional neurosis. Herzog rejects just this term. For Bellow, as for
the religious man, superego is not primarily equated with a usually
repressive society, not part of the Oedipal drama writ large. Aware of
"the harm done by people of high principles," Herzog nonetheless
records his dissent from the psychoanalytic view: "Instead of laying the
blame as Freud does on the excess of superego, I would say that the doing of good relieves the poor burdened human soul" (*B* 20.40, 195). For
Bellow, conscience remains intact as a means of individual assertion, in
an age where many have confused it with pleasure. Like the believer,
Bellow thinks that psychoanalysis undermines morality. Freud advocates
nothing. D. H. Lawrence was right in saying that this is why he can never
"get down to the rock on which he must build his church."[19] Rieff puts
it precisely in saying that Lawrence charges Freud with having "forgotten the prayerful attitude that man ought to have toward himself."[20]
Bellow's Gonzaga puts the contemporary lack of moral intensity more

dramatically: *"Go away. You have no holy ones"* (*SD*, 175). Though certainly
not in Lawrentian terms, it is fair to say that Bellow desires to express
the prayerful attitude. Augie March's sense of the amor fati as blessedness rather than indifference, Tommy Wilhelm's funeral parlor trans-
figuration, Henderson's self-proclaimed "mediumistic and attuned" soul,
Herzog's addressing God as "Thou," Sammler's knowledge of the contract, Citrine's musing on Humboldt's transcendence—all of these attest
to the prayerful attitude.

What, then, is the quality of Bellow's belief? Erich Fromm's distinction between authoritarian and humanistic religion takes us close to the
answer. The first involves self-abasement, subjection of the individual
to a higher end, the "fear and trembling" of contrition. The powers of
the self are projected onto God. The soul, or self, is slight compared to
life after death, or the Fatherland. Humanistic religion, on the other
hand, is "centered around man and his strength." It does, of course, imply a oneness with the "All," and it is "theistic"; however, it insists that
"God is a symbol of *man's powers.*"[21] Spinoza is an example. He affirmed
God's immanence but denied his transcendence (for which, we may note,
he was excommunicated). In the humanist perspective, as Fromm sees
it, the teachings of Buddha, Isaiah, Christ, Socrates, and Spinoza are the
same. In humanistic religion, "conscience is not the internalized voice
of authority but man's own voice, the guardian of our integrity. . . . Sin
is not primarily sin against God but sin against ourselves."[22] Obedience
is not the issue.

As a Jew out of the synagogue, a man who defines religious feeling
largely in reaction to a profound lack in the secular life in which he is
saturated, Bellow is certainly distant from authoritarian religion. Some
may think that he is distant from religion altogether, lacking in the commitment (which may necessarily include institutional involvement) that
makes it a way of life. Be that as it may, Bellow is more attuned to tradition than Fromm's distinctions will allow. For Bellow, God is not merely
a symbol of man's powers or a symbol of anything. God is not simply
immanent but transcendent and, usually, the Jewish God. He is "Thou"
but he is not, as Herzog puts it in manuscript, "God the Father, above
the clouds. I don't believe in that" (*B.* 18.12, 131). Conscience is man's
own voice but a voice with a transcendental yearning.

The ending of Herzog is perhaps the clearest case in point. Herzog
is not without some self-abasement (*"My face too blind, my mind too limited,
my instincts too narrow"*), but God, somehow personal, is defined in terms
of Herzog's emotional response to Him (*"Thou movest me"*). There is always the humanistic questioning (*"But this intensity, doesn't it mean anything? Is it an idiot joy that makes this animal, the most peculiar animal of all,*

exclaim something?"). Yet reason will take him only so far *("But I have no arguments to make about it"*). Just as his faith receives support from "nature" *("Something produces intensity, a holy feeling, as oranges produce orange, as grass green, as birds heat"*), his God concludes in man *("I am pretty well satisfied to be, to be just as it is willed, and for as long as I may remain in occupancy"*) (*H*, 340).

If Fromm's sense of the unity of spiritual worthies is rather indiscriminate, we may recall that Sammler's fascination with Eckhart and Citrine's with Rudolf Steiner is no less universalizing. Bellow's is not the belief of perfect faith. Faith may even surprise the Bellow protagonist, issuing usually from an unshakable sense of the ethical. "I wilfully misread my contract," thinks Herzog in a characteristic metaphor of obligation. "I never was the principal, but only on loan to myself," he continues, using a metaphor that Hattie Waggoner of "Leaving the Yellow House" also uses. She is on loan from her real, that is, unconscious self, the reservoir of her spirit. Herzog, however, is on loan from above rather than below: "Evidently I continue to believe in God. Though never admitting it. But what else explains my conduct and my life?" (*H*, 231). His subsequent recoil from murder is to make that explanation even more clear. Having reached a plateau of moral clarity, Herzog earns the right to correspond with God—a humanist assumption! The man of letters in the religious world. His words to God are very much those of humanist religion. *"How my mind has struggled to make coherent sense,"* says our seeker of the morally real. Contemporaneous as his words are, they have a trace of humility: *"I have not been too good at it. But have desired to do your unknowable will, taking it, and you, without symbols. Everything of intensest significance"* (*H*, 325f.). God is emotionally charged meaning, value, an immediate experience, an authentic illumination not to be diluted by constructs standing for something else (e.g., Freudian symbolism). This is not authoritarian religion but the humanist religion that equates God with the highest, purest feeling. He adds, with the post-Romantic, postmodern psychological fatigue not to be confused with religious self-abasement: *"Especially if divested of me"* (*H*, 326). Herzog's salvation is freedom from the cult of sensibility. In a draft of a letter to Monsignor Hilton, Herzog writes: *"If I had to put it in my own way,"* and he always does, *"I would say that to be inescapably closed up in a world of one's own making is hell"* (*B*. 18.10). Herzog knows the condition firsthand, and he calls the transcendence of it God.

"Love thy neighbor as thyself"—Fromm says that this is the essence of religion. But he didn't count on an era of self-hatred. There seems to be nothing in the humorless analyst that would put him in touch with our wrenching comedy on this subject. Herzog does pay more than lip-

service to "our employment by other human beings and their employment by us" as the "real and essential question" (*H*, 272), but he does
not have the answer. Nor do any of the later Bellow protagonists, much
as they may want it. Cain and Abel, rather than Oedipus, are central to
the Judeo-Christian tradition. The issue of responsibility for the other
person has always been a difficult one. "Am I my brother's keeper?" is,
in its original context, a rhetorical question raised by a maniac. All the
more reason that the answer must be yes. If the mutual love of brothers
is difficult, how much more difficult is that of neighbors. In *Civilization
and Its Discontents*, Freud says the Golden Rule is "impossible to fulfill."
Bellow would have to agree that "such an enormous inflation of love
can only lower its value,"[23] but he would reject Freud's contention that
it is "a commandment which is really justified by the fact that nothing
else runs so strongly counter to the original nature of man."[24] While not
so optimistic as Fromm, he is not so pessimistic as Freud.

Freud has contempt for what Fromm defines as humanist religion,
the poetized religion of "as if," God as symbol in a universe of tolerant
cultural relativism. The pious neurotics at least had belief, not just spiritual need. On this point it is important to emphasize that Fromm's humanism excludes actual belief but Bellow's does not. Bellow easily meets
Fromm's criteria for the religious mentality: (1) wonder (2) "ultimate concern" (Tillich) (3) oneness of separate self with All. The first two the
Bellow protagonist typically exhibits, the last less fully, though Bellow
dramatizes it shamelessly, if wryly, in *Humboldt's Gift*. Freud would have
said that Citrine can't let go of poppa and thus exhibits the infantilism
of the oceanic feeling. As for "ultimate concern," Freud writes to Marie
Bonaparte that, "The moment a man questions the meaning and value
of life he is sick, since objectively neither has any existence."[25] Man may
seek the light but it will only give him another insight into darkness.
On this assumption, wonder cannot be pristine but only an experience
of darkness overcome. Bellow would counter that these are prime illustrations of the usual psychoanalytic reductiveness. "You're a hard-nosed
man," shouts Bummidge to his "analyst." "Why do you prefer the ugli-
est interpretations? Why do you pollute all my good impulses?" (*LA*, 27).

Freud does acknowledge the civilizing tendencies of religion, even
in its most primitive form. In *Totem and Taboo* he writes, "It is difficult
to resist the notion that, long before a table of laws was handed down
by any god, these savages were in possession of a living commandment:
'Thou shalt not kill,' a violation of which would not go unpunished."[26]
Freud sees religion as the origin of ethics. Curiously, Freud comes back
every now and then to the one religious (cultural) commandment that
most fascinates Bellow, one that provides a stay against nihilistic chaos.

Even a tyrant or a dictator, says Freud in *The Future of an Illusion,* "has every reason to want others to keep at least one cultural commandment: thou shalt not kill." The alternative for Freud is intolerable. "How short-sighted," he says, "to strive for the abolition of culture! What would then remain would be the state of nature, and that is far harder to endure."[27] The state of nature for Bellow is not so nearly Hobbesian, though in *Mr. Sammler's Planet* and, particularly, in *The Dean's December,* it almost is. In any case, the prohibition against murder does not amount to religion.

There is an important distinction to be drawn in the ways Bellow and Freud view the act of murder. Freud sees all murder as part of the Oedipal drama, thereby shedding a brilliant light on, say, the Oedipal Dostoevsky. In his essay "Dostoevsky and Parricide," Freud considers *The Brothers Karamazov, Oedipus Rex* and *Hamlet* as Oedipal dramas which, being three of the greatest works of literature, lend indirect support to his interpretation of psychological experience. Of the murder in Dostoevsky's novel Freud writes, "It is a matter of indifference who committed the crime; psychology is interested only in discovering who desired it, and who welcomed it when it was done, and for that reason, all the brothers are equally guilty." Because of the Oedipal reality in Dostoevsky, "the criminal is to him almost a Redeemer, who has taken on himself the guilt which others would otherwise have had to bear. One need not now commit murder, after he has committed murder, but one must be grateful to him, because without him, one would oneself have to have been a murderer."[28] This interpretation can be documented in *The Brothers Karamazov,* which gives us a father well worth killing. But Freud makes virtually the same point in his discussion of tragedy in *Totem and Taboo,* where he speaks of the tragic hero in general. The primal crime underlies all: "In the remote reality it had actually been the members of the Chorus who caused the Hero's suffering; now, however, they exhausted themselves with sympathy and regret, and it was the Hero himself who was responsible for his own sufferings. The crime which was thrown on to his shoulders, presumptuousness and rebelliousness against a great authority, was precisely the crime for which the members of the Chorus, the company of brothers, was responsible. Thus the tragic Hero becomes, though it might be against his will, the redeemer of the Chorus."[29] Here as elsewhere, the brilliance of Freud's perceptions makes one feel that, anthropological evidence to the contrary notwithstanding, there must be a rightness to what he says.

Yet a crucial moral distinction remains. For Bellow, and for humanism generally, there is all the difference in the world between committing a murder and wishing to do so, between impulse and deed. Bellow has said that this is a distinction between the Jewish and Christian points of view: "The Jewish outlook is that unless you have actually committed the crime you are not guilty of it, no matter what you have thought or dreamed."[30] This is also the humanist and liberal view. Man may be vulnerable, the capacity for evil (*yetzer hara* in the old Hebrew expression) may be always present, but so is the capacity for good (*yetzer hatov*), and in the struggle between them lies the reality of moral life. For Freud and for a certain kind of Christianity, determinism or predestination essentially obliterated the distinction between wish and act. Nowhere are Bellow's humanist sympathies vis-a-vis Freudianism more clearly drawn in terms of moral emphasis. The assertions of free will in Bellow may be small but there is, for example, a crucial difference between Herzog's desire to murder and his decision not to. It is the criminal who is guilty, but we are not "equally guilty" (as Freud puts it). The problem is complex, for as Freud says in "Dostoevsky and Parricide": "A moral man is one who reacts to the temptation he feels in his heart without yielding to it."[31] In other words, Freud does make a distinction between what psychology is "interested in" and what morality is "interested in." Psychology is not ethics; health values are not moral values. Granted. But any system has moral implications and there is a key difference here: in Bellow there is the attraction of the good, in Freud the renunciation of the bad. As Rieff puts it: "Freud could not speak of the desire to be good in the same sense that he could speak of desiring what we have to renounce for the good. Surely this is one-sided. Aspiration may be as genuine as desire, and as original."[32] With his emphasis on the sway of the unconscious, Freud is nothing if not profound. But there can be the greatest depth in the obvious. Freud sees this when he considers biological desire (e.g., the babe at its mother's breast) but does not when he weighs moral desire. His dark view of human nature misses the profundity of simplicity. If the good can ever be considered simple.

Yet Bellow and Freud share a skepticism about the extremity of Dostoevskian goodness, that "rage for goodness so near to vileness and murderousness," as Albert Corde puts it (*DD*, 161). Neither is satisfied with the "murder-saviour" type, which Corde sees in the relatively moderate Toby Winthrop, and both see in Raskolnikov and Stavrogin. "It was foreign, bookish—it was Dostoevsky stuff that the vices of Sodom coexisted with the adoration of Holy Sophia," says Corde (*DD*, 130). Bellow characterizes this as abstract modern consciousness, but Freud has a clearer explanation of the phenomenon in its acute Dostoevskian manifestation. He is skeptical of penitence which "becomes a technique to enable murder to be done."[33] In *The Future of an Illusion* he states the social *raison d'etre* for "the sublime conclusion" of Russian mysticism "that sin is indispensable for the full enjoyment of the blessing of divine grace, and therefore fundamentally . . . pleasing to God." Freud says, "It is well known that the priests could only keep the masses submissive to religion by making these great concessions to human instincts."[34] Freud attacks the holy sinner as part of his argument to undermine religion, which he sees as authoritarian. Bellow, in his humanist stance, never without some skepticism about religion even in Sammler and Citrine, has Corde say, "So what was this pure-in-spirit bit? For an American who had been around, a man in his mid-fifties, this beatitude language was unreal" (*DD*, 130). Religion must meet the humanist requirement of reason.[35]

III

Despite this point of similarity, Freud's essay on "Dostoevsky and Parricide" illustrates still another sharp difference between Bellow and Freud, their relationship to art, literature in particular. Brilliant as it is, Freud's piece treats Dostoevsky more as a case than a writer. Freud finds Dostoevsky fascinating for the clarity with which he confirms the Oedipal drama. Freud's interest in content, then, is of a special kind. He has no interest in formal or stylistic matters and not even much interest in thematic ones. *The Brothers Karamazov* is mainly an instance of Dostoevsky's personality, particularly his neurotic configurations and how they damaged his artistic mission. The illumination of a psychoanalytically relevant pattern takes the place of moral and aesthetic evaluation of a work, which is why Freud may make much of a work that has little literary significance (e.g., Jensen's *Gradiva*). Freud gives us dazzling insights into Dostoevsky the neurotic, but he cannot really tell us why his work is good or bad, great or mediocre. In these ways, Freud's treatment of Dostoevsky is similar to his treatment of Leonardo. Freud is, in fact, uneasy with art. Otto Rank maintained that Freudian theory could not cope with the creative artist. And Freud seems to agree with him. It is in the essay on "Dostoevsky and Parricide" that Freud issued this famous disclaimer: "Unfortunately, before the problem of the creative artist, analysis must lay down its arms."[36] Why is this so? Because there is something about art that eludes the theory of unconscious determinism, there is something that is larger than Freud's system. This has for a long time been Bellow's opinion. And art is not, in his view, the only thing that is larger than Freud's system. As Herzog puts it (in manuscript), referring to just this remark, "Freud confessed he laid down his arms before the problem of art. He should have surrendered to all the mysteries of high inspiration, including the work of moral genius" (B.17.8). Again Bellow insists that there is an area of freedom that

Freudian rationalism does not comprehend. Lionel Trilling has written of the similarities between literature and psychoanalysis, which is "a science of tropes, of metaphor and its variants, synecdoche and metonymy."[37] And everyone knows Freud's claim that it was not he but the poets who discovered the unconscious. But what unconscious was it that "they" discovered? Not one that defines art as daydream, escape from reality, mild narcosis, or "substitute gratification" for "the oldest cultural renunciations."[38] Freud thinks it unfortunate that psychoanalysis must throw up its hands before "the problem" of art, but it is fortunate from the artist's point of view. Art is freedom of expression, health rather than sickness, genius rather than neurosis. Freud never grants to art the autonomy the artist gives it. He sees the imagination as a symptom of the unconscious. In this sense he values criticism over art. The interpretation of the subject is the key to art just as psychoanalysis is the key to the unconscious. As a novelist who values imagination, as a humanist whose art takes a particularly moral turn, as a human being who believes in the primacy of inspiration, Bellow could not agree with these formulations. "If I hold with Freud in anything," says Bellow, "I would hold with him in this one matter, that reality is a projection of something or other. Fictions are fascinating and relatively coherent projections."[39] He sees the novel, however, as a projection of "truth, or of reality," terms which do not correspond to Freud's idea of religion as a projection of revolt against the father or art as a projection of unconscious wish-fulfillment. To the term "truth" Freud prefers "fantasy."

Bellow's criticism of Freud does not break new ground as such. Rather it is a profound version of the familiar criticism Freud termed "unjust" in *The Ego and the Id,* when he said that "psychoanalysis has been reproached time after time with ignoring the higher, moral, supra-personal side of human nature." Freud claims that his critics ignore the nature of the ego and superego,"the representative of our relation to our parents."[40] But his ego-ideal, or superego, remains an outgrowth of Oedipal struggle. That is, Freud's moral world follows his limiting terminology, and it is a world which becomes increasingly claustral. Bellow is in essential agreement with Rieff's view of Freud as a modern thinker, as one who gives us a weak ego and an oppressive superego, with the nihilistic problematics this entails.

But Bellow is in radical disagreement with Rieff as to the consequences of seeing Freud this way. In Rieff's books on Freud and psychoanalytic theory, the author accepts with open arms the diminished concept of the self which it has been Bellow's task to repudiate. Where the protagonist of a Bellow work is typically a citizen-hero, Rieff speaks of a "citizen-patient." Although Rieff is wary of seeing "an admittedly sick society in terms of that subtlest ... authoritarian image, the hospital,"[41] this is exactly what he does. If one can speak of a sociologist of mind having a controlling metaphor, this is Rieff's: "In the emergent democracy of the sick ... [the] hospital is succeeding the church and the parliament as the archetypal institution of Western culture."[42] Freud is "the first out-patient of the hospital culture in which we live."[43] In *The Triumph of the Therapeutic*, Rieff predicts that "modern society will mount psychodramas far more frequently than its ancestors mounted miracle plays, with patient-analysts acting out their inner lives, after which they could extemporize the final act as interpretation." Rieff calls this "hospital-theater."[44] What Rieff considers serious, Bellow considers farce in *The Last Analysis*. The fruits of hospital culture may be strange. "We are, I fear, getting to know one another," says Rieff.[45] With his combination of elegance and lugubriousness, good will and fatalism, Rieff at times reminds one of no one as much as the old radio character Digby Odell, "your friendly undertaker," who nowadays would be reincarnated as your genial therapist. Freud saw ethics as a "therapeutic"[46]activity of the superego, assuming by this metaphor the sick person as the norm. Making the same assumption, Rieff sees any "system of moralizing demands" as "therapy," the "therapeutic" goal being "a manipulatable sense of well-being."[47]

It is precisely this view that Charlie Citrine attacks in *Humboldt's Gift* when Cantabile, looking through his library, asks about *The Triumph of the Therapeutic* (a phrase which first appears in Selma Fraiberg's negative review of Rieff's book on Freud). Citrine is quite clear about his dislike of the book: "It says that psychotherapists may become the new spiritual leaders of mankind. A disaster. Goethe was afraid the modern world might turn into a hospital. Every citizen unwell" (*HG*, 175). Rieff sees this new psychological man benignly as "the healthy hypochondriac."[48] Citrine can only wonder whether "hypochondria" is "a creation of the medical profession," concluding with a flourish:

> According to this author, when culture fails to deal with the feeling of emptiness and the panic to which man is disposed (and he does say "disposed") other agents come forward to put us together with therapy, with glue, or slogans, or spit, or as that fellow Gumbein [Harold Rosenberg] the art critic says, poor wretches are recycled on the couch. This view is even more pessimistic than the one held by Dostoevsky's Grand Inquisitor.... A natural disposition to feelings of emptiness and panic is worse than that. Much worse. What it really means is that we human beings are insane. The last

institution which controlled such insanity (on this view) was the Church. (*HG*, 175f)

Rieff inverts Pangloss so as to say that the therapeutic is the best of all possible worlds.

It is true, as Rieff claims, that "the understanding of normal character through the neurotic character, of health through sickness, is Freud's master trope."[49] This method surely is at the heart of Freud's genius, but it may, finally, give us a greater insight into sickness than health. Moreover, it may impose a modernist norm where none exists. The matter of Freud's master trope could be put quite differently. "Freud could build a theory of human nature," says Irving Kristol, "on the basis of his experience with hysterics and neurotics, a unique and strange achievement which testifies to our modern psychic equilibrium, whose fulcrum is at the edge of an abyss."[50] A skeptical humanist balance resides in this perspective, with which Bellow would be sympathetic. Rieff acknowledges that "there is a fatal lack of commitment about Freud's ideal type. To be busy, spirited, and self-confident is a goal that will inspire only those who have resigned the ghosts of older and nobler aspirations."[51] Yet Rieff willingly does so. Unlike Freud, Bellow constructs a past that he can honor, and he is in frequent, perhaps too frequent, correspondence with its ghosts.

IV

Though Bellow rejects Freudian thought in these fundamental respects, he is nonetheless sympathetic to and sometimes indebted to it in others. An admirer of Montaigne, an observer of local mores, Bellow is, like Freud, very well aware of the cost of the civilization he defends. A character like Artur Sammler knows a good deal about renunciation. Yet Freud's attributing all civilization to renunciation seems to Bellow unnecessarily severe. "Take what you want," says the Spanish proverb, "and pay for it." Freud is the genius of this theme, one which Bellow fully understands. No one is so taken up with psychic costs as Freud, our economist of the self. Indeed, he knows as well the cost of many things you never even get to "take." But it may be that life has its unexpected rewards, its serendipitous moments, its joys unmixed with pain. Or at least if not that a possibility of accomplishment for which one need not go halfway to castration. It may be that, with Augie March, one can perceive the blessedness in the *amor fati*. Or that, with Herzog, one can be moved by the principle of creation.

To the extent that Freudian disillusion is a repudiation of utopian progressivism, Bellow endorses it. Both reject Marx, knowing the essentialist wisdom of *plus ça change plus c'est la meme chose* (though Herzog feels or hopes that there are good human qualities yet to be discovered). They are both conservative liberals (if Freud can be called liberal in any sense) who place personality above politics, knowing, stoically, that the self must be defined in the face of constant crisis. Both recognize the need to recover instinct. Though Bellow thinks Freud inflates the pleasure principle, both abide by some version of the reality principle, preferring reason to primal energy. Yet Bellow gives much more to intuition and inspiration, is more trusting of emotional response. *"Trouve avant de chercher,"* says Charlie Citrine (quoting Valéry). "This finding before seeking was my special gift. If I had any" (*HG,* 73). Citrine's is the very reverse of the Freudian procedure. Given the Freudian system, the chances are that one will find what one is looking for, and what one finds will not be very nice. "We may reject the existence of an original, as it were natural, capacity to distinguish good from bad," says Freud.[52] Bellow is not so disillusioned, holding with Sammler that "we know." With his metaphors of contract and obligation, Bellow is more Jewish. Jokes and family feeling, integrity and argumentativeness may not a Jew make. Though these are more indicative than pinochle and cabanas, or sleeping on Saturday afternoon, Freud's Jewish identity remains much more problematic than Bellow's. But they both have one. As if in tacit homage, most of the Bellow protagonists have read Freud—even, in one manuscript, Eugene Henderson (*B.* 6.22, 323). And there is frequent reference in Bellow to psychoanalytic terminology. There may even be a rare instance of an image Bellow has taken over from Freud in his fiction, consciously or unconsciously.[53]

As a novelist who pursues self-definition partly through a recapturing of childhood experience, Bellow's occupation parallels Freud's. Both Freud and Herzog have their "personal histories, old tales from old times that may not be worth remembering" (*H,* 149). Both literature and psychoanalysis posit the primacy of emotion. To complement Bellow's humanism, Freud is more of a thinker than a scientist. He thought of himself as a humanist rather than a physician. Some Bellow characters, perhaps too many, read like case histories—Tommy Wilhelm and Dr. Adler being the most prominent—but Henderson, Herzog, Mady and Humboldt may be so considered. Herzog does not seem to mind, thinking jauntily, "If I am out of my mind, it's all right with me" (*H,* 18). He is diagnosed as a reactive-depressive. A certain psychological disarray is essential to Bellow's comic sense. More than this, there are times when we seem to be eavesdropping on an analytic session, as in the following reflection from Herzog: "What I seem to do, thought Herzog, is to inflame myself voluptuously, aesthetically, until I reach a sexual climax. And that climax looks like a resolution and an answer to many 'higher' problems" (*H,* 208). It is all the more significant that Herzog here is talking to himself, not to his analyst. Psychoanalysis has become part of personal style. In some of these "sessions," Herzog invokes the master, as when he records his guilt about being an apparition to Marco: "This particular sensitivity about meeting and parting had to be tamed. Such trembling sorrow—he tried to think what term Freud had for it: partial return of repressed traumatic material ultimately traceable to the death instinct?— should not be imparted to children, not that tremulous lifelong swoon of death. This same emotion, as Herzog the student was aware, was held to be the womb of cities, heavenly as well as earthly, mankind being unable to part with its beloved or its dead in this world or the next." But to Herzog, holding his daughter, the emotion is "tyranny" (*H,* 280). The first half of this idea comes largely from Freud's "Mourning and Melancholia," which is actually mentioned later in the novel when Herzog thinks that "the metabolic wastes of fatigue (he was fond of these physiological explanations; this one came from Freud's essay Mourning and Melancholia) made him temporarily light-hearted, even gay" (*H,* 302).

Though mentioned only in passing in *Herzog,* "Mourning and Melancholia" is more prominent in the manuscripts, elaborately pondered in a few versions (*B.*17.5; *B.*20.40; *B.*21.32). *"Dear Dr. Freud,"* the depressive Herzog writes in a letter, *"I have recently in a dark hour studied your essay on Mourning and Melancholia, as well as the papers of your colleague Dr. Abraham* . . . . As you might imagine I did not *read your essay by accident. Man prays in our religion (or former religion) for a 'new heart.' Radical determinism like yours offers no place for new hearts. But why else would anyone pray or seek light?"* To seeking light through prayer Freud would hardly be responsive, so Herzog pursues the therapeutic line:

> *The depressive character is narcissistic. It fears the disappearance of the beloved. Above all terrors it places the terror of abandonment and naked solitude. So with secret hate it cuts off the deserters. Who then reappears within—introjected as you say in your jargon. Then the voice of the love slain speaks continually within, and the depressive abuses and criticizes himself. You say then that the depressive is often able to state the truth about himself quite reliably and accurately, though he often overstates the case, and you add— it must have been irresistible—that it is odd to think that insights should be the result of disease. Or, truthfulness is a consequence of disease. But* my dear man, I am really very fond of that tart old man, *let us go back a bit. Is it possible that some people are born with a greater metaphysical terror than others, with less sheath or with (less) power to apprehend the*

> *inhuman and the void? William James makes room in his system for such*
> *types, whom he calls "tender-minded"... however I am grateful to you for cer-*
> *tain information, such as that the melancholic is abnormal in stripping his*
> *libido so rapidly from the deserting lover. Suffering from love yet intolerably*
> *cruel.... Have however some singular power that prevents me from laying*
> *my head docilely under your sober shade. One of these Moseses of whom you*
> *wrote—called meek. (B. 21.32, 235f)*

The prime clinical point is made briefly by Edvig in the novel (*H,* 53);
in manuscript we see Herzog virtually savoring the Freudian wisdom.
But with reservations, for Herzog rejects a priori Freud's "radical determinism" as he resists the illusion of total explanation in the diagnosis.
He sees just how his reaction to his recent marital disaster has to do with
"abandonment" (associated with fear of abandonment by the mother in
the earlier versions, as in Freud). He concurs that sickness can be the
blow that brings truth, but he attributes part of his depression to
metaphysical causes, causes in the nature of things, preferring to include
James's tendermindedness as a necessary element in the explanation,
thereby converting sickness into a form of ordinary consciousness.
Freud's tartness needs sweetening; even when Bellow is accepting him,
it is only a partial acceptance. But if *Herzog* shows how seriously Bellow
can take Freud, *The Last Analysis,* written at about the same time, shows
that farcical reduction of the claims of psychoanalysis was not far away.
Herzog's "singular power," his non-analyzable soul, will never let him
rest comfortably with Freud. As if to underscore his tenderminded perception, one more amenable to humanistic comprehension, Herzog signs
off, somewhat obscurely, as a meek Moses. The reference is to Freud's
Moses and Monotheism, which posits two Moses figures who are made to
become one: first, the masterful violent Egyptian who worshipped Aton,
and, second, the patient, "meek" Midianite who worshipped Jahve.[54]
Freud's book is fascinating but atypical in the sense that, as Rieff puts
it, "Freud acknowledges that civilization can be moved by spiritual as
well as instinctual discontents."[55] The book is indeed ingenious but eccentric, for against virtually all canons of evidence, it imposes the Oedipal
pattern as clearly as in *Totem and Taboo.* Our contemporary Moses does
not make much of it.

Though Herzog tells Dr. Freud that he is *"immersed in your Collected*
Papers" (B.18.18), though snatches of Freudian language appear in many
places in Bellow, usually seriously (sometimes comically, e.g., Hoberly's
unrequited love is now called "hysterical dependency" (*H,* 180)), though
Bellow recognizes the reality of *an* unconscious, of repression, of the psychological importance of childhood, of filial ambivalence, of behavior

conceived as conflict, nevertheless he can accept Freudianism as at best a partial explanation. Yet he too wants man to be the masculine achiever, and he sees sensuality as a temptation along the way; he too defines woman too quickly in terms of sensuality, and he fears too readily that he will be weakened by her. He too is puzzled by what "they want," though he has a much more contemporary sense of how the intellectual and sensual actually do mix in women. And Bellow is taken by that most Freudian of fables, the ant and the grasshopper. "The ant was once the hero, but now the grasshopper is the whole show," laments Govinda Lal (*MSP*, 216). Few people, it seems to Bellow, are willing to undergo the necessary renunciation which civilization demands. Immediate gratification has submerged higher purpose. For this perversion of his instinctual system, Freud is not responsible. Charlie Citrine is described by the post-Freudian analyst Ellenbogen as "an ant longing to be a grasshopper" (*HG*, 164). Not so, as a Freudian would understand. Perhaps the most enduring instance of Freud's influence on Bellow is the novelist's contempt for grasshopper culture. But, for Bellow, the Freudian instinctual system does not offer a strong enough moral counter to the demands of this culture. There is a lack of autonomy. Bellow sees that Freud wished to preserve human nature from cultural determinism, but he does not want to substitute for it a biological determinism. In a wise rabbinic commentary, it is suggested that God did not say "And it was good" after creating man because man's nature was not determined. The poets of Genesis knew what Freud did not, the pull of moral indeterminacy. Bellow possesses this knowledge.

Notes

1. Saul Bellow, *Herzog* (New York: Viking, 1964), 13; further parenthetical page references will be preceded by *H*. References to other Bellow works, with their respective abbreviations, will be from the Viking Press editions: *AM—The Adventures of Augie March* (1953); *SD—Seize the Day*, with three short stories (1956); *LA—The Last Analysis* (1965); *MSP—Mr. Sammler's Planet* (1970); *HG—Humboldt's Gift* (1975). The one exception to this Viking list is *DD—The Dean's December* (New York: Harper & Row, 1982).
2. "Notebooks," *Herzog* (B. 19.36, 113). Used by permission of Saul Bellow. All subsequent "Notebooks" citations will be given in the text. For a systematic critical use of these materials, see my *Saul Bellow: Vision and Revision* (Durham: Duke University Press, 1984).
3. Philip Rieff, *Freud: The Mind of the Moralist* (New York: Viking, 1959), 131.
4. Clara Thompson, *Psychoanalysis: Evolution and Development* (New York: Grove Press, 1950), 43.
5. Sigmund Freud, *Totem and Taboo*, trans. James Strachey (New York: Norton, 1962), 70.

6. Robert Boyers, et al., "Literature and Culture: An Interview with Saul Bellow," *Salmagundi* 30 (Summer 1975): 19. Hereafter referred to as *Salmagundi*.
7. Rieff, *Freud*, 43.
8. Philip Rieff, "Introduction" to D. H. Lawrence, *Psychoanalysis and the Unconscious: Fantasia of the Unconscious* (New York: Viking, 1960), viii.
9. One deep reader of a Freudian cast is John J. Clayton, in *Saul Bellow: In Defense of Man* (Bloomington: Indiana University Press, 1977). For him Augie March's "darkness" is the Terrible Father. Never mind that Augie does not really have a father; Henderson's and Herzog's will do. What is so "terrible" about Henderson's father? Doesn't Henderson try to reach his dead father with his violin playing? (Return of the repressed?) Is poor, vulnerable, dignified Father Herzog "terrible"? (Herzog's perfectly resolved Oedipus complex?) Clayton says that Herzog is ridden by Oedipal guilt and the resultant fear of castration and death. Therefore, the murder scene in *Herzog* is more of a father's act of vengeance, mimed by the guilty party to relieve himself. Gersbach is like Herzog, so that by not killing him Herzog is saying, father won't kill me. I'm safe (Clayton, 222). And more: "Underneath Moses Herzog is Stephan Rojack" (Clayton, 195). If *this* were true, he would have killed Gersbach and Mady. Herzog's saying that Gersbach "sought me in her flesh" is interpreted as follows: Gersbach does so just as Allbee sought Asa Levanthal in the body of the whore. In other words, he is a sexual object for Gersbach, and feeling this, Herzog experiences guilt. His sense of being a male whore is projected into the court case of Aleck-Alice, an actual male prostitute (Clayton, 231). A sense of victimization is involved, but is Herzog aware of being a male whore? Passionate about the dark motive, Clayton says that in *Mr. Sammler's Planet* "the black prince is acting out Sammler's buried self" (Clayton, 238). The proof of this is Sammler's getting upset at Eisen smashing the black man. Isn't the violence itself and all that it means a richly developed moral context enough reason for being upset? Freud cannot be held accountable for every application of his (or Jung's) ideas, but it was inevitable that his system would set this kind of response into motion. There have been more subtle applications.
10. Sigmund Freud, *Civilization and Its Discontents*, trans. James Strachey (New York: Norton, 1961), 13.
11. Ibid., 24f.
12. Bellow is hardly the first to question the Freudian unconscious in terms of motive. In Freud's Vienna, Karl Kraus, among others, made this criticism. He saw the unconscious as creative, healthy, fantastic, good. Jung saw the unconscious as something consciousness should strive for. D. H. Lawrence saw the unconscious or primitive motive as essentially good, though unlike Bellow, he saw this goodness as erotic.
13. Rieff, *Freud*, 215.
14. Freud, *Civilization and Its Discontents*, 65.
15. *Salamagundi*, 18f.

16. Sigmund Freud, "A Religious Experience," trans. James Strachey, in *Character and Culture*, ed. Philip Rieff (New York: Collier, 1963), 272f.
17. Sigmund Freud, *The Future of an Illusion*, trans. W. D. Robson-Scott (Garden City: Anchor-Doubleday, 1957), 85.
18. Henry Lowenfeld, "Psychoanalysis Today," *Partisan Review* 48 (Fall 1981): 446-55 *passim*.
19. In Rieff, ed., D. H. Lawrence, *Fantasia of the Unconscious*, 4.
20. Reiff, "Introduction" to D. H. Lawrence, ix.
21. Erich Fromm, *Psychoanalysis and Religion* (New Haven: Yale University Press, 1950), 37.
22. Ibid., 88.
23. Freud, *Civilization and Its Discontents*, 101.
24. Ibid., 66.
25. Quoted by Philip Rieff, *The Triumph of the Therapeutic* (New York: Harper Torchbooks, 1968), 34.
26. Freud, *Totem and Taboo*, 39.
27. Freud, *Future of an Illusion*, 22.
28. Sigmund Freud, "Dostoevsky and Parricide," *Art and Psychoanalysis*, ed. William Philips (New York: Criterion, 1957), 14f.
29. Freud, *Totem and Taboo*, 156.
30. *Salmagundi*, 16.
31. Freud, "Dostoevsky and Parricide," 3.
32. Rieff, *Freud*, 319.
33. Freud, "Dostoevsky and Parricide," 4.
34. Freud, *Future of an Illusion*, 67f.
35. In Bellow's manuscript, Herzog praises Jaspers: "Recently went through 'The Future of Mankind.' . . . Excellent man. . . . When good sense becomes sublime. Balanced faith based on reason" (*B*. 17.2). Jaspers' brand of existentialism does not offend him.
36. Freud, "Dostoevsky and Parricide," 3.
37. Lionel Trilling, *The Liberal Imagination* (New York: Doubleday Anchor, 1950), 61.
38. Freud, *Future of an Illusion*, 19.
39. *Salmagundi*, 18.
40. Sigmund Freud, *The Ego and the Id*, trans. Joan Riviere (New York: Norton, 1960), 25f.
41. Rieff, *Freud*, 243.
42. Ibid., 355.
43. Ibid., xiii.
44. Rieff, *Triumph of the Therapeutic*, 26.
45. Ibid., 22.
46. Freud, *Civilization and Its Discontents*, 101.
47. Rieff, *Triumph of the Therapeutic*, 13.
48. Ibid., 20.

49. Rieff, *Freud,* 45.
50. Irving Kristol, "God and the Psychoanalysts," *Commentary* (8 November 1949): 441.
51. Rieff, *Freud,* 55.
52. Freud, *Civilization and Its Discontents,* 79.
53. Compare *Herzog,* 232: "Sarah Herzog opened her hand and said, 'Look carefully, now, and you'll see what Adam was made of.' She rubbed the palm of her hand with a finger, rubbed until something dark appeared on the deep-lined skin, a particle of what certainly looked to him like earth," with Freud, *The Interpretation of Dreams,* trans. James Strachey (New York: Avon, 1965), 238: "My mother thereupon rubbed the palms of her hands together . . . and showed me the blackish scales of *epidermis* produced by the friction as a proof that we were made of earth."
54. Sigmund Freud, *Moses and Monotheism,* trans. Katherine Jones (New York: Vintage, 1939), 49.
55. Rieff, *Freud,* 281.

Saul Bellow and the Philosophy of Judaism

L. H. Goldman

I

Despite the varying methodological approaches tracing the progress of Jewish philosophical thought, the basis of the philosophy of Judaism is an ethical monotheism which is Bible-centered. It has been termed a "purposeful" philosophy which is concerned not with First Causes or the origins of creation but rather with the meaning of creation for man.[1] Consequently, it is fundamentally anthropocentric, providing reasons for man's existence and assuming and stressing "human confidence and sufficiency."[2]

Judaism is a legalistic religion encompassing a set of beliefs, rituals, and ethics which set the Jewish people apart from other nations, thereby assuring their own survival. These beliefs are set forth in the Torah and further developed in the form of both an oral and a written tradition which comprise the Talmud. The distinctive qualities of Judaism are its covenant with God, its humanism, and its emphasis on moral action.[3]

The first Jewish philosopher was Abraham, whose speculations concerning the universe brought monotheism to the world.[4] His purpose, however, was not theoretical. He was concerned with establishing a relationship between God and man.[5] Unlike the Hellenists. ancient Jewish philosophers (Talmudists) did not engage in theosophic speculations. These were considered mysteries beyond human comprehension.[6] They accepted the postulates presented in Scripture: God as Creator and man as subservient. They preoccupied themselves with interpreting the meaning of the commandments, with studying the law and its application to everyday life, with establishing the moral structure of the world. They were traditionalists. No doubt the earliest Jewish humanist philosophers were Hillel, the first-

First printed in *Studies in the Literary Imagination* 17, no. 2 (1984): 81–95.

century sage who, when asked to explain the Torah while standing on one foot said, "What is hateful to you do not unto your neighbor; this is the entire Torah. All the rest is commentary," and Rabbi Akiva, of the same period, who made the same assertion by suggesting that the fundamental principle and comprehensive teaching in the Torah is "Love thy neighbor as thyself" (Lev. 19:18).

The Jewish philosophers of the Middle Ages attempted to reconcile the unsystematic values of the Bible with the traditionalist philosophical speculations of the times. Their works form a body of apologetica. The most significant philosopher of this period was Moses Maimonides, a "supreme rationalist," an Aristotelian thinker, and still the best-known exponent of Jewish thought. His approach was not apologetic. As Hartman says, "his concern with philosophy was a concern with truth and not simply with demonstrating the merits of the Jewish tradition."[7] Maimonides contended that Judaism is a fusion of "philosophical spirituality and revealed law."[8] His *Guide of the Perplexed,* a rationalistic account of Judaism and a philosophical interpretation of the Bible, was translated from Hebrew into Latin in the thirteenth century and had a profound influence on Christian scholasticism. The Bible commentaries of Meister Eckhart, for example, owe their origins to Eckhart's contacts with Jewish philosophy, especially Maimonides's *Guide.*[9] Thomas Aquinas and Duns Scotus were also influenced by Maimonides.

During the modern period, from the eighteenth century on, a new movement within Judaism, Chasidism, developed. This was a folk movement aimed to fill the spiritual needs of the times. It was a movement born in adversity: the problems caused by the aftermath of the Chmelnicki massacres and the lack of proper leadership in the wake of the false Sabbetean and Frankist movements. The thrust of Chasidism is mystic, kabalistic, and emotional. It generates a mass appeal because it is non-intellectual and non-rationalistic. In fact, a sharp schism between the Chasidists and their opponents, the *Mitnagdim*—the intellectuals and rationalists—developed and continues to the present day.

In the mid-twentieth century the ethical values of Judaism were severely attacked by Hitler and his Nazi philosophy. Nazi philosophical thought did not appear spontaneously. It was nurtured during the gestation period of previous German philosophers. Hitler recognized that his war against the Jews was a war against twentieth-century humanism with the sole purpose of extirpating it at its roots: razing the humanism of Judaism and replacing it with a Nordic god of a Darwinian-Nietzschean-Wagnerian-Chamberlainian species. In 1936, in a paper read at Heidelberg University, Ernst Krieck, a Hitlerian professor of philosophy, noted: "The idea of humanism . . . is a philosophical principle of the eighteenth century caused by conditions of that time. It is in no sense binding upon us as we live under different conditions and under different fate."[10]

Jewish philosophy in the mid-twentieth century, after the Holocaust and after Auschwitz, has become more theosophic and thanatosophic. Humanists and theologians are trying to come to terms with the dichotomy of a God-centered universe and the Holocaust, which seemed to indicate to many the absence of God and the reign of nihilism. While the growth of Holocaust literature is burgeoning—diaries, testimonies, novels, and philosophic speculations—Saul Bellow's writings epitomize the moral outlook that is an integral part of the Jewish world view despite the cloud of death that hovers over the Jewish people. One of the striking contrasts between Bellow's philosophical stance and that of his contemporaries is that whereas most of the writers of the twentieth century nurture and agonize over a nihilistic outlook on life, Bellow's world view is refreshingly optimistic. This cleavage is caused in the main by Bellow's (subconscious) indebtedness to Jewish philosophers and possibly the influence of their writings on Christian thinkers with whom Bellow is familiar.[11]

Bellow presents a consistently Jewish philosophical view which is all-pervasive in his works. It takes the form of an ethical monotheism, essentially the ethical optimism expressed by Leo Baeck.[12] Bellow's source is not necessarily the works of Baeck, Maimonides, Buber, or other major exponents of Jewish philosophical thought. Bellow goes back to the original source, the Bible. His ethical optimism/monotheism is simplistic, yet sublime, capturing the essence of Jewish thought while suggesting a loss in the historical-evolutionary process. Appearing after Hitler's attempted obliteration of humanism, Bellow's works strive to reestablish the foundations of society by reaffirming the world's need for morality, for the return to the humanism of Judaism. Shiv Kumar has pointed out: "Judaism has recognized early in the history of mankind that the Faustian impulses in human nature will result in man's undoing if allowed a full rein."[13] Bellow, who has often said that the artist's purpose is a moral one, makes a conscious effort at world rehabilitation. Ethical and moral questions are at the core of his works.[14] His attitude toward his craft is that of the twentieth-century prophet, and his writing is tinged with self-evaluative Jewish humor. He refers to himself as "a sort of medium,"[15] and he says, "I really believe . . . that the individual has some permanent balance within himself. . . . That he knows right and wrong."[16] His obligation as a writer is to lead this individual in the proper direction. Bellow's works are polemical tracts that follow certain definitive axial lines of Jewish thought, especially in the presentation of God, man, and the universe.

II

The ethical monotheism in Bellow's novels indicates that there is a belief in God, that God commands a way of life for man which is moral and
humanistic. Although Bellow's ethical monotheism is devoid of all Jewish
ritual on the protagonist's part, it remains in his memory and relates to
another generation.

As was the mode of Jewish philosophers in the past, Bellow does not
engage in theosophic speculation. Even though his works are shaded by
the spectre of the Holocaust, his belief in the hierarchical structure of
the universe in which God is supreme and man is created in the image
of God with his place a little lower than the angels, remains central to
his philosophical view. Bellow's characters do not speculate about the nature of God—except for Herzog, who acknowledges his own belief in
God—nor attempt to prove His existence. That He is master of the universe
is a given, just as is the Jewishness of the Jewish protagonists.[17] They will
attempt to quell their nightly fears by suggesting that "God does not love
those who are unable to sleep,"[18] as does Joseph in *Dangling Man;* they
will plead for mercy, as does Tommy Wilhelm in *Seize the Day;* argue with
him as does Herzog; pray to Him as does Sammler; acknowledge their
life's contract as Herzog, Sammler, and Citrine do; or simply acknowledge
that "chaos does not run the show," thus never doubting or questioning
His existence, His omniscience, His omnipotence.

Accepting the presence of God in the universe also means accepting
His will, leading a good life, a virtuous life, an ethical life, a life imitative
of God as commanded in the Torah. A basic concept of Judaism is that
man is created in the image of God (Gen. 1:25); consequently he must
strive to emulate his Maker by sanctifying life. If life is sacred, then survival is a moral obligation. One of the most enigmatic aspects of the Jewish
people is its ability—despite pogroms, massacres, and holocausts—to survive. This tenacious clinging to life results from viewing life as a gift from
God which must be preserved at all costs. Bellow's novels are a form of
survivor literature, testimonials to life. Bellow's protagonists opt for life.
Hounded by terrifying beasts, either of the soul or of the flesh, either
Spirits of the Alternative, reality instructors, bitchy women, black thieves,
or WASP demons, they nevertheless overcome such traumas and move on
with their lives.

The sanctity of life, however, has to do not only with its innate sacredness but also with the quality of life. Hitler's dehumanization and attempted
destruction of the Jews of Europe was an attack on humanity, on the core
of existence. Bellow himself says that during the Holocaust, Germany waged
a war against the separate Self, "the individual's consciousness of his own

existence."[19] Likewise, Sammler says: "The best and purest human beings, from the beginning of time, have understood that life is sacred. To defy that old understanding is not banality. There was a conspiracy against the sacredness of life."[20] The problem of totalitarian governments, whether German or Russian, is the diminution of the self. Yet this is a problem not restricted to authoritarian states. Western culture after the Romantic period viewed man as Lilliputian, with the entire universe as his enemy. The basis of this view was Christian epistemology with its stress on fallen man and other-worldliness. Bellow's characters constantly contend with this devaluation of the individual: Joseph spars with the Spirit of Alternatives; Asa in *The Victim* struggles physically with Kirby Allbee; Herzog takes on all of Western civilization; Sammler was caught in the vertigo of the Holocaust and almost killed because he was a Jew; Charlie Citrine has to deal with Demmie Vonghel's Fundamentalist anxieties and inhibitions as well as Humboldt's fears of Nazis, the KKK, and the Protestant establishment.

Man is, in fact, commanded to "choose life" (Deut. 30:19-20). Jewish philosophy is a philosophy rooted in the temporal world of man. Its concerns by and large are for living life at its fullest, not as a "pyromaniac of the soul"[21] nor an ascetic but as one whose enjoyment of life acknowledges God's presence in the world.[22] Ecclesiastes states: "It is indeed God's gift to man, that he should eat and drink and be happy as he toils" (3.13).

The choosing of life is a participatory injunction involving not only the partaking of life's bounties but also the sharing of one's gifts with others. It involves the whole community of man. Hillel, the Jewish sage, says: "Do not separate thyself from the community." Only as a social being can man affirm the goodness that is in life and his love for his neighbor. Society attests to the unity of mankind which shares a common ancestry, the original family created by God.[23]

All of Bellow's heroes are ethical individuals. They are all social creatures. They love being with people. Solitude is an anathema to them. It is not a proper condition for man. Consequently, Bellow's novels end with the hero's reintegration, happily, into society. Joseph, pleased to terminate his position as dangling man, looks forward to army life; Asa, finally rid of his nemesis, Kirby Allbee, joyfully asks his wife to return; Augie, the most social Bellovian character, the *animal ridens*, is never without the company of people; Herzog, although he retreats to Ludeyville, looks forward to a visit from his priestess of love, Ramona; Sammler rejoins society prior to the events of the novel; Eugene Henderson ends up in Newfoundland, waiting for a plane that will return him to his home and his family; Citrine returns from his seclusion in Spain and affirms his contract with man and God as he reburies his one-time friend and mentor, Humboldt.

Also, bearing the Divine image means that man is unique; he has no exact duplicate, and it is incumbent upon him, therefore, to express his uniqueness and individuality. While expressing his individuality, man is given the freedom of choosing between good and evil, but he is encouraged to choose good, which is equated both with life and with God (Deut. 30:15, 19). This choice, or free will, the idea that an individual can choose between alternative actions, is a philosophic concept fundamental to Judaism. Out of this precept flows an entire system of behavior, of making proper choices, of becoming the author of an action, and being responsible and culpable for it. A. J. Heschel explains:

> All that exists obeys. Man alone occupies a unique status. As a natural being he obeys, as a human being he must frequently choose; confined in his existence, he is unrestrained in his will. His acts do not emanate from him like rays of energy from matter. Placed in the parting of the ways, he must time and again decide which direction to take. The course of his life is, accordingly, unpredictable; no one can write his autobiography in advance.[24]

The distinction between good and evil becomes the eternal conflict for man, but it is the good which echoes like a theme throughout Scriptures, indicating what man's choice should be. The first chapter of Genesis states "and it was good" six times and ends with the declaration: "And God saw everything that He had made, and behold, it was very good." From the beginning to the end, the focus is on the good, and it appears to be a quality present in all that God created. It is this appreciation of creation that leads to an optimistic outlook and a moral quest—"How should a good man live?"—on the part of Bellow's characters. The question itself assumes a moral responsibility for the choices that have to be made. These choices involve the heroes in difficult struggles and, at times, in harrowing experiences which ultimately shape their destiny.

In the philosophy of Judaism, life is viewed "as a network of continuity"[25] whereby the present is inexorably bound to the past. The Bible itself is the history of one family, the chronicle of its experiences through time. (Hitler attempted to break this continuity. What he inadvertently did was to establish another link in the continuum.[26]) Undoubtedly, the role of the family is paramount. The first commandment in the Bible is that of procreation. This acknowledges the realization that the family by means of the transmission of tradition creates the link between time and eternity. Although most of Bellow's protagonists belong to a fractured nuclear family, the Family is nevertheless of great importance to them. There is a strong attachment to children, a closeness to brothers, and a reverence for the past which each protagonist, through the course of the novel, attempts to reclaim for himself.

III

The greatness of Saul Bellow's art is by no means solely dependent on a system of philosophy. Even so, the philosophy of Judaism is part and parcel of his very being and manifests itself in the kind of writing he produces. Bellow has consistently rejected the category "Jewish-American writer" for himself. It is not a denial of his Jewishness, which he readily acknowledges. What he rejects is the categorization, which he views as a limiting factor. Bellow freely admits to his growing up in an Orthodox Jewish home, to Yiddish being his first language, to learning Hebrew in cheder.[27] He states that "at a most susceptible time of my life I was wholly Jewish. That's a gift, a piece of good fortune with which one does not quarrel."[28] It is rather one of "the foundations that I draw from in my art. . . . Certainly it exists within me, even as the events of childhood are impressed in every artist, if I may include myself in this category."[29] This foundation had molded his character, his mode of behavior, and his world view, and the process is reflected in the type of art Bellow creates. His ethical monotheism becomes part of his overall presentation, and it is visible in the encompassing metaphor he employs, the kind of protagonist he delineates, and the themes with which he concerns himself.

The originality of Bellow's writings is evident in that he eschews those sufficiently explored and exploited themes—exile, wandering, alienation. Joseph, in *Dangling Man*, says: "Alienation is a fool's plea." Bellow uses as his major theme the biblical narrative most expressive of the Jewish ethic: Jacob wrestling with the angel in the dark of night (Gen. 32:25).

The importance of this tale is in the statement it makes about man and life: it affirms the human qualities of man while attesting to life as a perpetual struggle. When Jacob walks away from the battle with his adversary, undefeated, he indicates that man's strength lies in his ability to persevere. That the trauma of the struggle nevertheless leaves its mark in the form of a lameness, a limp, suggests not only Jacob's imperfection but also his oneness with imperfect humanity. The concept that man is created in the image of God and yet is an imperfect creature (an idea basic to Judaism) is not a contradiction. Man shares with God the power of intellect, the ability to know that the divine element is in him and therefore he must choose a good life, one of dignity and self-respect; he must know himself and express his individuality, his uniqueness, that part of him which is uniquely divine. Yet he is fragile and must constantly battle the element in his personality which seeks to destroy this divinity.

The struggle with an adversary, one of the oldest ethical-literary themes, is usually depicted either theologically, as the temptation and the fall of Adam, or literarily, as Theseus's labyrinthine struggle with the minotaur. These express a typically non-Jewish ethos. Bellow's use of Jacob and the angel lends a specifically Jewish tone and perspective to his novels. His novels are not exercises in pessimism or nihilism. They are also unlike the naturalistic mode fashionable in the works of earlier writers. They represent Bellow's urgent desire to restore a balance to man's existence by reintroducing the humanism of his own heritage negated or neglected by certain promoters of Western culture.[30]

This biblical narrative usually appears as a covert metaphor in Bellow's works. It suggests the protagonist's quest and the problems he encounters, and it leads to the denouement and resolution. The quest for most Bellovian heroes is basically the same. It is not a search for identity, as some critics suggest.[31] It is rather a quest for a significant existence that would embrace their own identity, such as it is. Joseph, in *Dangling Man*, grapples with the Spirit of Alternatives in an effort to end his status as a "dangling man." His struggle with the darkness of his alter ego, within the confines of his own room, suggests Jacob's nighttime struggle with the angel. Joseph, like Jacob, emerges victorious. He ends the spurious freedom that plagues his existence and moves on with his life. Bellow's second novel, *The Victim*, presents not so much a quest as an ongoing clash of perspectives, one which ultimately results in the deadly nighttime confrontation between Asa Leventhal and Kirby Allbee. This is almost a recreation of Jacob's battle with his opponent, Esau. Here, too, Asa is victorious in ousting Kirby from his home, and both then continue on with their lives, Asa to a new job with the newspaper *Antique Horizons*—the name suggests all that Asa as Jew stands for—and to starting a family; Kirby, to a pause prior to capitulating to his personal destiny.

In both *The Adventures of Augie March* and *Mr. Sammler's Planet*, Bellow makes overt references to the Jacob narrative. Augie's contention is not in the form of an epochal battle which would determine his fate. Augie realizes that "a man's character is his fate." Therefore, his struggle is with "all the influences [that] were lined up waiting for" him. It is a lifelong challenge, and Augie confronts it with opposition and optimism. In a mood of depression, after his breakup with Thea, Augie attempts to rationalize and to comprehend man's existence and ultimately his own motives. He recognizes that the "struggle of humanity" is "to recruit others to your version of what's real,"[32] and he questions: "how many Jacobs are there who sleep on the stone and force it to be their pillow, or go to the mat with angels and wrestle the great fear to win a right to exist? These brave are so few that they are made the fathers of a whole people" (*AM*, 403).

Augie instinctively resists the influences that others seek to have over him. This opposition is a life-and-death contention because it potentially involves the obliteration of personality, the erasure of the uniqueness of the individual.

Sammler's situation is somewhat different. Because his struggle for existence took place prior to the events of the novel, he understands the ordeal others experience, especially Shula, his daughter. In a letter reassuring Dr. Lal that his manuscript is safe and also attempting to minimize Shula's theft, he says: "she dreams about the future. Yet everyone grapples, each in his awkward muffled way, with a power, a Jacob's angel, to get a final satisfaction or glory that is withheld."[33] In this work, Bellow defines his usage of the biblical episode, thereby suggesting its relevancy to his other works.

Although the corollary for Moses Herzog's plight is the biblical tale of Moses, Herzog's vying with his enemies—Madeleine, Gersbach, and Western culture—and his prevailing, though scarred, is an instance of the Jacob and the angel tale as well. Here, too, as in *The Victim,* there is a clash of cultures, and Moses must accept his own uniqueness—himself as a Jew—prior to securing his rehabilitation.[34] His recognition that Ludeyville was "Herzog's folly! . . . symbol of his Jewish struggle for a solid footing in White Anglo-Saxon Protestant America," and that his sinister war "defying the Wasp. . . . What a struggle I waged—left-handed but fierce"[35] was puerile, leads to his eventual recovery.

IV

The apocalyptic events of World War II, severing the universal umbilical cord, indicated the devastating results of a loss of societal connectedness and a loss of those imperatives that govern a harmonious world. Bellow seeks to ameliorate this trauma by reestablishing the nexus that binds men. Bellow's heroes, through language, thought, and action, attempt to rid themselves of the neutrality of science, so ruinous to world solidarity, and to recreate the bond of humanitarianism found in words such as "good," "humanity," "dignity," "responsibility."[36] These words have evolved into what European Jewish culture termed *menschlichkeit,* and they comprise much of the ethical optimism of Judaism. (It should be recalled that Nazism was diametrically opposed to the humanism of the philosophy of Judaism and sought, with the extinction of the Jewish people, to eradicate humanism as a world view.) A Jewish child's first commandment from his parents is, "Be a *mensch!*"—Be an ethical, caring human being! Bellow's characters are all that and more. They search for the answer to the question, "How should a good man live?" Yet they are not "good" men. Bellow has said, "I don't think I've represented any really good men; no one is thoroughly admirable in any of my novels."[37]; Bellow's heroes are flawed individuals, social, psychological, and emotional cripples, who attempt, through the course of a novel, to alleviate their condition. This condition, however, is what makes them human and joins them with the human struggle for survival and meaningful existence.

The characters Bellow creates are imbued with his ethical/optimism/monotheism. Bellow's protagonists are heroes—intellectuals (except for Tommy Wilhelm), sufferers, strugglers, survivors, believers. They are humanists: they are all concerned with dignity (their own and others), humanity (or lack of it), and community.

Joseph, in *Dangling Man*, is a war casualty who has not yet fought in the war. At the time we meet him, he is the personification of the diminished self of the naturalistic writers of twentieth-century American fiction. He is an irascible individual who cannot get along with anyone. His problem is too much freedom. The question of freedom becomes the primary theme in the work, a theme that Bellow will revert to again in *Herzog*. In *Dangling Man*, Bellow suggests that freedom consists in the ability to *choose* a course of action. Joseph begins to realize that his freedom lies in his choice or responsibility which confirms his relationship with society; Joseph's choice of enlisting into the army is an exercise of his freedom.[38] He also knows that restrictions add dignity to his life. He says: "a man must accept limits and cannot give in to the wild desire to be everything and everyone and everything to everyone" (*DM*, 101). His movement is away from denigration to acceptance of himself as a responsible individual. In addition to his self-deprecation throughout the work, Joseph is also concerned that "There is no dignity anywhere, nothing but absurd falsehood" (*DM*, 48). He is disturbed at the humiliation of Minna Servatius at her party. He says: "It is our humanity that we are responsible for . . . our dignity, our freedom" (*DM*, 167). He claims that his talent is "for being a good man," and a good man can live only as a responsible individual in a society.

Social responsibility, one of the minor themes in *Dangling Man*, becomes a major theme in *The Victim*. In this work, Bellow masterfully integrates a discussion of responsibility into the framework of a dialectic on anti-Semitism. Writing after the greatest outburst of anti-Semitism the world has yet witnessed, Bellow attempts to understand the anti-Semite, as well as responses to the anti-Semite, from a psychological and social point of view.

Bellow stresses the close relationship between social responsibility and individual responsibility. Such responsibility is inherent in a humanistic, non-deterministic philosophy, one in which the individual is accountable for his actions which stem from his freedom of choice. Leventhal reflects upon Schlossberg's statement that "It's bad to be less than human and it's bad to be more than human."[39] Then he declares that "human meant accountable in spite of many weaknesses" (*V*, 154). Asa, whom Bellow immediately establishes as a socially responsible individual (he takes care of his brother's family during Max's absence; he is mindful of those less fortunate than he who were not able to pull themselves together during the post-Depression period) is now confronted with an anti-Semite who claims to be Asa's victim. Kirby's rhetoric is typical anti-Semitic rhetoric. (The Nazis, too, claimed to be victims of a Jewish world conspiracy by referring to the infamous Protocols of the Elders of Zion.) Almost taken in by the absurdity of Kirby's charge, Asa recovers his equilibrium when he feels that Kirby attacks the moral sanctity of his home. At that point Asa begins to understand the connection between individual responsibility and human dignity. Asa, as did Joseph, moves from self-effacement to moral strength which adds a new dimension to his existence.

While *The Adventures of Augie March* is more expansive and lighter in tone, the tensions in this novel are similar to those of *The Victim:* a clash between deterministic and humanistic philosophies. Augie, a passive character who does not initiate new encounters or experiences but chances upon them through the machinations of others, nevertheless recognizes the importance of choosing one's own lifestyle, and he actively opposes the philosophy, the values, the standards that others live by. Augie struggles not only with opposing forces that seek to shape his destiny but for a fate "good enough." He is optimistic by nature and describes himself as an animal ridens, which he defines as someone who "will ... refuse to lead a disappointed life" or who laughs at nature which "thinks it can win over us and the power of hope" (*AM*, 599). He is a sensitive, caring, sentimental individual. Augie's upbringing is superintended in his formative years by Grandma Lausch, who preached to him what Augie (Bellow) terms a "kitchen religion," her form of Judaism which is a mixture of ethics and a homemaker's ritual. She advises him to be *"ehrlich"*—honest and respectful to people. Augie retains these values throughout his life. He has his lapses—he is involved in "illicit dealings" in Europe—but his conscience, his hope, and his search for a worthwhile fate ultimately govern his existence. As Augie concludes his memoirs, he looks forward to a settled life and having children, thus echoing the desire of every Jewish parent for one's own children.

Bellow's later works, *Herzog, Mr. Sammler's Planet* and *Humboldt's Gift,* are outspoken expressions of covenant Judaism as in each book man's life is viewed in terms of a contract with God, a contract which includes an attempt to reestablish the interrelatedness of the community of Man.

Melvin Bernstein claims that *Herzog* "is a testing of the Jewish definition of life and being, of purpose and death in the world—nothing less. It is a novel of ancient belief tested against modernism in the person of Herzog."[40] *Herzog* is a study of assimilation, and the theme suggested in the name of the hero, Moses, has to do with Jewish consciousness and with freedom.

Moses' bid for freedom is a release from the Egypt of the soul. During a crucial period when his life seems to be falling apart and he questions existence, Moses finds that those ideas that he accepted as a liberal intellectual, ideas that are the foundations of twentieth-century thought, including basic principles of Christianity and Romanticism, are actually detrimental to man because they seek transcendence of the human rather than ascendance within the human realm. Moses reflects, "I, a Jew . . . would never grasp the Christian and Faustian world idea, forever alien to me."[41] At this point, he recognizes the value of his own humanistic heritage. He believes in the essential value of the human being and cannot accept either the first fall of man or Heidegger's "second Fall of Man." Herzog is concerned that we live in "a society that was no community and devalued the person" (*H*, 201). He believes "brotherhood makes a man human" (*H*, 272). "When the preachers of dread tell you that others only distract you from metaphysical freedom then you must turn away from them. The real and essential question is one of our employment by other human beings and their employment by us" (*H*, 272). Freedom for Moses is the same as it was for Joseph: it is not an abstraction. It is the freedom to make intelligent choices within a society.

Moses is a *mensch*. He is compassionate. He is concerned with the dignity of the individual. He has suffered much, but he knows that "the advocacy and praise of suffering takes us in the wrong direction . . . . Suffering breaks people, crushes them, and is simply unilluminating" (*H*, 317).

At the beginning of the work, Moses describes himself as narcissistic, masochistic, anachronistic, depressive, jealous; these are life-negating qualities. His self-evaluative journey leads to the life-affirming declaration: "*Hineni!*" Moses at the end of his journey comes to the realization that life and death have meaning when seen in terms of a contract with God, whereby man is not "the principal, but only on loan" to himself, and his task is to "complete his assignment whatever that was" (*H*, 231). Herzog may not have a better understanding of himself, but he has come to a clearer understanding of existence. *Herzog* is Bellow's finest expression of ethical monotheism.

While all of Bellow's heroes are survivors of life's personal conflicts, Artur Sammler, in *Mr. Sammler's Planet*, is a survivor of the Holocaust. Through Artur Sammler, Bellow confronts the immoral mentality that gave rise to the century's greatest crime and pits this mentality against his own humanistic perception embodied in those values that he has previously clearly defined as Jewish.

Sammler, who has suffered the unbearable agony of the Holocaust witness, does not revel in suffering, yet he is sensitive to the suffering of others. Members of his circle of acquaintances, family and friends, confide their problems to him. His feelings, however, are focused on his dying nephew, i.e., his benefactor Elya Gruner, around whom his three-day odyssey revolves. Gruner is Bellow's "good" man. He is generous both to his children—to a fault—and to others; he is compassionate; he is sensitive, and his occasional digressions from the straight path attest to his humanity. He has led a good life and accepts his death as part of life, the termination of his contract on earth.

Both Sammler's Holocaust experience and his life in New York among his quasi-sane relatives suggest the theme of the work: madness. It is a mad world Sammler inhabits, where culture and education seem unrelated to one's way of life. The Germany which spawned some of the greatest thinkers of all time also propagated a "conspiracy against the sacredness of life" (*MSP,* 21). Yet Sammler, as do most of Bellow's protagonists, believes that chaos cannot determine human destiny. Chaos and madness may be all-pervasive, but ultimately each person fulfills his contract, as did Elya, which is a humbling and human experience.

Humboldt's Gift concerns contracts—gambling contracts, real-estate contracts, literary contracts, blood-brother contracts, drama contracts, marriage contracts—and their dissolution. The only one which cannot be dissolved is the heavenly one.

Bellow has often stated that *Humboldt's Gift* is a "comic book about death."[42] But death is not a subject for irreverent laughter. Death in *Mr. Sammler's Planet* is a serious matter. Sammler's Holocaust experiences and Elya Gruner's fate, treated with awe and sympathy, attest to this. In suggesting that *Humboldt's Gift* deals with the irreverence of death, Bellow points to the sanctity of life and the bonds that create the eternal link of man. Ultimately, death is meaningful only in its relationship to life, and Charlie's responsibility is not only to fulfill his own destiny "but to carry on for certain failed friends like Von Humboldt Fleisher who had never been able to struggle through into higher wakefulness."[43] Charlie renews his covenant with man and God when he reburies Humboldt in the Valhalla Cemetery to the melody of Menashe Klinger's singing. Charlie is aware of the "heav'nly harmony" of music and knows that "by means of music man affirmed that the logically unanswerable was, in a different form, answerable" (*HG,* 321), that is, "The dead shall live, the living die,/ And Music shall untune the sky."[44] Humboldt was "Goin' Home" to meet his

Maker. Such was "a man's assignment." Such will be Charlie's and for that matter Bellow's as well.

V

A number of critics have attempted to assess the Jewish content of Saul Bellow's fiction.[45] Many have been disappointed at the near-ancillary Jewishness that pervades his works. However, an understanding of the philosophy of Judaism will indicate that Bellow's perspective is unmistakably Jewish. Bellow writes in the manner of an Old Testament prophet, for Bellow is essentially a religious person and literature for him "is a way of coming closer to God."[46] Throughout his *oeuvre*, which comprises his "song of songs," Bellow's humanistic voice intones the anthropocentric concerns of his heritage.

Notes

1. Samuel Belkin, *Studies in Torah Judaism: The Philosophy of Purpose* (New York: Yeshiva University Press, 1958), 7-8.
2. David Hartman, *Joy and Responsibility: Israel, Modernity, and the Renewal of Judaism* (Jerusalem: Ben-Zvi Posner, 1978), 209.
3. Leo Baeck, *The Essence of Judaism* (New York: Schocken Books, 1948), 38-39.
4. Ben Zion Bokser, *The Wisdom of the Talmud: A Thousand Years of Jewish Thought* (New York: Philosophical Library, 1951), 83.
5. Belkin, 10.
6. Bokser, 84. Maimonides states that man attains the highest degree of knowledge of God when he comprehends that God is incomprehensible. Cf. *Guide of the Perplexed*, trans. from the original Arabic text by M. Friedlander, 2d ed., rev. (New York: Dover, 1956), I, chap. 54.
7. Hartman, 163.
8. Ibid.
9. See James M. Clark, ed. and trans., *Meister Eckhart: An Introduction to the Study of His Work* (New York: Nelson, 1957).
10. Quoted in Max Weinreich, *Hitler's Professors* (New York: Yivo, 1946), 21.
11. Irving Malin, "The Jewishness of Saul Bellow," *Saul Bellow: A Symposium on the Jewish Heritage*, ed. Shiv Kumar and Vinoda (Hyderabad, India: Nachson Books, 1983), 48. "Bellow's view of his heritage is . . . ambivalent," and he "does not approach his Jewishness in a consistent way." Although true from a theological or ritual viewpoint, this statement does not take into consideration Bellow's philosophical view.
12. Baeck, 86.
13. "The Hero as Prophet: A Study of Bellow's Fiction," *Saul Bellow: A Symposium on the Jewish Heritage*, ed. Shiv Kumar and Vinoda (Hyderabad, India: Nachson Books, 1983), 140.
14. See Michiko Kakutani, "A Talk with Saul Bellow: On His Work and Himself," *The New York Times Book Review*, 13 December 1981, 28.

15. See John Douglas Henry's interview with Saul Bellow, "Mystic Trade—the American Novelist," *The Listener*, 22 May 1969, 82.
16. Henry, 81.
17. See Bellow's statement in Esther Fuchs, "What Would a Jew Do Without Humor: A Conversation with Saul Bellow," *Maariv*, 13 January 1978, 37.
18. Saul Bellow, *Dangling Man* (New York: Vanguard, 1944), 123.
19. Saul Bellow, "Some Notes on Recent American Fiction," *Encounter* (1963): 23.
20. Saul Bellow, *Mr. Sammler's Planet* (New York: Viking, 1970), 22.
21. A. J. Herschel, *Man Is Not Alone: A Philosophy of Religion* (New York: Farrar, Straus & Young, 1951), 263.
22. Martin Buber, *On Judaism*, ed. Nahum Glatzer, trans. Eva Jospe, et al. (New York: Schocken Books, 1967), 220.
23. Bokser, 100.
24. Heschel, 207.
25. Elie Wiesel, *A Jew Today* (New York: Vintage Books, 1978), 7.
26. Sartre's idea that the Jew exists because of anti-Semitism negates his uniqueness and his identity as a Jew which is conferred upon him not by external conditions but by internal ones, by his covenant with God. This covenant predates both the term *anti-Semitism* and Christianity itself. See Bellow's statement on this in Gordon Lloyd Harper, "Saul Bellow," *Saul Bellow: A Collection of Critical Essays*, ed. Earl Rovit (Englewood Cliffs, N.J.: Prentice-Hall, 1975), 17, as well as Elie Wiesel's statement in *One Generation After* (New York: Pocket Books, 1978), 213.
27. See Fuchs's interview with Bellow in *Maariv*, 13 January 1978, 37.
28. Chirantan Kulshrestha, "Conversation with Saul Bellow," *Chicago Review* 23, no. 4 (1972): 15.
29. Fuchs, 37.
30. See Saul Bellow's "Nobel Prize Lecture," 12 December 1976.
31. See, for example, J. Bakker, "In Search of Reality: Two American Heroes Compared," *The Dutch Quarterly Review* 2 (1975): 145.
32. Saul Bellow, *The Adventures of Augie March* (New York: Viking, 1949), 402.
33. Bellow, *Mr. Sammler's Planet*, 129.
34. Harold Fisch, "The Hero as Jew: Reflection on *Herzog*," *Judaism* 17, no. 1 (Winter 1968): 43.
35. Saul Bellow, *Herzog* (New York: Viking, 1961), 309.
36. For a full discussion of the burden of language, see George Steiner, *Language and Silence* (New York: Atheneum, 1967), especially the essay, "The Hollow Miracle," 95-109.
37. Harper, 15.
38. It is not an accommodation as Marcus Klein says in "A Discipline of Nobility: Saul Bellow's Fiction," in *Saul Bellow: A Collection of Critical Essays*, 136; nor a defeat as Tony Tanner states in *Saul Bellow* (New York: Barnes and Noble, 1965), 23. Nor is it ambiguous, as Malcolm Bradbury suggests in *Saul Bellow* (New York: Methuen, 1982), 39.
39. Saul Bellow, *The Victim* (New York: Vanguard, 1947), 133.

40. Melvin Bernstein, "Jewishness, Judaism and the American-Jewish Novel," *Chicago Jewish Forum* 23 (1965): 281.
41. Bellow, *Herzog*, 235.
42. See Walter Clemons and Jack Kroll, "America's Master Novelist," *Newsweek*, 1 September 1975, 34.
43. Saul Bellow, *Humboldt's Gift* (New York: Viking, 1973), 383.
44. John Dryden, "A Song for St. Cecilia's Day, 1687," in *Selected Works of John Dryden*, ed. William Frost (New York: Holt, Rinehart and Winston, 1965), 75.
45. Cf. *Saul Bellow: A Symposium on the Jewish Heritage*, as well as L. H. Goldman, *Saul Bellow's Moral Vision: A Critical Study of the Jewish Experience* (New York: Irvington, 1983).
46. Rosette Lamont, "Bellow Observed," *Mosaic* 8, no. 1 (Fall 1974): 256.

Bellow and English Romanticism

Allan Chavkin

To people who really explain matters to us and reduce complications to simple truth, we owe everything. Our very lives.[1]

A prodigious reader who has been intrigued by the work of Rudolf Steiner, Wilhelm Reich, and many other modern thinkers, Saul Bellow is one of the most intellectual authors of the twentieth century, and one can see evidence of numerous philosophical influences on his fiction. Critics have found it difficult to delineate the complex sensibility at the core of his work. A key to this sensibility can be found, however, in his repudiation of what he considers to be "the Wasteland outlook" of modernism and in his allegiance to the older tradition of early nineteenth-century English romanticism.[2] Although critics have often mentioned Bellow's debt to romanticism, no one has discussed in detail this influence on his canon.[3]

Bellow never has explicitly stated that romanticism is a seminal influence on his canon, and it is impossible to argue with certainty that he deliberately adopts this outlook in his fiction. It is likely though that he instinctively turned to romanticism when he became disgusted with the "victim literature" of modernism.[4] The question of certifying direct influence in cases where influence is major, such as in this instance, becomes impossible because an author radically transforms a source, usually beyond recognition, when he makes it his own. Yet one should add that while one can not be certain that Bellow's romantic sensibility is largely a result of his deliberate borrowing from the early nineteenth-century English poets, there is no question that his knowledge of the works of these poets is enormous. In his canon one finds quotations not only from the major works of the romantics but also from their least read works that are seldom referred to by scholars.

In any case, Bellow's outlook can best be described as a romantic outlook that is strongly colored by his unique sardonic comedy. However, this romanticism was not evident at the beginning of his career. At that time,

First printed in *Studies in the Literary Imagination* 17, no. 2 (1984): 7–18.

Bellow was very much under the domination of "the Wasteland outlook"
and Dostoevsky's fiction, as seen in "Two Morning Monologues" (1941),
"The Mexican General" (1942), *Dangling Man* (1944), and *The Victim* (1947).
Some time in the late 1940's, he became disgusted with the depressive temperament these works revealed. *The Adventures of Augie March* (1953) and
Seize the Day (1956), as well as some short works written in the late 1940's
and in the next decade, represent his stated repudiation of both
Flaubertian pessimism and aestheticism (*PR*, 9-12). These works suggest
Bellow's deliberate rejection of the highly wrought, intricate form that he
associates with modernism. In contrast to his early works, he now affirmed
the worth of the ordinary individual and his everyday life. Like Wordsworth,
he had faith in the power of the imagination to liberate the alienated individual shackled by customary perception, distractions of everyday life,
and the drudgery of the daily routine; thus imagination could expand consciousness and lead toward a spiritual rebirth. In surprising variations,
this affirmative romantic theme became the central theme of Bellow's
canon.

Bellow turns instinctively to the traditions of comedy and romanticism
because of his dislike of what he considers to be the facile pessimism of
modern literature, a pessimism which has become, he suggests, a literary
convention in itself. According to Bellow, modern literature actually begins with the development of French realism in the middle of the
nineteenth century. This realism, which "challenges the human significance
of things," becomes the major event of modern literature (*PR*, 13). In this
tradition the romantic concept of the individual and the worth of everyday life become obsolete; in fact, modernism "is not satisfied simply to
dismiss a romantic, outmoded conception of the Self. In a spirit of deepest
vengefulness it curses it. It hates it. It rends it, annihilates it."[5] Despising
the romantic conception of the self, modern literature has, since Flaubert,
as Bellow argues, offered in its place a "myth of the diminished man":
"Common labor and humble life had their brief decades of glorification
at the beginning of the modern era. But after the Cotter and the Leech
Gatherer came the Man in the Crowd. In its Western form, realism made
the ordinary man extraordinarily limited—weak, sick, paltry, subject to
devouring illusion."[6]

Bellow rejects this view of human nature; unlike the modernists, he does
not desire to challenge the human significance of things but to affirm it.
He believes that they have not really examined the ordinary individual.
To probe the "souls" of "the baker's daughters" may allow us to see "reve-
lations and miracles."[7] His intention is to find "the extraordinary in the
ordinary," and he thinks that the power that can accomplish this task is
the imagination.[8]

Bellow believes that his faith in the imagination is not shared by contemporary society, which is materialistic and hostile to those who suggest ways of knowing that cannot be scientifically explained. The conflict is clearly elucidated in an important article of his published in 1975, aptly entitled "A World Too Much with Us."[9] He suggests that the problem that Wordsworth worried about in 1807, in which man squandered his powers in the dreary routines of daily life, has become much worse now. He implies that the task of the imagination has become much more difficult but all the more necessary. "The imagination I take to be indispensable to truth" (*W*, 5), he announces unequivocally, and he attacks the dominant attitude of contemporary society, which "greatly esteems action" and technical and scientific accomplishment but "takes little stock in the imagination or in individual talent" (*W*, 6).

According to Bellow, by ruling out certain kinds of knowledge and certain ways of knowing as illegitimate, we have created a "tedious rationality" that breeds boredom and other miseries. He recalls with admiration the British romantic poets with their faith in the power of the human mind: "Two centuries ago, the early romantic poets assumed that their minds were free, that they could know the good, that they could independently interpret and judge the entire creation, but those who still believe that the imagination has such powers to penetrate and to know keep their belief to themselves. As we now understand knowledge, does [the] imagination *know* anything? At the moment the educated world does not think so" (*W*, 6). Years earlier, in 1957, he had suggested that while "no one knows what the power of the imagination comes from or how much distraction it can cope with," its task was becoming increasingly difficult.[10] In 1965 he speculated: "I wonder whether there will ever be enough tranquillity under modern circumstances to allow our contemporary Wordsworth to recollect anything" (*PR*, 14).

Bellow finds the task of the imagination becoming increasingly more arduous, and one sees his romanticism becoming increasingly darker during the course of his career, though he does not return to the pessimism of his first two novels.

II

Although one can see the genesis of Bellow's romanticism in *The Adventures of Augie March* (1953) and *Seize the Day* (1956), his romanticism does not flower until *Henderson the Rain King* (1959). The themes of spiritual regeneration and the power of the imagination are treated specifically in romantic terms in this novel, where one finds important allusions to and quotations from the works of Blake, Shelley, Coleridge, and Wordsworth.

Jeff Campbell and Daniel Majdiak have shown that the single most important influence on the novel is Wordsworth's "Ode: Intimations of Immortality from Recollections of Early Childhood," for it provides the concept of spiritual growth that the novel adopts.

The novel also alludes to Conrad's *Heart of Darkness,* and Henderson's Conradian quest in the African wasteland is Bellow's version of what one learns from a descent into the nether regions of the soul. On his journey to "burst the spirit's sleep," as Henderson phrases it, borrowing the expression from the third stanza of Shelley's Dedication to *The Revolt of Islam,* he meets a parodic version of Kurtz (*HRK,* 160). Although Dahfu undeniably possesses the grandeur of mind that Kurtz is only reputed to possess, he does not resemble Kurtz in his descent into the depths of degradation. When Dahfu becomes Henderson's spiritual mentor, he helps Henderson overcome an excessive anxiety over death. Largely as a result of his meeting Dahfu, Henderson learns that his spiritual rebirth depends upon his recognizing the powers of the imagination, which Dahfu celebrates: "Imagination, imagination, imagination! It converts to actual. It sustains, it alters, it redeems!" (*HRK,* 271).

By the end of the novel, Henderson bursts the spirit's sleep and awakens to a universe redeemed by the imagination. The seemingly insatiable voice, "I want, I want," no longer haunts him.[11] He decides that the restless years of wandering are over and that he will enter medical school and acquire a useful profession. He can return to the woman he has abandoned because now he possesses "true feeling" for her, "call it love," though "the word is full of bluff," he says. Most important, Henderson, who was compelled to undertake his quest because of a profound alienation in a meaningless "universe of death," gains self-knowledge and feels reconciled to a world radiant with life and hope.

The ending of the novel deliberately echoes that of Wordsworth's "Ode." Henderson feels a solidarity with humanity, symbolized by his befriending, on the return home, a Persian orphan: "As for this kid resting against me . . . why, he was still trailing his cloud of glory. God knows, I dragged mine on as long as I could till it got dingy, mere tatters of gray fog. However, I always knew what it was" (*HRK,* 339). Henderson reaffirms here the idea of spiritual growth that one finds in the "Ode." Although aging results in the loss of the radiant vision of the child, there are compensations in one's maturity, increased capacity to love, and greater sensitivity to the suffering that is an inextricable part of the human condition. Moreover, the imagination can recapture, at times, the child's radiant perception. In short, the novel ends affirmatively rather than with the bleak vision of man's self-destructive quest for power that one finds in *Heart of Darkness.* On the contrary, Henderson comes to understand "that chaos doesn't run the whole show. That this is not a sick and hasty ride, helpless, through a dream into oblivion" (*HRK,* 175). Henderson's journey culminates in his awareness of man's nobility, largeness of heart, and power of mind.

Although one can also see such Wordsworthian humanism in Bellow's next novel, *Herzog* (1964) is a much darker novel than the one published five years earlier. The sardonic humor that somewhat colored the exuberant comedy of *Henderson the Rain King* entirely dominates the comedy of *Herzog.* Bellow's belief that "chaos doesn't run the whole show" is fervidly expressed in *Herzog*—its fervor is now provoked by a ubiquitous pessimism others feel toward the survival of Western civilization and its humanist values. The romanticism of *Herzog* serves as an antidote to the poison of "the Wasteland outlook," which is so pervasive that even people "who had never even read a book of metaphysics, were touting the Void as if it were so much salable real estate" (*H,* 93.) Herzog, a professor who teaches a course entitled "The Roots of Romanticism," disdains *"the cheap mental stimulants of Alienation, the cant and rant of pipsqueaks about Inauthenticity and Forlornness"* (*H,* 75).

Herzog has suffered real anguish, and he is rightly suspicious of those who revel in alienation, anguish, and despair. He is disturbed, too, at the bitter rejection and hatred of romantic humanism and warns at one point that one should not "sneer at the term Romantic," for romanticism preserved "the most generous ideas of mankind, during the greatest and most rapid of transformations, the most accelerated phase of the modern scientific and technical transformation" (H, 165). The Wastelanders who populate the world of *Herzog,* however, despise such "sentiments" as these, and their cynical animosity toward romanticism and its adherents is aptly symbolized in the novel by Herzog's discovering "a used sanitary napkin in a covered dish on his desk, where he kept bundles of notes for his Romantic studies" (*H,* 48-49). In short, the malice of the Wastelanders is literally brought home to him.

The problem for Herzog, then, is how to survive in a contemporary wasteland. His idealism has formerly proved disastrous, and with his private life as well as his career in disarray, he is on the verge of a mental breakdown. The relevance of his romantic humanist values in a society that finds them obsolete is not only a philosophical issue but also an issue that bears upon his daily life. The novel is, in fact, an elaborate meditation in which the professor probes the depths of his psyche, examines his past in intimate detail, and struggles, under much anxiety, to forge the disparate recollected fragments of his grim past into some kind of coherent whole. Like Wordsworth's *The Prelude,* the novel reveals the vicissitudes of the protagonist's mental state.

Fortunately, as Herzog recollects and reconstructs his past, it becomes clear that his beliefs do not have to be completely abandoned, only modified. Herzog's description of his proposed book on romanticism reveals the kind of modified romanticism in which Bellow believes and which he intends to express in the novel: "his study was supposed to have ended with a new angle on the modern condition, showing how life could be lived by renewing universal connections; overturning the last of the Romantic errors about the uniqueness of the Self; revising the old Western, Faustian idealogy; investigating the social meaning of Nothingness" (*H,* 39). Herzog never does write this book, but he does reveal in this description the relevance of romanticism to modern life. He suggests that mankind can overcome its excessive self-consciousness by achieving a marriage of mind and nature; can affirm the worth of the individual but avoid Faustian glorification of the self; and can establish a society based on brotherhood in place of the Hobbesian jungle that exists in contemporary society.

Bellow's belief that romanticism must be modified and made tough-minded enough to prevail in the modern wasteland becomes evident in Herzog's reflection on T. E. Hulme's attack on romanticism. Essentially, Herzog sympathizes with Hulme's dislike of a romanticism that is vague, escapist, ethereal, utopian, excessively emotional, and soft-minded. Yet he also disapproves of Hulme's "narrow repressiveness," his modernist view of man as an extraordinarily limited animal. Hulme's view of romanticism is a reductive view, for while it applies to second-rate works, such as Keats's *Endymion,* it does not accurately describe first-rate works such as Keats's odes or Wordsworth's "Ode," "Tintern Abbey," and "Resolution and Independence."

By the end of the novel, Herzog has achieved a tough-minded romantic sensibility that will enable him to survive in a harsh predatory society. He has abandoned his past idealism that made him vulnerable to exploitation, but he has also completely repudiated the Wastelanders' brutal "realism." His mental voyage has brought him to a Wordsworthian conclusion that everyday life itself is the highest good, and Bellow himself has said: "I think a good deal of *Herzog* can be explained simply by the implicit assumption that existence, quite apart from any of our judgments, has value" (*PR,* 15).

In Bellow's next novel, *Mr. Sammler's Planet,* the romantic humanist is a septuagenarian who is often pompous, self-righteous, and posturing. Artur Sammler is Bellow's crankiest humanist; his remarks occasionally verge on misogyny and misanthropy. A survivor of the Holocaust, he finds himself engulfed in the distractions of New York City, as he waits, full of anxiety, for the imminent death of his benefactor, Dr. Elya Gruner.

The romanticism of *Mr. Sammler's Planet* is somewhat different from that of *Herzog* and the preceding works, for the protagonist has strong intimations of eternity and confesses at one point that only the Bible and the thirteenth-century German mystic writers are interesting reading for him. This mystical inclination, which is to become even more pronounced in Bellow's next novel, was not of major significance previously. Yet the romanticism of this novel is not actually mystical, and despite Sammler's reading preferences, the book does not focus upon his mystical proclivity.

In fact, once again one finds a variation of the basic situation of *Herzog* and *Henderson the Rain King*. An alienated and death-haunted romantic humanist who is anxious that his values may make him vulnerable in a nihilistic wasteland, Sammler meditates upon the immediate past as well as the more distant past as he tries to create some kind of order out of chaos. The novel is a version of the characteristic genre of the English romantics—the discursive meditation. The real focus, as in so many romantic poems, is on capturing the process of the mind seeking to come to terms with its anxiety as it recollects, ponders, and endows the past with order and meaning. Two critics have acknowledged the novel's affinity with romantic theme and style. Contrasting *Mr. Sammler's Planet* and Norman Mailer's *An American Dream,* Susan Glickman has said that "if Mailer's God is energy and his experience of God orgasm, Bellow's divinity is Mind, and *his* experience of it, thought." Irvin Stock writes: "Bellow has a gift, reminiscent of Wordsworth, for evoking in his very sentence rhythms, as well as in his words, the *experience* of thought, the drama of its emergence out of the life of the whole man."[12]

Both Glickman and Stock associate the romanticism of this novel with the earth-bound romanticism of Wordsworth rather than with a visionary or apocalyptic romanticism. Sammler himself suggests that part of the reason for the decline of Western society is in its false or escapist romanticism. The pioneering walk on the moon becomes a metaphor for contemporary man's escape from the problems of the age. When Gruner's irresponsible son, a cold-hearted "high-IQ moron" (*MSP,* 177), tells Sammler that he has a reservation with the airlines for a future excursion to the moon, he is surprised at Sammler's lack of interest. Sammler explains: "I seem to be a depth man rather than a height man. I do not personally care for the illimitable.... I am content to sit here on the West Side, and watch, and admire these gorgeous Faustian departures for the other worlds" (*MSP,* 183-84). While he is impressed by the moon-walk, he remains dedicated to "this death-burdened, rotting, spoiled, sullied, exasperating, sinful earth" (*MSP,* 278).

The difference between Sammler's affirmation of the common life on "this death-burdened" earth and the public's rejection of it becomes clear when he observes the Manhattan crowd on the street. "The conviction transmitted by this crowd seemed to be that reality was a terrible thing, and that the final truth about mankind was overwhelming and crushing" (*MSP*, 280). For Sammler, this conviction is especially evident in modern man's penchant for role-playing. Sammler sees this role-playing, especially extreme in the youth cult, as a pernicious and perverse distortion of the function of the imagination.

The histrionic bent of the mob not only symbolizes the rejection of humanism and the acceptance of nihilism but also represents for Sammler a kind of madness. One sees almost all of the characters that Sammler is associated with in the novel as engaging in role-playing, including the licentious Angela, the irresponsible Wallace, and the eccentric Shula. No doubt the best example of the insane destructiveness of role-playing, Sammler implies, is that of Rumkowski, "the mad Jewish King of Lodz" (*MSP*, 230). His "play-acting" resulted in the murder of half a million people during World War II, when he helped the Nazis exterminate the Jews of Lodz.

At the end of the novel, Sammler prays for the soul of Elya Gruner, a man who did not engage in this "theatre of the soul" but who remained true to traditional humanist values as much as one possibly can in the spiritual chaos of modern society. It is these values, the great romantic positives, to which man must be true if his life is to be purposeful, Sammler implies. Yet, in the final lines of the work, he also suggests that each individual, by virtue of being human, has an intuitive awareness of transcendent reality. Even though some are not loyal to this reality, it exists. "For that is the truth of it—that we all know, God, that we know, that we know, we know, we know," Sammler says in his prayer that concludes the novel (*MSP*, 313).

The intimations of immortality that intrigue Artur Sammler increase in intensity in Bellow's next novel, *Humboldt's Gift* (1975). In fact, the protagonist Charlie Citrine spends much time pondering the anthroposophy of Rudolf Steiner. Some critics have argued that it is Steiner's anthroposophy that is the primary influence on the novel,[13] but such a conclusion is not justified by the text. While Citrine is exuberant at times over the transcendentalism of Steiner, he also mocks this nineteenth-century writer for some of his farfetched ideas. Moreover, it is important to recognize that Steiner's anthroposophy has its roots in English romanticism, and Owen Barfield, Steiner's apologist, whom Bellow interviewed while writing the novel, "repeatedly and consistently" associated Steiner's ideas with those of the romantic poets.[14] In short, the underlying sensibility of the novel and the source not only of the vatic poet Humboldt but also the ironic romantic writer Citrine, owe their primary debt to English romanticism.

As in Bellow's other works, it is a mistake to see any one ideology as providing the foundation upon which this novel is constructed. Yet having made the qualification, one can assert that the sensibility that pervades the work is essentially romantic. In various parts of the novel, Bellow quotes from or alludes to works of Wordsworth, Blake, Coleridge, Shelley, and Keats to suggest that a romantic sensibility is preferable to the gloomy modernist sensibility of contemporary society. Wordsworth's romanticism is of special importance in the novel, and John J. Clayton's claim that the "Ode: Intimations of Immortality from Recollections of Early Childhood" must have been very much in Bellow's mind as he wrote *Humboldt's Gift* helps one to understand the nature of the romanticism in the novel.[15] Bellow depicts the spiritual regeneration of Citrine in terms similar to those of Wordsworth's poem, and in fact *Humboldt's Gift* echoes the "Ode" at crucial points. The novel is a desultory meditation upon both the perplexing reality of death and the reassuring possibility of immortality that underlie the "Ode." At the core of this novel is a Wordsworthian faith in the power of the imagination to regenerate the death-haunted individual who has lost the "visionary gleam." Citrine's meditation upon death and immortality is prompted by his anguish over the premature death of his friend and mentor Von Humboldt Fleisher, a poet of immense promise. Both Humboldt's failure and Citrine's failure seem to support the view of the ubiquitous, Machiavellian "reality-instructors" who argue that romantic poets are not "tough enough" to prevail in a harsh society. Like *Herzog*, Citrine finds the cynical materialism of contemporary society unacceptable, yet he wonders if one can adhere to the higher values of the romantic poet in which Humboldt passionately believed.

The character of Humboldt somewhat resembles Bellow's personal friends John Berryman and Isaac Rosenfeld but is largely modeled on another friend of his, Delmore Schwartz, a poet who attempted to live up to the higher values of the romantic poet but failed to do so. James Atlas' biography of Schwartz reveals that the poet believed at times that art was not meant to provide a means to transcend reality but instead promised salvation in the everyday world. His Wordsworthian goal, which Bellow eventually embraced, "was to transmute the ordinary into something luminous and enduring"; yet, at other times, Schwartz succumbed to the notion that "the self-immolating powers of the imagination would lead him to some purer realm."[16] Eventually, he went mad and died prematurely.

Citrine's pondering of Humboldt's life and values enables him to attain a new awareness. Horrified by the "metaphysical assumptions about death everyone in the world has apparently reached, everyone would be snatched, ravished by death, throttled, smothered" (*HG*, 263), Citrine receives spiritual and moral guidance from Humboldt by means of a posthumously delivered letter. This posthumously delivered letter can be considered to be the turning point of the novel because it provides the impetus for his eventual decision to repudiate the materialism of "the reality-instructors" and to begin a new spiritual life. Bolstered and clarified by allusions to and quotations from Coleridge, Blake, and Keats, the letter warns Charlie not to succumb to a materialistic existence but to lead the life of the imagination. This message is stressed by Humboldt's quoting a passage from Blake's August 23, 1799, letter to the Reverend Dr. John Trusler, which contains the sentence: "And I know that This World Is a World of Imagination & Vision" (*HG*, 347).[17]

Dissatisfied with the current ideological package of "one-shot mortality," Charlie is intrigued with the idealism of Humboldt; he does realize, however, that he must retain a sense of irony or become self-destructive, as Humboldt did when he immersed himself in his idealism to an absurd point. Humboldt's idealism has its source in Wordsworth's "Ode," and Citrine decides to carry on this idealism but in modified form.

Charlie's spiritual crisis is prompted by an obsession over death, one which results in his disenchantment with the external world. In the course of the novel, he struggles to acquire a new consciousness and thereby gain "the faith that looks through death." His goal is to recover the child's immortal soul within him and thereby perceive the world with a child's sense of awe and enchantment as well as with the inner light which illuminates a dark world. At the opening of the work, he suggests that the process of regeneration is beginning: "I don't know how the child's soul had gotten back, but it was back" (*HG*, 3). The process of regeneration is not a smooth path, however, and the inner light that Charlie needs to recover fades when an acute awareness of mortality manifests itself. Wordsworth suggests in the "Ode" that the inner light that the child possesses dissipates as one grows older, but the imagination can enable one to recapture the child's soul within him, triumph over the anxiety of mortality, and view the world in all its radiance. Bellow's work reveals the same affirmative view.

At the end of the novel, Bellow implies that Citrine is on the correct road to achieving "the faith that looks through death." Reminiscent of the "Ode," the final sentence of the work invokes, with its symbolic flower, the possibility of spiritual rebirth. Although Citrine can never again perceive the world in the permanent "celestial light" of the child, the child's soul does survive within him, and Bellow implies that his protagonist is readying himself to blow the "imagination's trumpet" and "look again with open eyes upon the whole shining earth" (*HG*, 396).

III

Bellow's *The Dean's December* (1982) differs from his previous work in its preoccupation with social problems. Yet even here his romanticism is evident. Albert Corde, the protagonist of the novel, states that in the current moral crisis "the first act of morality was to disinter the reality, retrieve reality . . . represent it anew as art would represent it" (*DD*, 123). Bellow suggests that the imagination is the only force that can redeem reality from the "false consciousness" which has enveloped it and show man the way out of the contemporary morass (*DD*, 123). Occasionally alluding to and quoting from Blake, Shelley, Keats, and various heirs to English romantic tradition, Corde urges man to acquire a new kind of perception so that he can liberate himself from the mind-forged manacles that enslave him.

Corde's radicalism is implicit throughout Bellow's canon. Like Wordsworth, Bellow abandoned the role of political radical for the role of poetic radical with the goal of subverting false values. M. H. Abrams succinctly describes Wordsworth's task as one requiring the "absolute redemption" of his readers "by liberating their sensibilities from bondage to unnatural social-aesthetic norms and so opening their eyes to his own imaginative vision of a new world, in which men who are equal in the dignity of their common humanity are at home in a nature which, even in its humblest or most trivial aspect, is instinct with power and grandeur."[18] This description accurately describes Bellow's task as well as Wordsworth's. Like Wordsworth and most of the other nineteenth-century English romantics, Bellow calls for the liberation of the mind from the mortmain of custom and the slavery of routine perception. The individual needs a new kind of imaginative seeing without prejudices, preconceptions, abstract theories, or multitudes of facts. A twentieth-century romantic, Bellow reveals in his canon a qualified hope that man will redeem himself and his world by the powers of the imagination and thus reclaim the great positives of our Western past.[19]

Notes

1. From Bellow's unpublished manuscript of *Herzog*, Special Collections at the University of Chicago Library, Box 21, Folder 45, p. 375.
2. Saul Bellow, *Herzog* (New York: Viking, 1964), 75. Subsequent references to *Herzog* and to Bellow's other novels will be given parenthetically in the text with these abbreviations: *H—Herzog; HRK—Henderson the Rain King* (New York: Viking, 1959); *MSP—Mr. Sammler's Planet* (New York: Viking, 1970); *HG— Humboldt's Gift* (New York: Viking, 1975); and *DD—The Dean's December* (New York: Harper & Row, 1982).
3. Four critics examine the influence of romanticism on specific novels. See Daniel Majdiak, "The Romantic Self and *Henderson the Rain King*," *Bucknell*

Review 19 (Autumn 1971): 125-46; Jeff Campbell, "Bellow's Intimations of Immortality: Henderson the Rain King," *Studies in the Novel* 1 (Fall 1969): 323-33; Michael G. Yetman, "Who Would Not Sing for Humboldt?" *ELH* 48 (Winter 1981): 935-51; and Allan Chavkin, "Bellow's Alternative to the Wasteland: Romantic Theme and Form in *Herzog*," *Studies in the Novel* 11 (Fall 1979): 325-37, and his *"Humboldt's Gift* and the Romantic Imagination," *Philological Quarterly* 62 (Winter 1983): 1-19.

4. Gordon Lloyd Harper, "Saul Bellow: An Interview," in *Saul Bellow: A Collection of Critical Essays,* ed. Earl Rovit (Englewood Cliffs, N.J.: Prentice Hall, 1975), 12. Originally published in *Paris Review* 9, no. 37 (Winter 1965): 49-73. Subsequent references will be given parenthetically in the text with the abbreviation *PR.* Since the late 1940s, Bellow has repeatedly criticized modernism for its "Wasteland outlook" and its "victim literature." Even his earliest fiction (his "victim literature") contains criticism of this tradition.

5. Saul Bellow, *Recent American Literature* (Washington, D.C.: Library of Congress, 1963), 10.

6. Saul Bellow, "A Comment on Form and Despair,' " *Location* 1 (Summer 1964): 12, rpt. in *Herzog: Text and Criticism,* ed. Irving Howe (New York: Viking, 1967), 386-88.

7. Saul Bellow, "Where Do We Go from Here: The Future of Fiction," in *Saul Bellow and the Critics,* ed. Irving Malin (New York: New York University Press, 1967), 219. Originally published in *Michigan Quarterly Review* 1 (Winter 1962): 27-33.

8. Joseph Epstein, "A Talk with Saul Bellow," *New York Times Book Review,* 5 December 1976, 93.

9. Saul Bellow, "A World Too Much with Us," *Critical Inquiry* 2, no. 1 (Autumn 1975): 1-9. Subsequent reference to this article will be given parenthetically in the text with the abbreviation *W.*

10. Saul Bellow, "Distractions of a Fiction Writer," in *The Living Novel: A Symposium,* ed. Granville Hicks (New York: Macmillan, 1957), 6.

11. The phrase, which is repeated a number of times in the novel, has its source in Blake's caption for the ninth plate of For the Sexes: The Gates of Paradise. See *The Poetry and Prose of William Blake,* ed. David V. Erdman (Garden City: Doubleday, 1970), 261.

12. Susan Glickman, "The World as Will and Idea: A Comparative Study of *An American Dream* and *Mr. Sammler's Planet,*" *Modern Fiction Studies,* 28 (Winter 1982–83): 577; Irvin Stock, "Man in Culture," *Commentary* (May 1970): 93.

13. See, for example, Herbert J. Smith, *"Humboldt's Gift* and Rudolf Steiner," *Centennial Review* 22 (Fall 1978): 479-89. Bellow reveals a vatic impulse throughout his canon, though it is most pronounced in the fiction after *Mr. Sammler's Planet.* Nevertheless, this impulse is tempered by a strong skepticism and ultimately subsumed by a non-transcendental imagination that is anchored in the everyday world. Bellow describes this imagination as "a primitive prompter or commentator . . . telling us what the real world is" (*PR,* 10).

14. Yetman, 943.

15. John J. Clayton, *Saul Bellow: In Defense of Man*, 2nd ed. (Bloomington: Indiana University Press, 1979), 279.

16. James Atlas, *Delmore Schwartz: The Life of an American Poet* (New York: Farrar, Straus, and Giroux, 1977), 303, 379.

17. See *The Letters of William Blake*, ed. Geoffrey Keynes (New York: Macmillan, 1956), 35.

18. M. H. Abrams, *Natural Supernaturalism: Tradition and Revolution in Romantic Literature* (New York: Norton, 1971), 392.

The Symbolic Function of the Pastoral in Saul Bellow's Novels

Molly Stark Wieting

Most critics of Saul Bellow's novels have focused on the Jewish urban milieu. Indeed, with the exception of *Henderson the Rain King*—an inversion of the pattern typical of the other novels—the primary setting for Bellow's work is the city, Bellow's Chicago or New York, which comes alive as Bellow evokes sounds, sights, and impressions as perhaps no other American novelist has done. Yet in each of the novels one finds also a corresponding pastoral element, an excursion, either physical or mental, to an environment that is free from the clutter and chaos of the protagonist's urban existence. Whereas these flights to nature have attracted attention in individual novels, they have been virtually ignored as a pervasive pattern that forms a cohesive motif in Bellow's fiction.

The extent of the pastoral impulse determines the protagonist's confidence in dealing with the realities of his everyday world. Thus, the novels in which the pastoral is expressed strictly within the character's thought processes—*Dangling Man*, *The Victim*, *Seize the Day*, and *Mr. Sammler's Planet*—are invariably shorter and less optimistic in theme. Those novels, which devote more space to the pastoral and which allow the protagonist more freedom of movement—*The Adventures of Augie March*, *Henderson the Rain King*, *Herzog* and *Humboldt's Gift*—express exuberance in almost every respect. But all of these flights, Bellow implies, prepare the characters to return eventually to their natural habitat, the city.

The cities are, of course, among Bellow's most brilliant creations. With these he does more than simply reflect a vivid social and ethnic milieu—as important as that is; he also uses the urban world as a projection of his protagonists' fragmented lives. These characters have attitudes toward their environment that range from despair to acceptance, but they all

First printed in *Southern Quarterly* 16 (July 1978): 359–74.

81

identify with the chaos and clutter that they see around them. Joseph in *Dangling Man*, for instance, says that there "could be no doubt that these billboards, streets, tracks, houses, ugly and blind, were related to interior life."[1] He later confesses that he is a "chopped and shredded man" and the source of his fragmentation is "the public part of me . . . the world internalized" (165). Tommy Wilhelm is more despairing when he answers his father's accusations that he takes too many pills, "No, Dad, it's not the pills. It's that I'm not used to New York any more."[2] Another time, he maintains that his father's friend "was right about that in any big city and especially in New York—the end of the world, with its complexity and machinery, bricks and tubes, wires and stones, holes and heights. . . . You had to translate and translate, explain and explain, back and forth, and it was the punishment of hell itself not to understand or be understood" (83-84). In a more affectionate mood, Herzog drives around the Hyde Park area and describes *"his* Chicago—massive, clumsy, amorphous, smelling of mud and decay, dog turds; sooty facades, slabs of structural *nothing."* He muses that perhaps he is "as midwestern and unfocused as the same streets."[3] This preoccupation with the city as symbolic of the protagonists' inner states is precisely what makes the pastoral episodes loom so importantly in their minds.

Just as the chaos of city life mirrors the personal fragmentation of Bellow's characters, a "version of the pastoral," to borrow William Empson's phrase, symbolizes just the opposite—wholeness of spirit, order, and peace.[4] Like the earliest writers of the pastoral form, Bellow takes his characters away from the city to a simpler environment—or has them long for such a place—in order for them to undergo a temporary learning experience away from their more sophisticated surroundings. Bellow puts the longing for the pastoral in terms that are quite explicit when he has Augie March explain that he has grown up where there is "no shepherd-Sicily, no free-hand nature-painting, but deep city vexation."[5] And it is not coincidence that the despairing Tommy Wilhelm quotes "Lycidas" in a novel that ends at a stranger's funeral where Wilhelm sinks "deeper than sorrow through torn sobs and cries" as he approaches "the consummation of his heart's ultimate need" (118).

The relationship between the longing for a simpler place and the desire for inner harmony is further emphasized by the complexity of its treatment in *Mr. Sammler's Planet* and *Humboldt's Gift*, in which Bellow expresses the motif in cosmic terms. Whatever form the longing takes, all of the protagonists want relief from the pressures of the metropolis through flight to a place which provides a simpler, less complicated mode of existence, one which is harmonious with what they consider to be natural laws. Bellow's characters often discover something quite different from what they had expected; most learn that what they considered to be a search for inner peace often turns into a primitivism as discordant as the confusion of the city. Nevertheless, those characters who do make the quest—regardless of its outcome—are much more ebullient about life's possibilities in an urban society.

Of course, some of the protagonists in Bellow's novels—Joseph, Asa Leventhal, Tommy Wilhelm, and Mr. Sammler—do not get to make that journey. Limited to Chicago or New York, these compact works convey a pastoral impulse that gains importance only when viewed in context with longer works that give the characters more freedom of movement. Only in *Mr. Sammler's Planet* does one find a mature individual who has experienced the primitive qualities of nature before the novel begins and who is reluctant to indulge in pastoral dreams.

If there is any pastoral relief at all in *Dangling Man*, it occurs in conjunction with the seasonal cycle of nature which Joseph records in his diary. The account of his struggle begins in December with somber descriptions of Chicago's dreary winter and ends in April, the symbolic season of rebirth, with a hesitant acknowledgment of the beginnings of spring. The day before he enlists in the army, in fact, he notices that, in spite of the "impossible hope" of city clutter, "a few large birds, robins and grackles, appeared in the trees, and some of the trees themselves were beginning to bud." He sees a butterfly, hears the voices of children playing, and notes the brilliance of the sun in the streets. Upon returning to his room, he finds it "as full of this yellow as an egg is of yolk" (172–73). Just as Joseph's impression of spring is limited, however, so is his sense of personal fulfillment. His escape from Chicago through enlistment in the army and from the inner conflict that it represents is certainly no pastoral flight but an indication of personal failure. That it comes during the cyclic rebirth of nature makes his escape particularly ironic.

Neither does Leventhal find any satisfactory escape from the complexities of the city in *The Victim*. Only through his memory of a short stint with the civil service in Baltimore prior to the action of the novel does he find any kind of environmental relief. Leventhal remembers with longing his first meeting with his wife Mary. At a Fourth of July picnic on the Chesapeake shore they swam, participated in various sporting events, walked hand in hand together along the beach, and rode back to the city together on the boat. In such a relaxed atmosphere Levanthal "felt his spirits thawed out."[6] This calm interlude is cut short, however, by a temporary but violent argument with Mary, which sends him back to the city confusion of New York. A remnant of this earlier experience is still reflected in Mary, who is visiting her mother in Baltimore while

Levanthal remains in New York to struggle with the conflicts in the city. Even though order is restored after Mary's return, the novel ends on an ironic note, and the suffocating heat of New York rather than the beaches of Maryland represents Leventhal's final outlook.

Wilhelm, too, is denied pastoral relief in *Seize the Day*, a novella which, ironically, includes quotations from "Lycidas" and an elegiac ending. The most pathetic of Bellow's protagonists, Wilhelm readily admits his hatred of New York and reacts strongly to Mr. Perls's suggestion that he go to Florida where in off-season "it's cheap and quiet. Fairyland. The mangoes are just coming in. . . . You'd think you were in India" (39). The primary object of Wilhelm's pastoral dreams, however, is Roxbury, the town where he once retained a small apartment and where his girlfriend Olive lives. As he considers the complexity of his present situation, his thoughts drift to this rural atmosphere where "in late spring weather like this, he used to sit expanded in a wicker chair with the sunlight pouring through the weave, and sunlight through the slug-eaten holes of the young hollyhocks and as deeply as the grass allowed into small flowers. This peace . . . this peace was gone" (43). His mind again wanders to those less complex surroundings as he contemplates the problems of his stock investment:

> For several moments of peace he was removed to his small yard in Roxbury.
> He breathed in the sugar of the pure morning.
> He heard the long phrases of the birds.
> No enemy wanted his life.
> Wilhelm thought, I will get out of here. I don't belong in New York any more. And he sighed like a sleeper. (82)

Despite this longing, Wilhelm never actually experiences pastoral relief. He must come to terms with reality within the city, without the learning experiences proffered by the pastoral.

Mr. Sammler is, of course, a far more complex character. An elderly Polish Jew attempting to live an austere life in the chaotic extremities of New York in the sixties, he has neither the illusions nor the longing for an escape to nature. In fact, when his wealthy, promiscuous cousin tells him that she wants "to go to Mexico, to a hot place . . . where she could see something green," Sammler acidly replies, "Hot? Something green? A billiard table in hell would answer the same description."[7]

But then Mr. Sammler remembers his earlier experiences as a survivor of a concentration camp when he had to live by his own devices in a world that revealed primitive rather than bucolic harmony. After being blinded in one eye and left for dead during a mass murder in World War II, Sammler became a partisan in the Zamosht Forest. Living off the land as best he could, he coldly killed a man and took his clothes and food. Clearly recognizing that his lack of compassion was directly related to his primitive instinct to survive, he reflects, "The thing no doubt would have happened differently to another man, a man who had been eating, drinking, smoking, and whose blood was brimming with fat, nicotine, alcohol, sexual secretions. None of these in Sammler's blood. He was then not entirely human" (139). He remembers that when he finally appeared in the town, he was "wild, gaunt, decaying, the dead eye bulging—like a whelk" (140).

Thus Sammler has good reason for his skepticism about pastoral flights. His desire to find inner harmony in simpler surroundings has already been satisfied: "he had no drive for smashing through the masks of appearances. Not Me and the Universe.'" Knowing from experience that the flight into nature too often ends not in simplicity but in primitivism, he feels that man must live with dignity wherever he is. He must be "satisfied with such truth as one could get by approximation. Trying to live with a civil heart" (136). Although he continues to hold this view at the end of the novel, not even he can resist the fascination of Dr. Lal's theory of colonizing the moon—another version of the pastoral escape to simplicity.

Under the guise of helping him on a non-existent work about H. G. Wells, Sammler's eccentric daughter Shula steals the only copy of *The Future of the Moon*, a manuscript written by an exotic scientist from India. When Sammler reads the opening sentence which questions how long the earth could remain man's only home, he responds, "How long? O Lord, you bet! Wasn't it time—the very hour to go?" (51). As he ponders the specific scientific details of Lal's manuscript and the precise plans for its colonization, Sammler is not convinced that such a move would solve man's problem. "Distant," he muses, "is still finite. Finite is still feeling through the veil, examining the naked inner reality with a gloved hand. However, one could see the advantage of getting away from here, building plastic igloos in the vacuum, dwelling in quiet colonies, necessarily austere, drinking the fossil waters, considering the basic questions only" (53). Later in the novel, recoiling from the excesses of those around him, Sammler comes closest to succumbing to the possibilities of an escape from the complexities of the earth when he thinks, "So perhaps, *perhaps!* colonies on the moon would reduce the fever and swelling here, and the passion for boundlessness *and* wholeness might find more material appeasement. Humankind, drunk with terror, calm itself, sober up" (182).

Yet ultimately, Sammler rejects the pastoral hope. When his nephew Wallace asks him if he would sign up for a trip to the moon, Sammler replies that his travels are over. Instead, he maintains his belief that man must cope with life on the terms given him. At the end of the novel he, like Wilhelm, stands before the body of a dead man, but unlike Wilhelm, he is able to verbalize his understanding of the human plight. As he views the body of his relative Elya and considers man's attempts to deal with his life—superficial though they sometimes seemed—he says a prayer as much for himself as for Elya. Rather than attempting to escape the complexities of reality, "he was aware that he must meet . . . and he did meet the terms of his contract. The terms which in his inmost heart, each man knows . . . that we all know, God, that we know, that we know, we know" (313).

Mr. Sammler's Planet reflects Bellow's most highly developed use of the pastoral thus far. In the group of novels that tend to be compact and subdued in tone, Bellow has developed this motif from a single longing for an escape to nature and all it symbolizes to a sophisticated rendering of the complexities involved and the disillusionment that such a desire ultimately brings. A corresponding increase in the complexity of the pastoral occurs in the novels for which Bellow is more famous—those sprawling novels crammed with a gallery of characters, competing philosophies, and numerous episodes, both serious and comic. Among those episodes there is always a pastoral journey, and although the journey is not necessarily successful, there is a direct relationship between the actual journey and the protagonist's optimistic outlook at the end of the novel, often in spite of the facts of his situation. Beginning with the Mexican interlude in *The Adventures of Augie March* and continuing through Charlie Citrine's concern with the journey of the soul in *Humboldt's Gift*, Bellow treats the pastoral motif in a variety of increasingly complex ways.

The Adventures of Augie March, Bellow's first long novel, represents his first attempt to incorporate actual pastoral episodes. Although their use is minimal in this long, episodic work, it is central, for Augie, who refuses to settle for anything less than what he terms a higher fate, associates his confrontation of that destiny with pastoral experiences. The first such encounter and the subsequent retreat to the countryside occur when Augie, disillusioned with urban possibilities after his stint as a labor organizer, accompanies Thea, a wealthy but eccentric sports buff, to Mexico to train an eagle to hunt iguanas. Despite minor interferences, the first few days on the road are satisfying in their simplicity. Augie particularly recalls one afternoon while camping in the Ozarks when "the clouds, cattle in the water, things, stayed at their distance, and there was no need to herd, account for, hold them in head, but it was enough to be among them, released on the ground as they were in their brook or in their air" (330).

These idyllic moments are of brief duration, however, for after they pick up the eagle in Texarkana, the ideal of pastoral simplicity increasingly disintegrates into chaos. Their days and nights, which are consumed by the training of the eagle, gradually become more aligned with the savagery of nature than with its simplicity. This primitive disorder reaches a peak in Mexico with the eagle's failure at capturing live prey and Thea's new enthusiasm for hunting snakes, both of which are accentuated by the constant blare of fiestas. Augie describes the frenzy: "The band plunged in the *zocalo*, clashed, drummed, and brayed; the fireworks bristled and ran off in strings, the processions swayed around with images . . . . The energy for them [the fiestas] must have come from the olden-time worship of those fire snakes and smoke mirrors and gruesome monster gods" (372). Augie returns to Chicago, aware that his trip to Mexico with Thea has not brought the fulfillment he had hoped for, although it has enabled him to understand himself and those around him with a more perceptive awareness.

Yet Augie has still another illusory experience with the pastoral, although this time through a mental rather than a physical flight to the country. He is convinced that he can find an appropriate destiny by aligning himself with "axial lines," or natural laws, that appear to direct him to organize a school in a rural setting for children with special problems. This mental flight from the city, however, is just as illusory as his previous journey to Mexico. Instead of following such a plan, he marries and moves to Paris. Nevertheless, Augie refuses to give up hope, and his last buoyant affirmation of life occurs in a rural setting—a snow-covered field near a farmhouse in Normandy. He says, "Why, I am a sort of Columbus of those near-at-hand. . . . I may well be a flop at this line of endeavor. Columbus too thought he was a flop, probably, when they sent him back in chains. Which didn't prove there was no America" (536).

The use of the pastoral motif is developed extensively in Bellow's next long novel, *Henderson the Rain King*. In many ways, Henderson represents an inversion of the techniques that Bellow uses in his other novels in that the pastoral retreat rather than the city provides the dominant setting. Early in the novel Henderson attempts to escape the complexity and chaos of urban life by traveling to Africa, where he hopes to encounter a primitive simplicity. When he departs from the States, he leaves behind the world of actuality as well as the clutter of the city and begins a quest for spiritual truth. His journey is a symbolic one which takes him not only into the depths of the African continent but also into the recesses of his own psyche to discover the validity of the inner man. He attempts to describe the metaphoric nature of his travels when he insists that "living proof of something of the highest importance has been presented to me"; but an explanation is not easy, for "not the least of the difficulties is that it happened as in a dream."[8] Later, identifying the trip with his own thought processes, he says, "And believe me, the world is a mind. Travel is mental travel" (167).

What Henderson hopes to find both environmentally and psychologically is simplicity, harmony, order. Soon after his arrival in Africa he leaves the complex entourage of his friend and strikes out with only his guide Romilayu in an attempt "to simplify more and more," for his "object in coming was to leave certain things behind" (45). As he travels into the interior, he thinks that he has found the "prehuman past—the real past, no history or junk like that." Everything seems to be "so simplified"; in fact, he is sure that he has "gone clean out of the world, for as is common knowledge, the world is complex" (53). And nature does seem to speak to him directly as he awakes one morning in the Arnewi village. Deeply moved by the effect of the dawn on the white clay of the hut wall, Henderson senses "some powerful magnificence not human." He presses his face against the rose-colored wall, thinking to himself: "'*I knew* that this place was of old.' Meaning, I had sensed from the first that I might find things here which were of old, which I saw when I was still innocent and have longed for ever since, for all my life—and without which *I could not make it*" (100-102).

Despite this feeling of unity with nature early in his travels, Henderson gradually learns that the African way represents not simplicity but primitive chaos. And as he discards one by one the accoutrements of civilization, he finds himself facing a corresponding disorder within. Upon being drawn into their procession to the rain festival, he likens the confusion to urban chaos. He hears "a great release of sound, like Coney Island or Atlantic City or Times Square on New Year's Eve. . . . The frenzy was so great it was metropolitan. There was such a whirl of men and women and fetishes, and snarls like dog-beating and whines like sickles sharpening, and horns blasting and blazing into the air, that the scale could not be recorded" (169). Later, after he becomes rain king, Henderson is an involuntary participant in this savagery, and he learns that it goes beyond even the clutter of city life. As his clothes are stripped from him, he loses the last remnant of civilization and notes that "amidst those naked companions, naked myself, bare fore and aft in the streamers of grass and vine, I was dancing on burnt and cut feet over hot stones . . . I too cried Ya-na-bu-ni-ho-no-mum-mah!'" (198). His descent into the primitive is completed some time later when, submitting to Dahfu's persuasiveness, he imitates a lion. He admits, "And so I was the beast. I gave myself to it, and all my sorrow came out in roaring." Yet though he had "claws, and hair, and some teeth, and . . . was bursting with hot noise . . . when all this had come forth, there was still a remainder. That last thing of all was my human longing" (267). He then finally realizes that the incessant voice insisting "I want" is not a unique personal problem but the manifestation of spiritual yearning which is indicative of his humanity.

Having discovered that the flight to Africa cannot provide him with the simplicity and harmony for which he yearns, but that it can show him how to use creatively the chaos of life, Henderson is ready to return to the actual world of the city. As he leaves, he takes with him a lion cub, symbolic of both the primitive quality and the nobility of his African experience. On his way back to New York, Henderson celebrates his new affirmation of life with another type of pastoral experience. During a refueling stop in Newfoundland, he bounds over the frozen whiteness of Newfoundland and joyously acclaims his own spiritual "new found land."

In *Herzog* the primary setting shifts back to the city, but the pastoral excursions are still central to the novel. Bellow emphasizes their importance by placing both the beginning and the ending of the novel in a crumbling old house in Ludeyville, a rural town in the Berkshires. The short opening section establishes that Herzog is in Ludeyville and summarizes the frantic events that lead to his going there, events that are developed in the rest of the novel. One of the major episodes that Bellow explores for the first time in *Herzog* is the protagonist's early disillusionment with an escape to nature as an answer to his internal chaos, which he has associated with the pressures of urban life. When Herzog finally returns to his rural retreat, he is not attempting to find solace in nature itself but rather to transcend the natural world and commune with the spiritual world which he believes it to represent.

Herzog is initially disillusioned with a retreat to nature during the time when he and his second wife Madeleine lived there. Encouraged by the eccentric Madeleine, Herzog invested the last of his inheritance from his father to buy the house. In the pastoral simplicity of the Berkshires, he intended to complete his scholarly work. Instead, the idyllic setting brought only chaos. He was unable to complete his study because he had to spend his time renovating the house and writing articles to pay for his wife's extravagant purchases. His domestic happiness was shattered by Madeleine's stormy pregnancy and, as he later learns, her attraction to his friend Gersbach. As Herzog looks back on the Ludeyville interlude, he sees it not in terms of the pastoral relief that he had hoped for but rather as the beginning of the dissolution of his marriage, his career, and his sanity.

Thus Herzog has no illusions that his return to Ludeyville will provide any permanent answers, for he knows that the return to nature also has its primitive aspects. Attracted by a peculiar odor in the bathroom, he raises the toilet bowl and finds "the small beaked skulls and other remains of birds who had nested there after the water was drained, and then had been entombed by the falling lid. He looked grimly in, his heart aching somewhat at this accident" (312). Neither does he ignore the harshness of the human situation which will inevitably return to his life; he acknowledges that "the bitter cup would come round again, by and by" (326).

For the moment, however, he recognizes joy at being back at his rural retreat. His reaction upon seeing his shambling estate is *"Hineni!* marvelously beautiful it is today. He stopped in the overgrown yard, shut his eyes in the sun, against flashes of crimson, and drew in the odors of catalpa-bells, soil, honeysuckle, wild onions, and herbs" (310). His sense of personal fulfillment matches the beauty he sees around him. As he enters the house and opens the windows, "the sun and country air at once entered. He was surprised to feel such contentment ... contentment? Whom was he kidding, this was joy!" (313). He continues to muse about this new contentment as he sits in a lawn chair watching the setting sun and listening to the birds. He considers his own physical mortality and thinks,

> And inside—something, something, happiness ... "Thou movest me." ... But this intensity, doesn't it mean anything? Is it an idiot joy that makes the animal, the most peculiar animal of all, exclaim something? And he thinks this reaction a sign, a proof, of eternity? And he has it in his breast? But I have no arguments to make about it. "Thou movest me." (340)

Thus what Herzog wants is not an escape to the natural world but a transcendence of it.

In *Humboldt's Gift*, Bellow extends the transcendentalism of Herzog to even greater lengths and presents his most complex use of the pastoral motif. As with *Herzog* and *Mr. Sammler's Planet*, Bellow opens the novel with the protagonist's already having discovered that the journey to the countryside can result in the disintegration of the very peace and harmony that it was supposed to provide. In *Humboldt's Gift*, Bellow sends Charlie Citrine not only on a literal pastoral journey but also on a more direct spiritual quest—a sort of pastoral quest of the soul.

In this work the pastoral element not only is developed through the protagonist Charlie Citrine but is inextricably associated with Citrine's former mentor, the dead poet Von Humboldt Fleisher. As the young protege of Humboldt, Citrine had witnessed the older poet's early success, his retreat to a farm in New Jersey, his subsequent mental collapse, and later his pathetic death. Citrine had learned through his friend that a return to nature was no guarantee of peace and harmony. Citrine remembers that when he visited Humboldt, his friend "was all earth, trees, flowers, oranges, the sun, Paradise, Atlantis, Rhadamanthus. He talked about William Blake at Felpham and Milton's Eden, and he ran down the city. The city was lousy."[9] But Humboldt's work was suffering. Citrine muses, "Had he uttered the great words and songs he had in him? He had not. Unwritten poems were killing him. He had retreated to this place which sometimes looked like Arcadia to him and sometimes looked like hell" (25). The situation gradually worsened. Humboldt had frequent manic episodes, drove his wife to leave him through his groundless suspicions about her, and finally wound up a derelict in New York.

Citrine, then, has no illusions about the beneficent effects of a return to nature. He makes his distrust of the external world quite clear when he responds to a comment about the beauty of the French countryside: "But I had seen Beautiful many times, and so I closed my eyes. . . . The painted veil isn't what it used to be" (16). Yet Citrine struggles throughout the novel to discover man's relationship with nature. Referring to his earlier comments about French landscape, he suggests that "the veil of Maya" was wearing thin because man lacks "a *personal* connection with the external world." He refers to Rudolf Steiner's view "in spirit . . . a man can step out of himself and let things speak to him about themselves, to speak about what has meaning not for him alone but also for them. Thus the sun the moon the stars will speak to nonastronomers in spite of their ignorance of science" (202).

Citrine attempts to let nature speak to him as he imagines in detail a favorite object of meditation, a bush covered with roses. As he tries to concentrate on nothing but the rose bush and remember as many facts as possible about its growth process, he says he is "attempting to project myself into the very plant and to think how its green blood produced a red flower. Ah, but new growth in rosebushes was always red before it turned green. . . . I concentrated all the faculties of my soul on this vision and immersed it in the flowers" (223).

Citrine pursues this line of thinking with the eccentric Dr. Scheldt, a follower of Steiner's anthroposophy movement and a typical Bellow character who serves as part quack and part "reality instructor." Even though Citrine himself questions the extreme ideas of anthroposophy,

Dr. Scheldt functions as a sounding board for Citrine's views, which are a curious blend of Eastern mysticism and nineteenth-century American transcendentalism. He encourages Citrine's attempts to see the relationship between man and nature and approves of the direction of those thoughts. Citrine says such things as, "Let me see if I understand these things at all—thought in my head is also thought in the external world" and "The physical body is an agent of the spirit and its mirror. . . . The earth is literally a mirror of thoughts" (261-62). He pursues these ideas on his own later when he muses, "I had the strange hunch that nature itself was not *out there,* an object world externally separated from subjects, but that everything external corresponded vividly with something internal, that the two realms were identical and interchangeable, and that nature was my own unconscious being. . . . Each thing in nature was an emblem for something in my soul" (356–57).

But Citrine extends this mysticism even further: he wants the soul to transcend the physical and communicate with the spiritual; he wants to reach the souls of the dead. He explains, "Unless I had utterly lost interest in them [the dead], unless I were satisfied to feel only a secular melancholy about my mother and my father or Demmie Vonghel or Von Humboldt Fleisher, I was obliged to investigate, to satisfy myself that death *was* final, that the dead *were* dead. Either I conceded the finality of death and refused to have any further intimations . . . or I conducted a full and proper investigation" (263). Under the tutelage of Dr. Scheldt, he attempts to understand how the soul travels during sleep. Scheldt says, "The soul, when you sleep, enters the supersensible world, or at least one of its regions. To simplify, it enters its own element" (264). Later in the novel this exploration of the soul's journey is accompanied by the protagonist's actual movement to a simpler environment—a cheap pension in Madrid. In these simpler surroundings, Citrine concentrates on the communication with the dead he has especially loved—his parents, Demmie, and Humboldt. He says, "I, in the Pensíon La Roca, sent my intensest thoughts toward them with all the warmth I had. . . . Real questions to the dead have to be imbued with true feeling. By themselves abstractions will not travel. They must pass through the heart to be transmitted" (441).

But his pastoral journey—both physical and spiritual—is interrupted by a more immediate communication from the dead, one that provides a kind of comic relief from Citrine's philosophizing. Through a complicated chain of events, Citrine learns that Humboldt has left a legacy—a long letter and two movie scenarios, one that Citrine had collaborated with him on for fun many years earlier and an original one. Humboldt was so serious about their value that he had taken the precaution to send duplicates to himself by registered mail, duplicates that remained un-opened and that were included in the legacy to establish their author-ship. Citrine is moved to tears by the communication from his dead friend, but he considers the scenarios worthless. Through a comic series of events, he learns that one of the scenarios has been pirated and is a commercial success. Because of Humboldt's elaborate measures to es-tablish authorship, Citrine is able not only to collect royalties from the film but also to negotiate the sale of the second scenario. Thus he has, indeed, received a gift from the dead.

And the novel ends in this buoyant mood. When Citrine returns to the States briefly to settle his affairs, he has Humboldt's body moved from potter's field to the Valhalla Cemetery on a day early in April. A few flowers are blooming, and he is asked to identify them. He firmly establishes his urban roots by replying in the last sentence of the novel, "Search me.... I'm a city boy myself. They must be crocuses" (487).

Though the retreat to nature in Bellow's novels is often illusory, it signifies affirmation despite the harshness of life and extends hope in the face of disillusionment. The pastoral motif, then, symbolizes the pos-sibility of spiritual renewal.

Notes

1. Saul Bellow, *Dangling Man* (New York: Meridian Fiction, 1960), 24. Subse-quent references appear in the text.
2. Saul Bellow, *Seize the Day* (New York: Compass Books, 1961), 33. Subsequent references appear in the text.
3. Saul Bellow, *Herzog* (New York: Viking Press, 19645), 259. Subsequent refer-ences appear in the text.
4. *Some Versions of the Pastoral* (Norfolk, Conn.: New Direction Books, 1960). Leo Marx traces the significance of the pastoral in nineteenth-century American literature in *The Machine in the Garden: Technology and the Pastoral Idea in America* (New York: Oxford University Press, 1964), 3-33.
5. Saul Bellow, *The Adventures of Augie March* (New York: Compass Books, 1960), 84. Subsequent references appear in the text.
6. Saul Bellow, *The Victim* (New York: Compass Books, 1961), 15. Subsequent references appear in the text.
7. Saul Bellow, *Mr. Sammler's Planet* (New York: The Viking Press, 1970), 94. Subsequent references appear in the text.
8. Saul Bellow, *Henderson the Rain King* (New York: The Viking Press, 1959), 22. Subsequent references appear in the text.
9. Saul Bellow, *Humboldt's Gift* (New York: The Viking Press, 1975), 17. Subse-quent references appear in the text.

Women in Saul Bellow's Novels

Ada Aharoni

Some critics have asserted that Saul Bellow, throughout his novels, has failed to describe convincing women. One of these is Leslie Fiedler, who observes: "Indeed, the whole of Bellow's work is singularly lacking a real or vivid female character; where women are introduced, they appear as nympholeptic fantasies, peculiarly unconvincing."[1] And John Clayton remarks in relation to *Herzog*, "The women are creations of Herzog's masochistic imagination, not 'real' at all."[2] It is true that Bellow's artistic technique imposes some limitations on his portrayal of women characters, as we mainly perceive them through the minds of his male protagonists who often overshadow them; and because the narrators are men generally going through various existential crises, the female characters in comparison, often do not have the same depth of emotional, moral, and intellectual complexity as the heroes or anti-heroes. Furthermore, we sometimes get the impression that Bellow is more interested in illuminating certain societal attitudes towards women rather than fully delineating their characters.

However, having said that, the fact remains that Bellow through his thirty-eight years of writing, from *Dangling Man* (1944) to *The Dean's December* (1982), has given us a vast and rich gallery of convincing and vivid women of all kinds. His female characters are active, alive, creative, and outspoken. They are shown, for the most part, as forging meaningful lives for themselves, struggling, working, searching, growing, and achieving. There are modern "new" women and traditional old-world women, brilliant women and shallow materialistic ones, aging women who are trying to remain "girls" and young women who try to appear older, sensitive and insensitive women, kind and cruel ones—in one phrase—a whole world peopled by not only men but also by women.

First printed in *Studies in American Jewish Literature* 3 (1983): 99–112.

Some are two-dimensional and some are three-dimensional, but they're for the most part convincing characters vibrating with life. As it is not within the scope of this paper to describe fully the major types of women throughout Bellow's fiction, I have chosen to limit my analysis to a few of the central female characters appearing at different periods of his writing, and will especially dwell on Iva, Madeleine, Ramona, and Minna Corde, who through their character and behavior exemplify Bellow's masterful treatment of the characterization of women. This will also enable the tracing of the particular growth and development in the depiction of the female situation appearing throughout Bellow's works.

Dangling Man, Bellow's first novel, is written in the diary form, and we see the central female character the way her husband, Joseph, sees her and experiences her. Iva, therefore, remains two-dimensional, as we never hear her speak in her own voice, but we learn enough about her to give us a clear idea of her type of personality and her situation as a woman. Iva is young and energetic, and she dearly cherishes her independence. She works as a librarian, and is supportive of Joseph when he is unemployed and waiting for his call-up in the army. She suggests that instead of searching for new employment, Joseph should use the time to complete writing his book on Diderot, and that in the meantime they could live on her salary. Joseph is enthusiastic about this and grateful to Iva, but that is when their troubles begin.

Living on his wife's salary constantly gives Joseph the disagreeable feeling that he is "kept" by her. The sensation is further rubbed in by confrontations with her family who seem to accuse him of living at their daughter's expense.[3] He is also confronted with embarrassing situations, as with the bank manager who suspiciously refuses to let him cash Iva's paycheck. Here we feel Bellow is investigating what happens when the woman in the family becomes the breadwinner, and he is critically weighing the repercussions. This new situation adds to the tensions accumulated between Iva and Joseph in the past, and their relationship becomes endangered. One of the major sources of their misunderstanding was that Joseph had looked down on Iva's "superficial" interests such as "clothes, appearances, furniture, light entertainment, mystery stories, the attraction of fashion magazines" (65). He desperately tries to change her, and the more he tries, the more she resents it and rebels. We feel that Iva, after her long hours amid books and periodicals at the library, needs to relax at home with some lighter kind of reading and entertainment. But Joseph does not understand this. He reasons with himself that if he has not succeeded in changing Iva's tastes it is because women "were not equipped by training to resist such things . . . you might teach them to admire *Walden* but never convert them to wearing old clothes" (65).

According to Joseph, women behave the "superfluous" way they do simply because they have not been taught better. At this point, there is no attempt on his part as yet to understand Iva in terms of individual taste and in terms of a woman's own inner life. What is wrong in liking furniture, clothes, appearances and even mystery stories? Why should Iva be built on the model of the intellectual he would like her to be? Before the end of the book, Bellow will make his protagonist's view of women evolve during the seven months' span of his diary writing.

In her resentment of his attitude, Iva has gradually become estranged from him, and Joseph turns to another woman, Kitty Daumler, who becomes his mistress. However, in the course of his introspective exploration, when he is revising the whole meaning of the concept of "freedom," it becomes clear to Joseph that "a compact with one woman puts beyond reach what others might give us to enjoy" (67). Through this new insight, Joseph gains in knowledge not only of himself but also of Iva. According to Martin Buber, whom Bellow admires, "In order to be able to go out to the other you must have the starting place, you must have been, you must be, with yourself."[4] It is only when Joseph, through his introspective search, has been "with himself" that he can understand Iva, the other, better. The "other" or the "thou" in Buber is different than that in Simone de Beauvoir, who sees in the term "other" something derogatory—not only separate, but subsidiary and alien.

At that point, it penetrates Joseph's consciousness fully that Iva might not want to be changed, that her freedom is as dear to her as his is to himself, and he comes to the crucial realization that the ultimate quest for freedom, being common to all people, is a unifying element in human relationships. "The quest," Joseph writes in his diary, "is one and the same," and his conclusion is that because "the desire for pure freedom" is the same, "the differences in our personal histories, which hitherto meant so much to us... become of minor importance" (102). He admits that in trying to reform Iva's taste, he had "dominated her for years."

Thus, having gained a new insight into the essence of the concept of freedom, Joseph has more understanding and respect for Iva. He comments in his diary: "It was not evident that Iva did not want to be towed. Those dreams inspired by Burckhardt's great ladies of the Renaissance and the no less profound Augustan women were in my head, not hers. Eventually I learned that Iva could not live in my infatuations" (65). Joseph now understands that his aspirations for Iva were a response to masculine-centered values. Bellow brings his protagonist to a full realization that Iva is not only his wife, but a person in her own right, with tastes of her own and a personality of her own, and that he has to accept her the way she is. Thus at the outset of his brilliant literary career, Bellow already clearly shows his concern with relationships between men and women, and with the depiction of the female situation in modern life.

Ten years later, in *Herzog* (1964),[5] which is considered by most critics to be Bellow's masterpiece, we have a fascinating psychological study in Madeleine Herzog. Unlike Iva, Madeleine is three-dimensional, though she, too, is mainly described through the male protagonist's perception. We get an accurate and vivid description of how Herzog experiences her, but we also clearly see what she is like, for as Opdahl comments: "Although Bellow gives us only Herzog's view of Madeleine . . . the thoroughness of his portrayal of Herzog is itself a check on Herzog's view."[6] In his frantic attempt to be fair to her and to view her in an objective way, Herzog gives us a full, convincing, and vivid portrayal of Madeleine. Through his perception, we can not only clearly visualize Madeleine, but even see her side of the story too. Since it is Herzog, the hurt ex-husband who tells the story of his painful divorce with Madeleine, whom he still loves, his word must be taken with a grain of salt; and yet, underneath the male's point of view, we can also discern that of the female.

Madeleine, who is one of the most interesting of Bellow's women characters, is portrayed as brilliant, beautiful, ambitious, restless, aggressive, and outspoken. And throughout the novel, Herzog, who is painfully struggling to get rid of his passion for her, is in a constant conflict between his striving to be an objective observer and her presenting the subjective view of the hurt ex-husband who has been abandoned for another man. Trying hard to be fair to her, he admits that she has "great charm, and beauty of person also, and a brilliant mind" (5), but he often cannot help slipping back to his subjective view. He starts: "Quite objectively, however, she was a beauty . . . the bangs concealed a forehead of a considerable intellectual power," then he subjectively continues: "The will of a demon, or else outright mental disorder" (102). He admires not only her intelligence, her beauty, and her willpower, but also "the perfection of her self-control. She never hesitated. . . . It gave him a headache merely to look at her" (299–300).

In addition to the protagonist's view, Madeleine is also characterized through her relations with the various characters in the novel, and what they say about her. It is significant that most of the women in the novel admire Madeleine. Geraldine Portnoy says of her: "She is so vivacious, intelligent, and such a charmer. . . . It is extremely exciting to talk with her, she gives a sense of a significant encounter—with life—a beautiful, brilliant person with a fate of her own" (99–100). Joanna Russ comments that in general, "a woman who competes with men, finally becomes—

have we seen this figure before?—a bitch. Again."[7] And indeed, Madeleine is called a bitch by several men, who at the same time all admire her for her strength of character. For instance, the lawyer Sandor Himmelstein tells Herzog that she is "a strong-minded bitch, terrifically attractive. Loves to make up her mind. Once decided, decided forever. What a will power. It's a type" (82), and he argues with Herzog: "She's less of a whore than most. We're all whores in this world, and don't you forget it" (82). As a child, Madeleine had been sexually abused, which partly explains her sexual frigidity towards Herzog; but Herzog prefers to consider it "bitchiness" on her part. "She's built a wall of Russian books around herself . . . in my bed," he complains, and resentfully feels that her studies have invaded their most intimate privacy—their very conjugal bed. At that point Herzog had not yet realized the full impact Madeleine's "books" would have on their lives.

There is a basic antagonism between their marriage and Madeleine's studies. Like many modern intellectual women (we are told that she was a brilliant Radcliffe graduate), Madeleine finds that her family life does not give her sufficient scope, challenge, or satisfaction; she feels the deep need for further growth and for pursuing a career. Through Herzog's narration we can see that Madeleine, too, is going through a crisis and "rethinking everything." In her, we can perceive a woman in conflict who is having a hard time living with a husband she does not love and whom she tried to avoid. At the beginning of her marriage, she probably had hopes that Herzog would make some room for her career beside his own. But Herzog wants her to forego her own intellectual pursuits, to help him with his book on the romantics. He feels hurt, thwarted, cheated, and frustrated when she shows no inclination to do so, and goes on pursuing her own studies on Russian philosophy. Madeleine at that point has ceased to view herself as a function of the needs of a man who fails to satisfy her own deepest need.

This should have been a red light for Herzog to realize that something was wrong in their relationship, but he continues to show no interest in her studies and to regard them as if she were studying against him. When his friend Shapiro asks him what the title of her doctoral thesis is, he admits that he doesn't know what her research is about, but only vaguely knows that it has something to do with "Slavonic languages," or "Russian religious history (I guess)" (55). Yet he expects her to know everything concerning the new book he is writing on the romantics, and wants her to actively participate in it, under his own name of course. We know from him that he not only regards Madeleine as a "brilliant mind" (5), but that he has great faith in her probing and intelligent professional judgment. In several instances his male chauvinism is

blatant. In one of these, he admits that he had condescendingly "endured" her lectures on her research subject "many times, and far into
the night. He didn't dare say he was sleepy" because, he continues, "he
had to discuss knotty points of Rousseau and Hegel with her," as he "re-
lied completely on her intellectual judgments" (72). He fools her into
thinking that he is really listening to her plea for a second opinion about
her research—when his mind is far away from anything she has to say—
only because he needs to discuss his own ideas and intellectual interests
with her! We never hear about what Madeleine is talking to him "far
into the night," but we have the precise details of what he needed to
discuss with her. And then Herzog is surprised and deeply hurt when
Madeleine leaves him for Valentine, who shows much more interest in
her as a person and an individual.

Shapiro's visit to the Herzogs should also have been a warning sign
of how lacking and unfair Herzog's attitude is to his wife's studies. It
is only through Herzog's remembrance of Madeleine's conversation with
Shapiro that we hear about her intellectual interests and are surprised
to hear how well-read she is and what vast knowledge she has, ranging
over the Russian Church, Tikhon Zadonsky, Dostoevsky, Herzen, the
Revolution of 1848, Bakunin, Kropotkin, Comfort, Poggioli, Rozanov,
Soloviev, and Joseph de Maistre (70-72). Shapiro who is himself a learned
scholar, is very impressed by Madeleine's expertise in her field, her vast
knowledge, and quick mind. Herzog relates that Shapiro was delighted
with Madeleine and thought her intelligent and learned, and he sadly
admits to himself: "Well, she is." She and Shapiro conversed excitedly
and laughed gaily during their exchange of ideas, which made Herzog
jealous, resenting that she never laughed in this carefree way with him
and that the other two "found each other exceedingly stimulating" (70).

In his flashback of the visit, Herzog admits that Madeleine, "stuck away
in the woods," was avid for scholarly conversation and that she would
naturally find some interest in Shapiro who was well-read in her field,
and yet "he watched his wife, on whom he doted (with a troubled, angry
heart), as she revealed the wealth of her mind to Shapiro." He bitterly
describes this revealing of her mind almost as if it were an indecent act
or a bodily striptease. In his jealousy, he considers everything pertaining to his wife, including her mind, as his exclusive possession, which
should be revealed only to him and not to any Shapiro. Reflecting on
this, Herzog later admits to himself that he had never been as interested
in Madeleine's subject of research as Shapiro was. He relates that
Madeleine, when she had "enough confidence in Shapiro to speak freely
knowing it would be appreciated, genuinely" (72)—which implied a contrast with his own attitude—seemed "bursting with ideas and feelings."

Madeleine, watching the sullen Herzog, was hurt that he did not join in the lively conversation, and only sat there "like a clunk, bored, resentful," as if he wanted to prove that "he didn't respect her intelligence." Her offended look passed over her husband, as if complaining that he disdained her work and never really listened to her: "He wanted to shine all the time" (72), and resented the fact that it was her turn to shine. When Shapiro complimented her on her knowledge, "she was flattered, happy," and hoped her husband would change his attitude towards her studies when he felt that other people deeply appreciated her knowledge. But here again we witness a conflict between Herzog's objectivity and subjectivity. Even in retrospect he still tends to regard Shapiro and Mady's intellectual exchanges as mere "learned badinage" (76) or small talk. In his jealousy, he is convinced that Shapiro is more interested in Madeleine's physical beauty than her mind and hints that it is mainly her beautiful "behind" that he is really involved in.

When Shapiro suggests that they move to Chicago for Madeleine's studies, Herzog is infuriated, "Fill your big mouth with herring, Shapiro! . . . and mind your own fucking business" (74). He cannot envisage the possibility of moving to satisfy his wife's ambition for a career. His contemptuous attitude towards her studies drives Madeleine to pursue them still more intensely, to prove that she can succeed. Herzog keenly resents that and describes it as a cruel and exaggerated competition between them:

> I understood that Madeleine's ambition was to take my place in the learned world. To overcome me. She was reaching her final elevation, as queen of the intellectuals, the castiron bluestocking. And your friend Herzog writhing under this sharp elegant heel. . . . Madeleine, by the way, lured me out of the learned world, got in herself, slammed the door, and is still in there, gossiping about me. (76–77)

As if there were only one place in the academic world and that she has to throw him out, before she can usurp that place! Her knowledge is so threatening to him that he would much have preferred to keep her unlearned. From his point of view, if she has a thirst for knowledge he is ready to introduce her into his own intellectual pursuits (and exploit her intelligence for his own professional interests), and does not understand why she does not accept his benevolent offer and discard her career in favor of his.

Some critics have found Madeleine unsympathetic, cold, unstable, and neurotic. Leslie Fiedler, in *Love and Death in the American Novel*, says that Madeleine "seems a nightmare projection bred by baffled malice, rather than a realized woman; and Herzog's passionate involvement with her remains, therefore, unconvincing."[8] But Herzog's passion for Madeleine is the psychocenter of the novel, and if it were unconvincing, *Herzog* would not have been the masterpiece it has been acclaimed to be; neither would Bellow have received the Nobel Prize for literature, when his main opus is deemed to be "unconvincing." It is, on the contrary, only because Madeleine is such a lifelike character that Herzog's passionate involvement with her is convincing. As to her seeming "cold" and "unstable"—these are certainly the symptoms of the unfulfilled and unsatisfied woman, who feels she is not given the opportunity to "grow," and much of her frustrations stem from the fact that Herzog thwarts her intellectual drives and goals. Furthermore, certain critics, such as John Clayton, seem to overlook the fact that in stressing only the negative aspects of her character, they have probably been influenced by the hurt ex-husband's view.

Eventually, Herzog comes to realize that Madeleine must have suffered from his antagonistic attitude towards her studies and intellectual goals. The fear that her need for intellectual fulfillment was a compensation and a substitute for her lack of emotional fulfillment with him, had probably unconsciously caused him to be so contemptuous and antagonistic towards her studies and aspirations for a career. When he comes to see Edvig, and the psychiatrist asks him why he supposed her crisis happened, Herzog recognizes that it might have been caused by his contempt of her intellectual pursuits, which have given her the feeling that he was "disrespectful of her rights as a person" (58).

Yet, he persists in describing Madeleine as a domineering and cruel woman; but here again, his depiction is so extensive, that underlying his version, we also get hers. He recalls that she describes him as a tyrant (39, 191), and we see that to her he must have appeared just as cruel. Jack Ludwig rightly notes that Bellow must certainly be aware that Herzog is not much more moral than is Mady and Gersbach.[9] Mady writes to Herzog complaining that when she was in a room with him, he "seemed to swallow and gulp up all the air and left nothing for her to breathe" (191). She also resented the fact that he had adventures with other women (38), and as we learn from Herzog's conversation with Aunt Zelda, her accusations were well founded (39).

In his confrontation with Mady, Herzog seems to have wanted a wife, who, like his mother, was a Yiddishe mama who would have lived only for him and the children. But he had one of those in his first wife, Daisy, and he had left her precisely because of this: "I gave up the shelter of an orderly, purposeful, lawful existence because it bored me" (103). In a way, he is getting the same treatment from Mady as he himself has given to Daisy; but it hurts much more because he is the one who is abandoned, rather than the one abandoning. He also regrets his past attitude towards Sono, his Japanese mistress. He had been responsible for having kept her from returning to Japan and having made her disobey her father. Yet, when she had a severe attack of pneumonia for a whole month, he had not even gone to see her once. Thus Herzog comes to realize that he is not the only victim who has been caused to suffer rejection at the hand of a partner but that he too had inflicted suffering of the same kind on various women.

Madeleine held a different conception of a woman's life than either Daisy, Sono, or Herzog—yet he did not grasp that and was pained and bewildered by her attitude. Feeling that he had given her all that she could want, he considered himself "Madeleine's particular benefactor. He had done everything for her—everything!" (124). Mady keenly resents his patronizing attitude, and during one of their quarrels in the Berkshires, she cries out desperately:

> So now we're going to hear how you SAVED me. Let's hear it again. What a frightened puppy I was. How I wasn't strong enough to face life. But you gave me LOVE, from your big heart, and rescued me from the priests. Yes, cured me of menstrual cramps by servicing me so good. You SAVED me. You SACRIFICED your freedom. I took you away from Daisy and your son, and your Japanese screw. Your important time and money and attention. (124)

From her indignant outburst, we gather that Herzog had been cramming down her throat that she should be thankful to him as her generous benefactor for a long time before the disruption takes place until Mady could no longer take it. Another interesting point to notice here, is the development in the characterization. Unlike Iva, we often hear Mady talking in her own voice. Her sharp repartee, her witty dialogues, and arguments add an in-depth dimension to her characterization.

Why did Madeleine, who is in her early twenties, want to marry Herzog, her forty-four-year-old professor? She probably saw in him a father figure who would replace her own father whom she had lost to the theater. She also may have converted to Catholicism for the same reason, seeing in the Monsignor a father-figure with whom she could freely talk and confess herself—a close relationship she had never had with either of her parents. But we saw how Herzog responded to her need of talking—by tricking her into thinking that he was listening to her, so that she would then help him with his research.

Whereas Herzog disregarded Mady's intellectual aspirations, he complained to her that she neglected her household duties in Ludeyville. Mady retorts that she could not cope with the vast housework in the large derelict mansion: "It needs four servants and you want me to do all the work" (123). He resented the fact that she did not accept the subservient position he wanted to allocate her and felt that he was "a broken down monarch of some kind" (39). This is reminiscent of Henderson's attitude towards his wife, Lily: "I didn't like to see her behave and carry on like the lady of the house; because I, the sole heir of the famous name and estate, am a bum, and she is not a lady—but merely my wife—merely my wife."[10] Thus we see that domineering men and the attitude that women are second-class citizens abound among Bellow's protagonists.

There is also a kind of bafflement before the essence and definition of woman. Herzog, for instance, regards them as lurid kinds of vampires and "will never understand what women want. What do they want? They eat green salad and drink human blood" (42). In much the same vein, Tommy Wilhelm, the protagonist of *Seize the Day*, exclaims that he will never understand "women or money"[11]—the implication being that money and women are on the same level: inanimate, material matter, and mere commodities.

After two years of marriage, Madeleine cannot cope anymore with Herzog's domination and patronage. It is interesting to compare Madeleine's attitude to the divorce with that of Herzog's. She states in relief that the divorce was "the first time in her life she knew clearly what she was doing. Until now it was all confusion" (100). Herzog, on the other hand, goes to pieces. The climax of his struggle to overcome his passion occurs when he goes to shoot Madeleine and her lover in Chicago. However, when he watches through the window he sees a peaceful domestic scene: Mady washing dishes and cleaning the kitchen, and Valentine tenderly bathing Junie. This peaceful harmony brings a change in his attitude; he is confronted with an actual situation, two people in love living peaceably together, and not the monsters he had expected to find. He concludes: "Let the child find life," and as to the lovers, "if, even in that embrace of lust and treason, they had life and nature on their side, he would step quietly aside" (267). He has arrived at the full realization that Madeleine did not love him: "Madeleine refused to be married to him, and people's wishes have to be respected. Slavery is dead" (7).

After he has succeeded in uprooting Madeleine from his system, Phoebe asks him if he wants Madeleine back, and he answers frankly:

"I wish her a busy, useful, pleasant, dramatic life. Including *love*. The best people fall in love, and she's one of the best." Herzog has finally succeeded in freeing himself of his obsession for Madeleine,[12] and in so doing, he has given us one of the best feminine portraits in Bellow's works. Madeleine emerges as a "new woman" who makes her own choices and who ultimately takes her destiny into her own hands rather than being defeated by a patriarchal society. She embodies in her character and her actions the "free" woman who struggles to achieve her chance of growth and her goal of an independent career, as well as her goal of finding real love. Her true-to-life portrayal, her authenticity, and her vividness make her one of the best feminine portraits of her kind in modern American literature.

Ramona, the woman Herzog becomes involved with after Madeleine has left him is quite a different character. She combines the characteristics of the conventional Jewish wife—warm, gentle, loving, an excellent cook with genuine family feelings—with those of the modern woman: she is independent, hard-working, intellectual, and sexual. Herzog considers her a "sexual masterpiece" (67), and he compares her to the Egyptian goddess of fecundity, calling her a "priestess of Isis" (160). He also greatly admires her independent spirit: "She struggled, she fought. . . . In this world, to be a woman who took matters into her own hands!" (337). Ramona has already arrived at the goal of full personhood that Mady was aspiring to. She has already structured her life according to her own vision of authenticity, and Herzog admires her for it—when it is not at *his* expense that she has to achieve it! He also admires her wisdom, and in one of his mental letters, recognizing that she has done a great deal for him in striving to give him self-confidence again, he writes: "Dear Ramona—Very dear Ramona. I like you very much—dear to me, a true friend. . . . you have the complete wisdom" (15).

Ramona owns a flower shop which she runs herself and has in her very personality a "fragrant" quality. Thinking of her, Herzog praises her: "you're lovely, fragrant, sexual, good to touch—everything" (152). Nonetheless, there is a mock-heroic note in his description of the elaborate way Ramona dresses up for their sexual encounters, with her black lace underclothes and her alluring postures which make him think of a Spanish dancer or "devodorada." She "entered a room provocatively, swaggering slightly, one hand touching her thigh, as though she carried a knife in her garter belt" (16). The mention of the knife shows that his traumatic experience with Madeleine makes him regard women—even warm, gentle, and affectionate Ramona—as castrators. Typically, he is also suspicious of her ideology. She preached *"mens sana in corpore sano,"* (201)—a healthy soul in a healthy body—and had deeply absorbed the teachings of Marcuse, N. C. Brown, and the Neo-Freudians who believed the body is the instrument of the soul (208–9). She tells Herzog that the art of love is one of the most sublime achievements of the soul, and tries to teach him how to renew the spirit through the flesh—"the true and only temple of the spirit" (185). On the whole, however, Ramona delights Herzog, and he cries in admiration: "Bless the girl! What pleasure she gave him. All her ways satisfied him—her French—Russian— Argentine—Jewish ways" (200). At the end of the novel, we find Herzog preparing a meal for Ramona and picking flowers for her, things he had never done before for any of the other women.

It is interesting to note that whereas Madeleine complains that she cannot cope with the household chores in Ludeyville, when Herzog watches her through the window in Chicago with Valentine, she is wash- ing the dishes. In Ramona's apartment, Herzog himself wants to wash the dishes after dinner, for, he explains, "there is something about wash- ing dishes that calms me" (194). And at the end of the novel, when the reformed and out-of-crisis Herzog invites Ramona to dinner in his own house where he has cooked a good meal for her—he thinks: "She would help him with the dishes" (340). The point that Bellow is obviously mak- ing is that when the relationship between the couple is harmonious, the household chores do not represent a problem. Ultimately, in compar- ing the two women, and their situations in the novel—whereas Madeleine, in Evelyn Torton Beck's terms, refuses to inhabit the "background" of her husband's "foreground"[13] anymore—Ramona does not have to enter Herzog's background, as she has attained her own foreground. Bellow demonstrates that beautifully.[14]

In *Mr. Sammler's Planet* the three main women characters portrayed— Shula Sammler, Angela Gruner, and Margotte Arkin—are examples of hypochondria, sexual avidity, and distortions of values. Angela "sent money to defense funds for black murderers and rapists" (11); and Margotte, echoing Hannah Arendt on "the banality of evil," is full of pity and adulation for the romance and the glamour of criminals. Shula- Slawa has a split personality and is half mad. And as to the women stu- dent activists, Sammler has some hard things to say about them: "Females were naturally more prone to grossness, had more smells, needed more washing, clipping, binding, pruning, grooming, perfuming, and training" (36); as a result they suffered from a loss of femininity and self-esteem.

In *Humboldt's Gift*,[15] we find that the protagonist's "analytical skepti- cism" towards women is just as bad as Sammler's. Sammler at least was honest; Charlie Citrine is hypocritical and double faced in his dealing with women. On the one hand, he encourages the "passionate hypochon- dria" of women and presses them to tell him about their "tumors and their swollen legs. I wanted them to tell me about marriage, childbirth, money, sickness, and death" (13). And when they duly respond and open their hearts to him, he cynically classifies them "into categories as I sat there drinking coffee." His categories are all denigrating: "They were petty bourgeois, husband-killers, social climbers, hysterics, etc." (13). The women he frequents can in no way compare to the companionship of his male friends such as Humboldt, Shapiro, and Rahv whom he truly respects and esteems.

His friend George warns him against his wife's devastating influence: "You're not getting enough air with that woman. You look as if you're suffocating. Your tissues aren't getting any oxygen. She'll give you cancer." Charlie's sardonic answer implies that he sees in this destructive relationship a heavy cross he has to bear: "She may think she's offering me the blessings of an American marriage. Real Americans are supposed to suffer with their wives, and wives with husbands. Like Mr. and Mrs. Abraham Lincoln. It's the classic US grief" (43). The implication is that there should be no deception concerning the possibility of happiness in an American marriage.

Minna Corde in *The Dean's December* (1982),[16] is the most independent and high-powered woman character we have had till now in Bellow's novels. She is a world-famous astronomer, and in her portrayal, Bellow gives us a convincing illustration of what a strong, struggling, working, creating, "new" woman is. She is a fascinating character who has many complex angles in her personality and her relationship with her husband, Dean Albert Corde. As a successful career woman, she has a brilliant scientific mind. Having had the opportunity to make her own choices and to grow, she is fulfilled and satisfied, and fully involved with her research work. In addition to her strong will and intelligence, she is sensitive, thoughtful, and kind. Minna has achieved both goals of an independent, successful career, as well as the goal of finding real love with Albert. Like Ramona before her, Minna has arrived at the goal of full personhood that Madeleine and several other Bellovian female characters aspired to.

Dr. Valeria Raresh, Minna's mother, is also a woman of value. She had studied psychiatry and was well-versed in Freud and Ferenczi. In matters of self-respect she was a model for Minna even on her deathbed, in the Rumanian Communist Party Hospital in Bucharest.

Like the women characters before her, Minna, too, is mainly portrayed through the male protagonist's perception, and we rarely hear her own voice. We get a treatment of how Albert experiences her, how he thinks about her and her mother, and how he relates to the two, but we do not get the opposite treatment in full, except for some few passages where we hear Minna's voice. This complicates our comprehension of their real relationship and communication, and in some instances we are left to guess the extent of their involvement with each other. Gloria Cronin comments on this issue: "Like previous Bellow's heroes, Corde's first apprehension about the unknowability of truth is of the isolation of the human creature" (32).[17] And Mark Weinstein esteems that "throughout most of the novel, communication between the Cordes is subtle, ever-shifting, basically good" (71).[18] But is it?

A close analysis of the Cordes' relationship throughout the novel points to basic complications, some of them reminding us of situations and attitudes we have encountered in the previous books. Despite Minna's obvious qualities and qualifications, Albert seems to mock her involvement with her astrophysics research, and he often comments that she is more "in the stars" than on her planet. In his mind, a basic antagonism develops between his social pursuits and his fears for the decline of modern civilization—and her space pursuits. He doubts she had read his Chicago articles about the deterioration of the modern cities and the growth of crime. He attempts to involve her in his problems but is unsuccessful, because Minna has problems of her own—her astrophysics research and her mother's fatal sickness. Albert, like Herzog before him, cannot accept the fact that his own interests are not primordial in his wife's scale of values. He seems to have preferred a wife who thought and felt exactly like he. Yet he knew when he married Minna that she was a scientist with a career of her own and tastes of her own—why the disappointment and even, at times, bitterness? Like Herzog, who wanted Mady to forego her own intellectual pursuits to help him with his book, Corde feels thwarted and frustrated that Minna does not take his articles as seriously as he does and does not share his concerns and priorities. But Minna makes it clear that she has her own scientific priorities. He responds by considering her astrophysics research as a superfluous pursuit which had nothing to do with real life: "She did stars; human matters were her husband's field" (256). Yet we know that he has great respect for Minna and is even in awe of her vast scientific knowledge and her probing intelligence.

Corde's minimizing of Minna's scientific spatial research reminds us of Sammler's discussion with Professor Lal, when he tries to convince him that our planet had its own troubles which had to be cared for before we go to the moon. However, Corde does not give Minna credit for thinking otherwise, as Sammler does with Lal. Here too, as in the previous books, Albert tries to change Minna, not to convince her as with Lal, but to actually change her tastes and personality.

Joseph, too, had tried to change Iva, and had looked down on her "superficial interests," and Herzog had denigrated Mady's "badinage" with Russian philosophy. It is clear that the same male chauvinistic attitude towards the previous women characters is present in the case of Minna too, though her status is much higher than either the librarian Iva or the doctoral student Madeleine. Though she is a world-famous scientist, the protagonist's attitudes towards her is still aggressive and domineering. Corde, before the end of the novel, will learn the same lesson that Joseph did when he realized that "Iva could not live in my infatuation" (65), and that the freedom to pursue one's own personal interests and tastes is a unifying element in human relations.

Minna, unlike Madeleine, who as we have seen, refuses to inhabit the "background" of her husband's "foreground," does not even realize that this is what he expects of her. She is so engrossed in her work and career that it does not dawn on her that he could make such demands. Here too, as in the earlier novels, there is bafflement before the essence and definition of "woman." Albert regards her as not totally human and as distant and incomprehensible as a faraway star, who like "the beautiful Nadia Comaneci, did not need the support of the solid earth and preferred to live in the air, like a Chagall bride" (72). He describes Minna as an "innocent person" (256) and talks of her scientific research condescendingly, as if she were a child playing with a useless toy. However, he admits that when something is important, "Minna when she was brought back to earth could be a tigress" (72), as when she fights for her mother's life. This reminds us of the description of Denise in *Humboldt's Gift* as "a great beauty but not altogether human . . . exquisite and terribly fierce" (40).

Minna, feeling herself younger than her years, tries to impart that feeling to Albert, but he mocks her and callously remarks: "How could you deny the slippage?" He does not understand that what she is trying to do is to give him self-confidence. He often goes back to the fact that she did not comprehend fully what he was trying to accomplish in the Chicago articles. However, Minna loves harmony and quiet. She dislikes noise, disorder, notoriety, and any publicity. His Chicago articles and all the noise they create are against her very nature, but Albert does not understand this and is bitter. Knowing nothing about astrophysics, he does not ask her any questions about her work or try to learn anything about her concerns. On the other hand, he admits that she was tactful enough to let him tell her about Clemenceau or Jefferson or Lenin so that she could exclaim: "Really, I am so dumb!" This is when Albert enjoys her company most, when she pretends she is stupid. At those moments Albert feels: "You might love a woman for her tactfulness alone." She knows him better than he knows her and understands his craving for "macho" superiority, which she nobly grants him, despite the obvious disparity of knowledge and status between them. He is a dean of a college and a journalist, but she is a world-famous scientist.

Valeria's death results in Minna's emotional and physical deterioration, and her relationship with Albert, who does not try to comfort her, becomes a still more conflicted one. The major disruption in their relationship takes place when she asks him for support during her breakdown, and instead of giving it to her, he is amazed at her weakness and perplexity (256) over her mother's death and callously attacks her for choosing a career in the stars, which was an easy option: "It's the most seductive one. You learn to keep your humanity to yourself, the one who appreciates it best" (262). She cries in despair: "Why do you think you should tell me this now, Albert? I tell you how horrible my mother's death is, and the way you comfort me is to say everything is monstrous. You make me a speech." Her cry for help is a sign that she loves him and counts on him, but when she does not get any support from him, she tells him that she finds him a more emotional and strange person than she expected. But Albert thinks: "You couldn't fathom Minna's conceptions of strange and normal because she was so astronomical. The hours she spent with you, dear heart, were hours among the galaxies." But he admits that at times "she came back from space" (259).

Near the end of the novel, Albert and Minna are reconciled, as Minna recuperates from the shock of her mother's death and becomes her wise and conciliatory self again. Albert eventually accepts the fact that her cosmic work is primordial in her life, as she accepts that his sense of crisis of "the doomed populations of East and West" forces him to leave his work as Dean and go back to being a journalist again. Though he is still somewhat jealous and resentful of her deep involvement with that "zone of star formation waiting for her" (292), he concedes that even "if she would live for the sake of the stars, he didn't ask for more." And on her side she feels "she did have him, with all his troubling oddities, and he had her." Following her up to the top of Mount Palomar's huge telescope, he is full of awe for her competence, and he proudly regards her as his own representative among the stars, "those bright things so thick and close." At that moment we are witness to a real tender connection between Minna and Corde, but we are left with an uneasy feeling—will it last?

From Iva in *Dangling Man* to Minna in *The Dean's December*, Bellow has come a long way in his depiction of women characters. He has built a world of women, mostly as seen by men, and it illuminates a whole region of the relationship between men and women. When I asked Saul Bellow, at the International Conference on Saul Bellow's Work in Haifa (April

1987), if there was a possibility that his next protagonist would be a woman, his answer was: "Maybe. Women also wear trousers now; it's easier for me to understand someone who wears trousers."

Notes

1. Leslie Fiedler, *Love and Death in the American Novel* (New York: Stein & Day, 1967), 363.
2. John J. Clayton, *Saul Bellow: In Defense of Man* (Bloomington: Indiana University Press), 211.
3. Saul Bellow, *Dangling Man* (1944; reprint, New York: Signet, 1965). Hereafter Bellow novels are cited parenthetically.
4. Martin Buber, "Dialogue," *Four Existentialist Theologians*, ed. Will Herberg (New York: Doubleday, 1958), 174.
5. Saul Bellow, *Herzog* (New York: Viking Press, 1964).
6. Keith Opdahl, *The Novels of Saul Bellow* (University Park: Pennsylvania State University Press, 1967), 163-64.
7. Joanna Russ, "What Can a Heroine Do?" *Images of Women in Fiction*, ed. Susan Koppelman Cornillon (Ohio: Bowling Green University, 1972), 8.
8. Fiedler, 364.
9. Jack Ludwig, "The Wayward Reader," *Holiday* 37 (February 1965): 17–18.
10. Saul Bellow, *Henderson the Rain King* (New York: Viking Press, 1959), 6.
11. Saul Bellow, *Seize the Day* (1956; reprint, New York: Fawcett Crest, 1965).
12. Bellow has divorced four times. He married his first wife, Anita Goshkin, in 1937. Working on *Seize the Day,* he was waiting out the residence requirements for a divorce, and by the time it was published in 1956, he was remarried to his second wife, Alexandra Tschacbasor. When he wrote *Herzog,* he was divorcing for the second time. He married his third wife, Susan Glassman, in 1961, and was separated from her before *Mr. Sammler's Planet* was published in 1971. He married and divorced his fourth wife, Alexandra Ionescu Tulcea, a brilliant mathematician, of Rumanian extraction.
13. Evelyn Torton Beck, "The Many Faces of Eve: Women, Yiddish, and I. B. Singer," *Studies in American Jewish Literature,* ed. Daniel Walden, 1 (Albany: State University of New York Press, 1981).
14. For the description of additional women characters in Bellow until the publication of *Herzog,* see my Ph.D. dissertation: Ada Aharoni, *Saul Bellow's Introspective Fiction* (Jerusalem: The Hebrew University, 1974).
15. Saul Bellow, *Humboldt's Gift* (New York: Avon, 1976).
16. Saul Bellow, *The Dean's December* (New York: Harper & Row, 1982).
17. Gloria L. Cronin, "Through a Glass Brightly: Corde's Escape from History in *The Dean's December,*" *Saul Bellow Journal* 5,1 (Winter 1986): 32.
18. Mark Weinstein, "Communication in *The Dean's December,*" *Saul Bellow Journal* 5, 1 (Winter 1986): 71.

Saul Bellow and the
"Lost Cause" of Character

H. Porter Abbott

The novel of characters belongs entirely to the past, it describes a period: that which marked the apogee of the individual.

Alain Robbe-Grillet[1]

There is no reason why a novelist should not drop "character" if the strategy stimulates him. But it is nonsense to do it on the theoretical ground that the period which marked the apogee of the individual etc., is ended. We must not make bosses of our intellectuals. And we do them no good by letting them run the arts. Should they, when they read novels, find nothing in them but the endorsement of their own opinions? Are we here on earth to play such games?

Saul Bellow[2]

There is an elegiac quality in the transcript of "Character as a Lost Cause," a panel in *Novel's* tenth anniversary conference on current trends in novel theory (*Novel*, Spring 1978), as if the panelists were attempting to cope with life after the passing of the only one who had made life worth living. To call it elegiac is perhaps to overstate it. At least two of the panelists (Moynahan, Weinstein) were determined to say that the deceased was still around, that even in his absence he is present (though this is also characteristic of elegies). As they quite correctly imply, even the purest musicalizers of fiction, so distant from traditional novelists that almost all traces of family resemblance have been obliterated, depend on some idea of character to achieve their effects. Though it should also be entered into the record that, if modern fiction has its share of developing forms in which character is not central, the fiction of character has survived. There are, for example, writers like Katherine Anne Porter and Eudora Welty who seem to be entirely unembarrassed by the facility with which they create characters.

First printed in *Novel: A Forum on Fiction*, Vol. 13, 3 (Spring 1980): 264–83.

I would like to propose as an operating hypothesis for what follows
that what is distinctively modern about character is neither its trivializa-
tion, conversion into words, death, nor diminishment but the concern
for it that would lead to a panel on the topic. In this view, what has
changed—in the novel, as in meetings of humanists to discuss it—is that
character has become a subject. It has become a subject in part, perhaps,
because there is no longer any generally accepted synonymity between
character and human life itself. One can no longer take the existence
of character for granted. Whatever the cause, the tendency to make
character a subject can already be found extensively developed in
Conrad's sustained meditations through his agent, Marlow, on figures
like Kurtz and Lord Jim. In this essay, I want to show how it has been
developed by one contemporary novelist.

I

If the novel owes its existence to characters, then Bellow's first—
Dangling Man (1944)—had all the appearance of being his last. Late in
the book, Bellow's protagonist records two interviews he has with his
alter ego, a coy, rather pale Mephistopheles whom he calls *Tu As Raison
Aussi*. In these, Joseph sounds a theme that Bellow has never abandoned.
He manfully denies that it is impossible to be "human" in the present.
For that matter, the present, he argues, is hardly so bad as it has been
made out to be. " 'It's too easy to abjure it or detest it. Too narrow. Too
cowardly.' "³ As for "alienation," it is a vogue; one ought not to make
a doctrine of it. The problem with Joseph's argument is that almost everything else in *Dangling Man* appears to deny the argument's validity and
to support the currently popular hypothesis that the self—at least as it
made its appearance in the great literary documents of the past—is no
longer compatible with intelligence. Even in his imaginary interview,
while Joseph is sticking up for the old-fashioned authority of self, he
speaks of his yearning for an "ideal construction" or noble character
type that could serve him in the present as others had been served in
the past (" 'the Humanistic full man, the courtly lover, the knight, the
ecclesiastic,' " 93).

As he talks, the flow of Joseph's ideas generates the reason why, for
the one who thinks, a successful ideal construction is no longer possible.
Character is a product of belief and is sustainable only with the conviction that it is part of an enduring reality. To see it as purely the arbitrary
invention of one's own mind is to lose it. " 'But what of the gap between
the ideal construction and the real world, the truth?' " (93), Joseph asks.
No answer is provided. In this regard, Joseph's whole effort during the

nine months in which the novel takes place falls within the tradition of his modern ancestor, the underground man of Dostoevsky, who, like Joseph, yearns for character (even that of a lazy man—then he would know who he is, what to call himself) and who is prevented from having it, like Joseph, because he suffers from the "disease" of lucidity. Thus, Bellow's first effort as a novelist is a book that, implicitly at least, tells why he cannot be a novelist. Despite Joseph's protest, the book is very much in vogue, the static non-story of a mind in a room, a yearning for character in search of its type, a man so "alienated" that he is given to the gnostic fantasy that "his parents are pretenders; his real father is elsewhere and will some day come to claim him" (21).

This historical waning of character is directly linked in *Dangling Man* to the waning of confidence in reason. In the context of Bellow's canon, this is an important association. Bellow has been called both an intellectual novelist and an anti-intellectual novelist, a crisis of labeling attributable in part to his originality. Whatever one calls him, in his first book he pointedly underscored his independence from the primitivism of the American mainstream by making his protagonist a man of thought and a reader of books, with a special interest in the Enlightenment. And though Joseph has recently and somewhat inexplicably lost interest in books and given over his penchant for plans, he refuses to sacrifice his reason. The late collapse of rational hopes will not drive him into the opposite camp: "[W]hat are we given reason for? To discover the blessedness of unreason? That's a very poor argument" (90). Yet without some anchor beyond himself to which confidence in reason can be secured, Joseph's dilemma is exactly that of his crisis of confidence in character. "Out of my own strength it was necessary for me to return the verdict for reason, in its partial inadequacy, and against the advantages of its surrender" (46). He holds out valiantly against the seductions of *Tu As Raison Aussi,* but in the end, the case for the mind appears as hopeless as the case for character. On the last page, visiting his childhood room in his father's house, Joseph has a sudden vision of the transience both of his life as a child and of the very room itself. Shaken, he takes the experience for a forceful insight into the fundamentally gratuitous nature of all human arrangements.

> I understood it to be a revelation of the ephemeral agreements by which we live and pace ourselves. . . . Such reality, I thought, is actually very dangerous, very treacherous. It should not be trusted. And I rose rather unsteadily from the rocker, feeling that there was an element of treason to common sense in the very objects of common sense. Or that there was no trusting them, save through wide

agreement, and that my separation from such agreement had brought
me perilously far from the necessary trust, auxiliary to all sanity. (126)

To keep one's eye on the truth, in short, is to risk one's sanity. Reason,
which seeks the truth, must back off or be destroyed. At the end of the
book, Joseph asks to be inducted into the army. As he says, he has failed
to use his freedom. No character, no new Joseph, has flowered in the
hothouse to which he has confined himself. Instead his sense of himself
has become increasingly tenuous. In the process, his reason, poring over
the facts of his existence, has run a parallel course. To preserve both
his sense of himself and his sanity, Joseph abandons the authority of his
reason for the authority of society's arbitrary "agreements." He joins the
army.

There is one more notable way in which Joseph appears to fail. It is
worth discussing here for it, too, like the effort to stick up for reason,
is closely linked to Bellow's concern for character. This is Joseph's determination to engage in the overt expression of his feelings. As in the
aspect of Joseph's intellectuality, so in this regard too, the fledgling
novelist is declaring his arrival on the American scene *against* the prevailing mode. On page one, Joseph clearly informs us that he is *not* going
to be a part of the tight-lipped, Hemingway tradition; that he is not going to endure the "inhibitory effect" of "closemouthed straight-
forwardness"; that he is instead going to express his emotions and talk
at length about his inner problems. At the same time, he declares that
he is abandoning literary formality, the mandarin correctness and smooth
polish of craft that are very much a part of the stoic mode, and instead
is adopting the European tradition of the intimate diary, a necessarily
informal genre, adaptable to the spontaneous expressions of the inner
self. A writer of conscious self-indulgence, Joseph is almost as pugna-
cious as his opposition: "Most serious matters are closed to the hard-
boiled. They are unpracticed in introspection, and therefore badly
equipped to deal with opponents whom they cannot shoot like big game
or outdo in daring" (7).

There is probably a good deal of truth to the hypothesis that Bellow,
eighteen years after *The Sun Also Rises,* was letting Robert Cohn have his
own back.[4] But Joseph, who carries self-expression and lack of restraint
to the point of violence, who covers himself continually with shame, who
shows anything but "grace under pressure," is only vaguely a Jew in a
WASP world. His problems are the universal ones of trying to express
who he is and of not being inhibited by what family, friends, and society would like him to be. But expressing the immediate, passionate contours of who he truly is, fulfilling the ends of the *journal intime* to which

he has committed himself, assumes the availability of a self, which, as we have already noted, fails to materialize during his experimental confinement. In his case, formal unconstraint leads not to the searching introspection he spoke of at the start, but to an irrational and increasingly explosive belligerency that he records in his diary but rarely reflects upon. His violence, culminating in a brawl with a fellow boarder, finally demoralizes him and leads him to close down his experiment. Again, the book in this regard appears to declare its own failure. The emotional and expressive unconstraint that marked it at the start is abandoned at the end, the diary shelved, and Joseph joins the same army with which Hemingway himself was so closely associated. Indeed, though Joseph sets out to do battle with the Hemingway mode, he recognizes, not unsympathetically, that the mode itself is a response to the same frightening perception of human insignificance that he strives to overcome:

> Great pressure is brought to bear to make us undervalue ourselves. . . . We are schooled in quietness and, if one of us takes his measure occasionally, he does so coolly, as if he were examining his fingernails, not his soul. . . . Who can be the earnest huntsman of himself when he knows he is in turn a quarry? Or nothing so distinctive as quarry, but one of a shoal, driven toward the weirs. (79)

The immediate background for this passage is the war, but Joseph makes it clear that the war simply brings to focus the general dilemma of human beings trying to live in a vacuum, without belief. In such a world, one adopts the code of the Hemingway hero as an "ideal construction" both to give the illusion of being and to cut short any further discussion of the subject.

Part of the originality of Bellow's career is that it goes backwards. *Dangling Man* is his most modern book. In spite of its apparent failures on all fronts, Bellow did not become "post-modern," did not make those failures the basis of his future work. Instead, the life that Joseph fails to find in himself and that his immediate successors seek, grows up in abundance everywhere in the secondary characters of these busy novels, until finally, with *Henderson the Rain King*, the vividness and clarity of being that distinguish so many of Bellow's minor figures penetrate the central figure himself. These attributes, in fact, are what give *Henderson* a certain fraudulence, insofar as it pretends to be a *Bildungsroman:* because, for all Henderson's search for an "ideal construction" (in his mentor Dahfu's words, a "noble self-conception"), for all his despair over being a "becomer" rather than a "be-er," he is as sharply defined at the beginning of his narrative as he is at the end, equipped with an abundance of being on which his travels have little noticeable depth of effect. It is almost as if the theories of Dahfu were an appendage to the novel and that the real meaning and appeal of the work resided in the character of Henderson himself.

II

One principal condition of this reversion to character is the distinctively tentative quality of *Dangling Man*. Though the novel appears to conclude with a certain finality, it in fact takes no position in its final pages. This tentativeness is of a piece with an intellectual restraint in evidence throughout. It deserves discussion, not simply because it affects how we respond to the "argument" of the book, but also because it is yet another quality which is bound up with Bellow's regard for character.

To begin with, the aspects of the book which invite us to look at it as an argument are part of Bellow's reaction to the anti-intellectualism of American fiction. In his reaction, Bellow took for his model the European device of the diarist in his room, and it is more than likely that he had somewhere in his mind the ontological research carried out in *La Nausée*, Sartre's success of 1938. Like Roquentin, Joseph is a lapsing intellectual whose old modes of thinking have failed him (both diarists are in the process of giving up biographical studies of eighteenth-century figures). Like Roquentin, Joseph takes up writing his *journal intime* to get to the bottom of his crisis. Similarly, he is led to a wearying perception of inner formlessness; the city takes on the aspect of disorganized junk; and the host of minor characters are revealed to be consummate—and at heart desperate—self-deceivers. In the end, both protagonists revert rather abruptly to modes of absolute form (Roquentin to the traditional novel, Joseph to the army).[5]

But Bellow's relationship to literary tradition was, even at this stage of his career, quite sophisticated. If he went to Europe for a form commensurate with his aspirations, he went not as a thief but as an imitator.[6] Thus, in turning to Sartre's version of the diary novel, he is at once respecting it and revaluing it. Whether he was consciously attempting to create a mid-Atlantic form I cannot say, but certainly at the center of his revaluation of *La Nausée* is the figure of Joseph himself and in particular his relationship to the bleak insight that is the philosophical core of Sartre's novel. For where Sartre's hero bravely shoulders the burden of nothingness, Joseph resists it. He is a reluctant Roquentin. And though all the evidence appears to confirm the hypothesis that character, like all other form, is only the arbitrary invention of mind, Joseph leaves the case open. Where Roquentin sets out at the end of his book on a plan (to write a novel) that is predicated on the conviction he now has about life, Joseph abandons his diary with few convictions and no real plans. His decision to join the army is, as he says, a "move" in a game that is still in progress. His inquiry is far from complete: "The next move was the world's."

It may well be that Bellow had the conclusion of *La Nausée* in mind when he introduced the artist, John Pearl, into the collection of representative minor characters of *Dangling Man*. At the end of the former novel, Roquentin, listening to his favorite record for the last time, finds himself imagining the composer and the singer of the song working together on the twenty-first floor of a New York skyscraper. His last entry tells us that he has followed their lead, ascending to the *second* floor of the Hotel Printania to compose a story about "*quelque chose qui n'existerait pas, . . . belle et dure comme de l'acier.*"[7] Bellow situates his artist in a New York skyscraper *fifty-three* stories high and gives him an aesthetic credo that is broadly of the same type: "There is only one worthwhile sort of work, that of the imagination." It is a work that is "in the strictest sense not personel" (61). But this is an alternative that Joseph cannot allow himself, much as it appeals to him.

> It is an attractive idea, it confers a sort of life on him, sets him off from the debased dullness of those fifty-three stories. . . . [H]e has escaped a trap. That really is a victory to celebrate. I am fascinated by it and a little jealous. He can maintain himself. Is it because he is an artist? I believe it is. Those acts of the imagination save him. But what about me? I have no talent for that sort of thing. My talent, if I have one at all, is for being a citizen, or what is today called, most apologetically, a good man. Is there some sort of personal effort I can substitute for the imagination? (61)

His question goes unanswered. Though Pearl's (and Roquentin's) alternative, at least, is rejected, the fixed, unimaginative order of military discipline to which Bellow's diarist is delivered is not a matter of choice but, for the moment, passive acceptance.

Though Joseph, as he repeatedly describes himself, is a man of plans, a throwback to eighteenth-century rationalism who seeks a program of self-education and an ideal construction by which to identify himself as citizen and good man, there is no ideological fixity in *Dangling Man*. When it comes to reflecting on himself in his diary his thoughts are unsorted; he slips from one to the other with none of the Frenchman's ability to conclude. When Roquentin looks in the mirror (traditional in diary fiction), he sees the image of his own formlessness: "*au-dessous du singe, à la lisière du monde végétal, au niveau des polypes"* (31). The experience, like so many of the other experiences of defamiliarization recorded in Roquentin's diary, leads directly to the formulation of its nature and significance that takes place later in the city park. It becomes a part of what eventually emerges as the novel's thesis. Joseph's own mirror scene is by contrast pointedly restrained:

> I observed new folds near my mouth and, around my eyes and the root of my nose, marks that had not been there a year before. It is not pleasant to find such changes. But, tying my tie, I shrugged them off as inevitable, the price of experience, an outlay that had better be made ungrudgingly, since it was bound in any case to be collected. (115)

It is a determinedly modest passage. Where Roquentin finds an idea of self (that is, of its absence), Joseph notes in passing that he has aged. Abstract discourse, itself, seems to embarrass him. The most "intellectual" parts of the work, Joseph's conversations with *Tu As Raison Aussi*, read like elliptical parodies of their Dostoevskian equivalent. The final note is one of self-mockery:

> "How seriously you take this," cried *Tu As Raison Aussi*. "It's only a discussion. The boy's teeth are chattering. Do you have a chill?" He ran to get a blanket from the bed.
>
> I said faintly, "I'm all right." He tucked the blanket around me and, in great concern, wiped my forehead and sat by me until nightfall. (112)

Joseph's inability to develop his ideas in an orderly, systematic way and his general embarrassment about conceptual thought are, in their extremity, a reaction against his own recent experience of such thought in its most rigid and doctrinaire form. The exponent of rigidity in the novel is Comrade Jimmy Burns, with whom Joseph once had a close working relationship. Burns, when Joseph encounters him in a restaurant, refuses to recognize his backsliding former colleague. Joseph makes a scene and finally forces Burns to acknowledge his existence in what is the first of many instances in which Bellow records a basic antagonism between ideological thought and individual being. In *Dangling Man* this antagonism relates directly to the intellectual looseness of the novel itself. For all his egg-headedness, Joseph's failures of conceptual thought are what preserve him. At the end, the evidence against the self does not prevail because no "position" is taken. There is only the recognition that a certain experiment has failed. "Perhaps," says Joseph, "I could sound creation through other means" (126). At any rate, as he enters the army, the game is still in progress. And—who knows—it may not be too farfetched to see the quest of Eugene Henderson, ex-soldier, lover of military discipline and travesty of Hemingway the lion-hunter, as a sequel to that of Joseph the Dangler.[8]

III

The mid-Atlantic character of Joseph's intellect, its refusal to embrace the prevailing fashions of Paris or New York, anticipates one of the recurrent themes of Bellow's numerous essays and interviews. The theme is, simply, that there is a difference between thinking and having an idea. Under this heading, Bellow finds little to distinguish the cerebral French writer from his primitive American counterpart. They are both too easily impressed by ideas. Though this might be obvious in the work of the European, it is equally so in that of popular naturalists such as Farrell and Steinbeck. Much as they insist on "sitting on the curb playing poker and talking about whores,"[9] they submit to the restraint of a few ideas. They are didactic. Ideas weigh them down, often at great personal cost, for this is a sort of willful deracination of authors who are personally quite sophisticated: "We have developed in American fiction a strange combination of extreme naiveté in the characters and of profundity implicit in the writing, in the techniques themselves and in the language, but the language of thought itself is banned, it is considered dangerous and destructive."[10]

For his ideal in this regard, Bellow goes back to Shakespeare and Dostoevsky, who, as he says, were writers first, not philosophers. In his essay "Where Do We Go from Here?" he singles out Dostoevsky's performance in the Grand Inquisitor sequence as an outstanding example of thinking in fiction. As an individual, Dostoevsky has a set of Christian ideas which constitute a position. But in the Grand Inquisitor scene "he has in advance all but devastated his own position." This free opposition of ideas raises his work from the level of a tract to the level of art: "The opposites must be free to range themselves against each other, and they must be passionately expressed on both sides."[11] If Bellow's own works do not attain the complexity of argument found in Dostoevsky, the continuing dilemma of their conclusions—their resistance to interpretation—may well be a conscious formal strategy aimed at this effect. By the way they end, they avoid a reduction to idea. Thinking, in other words, is still in progress, and this, as Bellow states above, is part of the "art."

Another and more fundamental part of the art is emotion. Bellow returns to this point again and again. What thinking there is must, as he says of Dostoevsky, be "passionately expressed." "Nothing is legitimate in literature or any work of art which does not have the support of some kind of emotional conviction. The ideological conviction means almost nothing. The emotional conviction means everything."[12] The problem with the fiction of such novelists as Camus, Sartre, Mann, or Koestler is that it is "as strong as their intellectual position—or as weak."[13] Even in America, a heavy intellectuality has developed among both writers and readers, an unhealthy symbiosis, so that "books are strongly shaken to see what usable things will fall out of them to strengthen a theory or support some system of ideas," and "the poet becomes a sort of truffle hound who brings marvelous delicacies from the forest."[14] Not only does Bellow argue that ideas in fiction must be felt to be valid, but also he would agree, I think, that there is much in the author's craft and in the life imitated that has very little to do with ideas at all. His best and most forceful expression of this is still his early critique of popular New Criticism entitled "Deep Readers of the World Beware!"[15] His example in that brief essay is the bright student in the class who, reading that Achilles drags the body of Hector three times around the walls of Troy, finds in it a pattern of three rings rather than what it is—an expression of the anger of Achilles. Whether or not Bellow's accounting for this is correct (a keen insight, I think: the student is frightened by what he reads), an appropriate reading of *The Iliad*—at least of the scene referred to— puts this type of critic out of business. For the truth is that there is *no* idea expressed here, unless one wants to say that "Achilles is angry" qualifies as an idea. What is present is not an idea but a character, Achilles, at once inventing and revealing himself through the expression of his anger.

The example of Achilles throws a good hard light on the concern that underlies both Bellow's wariness of ideas and his conviction of the emotional primacy of the text. The concern is for a freedom that in Bellow appears coextensive with the self. By dragging the body of Hector three times around the walls of Troy, Achilles is, in a frightening way, expressing his originality. In so doing, he is at the same time expressing who he is. His being requires the creative freedom to surprise us. Thus, to overlook the centrality of the character in the scene who, powered by his feelings, invents himself—to appropriate him for a purely cognitive design as the student does—is to overlook that for which the scene was created.

The student's response to Achilles is a parody of the antagonism between selfhood and theory that Bellow first expressed in the fight between Joseph and Comrade Burns. In an interview for *Salmagundi*, he took it up from another perspective in some remarks on psychoanalysis.[16]

He dwelt on the case of a doctor who had written Freud about how he had lost his faith when, as a student, he had seen the body of a very beautiful old woman on the dissecting table. Freud's comment is that what the doctor had seen was "of course" his mother. Bellow's question is: "Was it not possible to experience beauty or pity without thinking of your mother, or without the Oedipus complex?" The rigidity of the theorist in this instance is a kind of intellectual fascism, for it denies the doctor his freedom to be himself. Freud does not literally presume to dominate the doctor, but he presumes to have the key to that by which the doctor is dominated. More disturbing still is the case of those who would give up their freedom to Freud: "I worry about these geniuses who create systems which then take the mind captive. It's very difficult to escape from any system of metaphors which successfully imposes itself upon you. You begin to think that way and pretty soon you can't think in any other way."

About the theorists who crowd his fiction, Bellow is much more ambivalent. He is, to begin with, intrigued by the fertility of mind that generates theories. But in addition, his own theorists generally express their originality in spite of their fondness for theory. In effect, they are made to fail as theorists. They are the kind of theorists that make genuine theorists shudder. We never see how their theories cohere, and this vital incoherence is itself an expression of the theorists' capacity to exceed their theories. Certainly the most benign example is Dahfu. His ellipticism and capacity to contradict himself are embedded in a richly expressive but often ungrammatical English. Moreover, as I have noted, Henderson is gifted with such fullness of being that he seems from the start a man basically immune to the domination of his mentor. His love and admiration for Dahfu are principally inspired not by his theories but by the dazzling man himself. Rightly so, for part of the attraction of such a character as Dahfu is his ability continually to surprise us. In this sense he is always ahead of our capacity to predict his behavior, given the fragments of his theory at our disposal.

The darker aspects of the theorist emerge in such figures as Tamkin and Bummidge[17] and, most appallingly, in the madman Basteshaw of *The Adventures of Augie March*. Basteshaw claims to have created life itself, and his plan for the future is a Utopia, imposed (like all Utopias) on humankind for its own good. His lineage goes back to *Frankenstein*, and he is produced with much the same cautionary intent. Adrift in the Atlantic on a lifeboat, Basteshaw literally ties Augie up. The episode is about as close to allegory as Bellow ever gets.

After *Dangling Man*, Bellow increasingly found in Jean-Paul Sartre an embodiment of intellectual pride. Sartre came to hold much the same status for Bellow as Freud did for Nabokov and for almost identical reasons. He is one of those "masterminds whose ideas ('class-struggle,' 'Oedipus complex,' 'identity crisis') come down over us like butterfly nets."[18] As in Nabokov's view of Freud, Sartre for Bellow is a kind of threatening clown, a figure of fun who is not all that funny. Funny, because he is like "the Swiftian philosopher extracting sunshine from cucumbers and getting spiders to manufacture silks"; unfunny, because in his rigid commitment to the "Larousse Syndrome" he is willing to sacrifice both his humanity and the humanness of others on the altar of concept. One consequence of this is Sartre's readiness to tell people who they are. This is the cause of a good deal of the anger he generates in Bellow, particularly as Sartre has, on more than one occasion, not only told the Jews who they are but has gone on to tell them how they should therefore behave as Jews. Bellow's anxiety on this score is as acute as it is when critics attempt to classify him as a Jewish novelist. There is perhaps something akin to Geronimo's fear of photographs in this. The fixity of the classification, like that of the photograph, obscures the originality which is so essential to Bellow's own sense of self.

IV

Bellow's sensitivity to the destructive power of fixed categories led him, in his work after *Dangling Man*, to draw a rather large circle around the self and post it. He has declared it a preserve not only from the depredations of ideologues and other theorists but even from his own reverential intrusion as a fictionist. The parable of this is his 1951 short story, "Looking for Mr. Green." It is the story of a social worker whose attempts to deliver a relief check to Mr. Green are subjected to a potentially infinite series of impediments. Late in the day, when Grebe believes he has at last ferreted out his prey, what emerges slowly into view down a stairway is not Mr. Green but a black woman whose name Grebe never learns.

> She was entirely naked, climbing down while she talked to herself, a heavy woman, naked and drunk. She blundered into him. The contact of her breasts, though they touched only his coat, made him go back against the door with a blind shock. See what he had tracked down, in his hunting game![19]

In mixed despair and relief, Grebe lets her sign for the check. "Whoever she was, the woman stood for Green" (107–8).

Nine years earlier, when he began writing his first novel, Bellow did not perhaps start with the clear perception with which "Mr. Green" concludes. But if he did not, *Dangling Man* evolved into a cautionary tale with essentially the same burden. The difference, and it is an important one, is that the object of the search in *Dangling Man* is the searcher's own self. As if Green were to seek Green. Looking into the "craters of the spirit," Joseph discovers nothing so distinguished as a self. He finds instead his double, Mr. Vanaker.[20] Vanaker is at once everything and nothing: a "werewolf," who, like Mr. Knott, the nonbeing in Beckett's novel *Watt,* is never the same thing twice. All we learn of Vanaker are tedious fragments of information as, for example, "that he is engaged to marry a lady of sixty who insists that he be converted to the Catholic faith," that he receives "large quantities of mail from the Masonic Scottish Rite" (21–22), that he moves his bed at two o'clock in the morning. He is, in short, that shabby disintegration of character that Joseph, brooding in the room next door, feels taking place in himself. Obviously, the anger that Vanaker arouses in Joseph is directly proportional to the intensity with which Joseph feels his devolution toward the state Vanaker represents. In his climactic fight with his double, Joseph exhibits the same noisy vulgarity for which he is fighting him. Joseph, keeping his own case open, will not allow that Vanaker is the truth about his interior self, but the fight precipitates the next move in his life, his volunteering for the army. In the context of Bellow's canon, Joseph is correct: Vanaker is not the final word. But the lesson of Vanaker is, in its essentials, the same as that of "Looking for Mr. Green": the self will not tolerate a frontal attack. Joseph's experiment has something of the moral quality of certain works in the hermetic/demonic tradition. Confined to his cell, he calls up out of his own power a sort of monster (parodied at one point when Vanaker actually starts a fire in his room—from which he emerges, singed, red-eyed, coughing).

If the novel and the later short story express the same conviction, it is necessary also to note that there is a big difference between the eroticism and sharp-tongued vitality of Mr. Green's surrogate and the ghostly, doglike shabbiness of Mr. Vanaker. For where the naked lady is a vibrant and exotic emblem of a self preserved, Vanaker is a trans-Atlantic idea of a self dissolved. The difference suggests an additional caution in the novel: that what Joseph seeks cannot exist in captivity. This applies to the literary document he is employing, too. However formless and spontaneous the non-art of his diary, its words will never accommodate what Joseph seeks. The apprentice novelist, no doubt, had the same revelation about what would happen to his craft if pursued further in the same

One of the accepted beliefs that McCarthy is contradicting is the Bergsonian one that the laugh aroused by the comic character is a laugh at its mechanical predictability, its machine-like and therefore unhuman quality. Such a laugh is necessarily tinged with contempt. We laugh to separate ourselves from the object of mirth.

Yet there is no real contradiction here, rather two fundamentally different kinds of character, for neither of which need one exclusively appropriate the designation "comic." Indeed, there are many examples of the latter (Bergsonian) kind at which one does not laugh at all, demonic characters who would impose their own predictability on others (especially fascinating to Bellow), or simply boring ones like those wholly predictable products of their needs and background whom late nineteenth-century novelists often found as necessary as furniture. The difference between free and fixed characters is Bellow's major subject in the work of his maturity.

The most focused study of the difference is Bellow's 1968 short story "Mosby's Memoirs." It is a good story to put beside *Dangling Man* because, like the earlier work, it features an autobiographer at work on the job of defining who he is. But where Joseph, a backsliding intellectual at the beginning of his career, seeks to discover himself in the formless mode of the diary, Mosby, a "fanatic about ideas" near the end of his career, is coldly embalming his public image in a highly formal mode patterned on the memoirs of Adams, Nicholson, Santayana, and Russell. The irony on which the story turns is that the "life" Mosby records is actually that of a dead man. The fantasy he has that he had already died years before in an automobile accident turns out to be more than a fantasy. At the end of the story, visiting a Zapotec temple reserved for human sacrifice and observing the mathematical precision with which it had been constructed, Mosby finds in it an image of the tomb he has constructed for himself and called his life. "A finished product, standing under the sun on large blocks of stone, on the stairs descending into this pit, he was complete. He had completed himself in this cogitating, unlaughing, stone, iron, nonsensical form."[22] Though he is not a comic character, Mosby epitomizes the abandonment of human freedom. The type is combined here with the type of the man of ideas, made especially treacherous in Mosby's instance because, at first look, he appears so independent, so free of party. Light years separate his cool sophistication and the subtlety of his thought from, say, *Dangling Man*'s Jimmy Burns and the political clichés in which the latter finds his "life." Yet they are brothers under the skin, for the motive behind their adopted rigidity is the same: a fear of the unpredictable. That which is beyond control appalls them. But in opposing it, they oppose that seminal freedom which, as I have argued, Bellow identifies with genuine selfhood. To Mosby, "liveliness, beauty, seemed very dangerous. Mortal danger" (151). He prefers to die by his own hand than to run the risks of being alive.

A second irony of "Mosby's Memoirs" is that a minor character in the Memoirs becomes a hero of the story. With cold premeditation, Mosby selects Hymen Lustgarten to serve as a comic diversion, "to relieve the rigor of this account of his mental wars" (156). What the story gradually reveals is that there is more than diversion involved here. Mosby must reduce Lustgarten by laughter because Lustgarten (the name is perhaps too emphatically suggestive) represents exactly the condition that it has been Mosby's lifetime effort to avoid. Lustgarten "didn't have to happen." As he is inexplicable, so he must be laughable. Still speaking of himself (as Adams) in the third person, Mosby stumbles momentarily over this tendency of his to reduce by laughter:

> At this time, Mosby had been making fun of people.
> "Why?"
> "Because he had needed to."
> "Why?"
> "Because!" (175)

Because, if he were to take Lustgarten seriously, his own fundamental lack of seriousness, the absurdity of his own life, would become apparent. Mosby flatly reverses Bergsonian theory ("Lustgarten didn't have to happen. And so he *was* funny" [175]) and in so doing preserves in himself the sterile elegance he later sees mirrored in the temple. Converting Lustgarten into mere comic relief is thus an act of aggression against Lustgarten. It continues into the Memoirs the concealed aggression that Mosby had engaged in when he had known Lustgarten.

Back then, Mosby had destroyed Lustgarten's marriage by teaching his wife (with whom Mosby slept) to laugh at her husband as Mosby did (a fact that goes *un*recorded in the Memoirs). What Lustgarten demonstrates is that there is a kind of freedom other than the drab and "terrible" freedom that Joseph created in *Dangling Man*. His self-expressive acts are as vivid and surprising as they are typical (in Paris, for example, sleeping at night in the Cadillac he has imported but cannot sell). At the end, this power is linked with suggestions of his fertility as we are surprised once again by Lustgarten, ascending on the wrong elevator. He tells of his new life—married again, children, running a laundromat in Algiers. "For Plato," notes Mosby, "this childbreeding is the lowest level of creativity" (172). In spite of his contempt, Mosby provides a lens through which we see the radiant contours of a free character. Lustgarten is the kind of "comic character" McCarthy distinguished from heroes and heroines—seen from the outside and thus preserved as an enigma. He is different from other sorts of character as well precisely because of the internal resourcefulness implied by the twists of his story. To Mosby, the artificer and man of exquisite form, this story appears to be a chaos of amusing but gratuitous accidents. "A man like Lustgarten," he thinks "would never, except with supernatural aid, exist in a suitable form" (168). What Mosby reveals is a basic misunderstanding of form. In all his surprising acts, Lustgarten is "in character," we recognize him, repeatable, familiar, at the very same time as we laugh with surprise. Like Achilles circling the walls of Troy, he invents himself through a collaboration with the discipline of his type.

VI

Superficially it would seem a much harder task to make the same case for *Herzog* as I have been making for "Mosby." *Herzog* has all the appearances of a very "modern" book in its excessive subjectivity, its rambling, inconclusive interior argument. Unlike "Mosby" in which Lustgarten is tracked by a kind of peripheral vision, *Herzog* takes place largely in the mind of its protagonist. His mental correspondence, which consists mainly of fragments of letters, seems, in its very plenitude, far more hopelessly disjunctive than Joseph's diary and has led at least one critic to see the book as yet another improvisation on the same journal form Bellow began with in *Dangling Man*.[23]

But the mere fact of a work's "interiority" is not in itself evidence for the dissolution of either character, the self, or the novel. Georg Lukács found in it one of the principal defining features of the novel. What Lukács required was that this interiority be embedded in a sequence of actions in the external world. And for all its steamy subjectivity, this is the case in *Herzog*. The book has plot—a comic variant of the revenge plot. Furthermore, plot and character mesh in precisely the symbiotic way James approved in "The Art of Fiction." Thus, *Dangling Man*'s airless, plotless, luxury of ontological freedom is replaced in *Herzog* by the immediate pressure of emotions that in turn arise from an action in progress. Herzog's revenge trip to Chicago, for example, is motivated directly by the things he sees and hears in the New York City Courthouse. The trial for a brutal child murder augments his fears for his daughter, while a host of grim details arouses his own nihilistic thoughts and suggests that anything (even murder) is permitted.

The point I would like to stress is that the reader is not the only one bent on interpreting these expressive acts with an eye to understanding the self that guides them. Herzog himself is reading Herzog. He reflects upon himself as he would upon a character. Thus, as confined as the book is to the interior Herzog, the mind we hear is continually engaged in trying to gain knowledge of itself by reading the acts it has a part in directing. Herzog has to pick up the gun, load it, go to Madeleine's house and sight Gersbach through the window before he knows for a certainty that he will not shoot him. As always, the act (or non-act) is "in character," fitting; and as always, it comes as a surprise. As he notes: "It was worth the trip."[24]

The stroke of genius in this particular scene is the vision of Gersbach which is the catalyst to Herzog's non-revenge. With the force of a revelation, Herzog sees in the man washing his (Herzog's) child the same qualities of freedom, inviolability, and enigma that he is continually rediscovering in himself. Gersbach, who up to now has been a caricature of the fixed, Bergsonian type, is for a moment converted into the kind of free character we have been discussing. Recognizing him as such, Herzog can no more impose his will on him than he can allow his various "reality-instructors" to tell him (Herzog) who he is. The physical act of dominating another by one's will (here, murder) is equated with the mental act of categorizing another according to one's ideology. As Herzog knows, the latter is a forerunner, a necessary preliminary, of the former. Conversely, the recognition of inner mystery is a possible stay against the violence of authoritarianism.

> Even that Gersbach, call him any name you like, charlatan, psychopath, with his hot phony eyes and his clumsy cheeks, with the folds. He was unknowable. And I myself, the same. But hard ruthless action taken against a man is the assertion by evildoers that he is fully knowable. They put me down, ergo they claimed final knowledge of Herzog. They *knew* me! And I hold with Spinoza (I hope he won't mind) that to demand what is impossible for any human being, to exercise power where it can't be exercised, is tyranny. Excuse me, therefore, sir and madam, but I reject your definition of me. (299)

VII

In his focus on character, Bellow weds not simply the personal and the political but with them the metaphysical as well. Herzog's meditations on himself culminate in a luxury of religious bewilderment. He makes no assertions, claims no beliefs. But clearly the final appeal of the emotions which in themselves constitute the mystery of his being arises from their metaphysical potential:

> But this intensity, doesn't it mean anything? Is it an idiot joy that makes this animal, the most peculiar animal of all, exclaim something? And he thinks this reaction a sign, a proof, of eternity. And he has it in his breast? But I have no arguments to make about it. "Thou movest me." (340)

This aspect of Bellow's continued study of character dominates his 1967 short story, "The Old System." In this tale, the lens is the even-tempered scientific mind of the geneticist Dr. Braun. The choice of mediator was a masterstroke of defamiliarization. For the cool, objective commander of computers, whose life has been dedicated to the study of the origin and transmission of human traits, the fierce lifetime battle and deathbed reconciliation of his cousins (Tina and Isaac Braun) is as baffling as anything he has seen under a microscope. He finds himself, for all his training, helpless to unriddle what appears to be their passionate and incorrigible folly. "Why these particular forms—these Isaacs and these Tinas?"[25]

> What the explanation might be, despite twenty-five years of specialization in the chemistry of heredity, he couldn't say. How a protein molecule might carry such propensities of ingenuity, and creative malice, and negative power. Originating in an invisible ferment. Capable of printing a talent or a vice upon a billion hearts. No wonder Isaac Braun cried out to his God when he sat sealed in his great black car and the freights rumbled in the polluted shimmering of this once-beautiful valley.
> *Answer me when I call, O God of my righteousness.* (58)

It almost seems to the geneticist that the genes have been preempted in their creative task by the individuals themselves, as if the very bulk of Tina were something which she herself had called into existence. "Some sub-office of the personality, behind a little door of the brain where the restless spirit never left its work, had ordered this tremendous female form, all of it, to become manifest" (65).

At the end of his revery, Braun is "bitterly moved" as he calls up the "crude circus of feelings" at play in Tina's Jewish deathbed scene. His bitterness is only in part the bitterness of frustration. In his noiseless apartment, the tepid modern man of thought recognizes the superiority of these people in the intensity of their passion—as if "once mankind had grasped its own idea, that it was human and human through such passions, it began to exploit, to play, to disturb for the sake of exciting disturbance, to make an uproar." What gives an even sharper edge to his bitterness is the recognition that, as they exceed him in their humanity, so too they may even exceed him in their knowledge—in the superiority of their ways of knowing to those of the scientist:

> And these tears! When you wept them from the heart, you felt you justified something, understood something. But what did you understand? Again, nothing! It was only an intimation of understanding. A promise that mankind might—might, mind you—eventually, through its gift which might—might again!—be a divine gift, comprehend why it lived. Why life, why death. (83)

VIII

The intensity of Bellow's interest in character—character conceived as a nexus of passion, enigma, freedom, and form—is behind many of the faults so often complained of in his work—sentimentality, infatuation with failure and suffering, sensationalism, repeated intellectual collapse. Though he has, since the imminent dissolution of character in *Dangling Man*, returned with enthusiasm to the limitations of type, the types he has favored for his protagonists have been pronounced failures of one kind or another: an assortment of clowns, schlemiels, "fuckynuckled" bumblers. The principal appeal of these types is that, through them, violation of normal human behavior—surprise—is an easily achieved effect. There is, of course, nothing new in having a bumbler for your protagonist. Its frequency of recurrence in the novel begins in the nineteenth century and begins for much the same reason it persists in Bellow: as part of a warfare against human predictability. The provincial awkwardness of Tolstoy's Levin, for example, his lack of urban grace, augments the vital distinction between him and Anna Karenina: a distinction between someone who is essentially free and someone who is caught in the relentless working out of laws of behavior. In *War and Peace*, Pierre is a more obvious example, through his mild clownishness, of this kind of augmentation of the sense of inner freedom. More explicitly, Dostoevsky's fondness for children, holy fools, and ridiculous men is part of a repudiation of theories of human predictability. The difference between these Russians (for whom Bellow has the greatest admiration) and Bellow is the extremity with which he feels the threat to which they were reacting. And the result of this has been, in him, a diminishment of context in favor of character as the phenomenon of principal interest. The rich fields of character in which the Russians placed their protagonists and through which they developed a correspondingly rich complexity of argument has given way in him to a focus on character itself, and principally on the element of surprise in character. Thus Bellow, whose apprenticeship and continuing effort as a novelist has been fed by a healthy opposition to the narrowness of American fiction, has made his own distinctive contribution to that narrowness.

Another aspect of this contribution is that the intellection of his "intellectual" novels performs basically a negative job of work. In his *Paris Review* interview, Bellow described Herzog as a man who "comes to realize that what he considered his intellectual privilege has proved to be another form of bondage."[26] Though Herzog is often motivated by ideas, much of his cogitation is a process of dealing "with the ideas in negative fashion. He needs to dismiss a great mass of irrelevancy and nonsense in order to survive." In so describing his work, Bellow interestingly (and with a certain ironic relish) appropriated the term *Bildungsroman*: "Any *Bildungsroman*—and *Herzog* is, to use that heavy German term, a *Bildungsroman*—concludes with the first step. The first *real* step. Any man who has rid himself of superfluous ideas in order to take that step has done something significant." But a glance at the tradition that extends from *Wilhelm Meister* to *The Magic Mountain* is sufficient to show that Bellow's stress in describing his work as a *Bildungsroman* is skewed to meet the specifications of his own mid-Atlantic variant of the form. It is a form adapted to meet the needs of an author under siege, who feels in a narrower, more acute way than his European predecessors a threat to the self: a threat which derives from a perverse relationship to ideas.

For this reason, most of the secondary figures in the book, for all their superficial differences, represent the same basic illness. The "intellectuals" in the novel are the worst offenders because they are the most pretentious. Epitomized by Herzog's mad ex-wife Madeleine, their intellection is shown to have little to do with thought and much to do with an obsession with ideas, which they take on in the manner of religious converts. But just as Bellow has, in his various essays and interviews, described American and European novelists as brothers in their regard for ideas, so these intellectuals with their imported beliefs are the immediate kin of such pure products of the American scene as Herzog's lawyer, Sandor Himelstein ("Facts are nasty"), and his current lover, Ramona ("If only you would learn to trust your instincts"). All of them are possessed by reigning ideas that they impose on reality. All of them stake a claim on Herzog, defining him according to these ideas. Thus Herzog wages his battle against the tyranny of ideas on two fronts, within and without.

Both the emphasis and the corresponding limitation of the form fit that other notable mid-century attempt at an American *Bildungsroman,* Ralph Ellison's *Invisible Man.* Like *Herzog,* Ellison's novel records a retrograde quest in which the protagonist disencumbers himself of a succession of false ideas of self. By the end of the novel, he has accomplished Bellow's "first step." Though he is more a potentiality at that point than a character, it is clear that character is the object and that Ellison, like Bellow, identifies genuine character with freedom.[27] Ellison could also, like Bellow, be described as someone consciously engaged in resisting American provincialism by synthesizing American and European traditions. Yet, even in their "mid-Atlantic" aspect, the bias in both works is basically American. Call them *Bildungsromane;* but x-rayed, they show essentially the same bone structure as *Huckleberry Finn.* Like their "Primitive" American forerunner, they are preeminently novels of *un*learning, a process of divesting oneself of ideas in order to reach essential internal knowledge. Twain in his stress on the internal authority of the self was a blood relation of his Transcendentalist contemporaries. In Bellow and Ellison there is, I think, no diminishment of the tradition, simply an increasing sense of urgency which, as I have been arguing, has led Bellow to make character his subject. Herzog's victory at the end, however precarious, is to have found his way back to what he is. In his country cabin, like Thoreau before him, he finds his end in his own Being: *"pretty well satisfied to be, to be just as it is willed, and for as long as I may remain in occupancy"* (340).

Notes

1. Alain Robbe-Grillet, *For a New Novel,* trans. Richard Howard (New York: Grove Press, 1965), 26.
2. Saul Bellow, *Nobel Lecture* (Stockholm: U.S. Information Service, 1977), 10.
3. Saul Bellow, *Dangling Man* (New York: New American Library, 1965), 91.
4. "The dangling man, Joseph, might be characterized as a sensitive and intelligent Robert Cohn who did not go to Princeton." Jonathan Baumbach, *The Landscape of Nightmare: Studies in the Contemporary American Novel* (New York: New York University Press, 1965), 36.
5. For more similarities and somewhat diffferent slants on their significance, see John J. Clayton's *Saul Bellow: In Defense of Man* (Bloomington: Indiana University Press, 1968), 57–59, 120–22; and Keith Opdahl's *The Novels of Saul Bellow* (University Park: Pennsylvania State University Press, 1967), 31–49.
6. Much like epic poets, Bellow consciously "competes" with his predecessors, adapting work to his own ends in a way which declares both respect for the model and pride in his own achievement. The relationship can be found between his next novel *The Victim* and Dostoevsky's *The Eternal Husband,* and

between his short story "The Gonzaga Manuscripts" and James's *The Aspern Papers*. More broadly it can be found between *The Adventures of Augie March* and the picaresque tradition, and between *Herzog* and the epistolary tradition. Much of this is playful and consistent with his love of gentle travesty (in *Henderson,* the medieval bestiary; in *Seize the Day,* the Renaissance unities of time, place, and action). All of this in turn is part of Bellow's attempt on a number of fronts to resist American literary provincialism.

7. Jean-Paul Sartre, *La Nausée* (Paris: Gallimard, 1938), 250.

8. Not a whimsical suggestion. Note that both men have the same problem of coping with their often destructive violence. Henderson fears that his yelling may have killed Miss Lenox, but may not Joseph have hastened the death of Mrs. Kiefer by the vehemence of his last outburst against Mr. Vanaker?

9. Sanford Pinsker, "Saul Bellow in the Classroom," *College English* 34 (1973): 976.

10. Saul Bellow, "Where Do We Go from Here: The Future of Fiction," in *To the Young Writer,* ed. A. L. Baker (Ann Arbor: University of Michigan Press, 1965), 144.

11. "Where Do We Go from Here," 146.

12. Robert Boyers, "Literature and Culture: An Interview with Saul Bellow," *Salmagundi* 30 (Summer 1975): 14.

13. Saul Bellow, "The Writer as Moralist," *The Atlantic Monthly,* March 1963, 62.

14. Saul Bellow, "A World Too Much With Us," *Critical Inquiry* 2 (Autumn 1975): 9.

15. *New York Times Book Review,* 15 February 1962; rpt. in *Herzog: Text and Criticism,* ed. Irving Howe (New York: Viking Press, 1976), 365–68.

16. "Literature and Culture," 18–19.

17. For a good discrimination between the intellection of Bummidge and Herzog see Ronald Weber, "Bellow's Thinkers," *Western Humanities Review* 22 (1968): 305–13.

18. This and the following quotations come from ten pages Bellow devotes to Sartre in *To Jerusalem and Back* (New York: Knopf, 1976), 118–28. For more on Sartre see *Writers at Work,* 3rd ser. (New York: Viking Press, 1968), 194–95, and "A World Too Much with Us," 4–5.

19. *Mosby's Memoirs and Other Stories* (Greenwich, Conn.: Fawcett, 1968), 106. Bellow provides a gentle roasting of the "Larousse Syndrome" through one of the people Grebe does find. Mr. Field will not accept his check until he has proven to Grebe who he is. He does this by laying all his papers of identification out in a circle: "Social Security card, relief certification, letters from the state hospital in Manteno, and a naval discharge dated San Diego, 1920. . . . There's everything I done and been. Just the death certificate and they can close the book on me'" (100).

20. The evidence for doubling here is almost needlessly elaborated. Bellow even has him steal Joseph's socks—not the finest apparel.

21. Mary McCarthy, *The Humanist in the Bathtub* (New York: New American Library, 1964), 211-12.

22. *Mosby's Memoirs,* 176.

23. Earl Rovit, *Saul Bellow* (Minneapolis: University of Minnesota Press, 1967), 24–25.

24. *Herzog: Text and Criticism,* ed. Irving Howe (New York: Viking Press, 1976), 258.

25. *Mosby's Memoirs,* 83.

26. This and the following quotations are from *Writers at Work,* 193–95.

27. Bellow reviewed Ellison's novel for *Commentary* (June 1952) and called it "a book of the very first order, a superb book." In his review, Bellow focused on Ellison's staunch rejection of determinisms of all kinds—one of a number of concerns the two authors share. For another, Bellow's indignation at Sartre for telling him how to act as a Jew is equalled if not surpassed by Ellison's at Irving Howe for telling him how to act as a negro (see Ralph Ellison, *Shadow and Act* [New York: New American Library, 1966], 113–47).

Saul Bellow and
the University as Villain

Ben Siegel

Few American novelists talk and write about the university as much as
does Saul Bellow. Certainly no other subject stirs in him equal rancor
and resentment. He reiterates his unhappiness with the university in lecture and interview, essay and fiction. He has done so since early in his
career. His views are not totally consistent, but they are clear and un-
compromising. Bellow does not underestimate the university's importance. He knows this country's literary activity is not concentrated in
New York or Chicago or any city, and its literary intellectuals are not
molded on Grub Street or in Bohemia. They are shaped in the university, he admits, with Bohemia itself now "relocated . . . near to university campuses."[1] His attitude suggests a familiar paradox. Like many
American novelists and poets, Bellow remains rooted in academe while
making it a frequent target. He refers to himself as a "professor" and
reportedly complains at campus events lacking any "special provision"
for faculty. Where faculty privileges are concerned, Bellow proves, according to Mark Harris, "rather caste minded, petulant, peevish, especially when he . . . [is] inconvenienced." He thinks "that someone should
always be handy to assist him."[2] Yet he attributes much of what is wrong
with this nation's culture, especially its literary culture, to the university
and its professors.

I. Professors and the Literary Situation

In *Seize the Day* (1956) Bellow describes the type of individual who becomes a professor. Tommy Wilhelm recalls with distaste his cousin Artie,
who has been "an honor student at Columbia in math and languages.

First printed in somewhat different form in *The Missouri Review* 6 (Winter 1983):
167–88.

That dark little gloomy Artie with his disgusting narrow face, and his moles and self-sniffing ways and his unclean table manners, the boring habit he had of conjugating verbs when you went for a walk with him, 'Rumanian is an easy language. You just add a *tl* to everything.' " This same pitiful Artie was now a respected professor. "Not that to be a professor was in itself so great. How could anyone bear to know so many languages? And Artie also had to remain Artie, which was a bad deal. But perhaps success had changed him. Now that he had a place in the world perhaps he was better. Did Artie love his languages, and live for them, or was he also, in his heart, cynical? So many people nowadays were."[3]

Cynical or not, professors like Artie bear prime responsibility for America's "literary situation." This Bellovian phrase covers not only recent writers and writings but also the several decades of postwar media intellectuals shaping the country's thought and expression. Since World War II, American universities have littered the cultural landscape "with small Daedaluses who teach literature, edit magazines, write critical articles and can be seen swarming far from Crete or Dublin."[4] But then Bellow is not certain this country even has a "literary situation." What it does have resembles more a sociological, political, or psychological situation, with some literary elements. "Literature itself has been swallowed up" in the last three decades. Just prior to the Second World War, America's "highbrow public" was small, but after the war, thanks to the G. I. Bill, it exploded with a "new class of intellectuals or near-intellectuals." A college degree indicates, if nothing else, Bellow notes, an "exposure to high culture" and its creators or purveyors. The poems and novels these students read were written by "highbrow geniuses—disaffected, subversive, radical." Rejecting all "average preferences" (*CC,* 2) for their own singular ones, these modern masters infused the young with their own radical disaffection.

The new graduates formed in turn a serious "minority readership," but one different in taste and size from "that handful of connoisseurs that had read *Transition* in the twenties and discussed 'significant form.' " Now America had a large literary community, but a bad literary culture. Yet if deficient in taste, this community or audience proved insatiable in its cultural hunger, viewing literature as both "swallowable" and "enormously profitable." Its members contributed to the "university boom" and to the expansion of journalism and publishing.[5] Hence the postwar years found the universities newly prosperous and at the center of an enlarged but artificial "literary culture." Bellow claims that in the fifties and sixties the campus became "what Paris was to Fitzgerald and Hemingway in the twenties." He realizes "Ann Arbor and Iowa City are not Paris," but then "Paris isn't Paris either," its old cultural glamor gone with Gertrude Stein, Joyce, and Gide. Indeed, all of culture's great "national capitals" (*SDL,* 17) are gone, so artists and writers have turned for "asylum" to the universities and transformed them into "the sanctuary, at times the hospital, of literature, painting, music, and theatre" (*CN,* 169).

Still, if writers find shelter on campus, they are not truly comfortable there. One source of discomfort is their sensitivity to the popular conviction that "the intellectual life is somehow not virile. Artists and professors, like clergymen and librarians, are thought to be female." This popular view, observes Bellow, forces the artist to present himself as a man of the people and to downplay his true concern with thought. "Maybe that's why we don't have more novels of ideas" and why this society's truly powerful men "hold writers and poets in contempt." These leaders find in modern literature little evidence "that anybody is thinking about any significant questions."[6] The trouble, in this "vague and shifting" time, is that novelists and poets are not clear as to their obligations. Any writer able to do his society some good, Bellow reasons, should do it. But writers seldom think of themselves as society's shields against barbarism. Generally they think about stories they are or should be writing. Their "cultural assignment" results less from their thinking than from that of professors. If a few writers believe their efforts belong to society, most simply do not care.

How does Saul Bellow view his cultural obligation? "Sometimes I'm on one side of the matter and sometimes I'm on the other. Occasionally I worry about what's happening to culture in the United States, but on other days I think there is no culture in the United States, and there's no point in worrying about it."[7] His fiction and essays do not reflect this cavalier attitude. Instead, they reveal Bellow's deep concern for the nation's intellectual life, on campus and off. He emphasizes repeatedly how damaging to humanistic thought is the university's increasing commitment to technology and to the sciences, physical and behavioral. No respectable campus today lacks "computers, atom smashers, agricultural researchers, free psychotherapy, technocratic planners, revolutionary ideologists." Ideas are flattened, packaged, devalued. So are standards and lifestyles. Every campus has "everything, including bohemia," or, to be precise, bohemia may have the university. Either way, the campus "is being thoroughly bohemianized" (*CN,* 169–70).

II. The University and Its Literary Magazines

The commitment of universities to technology and bohemianism was only indirectly responsible for weakening contemporary culture. But universities contributed directly to the destruction of the nation's "in-dependent literary culture" when they bought up most literary publica-tions during the fifties and sixties. They did so without calculation, but their innocence made little difference. Championing the avant-garde in all its forms, the universities gathered the most adventurous literary maga-zines and journals and sponsored the most experimental theatre and dance, music, and painting. "They had it all," so unaffiliated writers soon had "no extra-institutional and independent environment."[8] The danger of such academic absorption is exemplified for Bellow by certain liter-ary periodicals and underground papers edited by "brutal profs and bad-tempered ivy league sodomites" (*CN,* 164). These sorry academics or quasi-academics disseminate their personal (if borrowed) cultural ideas through the captive quarterlies, which now function as "attitude sources." Such publications serve graduate students and young intellectuals as *Vogue* and *Glamour* serve working girls and housewives: they teach read-ers the "in-things" and "out-things." They supply not art but "art-discourse" (*SDL,* 21), as well as prepared views for fashion or discussion.

Reading these quarterlies Bellow feels "first uncomfortable, then queasy, then indignant, contemptuous and finally bleak, flattened out by the bad writing." Who reads this stuff? Do cultivated housewives and graduate students eat "these stale ideological chocolates?" Customers and responsible individuals must pay the bills. Still the universities bear major responsibility. For literary publications are now almost all "university subsidized, as what is not these days" (*CN,* 164, 169).

To illustrate the fallen state of literary magazines, Bellow goes after several old adversaries—the *Partisan Review* and two of its editors, William Phillips and Richard Poirier. Bellow had published his early stories in *PR* and in the forties and early fifties was an accepted member of the *"Partisan Review* crowd." His break from that coterie marked a turning point for him. In a recent interview Bellow described himself arriving in New York in the 1940s as a "young hick" set on "going to the big town and taking it." He was drawn to *PR*'s writers and their "sense of commu-nity." His new friends, among them Delmore Schwartz, Clement Greenberg, Meyer Schapiro, and Dwight MacDonald, "were not always friendly friends, but they were always stimulating friends." Bellow ap-preciated "the open spirit of easy fraternization" that animated their discussions. Politics, generally in the form of Marxism, tended to be mostly theoretical. In the late fifties and the sixties, however, the world darkened, and the New York intellectual mood changed. During that time "a new generation turned up." Many newcomers out of Columbia University were students of Lionel Trilling. They moved "into enterprises like *Commentary*—and suddenly the whole atmosphere in New York became far more political than it had been before."[9] Groups such as "the New York poets, the *Commentary* group, *The New York Review of Books* group, the people around Stanley Kunitz and Cal [Robert] Lowell" were formed.[10]

Bellow did not want to become embroiled "in the literary life and its rackets" and avoided choosing sides. Looking back, he explains:

> People have said in their memoirs that I was guarded, cautious, career-oriented, but I don't think that's so—after all, there was nothing easier in New York during those days than the life of the extremist, and that's continued to be so. I was not comfortable with the extremist life, and so I thought I might as well go back to the undiluted U.S.A., go back to Chicago. It's vulgar but it's vital and it's more American, more representative.[11]

By the mid-1960s his *Partisan Review* phase was history. The magazine and its staff, not to mention the New York intellectual scene, had experienced many changes. A decade later Bellow launched attacks against *Partisan Review*, and William Phillips, Richard Poirier, and other of its editors and contributors. His action was likely instigated by Poirier's mean-spirited *PR* review of *Herzog* in 1965. In his 1971 essay "Culture Now," Bellow argues that reading William Phillips's article on Susan Sontag "is much like trying to go scuba diving at Coney Island in urinous brine and scraps of old paper, orange rinds and soaked hot dog buns." Its sorry babblings remind him that "one of the nice things about *Hamlet* is that Polonius is stabbed." Phillips does rate a few merit points from Bellow. An oldtimer, he helped found a magazine that published the nation's best writers and poets from the 1930s through the 1950s. But his own prose is deplorable. "What writing!" Bellow laments. "Eleanor Roosevelt wrote far better in *My Days*." Richard Poirier also gets his lumps. "The new regime of Mr. Poirier has not improved Mr. Phillips' style. Mr. Poirier has made *PR* look like a butcher's showcase, shining with pink hairless pigginess and adorned with figurines of hand-carved suet which represent the very latest in art, literature and politics. Hoarse Mr. Phillips also is up to date, and gives the *dernier cri*" (*CN*, 164–65).

Shifting from Phillips's prose to his critical views, Bellow scoffs at his reference to an inactive audience as an "inert voyeuristic mass." As a creative artist or "virtuoso," Bellow expects a receptive but not an "active" readership or audience. He accuses Phillips of dismissing as perverse the spectator who sits still by insisting everyone *do* something, grab "a piece of the action." Phillips contends, according to Bellow, that every person "must create," as all true art is a collaboration and the only true artist is "the public itself" (*CN*, 165–66). Bellow rejects this confusion of actor and spectator and, by extension, writer and reader. Phillips's new political stance also angers him. A lifelong Marxist ideologue, he now embraces a New Left devoid of theory or program. Phillips is convinced, quotes Bellow, " 'that only an antitheoretical, antihistorical, non-Marxist, unstructured movement like that of the youth today could have created a new left force in the West.' "[12] This declaration, "in its idiocy," is for Bellow "really rather touching." One must realize, he observes, that "in surrendering his Marxism," Phillips is rejecting "forty years of his life." Why? Bellow's guess is that Phillips fears he may not be making it with the young and that New York radicals will dismiss him as "a silly dry old stick who is out of it" (*CN*, 166). Bellow expands upon this attack later while implicating the universities in the destruction of the "literary situation." Rutgers University acquired *PR* just as its founding editors were succumbing to age and fatigue. Taken over by new people, the magazine quickly grew "very corrupt and doddery."[13]

The old animosities were stirred anew by Poirier's 1975 partly revised review of *Herzog*. In his opening paragraph, Poirier describes *Herzog* and *Mr. Sammler's Planet* as "efforts to test out, to substantiate, to vitalize, and ultimately to propagate a kind of cultural conservatism which [Bellow] shares with the two aggrieved heroes of these novels, and to imagine that they are victims of the cultural debasements, as Bellow sees it, of the sixties."[14] Not given to forgetting or forgiving, Bellow used a recent interview to strike back:

> People who stick labels on you are in the gumming business. . . . What good are these categories? They mean very little, especially when the people who apply them haven't had a new thought since they were undergraduates and now preside over a literary establishment that lectures to dentists and accountants who want to be filled in on the thrills. I think these are the reptiles of the literary establishment who are grazing on the last Mesozoic grasses of Romanticism. Americans in this respect are quite old-fashioned: they're quite willing to embrace stale European ideas—they should be on 10th Avenue where the rest of the old importers used to be.
>
> They think they know what writers should be and what writers should write, but who are these representatives who practice what Poirier preaches? They're, for the most part, spiritless, etiolated, and the liveliest of them are third-rate vaudevillians. Is this literary life? I'd rather inspect gas mains in Chicago.[15]

Shoddy thinking and writing typify not only *PR*, says Bellow, but also most quarterlies, the "university subsidized" ones in particular. The academic publications share with popular magazines like *Playboy, Esquire,* and *Evergreen Review* a bohemian disdain for serious art. Despite surface differences, they all swing "against a background of high or formerly high culture" (*CN*, 171–72). A Leslie Fiedler article in *Playboy* offers an example. In his "Cross the Border, Close the Gap," Fiedler charges Bellow (as well as John Updike, Mary McCarthy, and James Baldwin) with writing "old novels." Without mentioning the critical jab, Bellow attacks Fiedler's desire to "close the gap between high culture and low, belles-lettres and pop art."[16] He resents this call, as he puts it, "for more obscenity, more of the *mantic,* the *mad* and the *savage.*" Why does Fiedler advocate the standards of "pop art," asks Bellow, and of "the media-managing intellectuals"? His own class interests are at risk. His pupils are among the "college-educated swinging, bearded, costumed, bohemianized intellectuals [who] are writing the ads, manufacturing the gimmicks, directing the shows, exploiting the Woodstocks." A partisan rather than an objective observer, Fiedler is pushing "his own product" by rating "the worst sins of the masses . . . [above] the dead virtues of high culture" (*CN*, 172–74). His call for new literary standards derives from the popular conviction that literary modernism is dead. The age of Proust, Mann, and Joyce, as well as T. S. Eliot and Paul Valery has been replaced by a new "postmodernism," and this new era, according to Fiedler, demands a "death-of-art criticism." Those writers not fortunate enough to be under thirty-five have to be "reborn" to become relevant to the moment and the young.

Bellow finds Leslie Fiedler's theories to be as "dismal" as they are amusing. They are too close "to madness" for Bellow "to keep smiling." Even worse, this madness is old and unoriginal, offering implications of fascism instead of wit. Fiedler may intend only to scare the reader over thirty-five with talk of the death of his mind and imagination. In past years Leslie Fiedler, says Bellow, most likely would have written for Hearst's Sunday supplement. His undeniable "hatred of liberalism, love of an imaginary past (Cowboys and Indians), somnambulistic certitude, praise of tribalism and of Dionysiac excesses, the cult of youth, the chastising of high culture by the masses, the consecration of violence— all . . . suggest fascism." Hence history is important to Fiedler for its disposable elements. "Considerations of style, quality or degree are irrelevant." What this professor advocates is part of "an old story—an ancient religious belief, really. Destruction purifies." Jung and Lawrence, among others, have repeated this myth: "after the holocaust, the Phoenix . . . after Death, Resurrection" (*CN*, 173–74). By urging his readers to "shake off the dead past" and to rely solely on the future, Fiedler perpetuates this old motif.

So Fiedler is for Bellow merely one more intellectual opportunist. Equally opportunistic was another renowned professor—the late Marshall McLuhan. A high-pitched McLuhan review of a Mick Jagger film reveals to Bellow what the avant-garde and Ph.D. literature programs have combined to give this society: "apocalyptic clichés; a wild self-confidence; violently compact historical judgments; easy formulas about the 'cancellation of a world.' " Can anyone miss in McLuhan's views (all copyrighted by McLuhan Associates Ltd.), asks Bellow, "the presence of money"? In America time and recognition alter all, even the most perceptive. McLuhan, who long warned this country of the media's seductive powers, finally seemed himself "a medium." The avant-garde may have formed him, so that he "started out esoteric," but he ended up speaking "to a great public." Ours is "an amazing country," concludes Bellow. Even McLuhan did not "know the half of it" (*CN*, 163–64). As a result he was absorbed and transformed by the very forces he opposed.

III. Antiquarians and Moderns

Most literature professors, Bellow realizes, are neither populists like Leslie Fiedler or Marshall McLuhan nor advocates of a New Left like Poirier and contributors to *PR*. Still, they are primarily responsible for the university's pernicious influence on literary thought and culture. He divides professors into two general types. The first is the "antiquarian," who, in his concern with the classics, serves as our "custodian of the cultural valuables." He and his colleagues insist that these heirlooms have been so "edited and catalogued, [and] sufficiently described" that there is "little more to do about them." Nurturing a "modest pride," they feel "separated from the unseemly, thrashing, boring, dangerous world." They resolve to hand over their cultural treasures only to the next generation's "qualified curators" (*SDL*, 21). These "stony old pedants" amuse Bellow. Two generations back they "refused to discuss anyone newer than Browning." A small minority, he admits, are "quite useful; others are harmless enough, textual editors, antiquarians and fuddyduddies. Others are influential interpreters. Or misinterpreters" (*CC*, 2). Over all, however, the antiquarians are no longer significant. Their power was broken in the 1930s, he declares, when the universities turned to modern literature and contemporary writers.

So Bellow's anger is reserved for the second academic species: the modern lit prof. He (always *he*, never *she*) and his thousands of colleagues turn out the "millions of graduates in literature" (*CC*, 2). Not only do they deal in the recent literary masters, but these profs often also take the same figures as role models. "When I was an undergraduate," Bellow recalls, "there were teachers of literature who looked Tennysonian, Browningish, Swinburnian, pre-Raphaelite or Celtic Twilight." Later many were influenced by Hemingway, a highly popular model. Some profs who grew up in the twenties opted for "the Fitzgerald style of the sad young man who drank too much and had a nutty wife. (Many wives obliged.) Now we have Lawrentian profs, Dylan Thomas profs, Becketts, Ionescos and Mailers, wood-demons, sons of Pan Dionysians, LSD god-seekers." Many Americans encourage this role playing. Conditioned to consume good things and to make them their own, such people render culture and cultural models "personally applicable" (*SDL*, 21).

Yet these modern lit profs, like the antiquarians, also wish to keep any literary culture limited and manageable. So they proclaim the novel's imminent demise and that of literature in general. Such academics are for Bellow much like property owners. "They have their lots surveyed. Here the property begins and there it ends. A conservative instinct in them, which every lover of order will recognize and respect, resists extension, calls for limits." They are vocal and numerous. "For every poet now there are a hundred custodians and doctors of literature, and dozens of undertakers measuring away at coffins." These crepe hangers affect both students and writers, with the literature students lining up happily. " 'Thank God!' they say, 'it's over. Now we have a field. We can study.' " Their attitude is understandable. Libraries and secondhand bookstores are packed full, as is "the physical universe [that] overwhelms us with its immensities." Must man's writing "flood us as well?" Still, Bellow cannot help wondering whether novels can be studied or even read with much profit if writers do not continue to write them. "Not professional study but imagination," he warns, "keeps imagination alive." The trouble is that by such negative talk the novelist is affected and made uneasy. "Trained to take words seriously," he assumes he is hearing serious words. "He believes it is the voice of high seriousness saying 'obsolete. Finished.' " What if the voice were to prove "the voice of low seriousness instead?"[17]

The role playing and dire prophecies of such people are bad, but even worse is their ineptitude. Bellow is astonished "at the ignorance of learned people." Many who teach literature or writing are so poorly prepared that they should attempt a novel simply to grasp how a book is constructed. "I suppose that the maker of a thing, however clumsy he may be, acquires a sort of knowledge for which there is no substitute."[18] If the knowledge of university scholars is defective, their prose is more so. Most of it—literary and non-literary—lacks "poetry." During the past half-century, academic jargon has grown steadily more deviant. While he can appreciate the knowledge of this country's highly intelligent economists, sociologists, lawyers, historians, and scientists, Bellow reads their prose "with the greatest difficulty, exasperated, tormented, despairing."[19]

Yet even if tin-eared, these societal specialists do not offer the major danger, "the academic danger." The humanities profs pose much the greater risk. These "humanist intellectuals" have stirred Bellow's strong dislike through the years. His next-to-latest novel, *The Dean's December,* makes clear that his feelings about academics, especially those in the humanities, have changed little. He reasserts his dissatisfaction with the intellectual rigidity and parochialism of both scientists and humanists, but he is, as always, more bitter toward his humanities colleagues. Geologist Sam Beech invites Bellow's hero, Albert Corde (a veteran journalist turned professor and college dean), to help turn his scientific findings into a prose accessible "not only to the general public . . . but also to the Humanists." Corde is puzzled. "Who were these Humanists, and why should Beech imagine that they were a group to whom any case could be stated? And if there was such a group, why should it be inclined to pay attention to Corde? He considered how to discuss this with a geologist like Beech. 'You want to understand humanist intellectuals? Think of the Ruling Reptiles of the Mesozoic [Age].' "[20]

Corde is not suggesting humanists alone are flawed in thought and knowledge. Scientists, too, are shortsighted and insensitive to many moral and aesthetic implications of their own efforts. He reasons that "if pure scientists had really understood science, they would have realized the morality and poetry implicit in its laws. So it's all going to run down the drain, like blood in a Hitchcock movie." But the humanists, of whom more is expected culturally, "also have flunked the course. They have no strength because they have no conception of what the main effort of the human mind has been for three centuries and what it has found" (*TDD,* 228).

What most annoys Bellow about these tenured faculty humanists is that despite their ignorance they never suffer writer's block and are able always to supply literary articles so cheaply they have "all but wiped out . . . professional competitors." They want to wrench literature from writers and keep it for themselves. They remind Bellow of "the British princess who said to her husband during the honeymoon, 'Do the servants do this too? Much too good for them.' " These professors and their disciples (the next crop of literary intellectuals) are convinced literature is much "too good for contemporary novelists, those poor untutored drudges." Identifying with figures like Henry James and James Joyce, Marcel Proust and the French symbolists, they offer themselves as each master's only true heirs and agents. Their stance enables them to "enjoy a certain genteel prestige. They are the happy few" (*CC*, 2). What are these cultural impresarios doing with their appropriated literature?

> Why, they talk about it; they treasure it; they make careers of it; they become an elite through it; they adorn themselves with it; they . . . take masterpieces and turn them into discourse in the modern intellectual style. I'm against that, of course. I am not for the redescription of *Moby Dick* by Marxists and existentialists and Christian symbolists, respectively. What does that do for *Moby Dick* or for me? It doesn't do anything. It only results in the making of more books—King Solomon has already warned us against that in Ecclesiastes.[21]

IV. Academics as Critics

Issues more serious than the mere accumulation of needless reading matter are involved here. This academic redescribing of basic texts, by relating them to myth, history, philosophy, or psychology, Bellow complains, renders them "less accessible" to readers. It means that for human emotion or response professors "substitute acts of comprehension" (*CC*, 2). They are obsessed with meaning, especially hidden meaning. They are convinced fiction is not to be taken literally. They resemble for Bellow those Christian fathers who expected Scripture to "yield the higher meanings." Yet such academics are not, like church fathers, nurturing "sublime conceptions of God and Man." If they were "moved by the sublimity of the poets and philosophers they teach, these humanities profs would be the university's most fervent and powerful members." Instead they rest at "the lower end of the hierarchy, at the bottom of the pile" (*SQA*, 55–56).

What fervor academics can muster they devote not to creating imaginative literature but to "manufacturing 'intellectual history.'" In a position to recruit writers and artists who best meet their needs, they fashion a congenial subculture for themselves and their students. They consider seriously only books whose "attitudes, positions or fantasies" please them, even if such books are "little more than the footnotes of fashionable doctrines" (*CC*, 45). For these works are now "their material, their capital." Taking from them what they need for their journalism or social critiques, they produce "hybrid works." These efforts are "partly literary" and occasionally interesting, but mostly they reveal contemporary literature's "decadence or obsolescence." The professors want people to think they are lifting modern literature into "a higher, more valuable mental realm, a realm of dazzling intellectuality" (*CC*, 2, 44). They are not.

Despite this culture capitalism, Bellow does not oppose proper literary discussion. "[T]here's no reason why people shouldn't talk about books. There is a prerequisite, though, which is that they should be deeply stirred by the books. They should love them or hate them." But they should "not try to convert them into . . . chatter. . . . [S]o much of literary criticism is babbling." He refers here to those critics who "translate" important books by writing them again in their own "fashionable intellectual jargon." The books that result "are no longer themselves. They have been borrowed by Culture, with a capital C." Such borrowings move Bellow to distinguish between two types of art. One type has a "direct effect on people." The other type proves "a cultural commodity [and] . . . a fertilizer for the cultivation of languages, vocabularies, intellectual styles, ornaments, degrees, honors, prizes, and all the rest of that. That's Culture with a Capital C." A recurrent process, its prime model has been "the Christian religion, which started with faith and ended with churches."[22] Such transmuting of the spirit into the text is seldom uplifting.

Bellow guards against becoming himself a Culture object. "I think we must all be on guard against it," he warns. "I don't want to become a support of the new clergy. Why should I? It's none of my business!"[23] What is his business? To sound the alarm. In recent years this classroom clergy has obscured the connections between the literary present and past, between contemporary writers and their predecessors. Such teachers have "miseducated the young," he declares, neither developing their tastes nor creating a public sensitive to the arts. Instead they have contributed to their students'—in Thorstein Veblen's phrase—"trained incapacity" (*CC*, 45) by reducing novels to cultural objects and dehumanizing art. In fact, Bellow suggests that the "dehumanization of art" that Ortega y Gasset lamented may well result from those pressures for meanings university intellectuals exert upon art. Each literary generation cherishes the novel as a cultural object of high importance. But each treats it also as a historical artifact whose "ideas . . . symbolic structure . . . position in the history of Romanticism or Realism or Modernism . . . [and] its higher relevance require devout study" (*SQA*, 55).

Bellow does not deny the merit of literary study and analysis. Even redescriptions and labels can be "intriguing and useful," he admits, but Americans often overdo "this comedy of terms. We pay psychologists to penetrate our characters and redescribe them to us scientifically . . . . We are delighted to hear that we are introverted, fixated, have a repression here, a cathexis there, are attached to our mothers thus and so." We pay happily for cultural or personal analyses, but they have little to do with novels and novelists. Writers and readers—unlike professors—

desire from literature "the living moment." They wish to read about "men and women alive—a circumambient world." Instead of such vital responses, students and readers get from professors laborious explications. These academic critics restate and redefine "everything downward, blackening the present age and denying creative scope to their contemporaries" (*CC*, 2). Bellow considers their criticism too "linear" or "sketchy." A novelist does not "feel he's got anything until he has it in all the density of actual experience. Then he looks at a piece of criticism, and all he sees is the single outline of thought. It's not the same thing. And you can't deal with a phenomenon that way. So he never really trusts criticism, because it lacks the essential density."[24]

Yet the "cultural bureaucrats" on campus shape things to their liking by ignoring all contradictions, aesthetic or social. They are bothered little, therefore, by gaps between their theories and practices. For instance, they "have absorbed the dislike of the modern classic writers for civilization. They are repelled by the effrontery of power and the degradation of the urban crowd. They have made the Waste Land outlook their own." At the same time, these university functionaries accumulate "money, position, privileges, power." They enroll their children in private schools and enjoy "elegant dental care ... [and] jet holidays in Europe. They have stocks, bonds, houses, even yachts, and with all this, owing to their education, they enjoy a particular and intimate sympathy with the heroic artistic life. Their tastes and judgments were formed by Rimbaud and D. H. Lawrence. Could anything be neater?" (*CC*, 44). The force of this argument is perhaps lost on the bemused college teacher reading this glittering catalogue of his wealth and power, his jet holidays and his yachts; he can only wonder where Bellow encounters such privileged academics—or the "middle-class writers" against whom he levels similar charges.

But the hypocrisy of literature professors concerns Bellow less than does their intellectual rigidity. Their actions in and out of class result largely, he insists, from the tenured stability and confidence they gained from huge postwar enrollments. Lionel Trilling voiced a similar complaint, Bellow points out, in *Beyond Culture*, where he dismissed as culturally flawed the student hordes then exposed to modern classics.[25] These graduates convinced Trilling a literary education could be "a mixed blessing" (*CC*, 44), as the critics, writers, and executives sent by English departments into society were too ill-prepared to contribute intellectually. Still they helped change, by sheer numbers and needs, both the literature curriculum and the reading public. They demanded that contemporary literature be part of the curriculum. Before them, every educated person was thought capable of reading a novel without the help of "ten manuals." But burgeoning classes enabled faculty members to assert their intellectual authority by implementing "a gloomy prepara-tory region, a perfect swamp," that every student has to cross before he can "open his *Moby Dick* and read 'Call me Ishmael.' " The result of this is that "He is made to feel ignorant before masterpieces, unworthy, he is frightened and repelled." At best this method "produces B.A.'s who can tell you why the *Pequod* leaves port on Christmas morning. What else can they tell you? No feeling for the book has been communicated, only a lot of pseudolearned interpretations" (*SQA*, 55).

V. Readers, Writers, and University Intellectuals

Critical of postwar education, Bellow found instruction little better in his student days. His unhappiness with professors stems in part from his own undergraduate experience, which he feels helped confuse his natural interplay of ideas and emotions. To this day, he states, "I avoid the assumption that I know the origin of my own thoughts and feelings. I've become aware of a conflict between the modern university educa-tion I received and those things that I really felt in my soul most deeply." He now trusts increasingly the impressions of his soul, despite being taught he has no soul. "The soul is out of bounds if you have the sort of education I had. I got my bachelor's degree as an anthropologist. And I read Marx and Bertrand Russell and Morris R. Cohen. I read the logi-cal positivists. I read Freud and Adler and the Gestalt psychologists and the rest. And I know how a modern man is supposed to think. . . . [Charlie Citrine, the hero of *Humboldt's Gift*,] says, 'If you put a test before me I can get a high mark, but it's only head culture.' The fact is there are other deeper motives in a human being."[26]

Bellow is hardly alone in his confusion. His encounters with readers suggest their educations have proved even less adequate than his own. Always grateful to learn someone expends the time and trouble to read his books, he is "also a bit depressed" when a reader asks, " 'What does it mean?' As if a novel were a puzzle, or a code, to which only the author and certain highly erudite readers had the key."[27] This question offers him further proof of the "demoralizing effect" of literature teaching in the universities. "Things are not what they seem," students are taught, and unless things "represent something large and worthy, writers will not bother with them. Any deep reader can tell you that picking up a bus transfer is the *Risemotiv* when it happens in a novel. A travel folder signifies Death. Coal holes represent the Underworld. Soda crackers are the Host. Three bottles of beer are—it's obvious. The busy mind can hardly miss at this game and every player is a winner." How then are readers to approach a work of fiction? "Are we to attach meaning to whatever is grazed by the writer? Is modern literature Scripture? Is criticism Talmud, theology? Deep readers of the world, beware! You had better be sure that your seriousness is indeed high seriousness and not, God forbid, low seriousness."[28]

Equally troubling is the sad truth that many writers contribute to this mystification process. Like the academic critics, these novelists, by relying as much on symbols and analysis as on imagination, also help to separate literature from life and to weaken a basic literary function—the raising of moral or social issues. Claiming to feel "no such temptation" to symbolize, Bellow complains that many writers do. "Take somebody like Joyce, especially in *Finnegans Wake*. He is writing for a small public of intellectuals—of highly skilled readers, people who know the history of modern literature and are amused by puzzles. The same thing is true of Thomas Mann. Of Eliot. Of all the small public writers."[29] These writers want their writings to be "a little deeper than average," so they pander to the "deep readers." In fact, this century's best poets and novelists, led by James Joyce, have promoted "this deep reading." So they should not complain or expect critics to downplay their symbols, much less ignore them or view them as "accidental."

> A true symbol is substantial, not accidental. You cannot avoid it. You can't take the handkerchief from *Othello*, or the sea from *The Nigger of the Narcissus*, or the disfigured feet from *Oedipus Rex*. You can, however, read *Ulysses* without suspecting that wood shavings have to do with the Crucifixion or that the name Simon refers to the sin of simony or that the hunger of the Dubliners at noon parallels that of the Lestrigonians. These are purely peripheral matters; fringe benefits, if you like. The beauty of the book cannot escape you if you are any sort of reader, and it is better to approach it from the side of naiveté than from that of culture-idolatry, sophistication, and snobbery. (*DRWB*, 365–67)

This emphasis upon symbols (substantial or peripheral) has produced a readership that prefers meaning to feeling. Students learn to do what "most civilized people do when confronted with passion and death. They contrive somehow to avoid them." So do writers. They publish novels woven entirely of abstractions or meanings. Oh, meanings may be important, Bellow admits, but the "need for concreteness, for particulars, is even greater. We need to see how human beings act after they have appropriated or assimilated the meanings. Meanings themselves are a dime a dozen. In literature humankind becomes abstract when we begin to dislike it." What is to be done? Bellow is specific: "We must leave it

to imagination and to inspiration to redeem the concrete and the particular and to recover the value of flesh and bone." Just as they are, flesh
and bone and life's other commonplaces "are mysterious enough"
(*DRWB*, 368).

No matter how unhappy with symbolist or "abstract" writers he may
be, Bellow is most angry with the academy. In *The Dean's December* he up-
dates his disenchantment with academics and their former students, the
media intellectuals. His secondary commentator here is Dewey Spangler,
a noted journalist and childhood friend of protagonist Albert Corde.
In his newspaper column Spangler quotes Corde's private comments and
interprets his public ones on the media and on his fellow professors:
"Professor Corde is very hard on journalism, on the mass media." He
accuses journalists of failing "to deal with the moral, emotional, imaginative life, in short, the true life of human beings." They employ their great
influence, Corde charges, to prevent "people from having access to this
true life. What we call 'information' he would characterize as delusion. . . .
[He] thinks that public discussion is threadbare . . . that our cultural
poverty has the same root as the frantic and criminal life of our once
great cities." For this the Dean blames the communications industry, seeing it as the breeder of "hysteria and misunderstanding" (*TDD*, 301).

But if tough on the media, the Dean is tougher, Spangler observes,
on university intellectuals. Corde has expected much of them, believing
their "privileges" obligated them to be different from everybody else.
They have disappointed him by not accepting their differences and not
making the cultural contributions society needs. Their challenge was "to
produce new models," but these humanists have failed to "lead the public." They have not clarified society's "principal problems" nor depicted
"democracy to itself in this time of agonized struggle." In short, the
professors, as Corde sees them, have been as dominated by consensus
or public opinion as their fellow Americans. So instead of "irradiating
American society with humanistic culture," these academics have
revealed themselves to be "failures and phonies" (*TDD*, 301–2).

Spangler suggests that Corde, by revealing his disappointment in two
Harper's articles, "must have offended his colleagues deeply." He then
adds mischievously that his friend may not appreciate "the magnitude
of the challenge" facing professors. Who is capable, after all, of making
"high human types of the business community, the engineers, the politicians and the scientists? What system of higher education could con-
ceivably have succeeded?" But Dean Corde, declares Spangler, "is
unforgiving. Philistinism is his accusation. Philistine by origin, humanistic academics were drawn magnetically back again to the philistine core
of American society. What should have been an elite of the intellect

became instead an elite of influence and comforts." The Dean does not claim the professors could have stopped cities from decaying, Spangler concedes, but he does feel "they could have told us . . . what the human meaning of this decay was and what it augured for civilization." Corde is angry because scholars who supposedly "represent the old greatness" failed to "put up a fight for it. They gave in to the great emptiness. And 'from the emptiness [Corde has written] come whirlwinds of insanity' " (*TDD*, 302–3).

Pondering Spangler's summary, Corde realizes his private statements will cost him his job. "By a process of instantaneous translation," he reads them with the eyes of his Provost and colleagues, and he decides "the trouble is all in the nuances. Oh, the nuances!" Yet he knows his old crony has caught his basic hostility to academia. Even missed nuances cannot mitigate the caustic jibes Spangler quotes. Typical is his observation that while most professors do work hard, "a professor when he gets tenure doesn't *have* to do anything. A tenured professor and a welfare mother with eight kids have much in common" (*TDD*, 303). But if Albert Corde is embarrassed, Saul Bellow is adamant. Such views are his own, and he has altered them little over the years. Indeed, few academics of conscience, he suggests, should deny their painful validity.

VI. Making a Go of It

Despite the rigidity of the university and its professors, Bellow finds self-defeating the acceptance by many American writers of the popular stereotypes of "professors, clergymen, artists and all males in 'genteel' occupations as women, not men." Nor are such writers helped emotionally by their failure to find on campus adequate cultural compensation for this psychic abuse. They expected the university to offer "a unified intellectual life" rather than "dispersed specialties." Under ideal conditions a common integrated culture could "coalesce about university-sheltered artists," Bellow concedes, but such conditions are not likely. Instead, universities and government agencies, channeling their interests and rewards into the most practical areas, intensify the differences between humanists and those in the hard sciences. The physics professor, for instance, is reassured by his "sense of being needed (by the Air Force and the Navy and Oak Ridge)"; the literature professor, however, may feel "he is foolishly watching the rats in the vegetation while he ponders the problems of Hamlet's uncle." He has no visible connection "to the gas tanks behind him and Sputnik overhead." Hence he and the other humanists "often have a keen sense of their inferiority to the great mass of Americans. Is the real realer where the mass is thicker? So they seem to believe." They also may believe that it is "shameful for grown men ... [to be] sitting with a parcel of kids in a corner."[30]

This defeatist attitude helps explain why writers find in English departments "discouraged people who stand dully upon a brilliant plane." These sad individuals may be "in charge of masterpieces," but they are "not themselves inspired." Still, no determined, lively writer, declares Bellow, need reject a faculty position. "If he knows his own mind and if the university thinks it can get along with him—well, why not?" He may not only make a go of it, but he may also find in university communities good conversation and even perhaps a Whitehead or Einstein who will prove "as well worth writing about as [any] saloon-keepers or big game hunters." Everything rests with the writer, with the energy he has "the boldness to release" or the environmental restraints he can disregard. He needs to ask himself whether he can be bold in Greenwich Village but not on campus. Does it matter whether he is on land or sea? Can he display courage in the mines or on an assembly line but not in "the literary life"? An occasional writer does love "to knock around" in rough company. If so, he should feel free to do so. Certainly he should feel as free as did Walt Whitman to "go into the streets, ride up and down Broadway or go and dig clams." But he should never do "these things deliberately ... [or merely] for the sake of writing" (*UV*, 362). In short, a writer should do what he feels necessary, but he cannot rely upon any formula or prescription.

Yet, if upbeat about the dedicated writer resolving his internal difficulties, Bellow is less sanguine about the external pressures confronting him. Serious writers are beset by an array of scholars, historians, and teachers who have educated and now dominate the reading public. This highly critical readership also includes psychologists and psychotherapists, ideologists and various other "professional custodians of culture." Together these "shapers of the future" pose countless questions to satisfy themselves about which writers merit attention. But the fiction writer and poet, Bellow observes, can respond to such queries only "with sadness and sighs."[31] They appear to have little else to offer so pragmatic an American reading public in these technological times.

For campus writers such problems of relevance are compounded. Isolated in English departments, with little access to the sciences or other hard disciplines, they are unable or unwilling to formulate new literary ideas. Instead they follow the lit profs and derive their cultural concepts from the modern classics they grip so stubbornly. They merely restate then "the Eliot view, the Joyce view, the Lawrence view." They also are satisfied merely to prepare students for an expanding culture's new power positions. In short, they wish to exploit only what is already there.

They themselves are what is new. "They are the brilliant event, the great result of modern creativity." They wear modern artistic and literary trappings as comfortably "as young ladies wear their plastic Mondrian raincoats" (*SDL,* 18, 21-22). This resistance to new ideas by writers and teachers has brought little change to American literary thought during the past half-century. They rarely challenge the "modernist orthodoxy" dominating most English departments. These departments serve the literary young as their cultural settings or "Paris substitutes," but they limit their creative potential.

Sadly enough, the universities want things this way. They do not hire these new people to think creatively but only to turn students into professional writers. The schools wish them also "to bring the art-life to the campus. Bohemia. Not the vices, just the color of Bohemia." In fact, the writer new to campus finds the lit profs and some philosophers and theologians acting like writers. Should he compete with them? No, says Bellow. He should "sit down, apart, and think things over quietly" (*SDL,* 20). He might reflect on those societal pressures that try a man's soul, especially his own. He should not expect help: the old lit profs will not admit he exists, while the modern lit profs may make him wish he did not. The philosophers and theologians, however, will welcome him. They also will use him, as they try to include what he writes in their diagnoses of man's spiritual disorders. But while he may add to their existential evidence, the young writer is not likely to learn much from them.

So he and all the creative people on campus should keep their expectations down and guards up. They should resist becoming comfortable. Some, understandably, may become teachers and others, scholars (*SQA,* 60), but none should deteriorate into arid pedants or posturing radicals. The trouble is that writers (older and younger) have a feeble grasp of the social changes giving universities their new "revolutionary power." University-trained intellectuals dominate industry and education, politics and city planning. Yet their innocence impedes literature teachers and writers in making humanistic use of their students. Instead, these campus humanists fall prey to a studied but empty radicalism. "But it is only the manner that is radical. Few things can be safer, more success-assuring than this non-threatening radicalism." Endangering no one, it relies, "at bottom, on the stability of institutions" (*SDL,* 26).

In fact, recent radicalism has had no home other than the university. Why? To Bellow the reason is obvious. Having inherited a romantic tradition essentially "anti-authority," or at least "hostile to institutions," writers, unlike most academics, enjoy little tranquility in their campus sanctuary. Their psychic unrest or "bad conscience" pushes them into "exaggeratedly radical attitudes" (*SDL,* 25–26) and into positions of social

concern. So they invent "a false radicalism," while lacking any coherent
idea of what "they are opposing or upholding as radicals." They are more
concerned with "style than substance." Too often they nurture feelings
"of being Promethean when they're only having a tantrum."[32] The public compounds their confusion by turning them into popular figures and
convincing them their political gestures should not be confined to campus. Such literary radicals, Bellow warns, should realize that a forced
social involvement can be ruinous. But then so can a comfortable withdrawal. Jose Ortega y Gasset criticized Goethe, recalls Bellow, for settling
down in Weimar. Ortega believed a poet should consent to be home-
less. Bellow will not go that far. Poets are not easy "to prescribe for,"
he cautions, whereas critics "love to have their hearts wrung" by the
disasters befalling a great artist. Still he wonders if the university is not
"simply Weimar in another more disgusting and intensely more bourgeois form?" Certainly campus writers in their radicalism often reveal
traces "of such Weimar fears" (*SDL,* 25).

But most American writers, he admits, have little reason not to opt
for the good life. Most are from this country's middle class, and it has
shaped and justified their intellectual corruption and hypocrisy. For
shielded by middle America's comforts and benefits, these writers indulge an "unearned bitterness" by decrying modern man's moral and
aesthetic flaws. Educated America pampers its offspring by offering them
"the radical doctrines of all the ages" without teaching them that these
doctrines "in their superabundance only cancel one another out." The
middle class also trains its literary young "in passivity and resignation
and in the double enjoyment of selfishness and good will." It tells them
to enjoy everything life offers. "They can live dangerously while manag-
ing somehow to be safe. They can be . . . bureaucrats and bohemians. . . .
[They may] raise families but enjoy bohemian sexuality . . . observe the
laws while in their hearts and . . . social attitudes they may be as subversive as they please." In short, they can be "conservative and radical" and
about anything else they wish to be. What these writers are not taught
is "to care genuinely for any man or any cause."[33] Does Bellow speak
here only of cynical journalists and life-hardened novelists? He does not.
"I have known blue-eyed poets apparently fresh from heaven, who gazed
at you like Little Lord Fauntleroy while thinking how you would look
in your coffin."[34]

His point is that neither novelist nor poet should blame only the
university for his moral confusion. For what happens on campus ultimately reflects what happens—or does not happen—off campus. The
creative writer who does not find in the university community an edifying

interchange of thought and feeling will not find it in society. Universities may be this nation's cultural "warehouses," says Bellow, but they do not sever anyone's moral ties to the community. Europeans see this more clearly than Americans. In Europe, writers long have come from the better-educated, socially involved classes, and they know academic life seldom differs greatly from "real life." But American intellectuals always imagine that their education removes them from ordinary events. This attitude is for Bellow "unjustifiably romantic." He points out that universities alone harbor the poets, humanists, and scholars upon whom (with all their faults) Walt Whitman, in *Democratic Vistas,* placed the responsibility of formulating the archetypal man as American. This humanistic task is a difficult one, but then so is living a moral life, off or on campus. "Let us imagine," Bellow suggests, "a man who lives in Akron, Ohio, and teaches the history of the Italian Renaissance. It is dreadful to think what he has to reconcile. Or he teaches ethics, and takes part in department politics. He behaves shabbily and his own heart cannot bear the contrast. What I am trying to say is that certain ideas can't be held idly. Attempted containment of them is ruin" (*DFW*, 24). So university people must adhere to their vaunted humanistic standards in community as well as faculty matters.

Conversely, American society must be more generous to its writers. The late Harvey Swados stated this pointedly. "In a society which babbles interminable platitudes about battling for the minds and hearts of men," he noted, "even while it demonstrates in a thousand ways that it values the football coach and the sales engineer above the novelist and the poet, we can expect nothing but a continuation of the circumstances which drive the novelist not only into a marginal position—bad enough in itself—but into marginal utterances." These platitudes and hypocrisies produce "the false dichotomy between 'affirmative' and 'negative' writing and the vicious spiral of neglect" that isolate the writer even more and cause him "to feed on himself and his similars instead of on the social body for his material." Then the deplorable economic situation that results "from his isolation forces him into the insulated little world of the university." There the creative writer produces works that the critics receive "not with interest, attention or even compassion, but also with envy and malice." They treat his efforts not merely with "scorn" but "as an opportunity for self-aggrandizement."[35]

Harsh charges these, but Saul Bellow and so many other novelists and poets echo them so frequently they cannot be ignored. All who care about the university and its moral health, and about the creative people it harbors and abuses, must ponder them carefully.

Notes

1. Saul Bellow, "Cloister Culture," *New York Times Book Review*, 10 July 1966, 2. Subsequent references to this source, abbreviated as *CC*, are given parenthetically in the text.
2. Mark Harris, *Saul Bellow, Drumlin Woodchuck* (Athens: University of Georgia Press, 1980), 154.
3. Saul Bellow, *Seize the Day* (New York: Viking Press, 1956; New York: Viking Compass Books, 1961), 16.
4. Saul Bellow, "Skepticism and the Depth of Life," in *The Arts and the Public*, ed. James E. Miller, Jr. and Paul D. Herring (Chicago: University of Chicago Press, 1967), 25. Subsequent references to this source, abbreviated as *SDL*, are given parenthetically in the text.
5. Saul Bellow, "Culture Now: Some Animadversions, Some Laughs," *Modern Occasions* 1 (Winter 1971): 162. Subsequent references to this source, abbreviated as *CN*, are given parenthetically in the text.
6. Jane Howard, "Mr. Bellow Considers His Planet," *Life* 3 April 1970, 60.
7. Robert Boyers *et al.* "Literature and Culture: An Interview with Saul Bellow," *Salmagundi* 30 (Summer 1975): 6.
8. Boyers, 12–13.
9. Michiko Kakutani, "A Talk with Saul Bellow: On His Work and Himself," *New York Times Book Review*, 13 December 1981, 29.
10. William Kennedy, "If Saul Bellow Doesn't Have a True Word to Say, He Keeps His Mouth Shut," *Esquire*, February 1982, 54.
11. Kakutani, 29.
12. See William Phillips, "Radical Styles," *Partisan Review* 36, no. 3 (1969): 397. For Phillips's response to Bellow, see his "William Phillips Answers Saul Bellow," *Intellectual Digest*, October 1971, 4.
13. Boyers, 13.
14. Richard Poirier, "Herzog, or, Bellow in Trouble," in *Saul Bellow: A Collection of Critical Essays*, ed. Earl Rovit (Englewood Cliffs, N.J.: Prentice Hall, 1975), 81. See also Poirier's earlier version, "Bellows to Herzog," *Partisan Review* 32 (Spring 1965): 264–71.
15. Kakutani, 28.
16. Leslie Fiedler, "Cross the Border, Close the Gap," *Playboy*, December 1969, 252, 230.
17. Saul Bellow, "Distractions of a Fiction Writer," in *The Living Novel: A Symposium*, ed. Granville Hicks (New York: Macmillan, 1957; New York: Collier Books, 1962), 27. Subsequent references to this source, abbreviated as *DFW*, are given parenthetically in the text.
18. John Enck, "Saul Bellow: An Interview," *Wisconsin Studies in Contemporary Literature* 6 (Summer 1965): 158.
19. Saul Bellow, "Some Questions and Answers," *Ontario Review* 1 (Fall–Winter 1975–76): 59. Subsequent references to this source, abbreviated as *SQA*, are given parenthetically in the text.
20. Saul Bellow, *The Dean's December* (New York: Harper & Row, 1982), 136.

Subsequent references to this source, abbreviated as *TDD*, are given parenthetically in the text.

21. Jo Brans, "Common Needs, Common Preoccupations: An Interview with Saul Bellow," in *Critical Essays on Saul Bellow*, ed. Stanley Trachtenberg (Boston: G. K. Hall, 1976), 61.

22. Brans.

23. Brans, 61–62.

24. Brans, 68.

25. See Lionel Trilling, "The Two Environments," in *Beyond Culture: Essays on Literature and Learning* (New York: Viking Press, 1965), 229–33.

26. Brans, 58–59.

27. Joseph Epstein, "A Talk with Saul Bellow," the *New York Times Book Review*, 5 December 1976, 34.

28. Saul Bellow, "Deep Readers of the World, Beware," the *New York Times Book Review*, 15 February 1959, 34. Subsequent references to this source, abbreviated as *DRWB*, are given parenthetically in the text.

29. Brans, 62.

30. Saul Bellow, "The University as Villain," *The Nation*, 16 November 1957, 362. Subsequent references to this source, abbreviated as *UV*, are given parenthetically in the text.

31. Saul Bellow, "Machines and Storybook: Literature in the Age of Technology," *Harper's*, August 1974, 54. Subsequent references to this source, abbreviated as *MS*, are given parenthetically in the text.

32. Nina A. Steers, "Successor to Faulkner? An Interview with Saul Bellow," *Show* 4 (September 1964): 37.

33. Saul Bellow, "Some Notes on Recent American Fiction," *Encounter*, November 1963, 26.

34. Saul Bellow, "John Berryman," Foreward to John Berryman, *Recovery* (New York: Farrar Straus and Giroux, 1973), ix.

35. Harvy Swados, "The Image in the Mirror," in *The Living Novel: A Symposium*, ed. Granville Hicks (New York: Macmillan, 1975; New York: Collier Books, 1962), 182–83.

SPECIALIZED
ESSAYS

The Dialectic of Hero and Anti-Hero in *Rameau's Nephew* and *Dangling Man*

Jo Brans

He has no greater opposite than himself.[1]

Scratch an anti-hero and you are apt to find a failed or disillusioned or untimely hero. Don Quixote, for example, can be viewed as a man in whom heroic ideals, which exist in the mind, become ridiculous because they are vestiges of an earlier age and because they do not agree with the evidence of the senses, with flesh and blood reality. But is the Don a hero for his intentions or an anti-hero for the absurd actions into which those intentions lead him? And is Quixote's squire, Sancho Panza, to be praised for his usual practicality or condemned for his lack of vision? Critical judgment of the last three centuries has varied considerably in answering these questions. Our safest bet is to regard *Don Quixote*, as Elias Rivers does, as a "dialectic of hero and anti-hero." After all, says Rivers, Sancho "dreams of governing an island and learns to use his master's literary rhetoric"[2] whereas Quixote several times becomes commonsensical and finally faces death free of all of his former illusions, which Sancho begs him to retain. In short, although the two represent polar attitudes toward the meaning and purpose of human life, they also borrow attitudes from each other. Neither is a hero, neither a confirmed anti-hero. They coexist, that is all, and form together the complicated being, man.

If our schema-minded literary ancestors like to externalize the two views of life in separate characters, as in the Don and Sancho, in order to dramatize the relationship between the two, the twentieth century has, after Dostoevsky, internalized the conflict in one almost schizoid protagonist. Never is the shift from externalization to internalization more apparent than in a comparative study of Diderot's *Le Neveu de Rameau*

First published in *Studies in the Novel* 16, no. 4 (Winter 1984): 435–47.

written near the close of the eighteenth century, and Saul Bellow's 1944 novel, *Dangling Man*, on which Diderot had a great impact.

In *Rameau's Nephew*, the characters of hero and anti-hero are externalized and nicely balanced: the hero, Diderot-Moi, a high-minded philosopher and writer, wills his life according to fixed moral principles, and the anti-hero, Lui, an opportunistic musician, floats in the rugged channels of a deterministic sea. In form, the book is a novelistic play or dialogue between Moi and Lui. As a dialogue, it posits no conclusion; neither Moi nor Lui clearly wins. They meet by chance, argue about their respective roles in society and their ideas of life, and go their separate ways, enlarged but not enlightened.

In an interview in 1976, Bellow told me:

> I read *Rameau's Nephew* when I was very young and I got terribly excited by it. I thought it was just a marvelous book. I especially admired the speed and energy of the formulations and Diderot's talent for hitting all the high spots without any waste of time, and the amount of feeling. It just made a great impression.
>
> It was also a way of combining the writing of a story with a great deal of thought, not philosophical thought but the thought of an imaginative man about someone's career and about what it meant to be a parasite and a failure in an elite society and to be low man among the aristocrats. All of that really appealed to me.[3]

Because of this appeal, in his first novel, *Dangling Man*, Bellow recreates the dialectic of hero and anti-hero used by Diderot—with a difference. Although in Diderot's work Moi admits to having thoughts which he keeps to himself like those which Lui expresses, the two men are separate, and their moral characters are distinct. But Bellow internalizes the opposition of the two in his protagonist, Joseph, who embodies at once the high-mindedness of Moi and the low opportunism of Lui. Other characters reflect various aspects of Joseph's personality, but the conflict in the novel is essentially an internal conflict in Joseph himself, who is, as I see it, both hero and anti-hero.

Bellow's interest in Diderot's book was to extend over more than thirty years. In 1975, he was still urging it on his friends as reading material,[4] perhaps because in writing *Humboldt's Gift*, which was published that year, he had been engaged once again in creating an anti-hero, whom he called Rinaldo Cantabile, and who is similar to Diderot's Nephew. Cantabile, a real thug, is not a musician like the Nephew, but he admires the arts. Bellow slyly acknowledges the connections between the two characters, as well as Diderot's continuing influence, by giving Cantabile his musical name. Bellow goes on to make the acknowledgment overt. Charlie Citrine, the novel's hero, reflects: "Cantabile . . . had reached the stage reached by bums, con men, freeloaders, criminals in France in the eighteenth century, the stage of the intellectual creative man and theorist. Maybe he thought he was Rameau's nephew . . . ."[5]

In *Humboldt* Bellow allows Charlie, the Moi character, a solid and, for the reader, a satisfying victory over Cantabile. Charlie defeats Cantabile morally and bests him financially. At last he simply says to his obstreperous, bullying acquaintance, "Now go away, Cantabile, our relationship has drawn to a close. Let's become strangers again."[6]

"Diderot holds himself too much aloof and reserved in *Rameau's Nephew*," Bellow said in the interview we did a year after the publication of *Humboldt's Gift*. His youthful admiration for Diderot was perhaps at this point somewhat tempered by the experience of having written nine novels of his own about which critics have often made similar complaints. Bellow was candid about this flaw in his own work, admitting with amused chagrin, for example, that Sammler's misanthropy has all too frequently been regarded as the misanthropy of the author. "*Sammler* would have been a better book," he claimed elsewhere in the interview, "if I had dealt openly with some of my feelings, instead of filtering them through him," and went on to describe *Mr. Sammler's Planet* as "a sort of exotic report on life in the United States," limited by the eccentric point of view of its protagonist.[7] One would imagine that Charlie's decisive victory over Cantabile in *Humboldt* is meant to provide a corrective to an ongoing tendency toward ambiguity in Bellow's work.

Certainly everything in *Dangling Man* is filtered through Joseph, and the reader, like its hero, "dangles" a bit because the book lacks an objective stance from which one can judge Joseph. At the end of the novel, Joseph takes action which looks superficially like heroism, but his ironic description of it leaves the author's meaning questionable. Diderot's dialogue is of course purposely inconclusive. Moi describes the encounter with Lui and so controls the point of view, but Lui is an often sympathetic and always credible character who is allowed to speak for himself in full self-revelation. From the evidence in *Rameau's Nephew* and *Dangling Man*, one concludes that Diderot and Bellow have represented alternative ways of thinking and behaving which are visible in the world and present in the individual psyche. In literature as in life, we must choose.

Yet how can one choose? The two books pose the same insoluble problem: which is more important, submission to the human community, without which civilized life is impossible, or protection of the integrity and uniqueness of the self? Dubious as the apparent value judgment in the traditional definitions may be, the hero is he who

embodies and preserves the highest values of the community, the anti-
hero he who marches, or dawdles, to a different drumbeat, the cadence
of his own iconoclastic sensibility.

I

Rameau's Nephew is set in the French Enlightenment, that unprecedented age of "light" when human reason and universal nature promised
to work together for man's perfectibility. Diderot began the book in his
maturity, sometime between 1761 and 1764, when he was close to fifty.
The task of the *Enclyclopedia* was drawing to a close, and he could turn
from his public life to the private and secret writing, published posthumously, by which we today know him best, though few of his contemporaries had any idea of its existence. *Le philosophe,* as his friends called
him, perhaps intended the secrecy for reasons which become obvious
in *Rameau's Nephew.*

The first paragraph of the book invites us to take a particular view
of the dialogue which follows. Diderot, or Moi, speaks of discussions he
regularly holds with himself on "politics, love, taste, or philosophy." He
believes in giving his mind "free rein," he confides, "to follow any idea,
wise or mad, that may come uppermost" (8). Two paragraphs later, the
bizarre figure of the Nephew appears as if to personify the mad ideas
the philosopher himself has. Although Moi assures us stiffly that he has
"no great esteem for such eccentrics," he does occasionally welcome
Rameau if only because the Nephew "breaks the tedious uniformity which
our education, our social conventions, and our customary good manners have brought about." Critics have suggested that in fact both characters are Diderot; Moi is Diderot the Moralist and Lui is Diderot the
Determinist.[8] Such a dichotomy seems too fixed for the intellectual push
and pull of the dialogue. Rather, the hero of society simply needs a
reminder of alternatives. According to Moi, Rameau is "like a grain of
yeast that ferments and restores to each of us a part of his native individuality" (9–10).

We detect immediately a deep confusion or ambivalence in Diderot-
Moi in regard to the Nephew-Lui. Moi condescends to Lui, repeatedly
calling him "dear fellow," and, when Lui scores a point, insulting him
with, "That is infinitely truer than you think" (14). Ironically, Moi counsels Lui to stick to his role of parasitical grubbing and bootlicking in
the household of Bedin, Lui's patron, so as not to upset the general harmony of society. He is "overcome" by the mixture of "cunning and base-
ness," "turpitude and frankness" he finds in Lui (23). Lui is of a lower
order than himself. Yet he sincerely admires Lui for the originality of

his opinions and his honesty in expressing them, his realism, his ability to "see straight" without the blinders of fixed ideas or "universal ethics" (33). Moi is also honest; he admits that he too is "far from despising sensual pleasures" of food and wine and women, though he prefers more virtuous pastimes (36). In fact there is a kinship between Moi and Lui which Moi honorably acknowledges:

> There was in all he said much that one thinks to oneself, and acts on, but that one never says. This was in fact the chief difference between my man and the rest of us. He admitted his vices, which are also ours: he was no hypocrite. Neither more nor less detestable than other men, he was franker than they, more logical, and thus often profound in his depravity. (74)

In spite of both his condescending airs and his genuine admiration, Moi evidently fears the inroads that contact with Lui's sophistry might make into his own delicately balanced moral philosophy. Over and over he evades discussion and changes touchy subjects: Lui's calculated pimping for a young aristocrat (22-23), Moi's own poverty (26), the difficulties of childhood education (27), Lui's admiration for successful evil (61–62). Whatever Moi finds uncomfortable he skirts, subtly turning the dangerous conversation back to other grounds, especially to music. Evidently the safest arena for the meeting of the two aspects of personality is in art.

Moi's philosophy is simple, but austere. He believes in security, decorum, and the established order. He is a Platonist, accepting the imperfections of earth as proof of the excellence of heaven. Above all, he believes in the human will toward goodness, and he counters Lui's cynicism and determinism with repeated expressions of this belief: "One can rise above one's fate" (37); "If I were in your place, I wouldn't take it all for granted, I'd try" (79); and "Whatever a man tries, Nature destined him for that" (82).

Moi's earlier evasions have, however, made us alert to his more deep-seated evasion, an evasion of life itself, and we are not surprised when he finally pleads exemption. To Lui's catalogue of the encroaching trivia of everyday life, Moi exclaims, "It would be better to shut oneself up in a garret, eat a dry crust, drink plain water and try to find oneself" (78). He will meet life on his own elevated terms, or not at all.

To Moi's condescension, Lui retaliates with sarcasm. He addresses Moi as "Master Philosopher" and with mock deference inquires, "Would it be possible by dint of humble supplications to ascertain from his excellency the Philosopher the approximate age of his honorable daughter?" (27). But in fact he has little use for any philosopher; he is a realist, well acquainted with all manners and conditions of men. In response to Moi's Platonic and Enlightenment assumption that all men through reason seek virtue, Rameau answers, "But virtue and philosophy are not made for everybody" (34), and advances his own theory that as there are grammatical idioms which are deviations from universal grammar, so there are moral idioms, deviations from universal morality. The most idiomatic of men, he confronts the hero of Enlightenment values with his eccentric and anti-heroic personality.

In his mind, Lui is not perfectible. He sees himself as the victim of forces beyond his control which he calls variously "chance" (29), "Nature" (45), "accidents" (47), "fate" (72), and he views this all-inclusive determinism as physiological, environmental, and genetic:

> It must be that virtue requires a special sense that I lack, a fiber that has not been granted me. My fiber is loose, one can pluck it forever without its yielding a note. Or else I have spent my life with good musicians and bad people, whence my ear has become very sharp and my heart quite deaf. And then there is heredity. My father's blood is the same as my uncle's; my blood is like my father's. The paternal molecule was hard and obtuse, and like a primordial germ it has affected all the rest. (71–72)

As a matter of fact, he tells the scandalized Moi, "The best order, for me, is that in which I had to exist—and a fig for the most perfect world if I am not of it. I'd rather *be* . . . " (16). The "I" is primary.

What Strugnell has called "roguery raised to the level of a metaphysics" has made Rameau a social parasite who has been mechanized and bestialized by his life. As a mechanical creature, the rightful inhabitant in some ways of the world-machine of the Enlightenment, he follows the course of least resistance: "And then I was hungry and I ate when I had the chance. After eating I was thirsty and I have occasionally drunk. Meanwhile my beard grew and when grown I had it shaved" (11). Like a pet dog, he takes what comes his way:

> My people . . . missed every moment I was away from them. I was their dear Rameau, pretty Rameau—*their* Rameau—the jester, the buffoon, the lazy dog, the saucy rogue, the great greedy boob. Not one of these epithets went without a smile, a chuck under the chin, a pat on the back, a cuff, a kick. At table it was a choice morsel tossed to me . . . .
> (19)

Yet even this abject being, this "person of no consequence," has heroic aspirations. He wants above all to be a musical genius, and he has mastered the techniques and maimed his hands in the effort to succeed. Musically, Lui has discrimination: he admires those heroic musicians who are leading the musical community to new heights. But he lacks genius and considers himself fit only for teaching and parody. On one occasion he treats Moi to a virtuoso performance which has more feeling than form. Moi's reception is ambivalent: "Did I admire? Yes, I did admire. Was I moved to pity? I was moved. But a streak of derision was interwoven with these feelings and denatured them" (67).

Failing to be a musical genius, Lui has tried to be a genius of corrupt expediency. He patterns himself after Bouret and other great men of the profession of parasitism and thinks of himself as incarnating the values of a corrupt society; that is, he wants to be the hero of an anti-heroic society. To satisfy human needs, every man takes a position in a rigidly choreographed social dance. The point is to be good enough to get "a good bed, good food, warm clothes . . . plenty of rest, money, and other things that I would rather owe to kindness than to toil" (85). He is a self-avowed "superior moralist" of his social milieu.

Even here, as Moi is quick to note, Lui has lacked the integrity of character of the great. Before this chance meeting, Lui has forfeited his position with Bertin because of an innate—and unwelcome—dignity which will allow him to crawl only at his own pleasure, not on somebody else's order. "That's the worm's natural gait and it is mine, too, when we are left alone, but we turn and rear, both of us, when stepped on" (40). His ego means more to him than the successful parasitism which would make him, like Bouret, a hero of vice, a "great criminal" (58). To have freedom of personality for Lui is to accept anti-heroism.

II

The action of *Dangling Man* opens in Chicago in December, 1942. Joseph, the protagonist, has quit his job the previous May to wait for the draft. Although he is 1A, the call does not come. For seven months he has been jobless, supported by his wife, free to do "all the delightful things" he cannot do in the army (11). That is, he "dangles." Before he began to dangle, he was writing an essay on Diderot, part of a series on philosophers of the Enlightenment, and he originally plans to finish that. If to the reader such a series seems a somewhat quixotic project to work on during a world war, that is Bellow's intention.

For even more obviously than Diderot does, Bellow invites us immediately to look for alternative aspects of character in Joseph, and affords

us the means in the first-person journal form of the novel. As bleak himself as the winter landscape beyond his tomblike room, Joseph records
that he has deteriorated in his isolated state; in the fourth entry, he
describes himself as two-fold, the "older" Joseph who reads Enlightenment philosophy and his present dangling self. The older Joseph has
heroic principles. An attractive, gentlemanly amiable though reserved
historian, he has a "general plan" for his life, into which "have gone his
friends, his family, and his wife" (29). He wants to preserve himself, his
integrity, but he believes in compromise and manages to think of himself simultaneously as a scholar, a social idealist, and an excellent em-
ployee. For a time he was a Marxist, led to Marxism by a reforming
Platonism. His disappointment in that camp has caused him to think
instead in terms of a "colony of the spirit," peopled by those who are
as sensitive, moral, and pacific as he is, though he has begun to have
misgivings about that program also (39-40). He wants to help the world:
to improve his wife, to inspire his friends, to find the good life. In fact,
he is like a younger version of Diderot-Moi.

Then the abortive draft call and his subsequent situation lift Joseph
into the leisure for a quest, the traditional task of the hero. His quest,
philosophical rather than physical, takes the form of several inquiries
into the nature of human life. First he tries "to find clear signs of their
common humanity" in other people (25). Then he asks, "How should
a good man live; what ought he to do?" (39). And finally, "I must know
what I myself am" (119). Thus, in his dangling state, alone in his room
for ten hours a day, Joseph attempts to follow the advice of Diderot-Moi
"to shut oneself up in a garret, eat a dry crust, drink plain water and
try to find oneself." As Moi's advice presages, the object of Joseph's quest
gradually narrows from common humanity to the single good life to self-
knowledge.

But when the hero begins to ask questions, especially such questions
as these, each of which diminishes in scope from the last, hero subtly
shifts into anti-hero, and the other Joseph emerges, self-indulgent, immoral, violent, anti-heroic to the core. The former pacifist has fourteen
quarrels in succession; he has a mistress; he eats too much, quits writing, sleeps late, reads the newspaper front to back, gains weight, sinks,
as he himself recognizes, into Hobbes's "nasty, brutish, and short" realities of purposeless existence (56).

Joseph thus develops the faults both of Moi, Diderot's hero, and Lui,
his anti-hero. Because, like Moi, he has sought the philosopher's exemption from the encroachment of ordinary human burdens and cares, he
has separated himself from the cycle of nature and the cycle of human
life. He lives in a vacuum. Reading Goethe, Joseph comes across a

paragraph which Bellow uses as a motif in the novel to point to Joseph's alienation: "All comfort in life is based upon a regular occurrence of external phenomena. The changes of the day and night, of the seasons, of flowers and fruits, and all other recurring pleasures that come to us . . . —these are the mainsprings of our earthly life" (18). Joseph has always been aloof to this seasonal change anyway; in the middle of winter, he tells us, he could convince himself it was July and vice versa (13). In this winter of his discontent he also misses one human recurrence after another: Christmas is spoiled by his selfishness, New Year's Eve passes without revelry, and on January 2 he realizes the problem completely:

> But what such a life as this incurs is the derangement of days, the leveling of occasions . . . [so that] days have lost their distinctiveness . . . . But now they are undistinguished, all equal, and it is difficult to tell Tuesday from Saturday . . . . It is possible that that is one reason why I have been creating agitation . . . . I am tired of having to identify a day as "the day I asked for a second cup of coffee . . . ." (81–82)

Even his sixth wedding anniversary goes awry, marked gloomily by Joseph's "prevision" of death (77).

Because Joseph places inordinate value on his own freedom and individuality, he has been brought, like Lui, to parasitism and solipsism. He preys on his wife Iva (I've a wife), seeing her only as an extension of his personality, and depending on her as financial support and emotional bulwark. Like Euripides's Admetus, the unyoked man, Joseph accepts his wife's sacrifice gladly. Bellow gives a metaphor for Joseph's self-absorption. Going to his mother-in-law's kitchen for a glass of orange juice, Joseph sees "a half-cleaned chicken, its yellow claws rigid, its head bent as though to examine its entrails . . . . Beside it stood the orange juice, a brown feather floating in it. I poured it down the drain" (24). Staring perpetually at his own innards as the ancients studied entrails for a hint of the future, Joseph is as dead as the fowl, and the stray feathers spoil the most reliable pleasures of daily life.

Like his biblical counterpart, Joseph interprets dreams, though only his own; they are all of universal death and destruction and his alarming exemption and neutrality. Through the horror in them and the glimpse they give of the subconscious from which they come, he understands the limits of reason, the limitations of the philosophical life:

> My beliefs are inadequate, they do not guard me. I think invariably of the awning of the store on the corner. It gives as much protection

against the rain and wind as my beliefs give against the chaos I am
forced to face. "God does not love those who are unable to sleep
soundly," runs an old saying. (123)

At this low point of the collapse of his spiritual values, Joseph meets
his Nephew. His name is Alf Steidler, and he is an old acquaintance.
Joseph comments: "Whenever I meet Steidler, I think of Rameau's
nephew, described by Diderot as ... *un (personnage) composé de hauteur et
de bassesse, de bon sens et de déraison'* " (127). If Steidler is Lui, Joseph must
be Moi, and there exists from Diderot an acknowledged kinship. Various characters in the novel reflect Joseph. Iva is his possession. As Marcus
Klein has pointed out, old Vanaker represents what Joseph might become in complete freedom, "ordinary free self-hood."[10] His niece Etta,
the "little animal," not only looks like Joseph but is as selfish as he is,
so that when he beats her he is punishing himself (70). His brother Amos
and his friend Adler are the war profiteers he disdains to be but subtly
is; in another friend Abt, and in Abt's victimization of Minna, we see
Joseph's attitude toward Iva; and in John Pearl, the artist, Joseph recognizes an alternative self he longs for but cannot be. But in Steidler he
is brought face to face with the worst of himself, with the physical realities of his philosophical posturing.

Like Joseph, Steidler has missed the draft, having conned himself out
of the service. He is an opportunist, a grafter, and a leech. As Joseph
is a failed philosopher, Steidler, like Lui, is a failed artist. Completely
cynical about human dignity and the possibility of truth, Steidler prides
himself on his conquest of women. To Joseph's horror, Steidler recognizes in Joseph a like soul. A buffoon himself, he finds the serious Joseph
hilarious. Uncomfortably Joseph realizes that Steidler "exaggerates, but
he does not lie" (134). Feeling that he and Steidler in their meetings are
accomplices, "practicing some terrible vice together" (148), Joseph is
struck with the necessity of finding an alternative to the life into which
he has fallen.

From the recesses of Joseph's being, the Spirit of Alternatives, *Tu As
Raison Aussi,* comes to him. The Spirit does not so much suggest as
respond, but through his wise mediation Joseph is led to see that instead
of his extensive philosophical preparation to live, he should be preparing himself to die. *Tu As Raison Aussi* can be viewed as a spirit of
Mephistopholean negation or as a healthy antithesis to Joseph's Faustian
quest. Death is the great fact of life, says the Spirit, an idea Bellow underscores by presenting a number of off-stage deaths of various kinds.
Jefferson Forman's sacrificial death in the service, the spontaneous death
of a man of action, shames Joseph into his first understanding that he

would rather be a victim of the war than a profiteer. As old Vanaker's ignominious life gives us a grim prognosis of Joseph's impending future, in the sudden fall of the anonymous man on the sidewalk as Joseph hastens to meet Iva on their sixth wedding anniversary, he has a "prevision" of his own death (116). The man even wears a watch like that of Joseph's father, reminding us that as a boy Joseph has seen his own mortality in a portrait of his dead grandfather. I have already mentioned Joseph's dreams of death, of the dead in a slaughterhouse, of the dead from a massacre, of his own solitary and accidental death. Death is ever-present in Joseph's unconscious, though he tries to think his way clear of it. The most important death takes place stage by stage throughout the entire novel. As Joseph slowly returns to life, his landlady, old Mrs. Kiefer (key for), dies lingeringly. Hers is the exemplary way to die. After a lifetime of service to others, she dies surrounded by loving family and friends, and her funeral is a dignified ceremonial. As her life has meant something, her death has grandeur also.

Joseph achieves two important realizations: that he cannot be free except in giving himself away, unlocking "the imprisoning self" that keeps him "impure and unknowing, turning inward and self-fastened"; and that his quest is the common human quest, no matter what its immediate object may be for others: "We are all drawn toward the same craters of the spirit—to know what we are and what we are for, to know our purpose, to seek grace" (154). Recognizing that his destiny is also the common human destiny, that, as the Spirit tells him, "Everybody else is dangling, too" (165), Joseph rejoins his race. In the spring of the year he, too, is reborn. He elaborately celebrates the first day of spring by walking in the park in his spring coat. But celebrating life means accepting death. Like Mann's Hans Castorp, Joseph descends from his mountaintop into the "universal feast of death" and urgently requests his draft board to call him into selective service.

But first we are confronted with one other Bellow metaphor for Joseph's life, the Christian Science pamphleteer who hands out health-giving advice, meanwhile growing sicker and more wasted by the day herself. It is worth noting that her beliefs sell for the same as Herzog's: "What this country needs is a good five-cent synthesis." For beliefs alone are worth little. They do not work independent of action; Joseph and Herzog and Sammler all must come back to the validity of immediate human experience, of the shared life of the species caught in its cycle of birth and life and death. For each of these heroes, and I use the word precisely, the return is a defeat, but a necessary, enlivening defeat. Joseph's last journal entry sounds relieved but chagrined:

> This is my last civilian day . . . . I am no longer to be held accountable
> for myself; I am grateful for that. I am in other hands, relieved of
> self-determination, freedom canceled.
>   Hurray for regular hours!
>   And for the supervision of the spirit!
>   Long live regimentation! (191)

But he has made the only choice Bellow will allow him, in order to escape the desperate straits of anti-heroism.

III

Neither *Rameau's Nephew* nor *Dangling Man* concludes with a trumpet
blast of bravura heroism. Though Moi deals stout blows throughout the
dialogue and earns respect for his high ideals and solid character, he
is several times during this battle of wits defeated by Lui. Moi's insularity
and näiveté go down before Lui's wide experience and particular
knowledge of society; his evasions before Lui's unabashed acceptance
of himself; his moral snobbishness before Lui's resilience and sheer
energy. Lionel Trilling reminds us that Hegel regarded Lui as the hero:

> It is therefore not Diderot-*Moi,* not the *philosophe* with his archaic
> love of simple truth and morality, with his clearly defined self and
> his commitment to sincerity, who, for Hegel, commands esteem.
> Rather, it is Rameau, the buffoon, the flattering parasite, the com-
> pulsive mimic, without a self to be true to: it is he who represents
> Spirit moving to its next stage of development.[11]

Joseph rushes off to arms and the manhood of "hardboileddom" he
so disdained initially, but his advance looks suspiciously like retreat. Will
it be possible for him to be what Socrates was, as he tells Amos, a
philosopher temporarily serving public need as a hoplite, an ordinary
foot-soldier? He hopes so: "perhaps the war could teach me, by violence,
what I had been unable to learn during those months in the room.
Perhaps I could sound creation through other means. Perhaps" (191).
But "perhaps" three times in a row makes the hope seem wistful and
insubstantial.

Nor does anti-heroism win the day, either day. In the midst of
Rameau's degradation and corruption, shreds of the old order of dignity and decency remain; he will crawl only by desire, and he grieves
over his failed art and his lost love. Throughout the process of Joseph's
deterioration, the dangling man never ceases to ask the questions
that matter. As the hero is necessary so that the human community

may continue, the anti-hero assures the human quality that comes with questioning.

Notes

1. Denis Diderot, *Rameau's Nephew and Other Works,* trans. Jacques Barzun and Ralph H. Bowen (New York: Bobbs-Merrill, 1964), 9. All other references are from this edition. All references to *Dangling Man* are taken from Saul Bellow, *Dangling Man* (New York: The Vanguard Press, 1944).
2. Elias L. Rivers, "The Anti-Hero in Spain," *The Anti-Hero: His Emergence and Transformations,* ed. Lillian R. Furst and James D. Wilson (Atlanta: Georgia State University Press, 1976), 26.
3. See Jo Brans, "Common Needs, Common Preoccupations," *Southwest Review* (Winter 1977), for an abridged form of this interview. The entire interview, which includes the section quoted here, can be found in "A Feeling for Where the Nerves Lie," in my *Listen to the Voices* (Dallas: Southern Methodist University Press, 1988), 27.
4. Walter Clemons and Jack Kroll, "America's Master Novelist," *Newsweek,* 1 September 1975, 39.
5. Saul Bellow, *Humboldt's Gift* (New York: Viking, 1975), 174.
6. *Humboldt's Gift,* 483.
7. *Listen to the Voices,* 23–24.
8. See, for example, C. J. Greshoff, *Seven Studies in the French Novel* (Cape Town: A. A. Balkema, 1964), 17.
9. A. R. Strugnell, "Diderot's *Neveu de Rameau:* Portrait of a Rogue in the French Enlightenment," in *Knaves and Swindlers: Essays on the Picaresque Novel in Europe,* ed. Christine J. Whitbourn (New York: Oxford University Press, 1974), 107.
10. Marcus Klein, "A Discipline of Nobility: Saul Bellow's Fiction," in *Twentieth Century Views: Saul Bellow,* ed. Earl Rovit (Englewood Cliffs, N.J.: Prentice-Hall, 1975), 148.
11. Lionel Trilling, "The Honest Soul and the Disintegrated Consciousness," in his *Sincerity and Authenticity* (Cambridge: Harvard University Press, 1972), 44.

Bellow's More-or-Less Human Bestiaries: *Augie March* and *Henderson the Rain King*

Michael O. Bellamy

It is a minor character in *The Victim* (1947) who most trenchantly identifies the central preoccupation of Saul Bellow's fiction. Schlossberg claims that man's most pressing obligation is to find out what kinds of behavior—and by implication what aspirations—are appropriate for human beings: "It's bad to be less than human .... Good acting is what is exactly human .... More than human, can you have any use for life? Less than human, you don't either."[1] At one extreme of the enormous spectrum of possibilities is the desire for transcendence, immortality, apotheosis. At the other end is the passive acceptance, even the downright celebration, of the most degrading kinds of behavior that human beings are so often capable of enjoying. *Mr. Sammler's Planet* (1969) is a clear illustration of Schlossberg's observation in that it scrutinizes both the excesses of "more" and the deficiencies of "less." The desire to be more than human is represented by the theme of the exploration of outer space. This attempt literally to transcend the human condition is consistently viewed from the perspective of Mr. Sammler's gentle irony. His planet is clearly the earth; his corresponding philosophical emphasis is on man's immanence in nature. At the other extreme from this scientific endeavor to overcome the limits of nature are Sammler's friends and relatives, those sixties-style, New York manic eccentrics whose moral and aesthetic credo seems to be that "less is more." For those devotees of the excremental vision, Sammler has nothing but scorn. For them he reserves not gentle irony but fierce invective.

But the emphasis in *Sammler,* and in Bellow's fiction in general, is not on the differences between attempts to be more than human and attempts to be less than human, but rather on their virtual identity. Whether Henderson is raising pigs as an act of sacrilegious defiance or

First printed in *Ball State University Forum* 23, no. 1 (1982): 12–22.

assuming the role of the Messiah by trying to overcome a plague of frogs, the motivations and the results are the same. Whether, in other words, the behavior can be characterized as more or as less than human, the ultimate aspiration is for apotheosis. As the motive is always a desire for transcendence, so also the result is always degradation. If, then, the aim of "more" and "less" is to be more than human, the end result of "more" and "less" is to be less than human. As Schlossberg implies, "more" and "less" converge at the point when both extremes lack "any use for life." Proponents of transcendence share the idea that they are too good for life, when in fact they are not good enough. Thus Henderson's initial reluctance to conform with African ritual by wrestling with Itelo is not, as he at first thinks, because he is "too high on the scale of civilization"[2] but rather because he is too low to bother to struggle.

The question that remains is how Bellow goes about determining precisely "what is exactly human" when he gets down to specific cases. One of his favorite and most effective ways of exploring this question is his habit of comparing man to his fellow creatures, a device which provides a kind of scale of creatures, a chain of living beings against which to measure what truly is human. His bestiaries, *Augie March* (1953) and *Henderson the Rain King* (1959), serve another function that is equally important in defining what truly is human. The enormous number and variety of animals in these two novels points us toward Bellow's belief in man's immanence within nature. We are reminded by the ubiquity of these creatures that man is himself a creature whose nature is to be assessed not only *over against* the animal kingdom, but also *within* the animal kingdom in terms of the way he interacts with his fellow creatures. Animals tend to undermine man's numerous schemes for transcendence by reminding Bellow's characters of their creaturehood, especially at those heady moments when they would most like to forget it.

Perhaps the most spectacular of these moments is in *Augie March* when Thea Fenchel tries to achieve apotheosis through a scheme that involves the use of animals. All the ironies of this endeavor to escape nature through nature come home to roost. Thea's idea is to resurrect an avatar of Quetzalcoatl, the Aztec plumed-serpent deity, by training a haggard eagle for hunting iguanas, ancient reptiles that exude their "snaky" odor in the primordial jungles of Mexico.[3] In fact, the irony of Thea's bizarre scheme to "catch up with legends *more or less*" (333, emphasis mine) is apparent even before she and Augie depart for their disastrous escapade in Mexico. "More" does indeed become "less" in Thea's dismal failure to reenact this legend.

The episode most immediately recalls D. H. Lawrence's *The Plumed Serpent* (1926), a novel in which the significance of the bird-reptile deity is never really resolved. Far more satisfying and revealing, especially with respect to Bellow's attempt to define what is human, is the light shed on this episode by the writings of Friedrich Nietzsche. In *Thus Spake Zarathustra,* as in most of Nietzsche's works, the call is for an *Ubermensch,* or a superman, to take the place of the defunct Christian god. The specific allusion in Thea's endeavor to Zarathustra's is in the prophet's original determination to come down from the seclusion of the mountain and reincarnate as man; Zarathustra's visible manifestation among men is to be in the company of his emblematic animals, or as he puts it, "my eagle and my serpent."[4] Thea's bird/reptile construct is evocative of this desire for transcendence, both in the emblematic significance of her animals and in the very flight of the eagle.

Thea's name, which means "divine," is itself indicative of her desire for apotheosis. She is, in fact, a sort of *"Uberfrau."* To her credit is her extraordinary physical courage, a courage she manifests with aplomb, whether she is handling poisonous snakes or haggard eagles. She is also fearless about the opinions of other people, fully "prepared for the extremest test of her thoughts" (316). Her "extremely high standards" (379) reflect her belief in "something better than what people call reality" (316). The less attractive side of these exacting expectations is her habit of applying them to others, whose "monkey games" (351) are seen as typical of "mere humanity" (401). The problem with Thea's standards is the impossibility of fulfilling them. The metaphor for this danger in *Zarathustra* is the tightrope, and the man who would transcend by leaving the earth is, as Nietzsche reminds us, in the most precarious of positions: "Man is a rope, tied between beast and overman [superman]—a rope over an abyss. A dangerous across, a dangerous on-the-way, a dangerous looking-back, a dangerous shuddering and stopping" (126).

Thea's failure to walk the tightrope of transcendence is implicit in the very properties of her eagle/iguana, plumed-serpent construct. Ideally, the composite bird-serpent is an emblem of periodic regeneration, as the bird moults and the reptile sloughs its skin. The union of these two creatures is also indicative of a divine synthesis of the antithetical realms they inhabit; the eagle soars above man, while the serpent crawls below him on, or even under, the earth. The plumed serpent, then, represents a reconciliation of man's highest aspirations and his lowest desires in a kind of Hegelian synthesis. The problem with this kind of synthesis is that it fails to subsume the middle term between "more" and "less" than human—humanity itself.

The consequences of leaving out this middle term are ironically apparent in the failure of the eagle to live up to Thea's "inhuman" expectations. When the iguana counterattacks, Caligula, as Augie calls this dreaded bird, retreats. This humiliation brings Thea down to earth, even as the eagle takes off. But the discovery that the eagle is really a "chicken" (355) is not the first indication that identifying Caligula solely with his awesome power, his potential for transcendence, or even his demoniacal ruthlessness, is naive. True, satanic possession is often associated with excrement; nevertheless, the constant association of the eagle with defecation undermines his "dignity" long before his retreat from the iguana. When Augie describes Caligula's quick "squirt of excrement" (334) or tells us, over and over again, that "the toilet became the eagle's mews" (343), we are reminded more of Caligula's creaturehood than of his satanic demeanor. If we dwell upon Augie's insistence that the bird is Thea's, we are being informed, in a roundabout way, of a function all creatures must perform in order to live. If, in other words, one is to have any use for life, one must not forget, however humbling it may be, what even Swift's Celia must do in her mews. To ignore this fact of life is, as Schlossberg puts it, not to have any use for life. Ultimately, it hardly matters whether we call such an attitude toward defecation more, or less, than human.

Even more revealing than the humbling aspects of Caligula's behavior is what Augie comes increasingly to realize: "the humane side of" the entire Quetzalcoatl endeavor (356). It is Thea who draws attention to what she thinks is Augie's illicit tendency to "humanize" (349) animals by expressing "sympathy" (347) for them. Even the lizard she uses for Caligula's "target practice" elicits Augie's pity. But if Thea is consistent in ridiculing this sort of "sentimentality," she is guilty, in her own way, of the pathetic fallacy, or in other words, of imposing her human expectations on the animal kingdom. It is typical of Thea that this flaw is revealed at a moment of stress. Thus, when the eagle fails, she calls him a "bastard" (348) and a "coward" (354), terms which can only be applied to human beings that fail to measure up to human expectations. By her own admission, Thea's attempt to transcend the condition of "mere humanity" (401) by subduing, or manning nature in the "person" of Caligula, is absurd; ironically, she fails to overcome her own human nature to the precise extent that Caligula is himself "human." Conversely, it is nonsense to talk of "manning" or conquering nature when man is himself one of nature's creatures. Augie, who comes to see even the "humane side" of Caligula—he later calls him merely "the eagle"—sums up the interdependence of man and beast by describing Thea's rage at the eagle's retreat in this way: "Well, it was hard to take this from wild nature, that there should be humanity mixed with it; such as there was in the beasts that embraced Odysseus and his men and wept on them in Circe's yard" (355).

Consistent with the unresolved duality of Thea's construct is the reason for her romantic breakup with Augie. Ultimately, they both find they
are unable to sustain the high standards requisite for the intensity of
their relationship. In this respect, the iguana's attack on the soaring eagle
represents the flesh undermining the spirit's aspiration. The failure of
the venture is reflected in the termination of Augie's and Thea's liaison;
more specifically, what precipitates their separation is Thea's sexual
jealousy, an especially ironic emotion in the light of Nietzsche's exhaustive analysis of *Ressentiment,* man's lowest vice. In the heat of the moment,
Thea forgets her own high standards; in fact she reveals that they do
not apply when it comes to her suspicions about what Augie has been
up to with another woman: "Don't," she pleads with Augie, "ask me to
be superhuman" (394). The destruction of her hopes reminds us that
her god was, after all, a pastiche god, or a "dirty bastard" (348), as she
calls him at the moment of his failure, and that as such, the bird-god
was bound, like her relationship with Augie, to fall apart at the first moment of disillusionment.

Augie's observation that "the beauty of it [Thea's scheme] is harmed
by what it suffers on the way to proof" (316) is only partly relevant. The
most profound flaw in Thea's design is apparent at its very inception.
The problem at the origin of her plan is especially significant, as originality is of crucial importance in any Romantic program of transcendence. To achieve apotheosis one must obviously escape tradition as we
know it; but of course Thea's recourse to the Quetzalcoatl legend is anything but original. What she is actually trying to do, as Augie points out,
is catch up. Augie describes the contemporary manifestations of this
legend: "Hereabouts, worshipers disguised as gods and as gods in the
disguise of birds, jumped from platforms fixed on long poles, and glided
as they spun by the ropes—feathered serpents, and eagles too, the *vola-*
dores, or fliers. There still are such plummeters, in market places, as there
seem to be remnants or conversions or equivalents of all the old things"
(338).

In fact, even Thea's eccentric attempt to enact the Quetzalcoatl legend
is not unprecedented, as she adopts the idea from a couple of Americans, whose recent success, incidentally, further emphasizes her failure.
Given this derivative quality, we should not be astonished to discover
that Caligula's so-called "original eyes" (330) are actually bedimmed by
a more complicated "human" vision.

Thea can respond to this dilemma in two ways, neither one of which
is very satisfying: she can either ignore the problem of originality by working frankly within a tradition, or she can avoid tradition by cultivating
eccentricity for its own sake. She chooses the first alternative throughout

the Quetzalcoatl episode. The irony of this failure to be original is implicit in her reference to the "monkey games" (351) of those she despises, or more specifically, in the significance of the Kinkajou, or pet monkey, that is kept by the "Pan American Bums" (413) who hang about the same area of Mexico where Augie and Thea try to hunt iguanas. Monkeys are at once the antithesis of the envisioned superman—the creatures at the end of a sort of evolution in reverse—and famous for their tendency to imitate. Seeking originality, Thea eventually cultivates eccentricity in what turns out to be unconscious self-parody. After losing interest in iguanas, she immediately goes after "wild pigs" (364), an implicit indication of her Circean role with respect to Augie during their sojourn in Mexico. Easily bored, she then takes up poisonous "snakes" (369), marine monsters—"a creature puffed up in scales, warty as a pickle, gray, with skinny gray wattles, and tickle claws, breathing on its belly" (410), and finally "some rare flamingos" (410). (Later still, she even collects another husband.) Her hunger for these wild, rare, and dangerous animals becomes a grotesque demonstration of what is eccentric, reptilian, even poisonous, about herself. Schlossberg's "more or less" paradigm is again useful, as Thea's schemes subsequent to the Quetzalcoatl affair reduce the idea of "more" to its quantitative aspect so that more, or even more kinds of, animals represent less purpose in that act of gathering a menagerie. The fall is from the sublime aspirations of the Quetzalcoatl legend to the absurd collection of poisonous reptiles and odd birds as an end in itself.

Thea's disappearance from the novel does not signal the end of Bellow's exploration of the implications of Nietzsche's ideas about transcendence. After his return to Chicago, Augie works as a research assistant for a crack-brained millionaire, who has undertaken the superhuman task of writing an encyclopedic opus which is to incorporate all human knowledge. The teutonic scholar who undertakes this Faustian endeavor is heavily influenced by the ideas of Nietzsche, especially his attack on Christianity and his contention that man must fill the vacuum created by the death of God. Augie quotes Robey, the stuttering eclectic, would-be *Ubermensch*, and then summarizes his habitual diatribes:

> "Man will accept death. Live without God. That's a b-brave project. End of an illusion. But with what values instead?" . . . He was saying that Christianity originally was aimed at the lowly and slaves, and that was why crucifixion and nailing and all such punitive grandeur of martyrdom were necessary. But at the pole opposite, the happy pole, there ought to be an equal thickness. Joy without sin, love without darkness, gay prosperity. Not to be always spoiling things.

> Oh great age of generous love and time of a new man! Not the poor,
> dark, disfigured creature cramped by his falsehood . . . deeper than
> a latrine in jealousy, dead as a cabbage to feeling, a maggot to beauty,
> a shrimp to duty, spinning the same thread of cocoon preoccupa-
> tion from his mouth . . . . Drilled like a Prussian by the coarse holler-
> ing of the sergeant fears. Robey poured it on me. He let it come down.
> (441–42)

Robey is himself the most obvious indication that something is radically amiss with his enterprise. Augie not only assumes that his employer's
eccentricity verges on madness, he is also disgusted by Robey's entire
demeanor. Again, we are presented with the less-than-human endeavor-
ing to undertake the more-than-human:

> I found myself face to face with this man Robey in his house on the
> lakefront. And what a face it was—what an appearance! Big, inflamed,
> reticent eyes, a reddish beard, red sullen lips, and across his nose
> a blotch; his stutter was bad; when it really caught him he made a
> great effort, fixed his soul, and twisted his head while his eyes took
> on this discipline and almost hatred. (439)

Robey, like Thea, is a great collector; also, as with Thea, the mere accumulation of items becomes an end in itself. Again, more becomes less.
In Thea's case, it is rare animals, while in Robey's it is "lavish collections
of screens, antiques, iron, Russian sleighs, hanks and tails of helmets,
and mother-of-pearl boxes" (441). But most important of all, Robey collects facts. Not surprisingly, Augie never exactly understands what it is
that Robey is trying to do with all this information, just as he is incapable
of fathoming the reason for Thea's untiring collection of animals. This
emphasis on quantity, rather than quality, is thematically related to Thea's
and Robey's seemingly inexhaustible supply of money. Both respond to this
wealth irrationally: Thea is a spendthrift, while Robey is a miser. But
an even more important connection between these two seemingly different characters is implicit in the scene in which Augie discovers Robey
enacting his own grotesque version of Thea's sublime hunt for iguanas:

> I found him standing on a kitchen chair, wrapped in his bathrobe,
> pumping Flit into a cupboard while hundreds of roaches rushed out
> practically clutching their heads and falling down from the walls.
> What a moment that was! He wildly raised hell as he worked the spray
> gun, full of lust, and breathed as loudly as the spray itself while the
> animals landed as thick as beans or beat it, crazy, like an Oklahoma
> land rush, in every direction. (444)

Thus, Robey, the debased predator wrapped in his winglike robe, a "superman," a cormorant "raising hell," descends upon the cockroaches, those ancient insects, whose crazy flight grotesquely resembles Augie's description of the breathtaking flights of iguanas down the mountainside:

> The lizards were really huge, with great frills or sails—those ancient membranes. The odor here was snaky, and we seemed in the age of snakes among the hot poisons of green and livid gardenias. We waited, and the cautious kid went to poke under the leaves with a long pole, for the iguanas were savage. Then on a ledge above us I saw one who looked on, but as I pointed him out we saw the Elizabethan top of him scoot away. These beasts were as fast and bold as anything I had ever seen, and they would jump anywhere and from any height, with a pure writhe of their sides, like fish. They had great muscles, like fish, and their flying was monstrously beautiful. I was astonished that they didn't dash themselves into pellets, like slugs of quicksilver, but when they smashed down they continued without any pause to run. They were faster than the wild pigs. (353–54)

If Robey's tirades about the *Ubermensch* make a mockery of Nietzsche's ideas, Augie's enlistment in the merchant marine at the outset of World War II is a reminder that other uses of the German philosopher's ideas have been anything but humorous. On his first voyage, Augie's ship is torpedoed and sunk. He and the ship's carpenter, Basteshaw, the sole survivors, drift in a lifeboat for several days in the Pacific. During this interlude, Basteshaw describes his attempt to make man over in a new image. The most revealing circumstance of Basteshaw's attempt to synthesize a higher form of life is that it follows his failure to find out first what, in fact, it means to be a proper human being. The attempt to be more-than-human is motivated by, as Basteshaw puts it, his failure "to be cast in the mold of true manhood. But who is cast in this mold? Nobody knows" (504). If, in other words, one can't be a proper man, why not strive to be a superman? If one cannot discover how to be a proper *mensch*, why not become the *Ubermensch*? This is the familiar theory of transcendence that less is more. Basteshaw presents Augie with a version of this proposition, employing the same upside-down logic, telling him he can make him "wiser than the Sphinx" (508). If the answer to the Sphinx's riddle is man, Augie's knowledge will involve the superman. This curious conversation takes place, it should be remembered, while Augie and Basteshaw cling precariously to existence in a lifeboat after a fascist government has brought about the destruction of their vessel, killing everybody else aboard. The irony of this situation can be compared to an image in which Augie refers to the outcome of the fascist

dream of improving the human race. In this case, less-than-human behavior, ostensibly justified by more-than-human goals, is signified by turning fascism, in the person of Mussolini, upside down—"that same
Mussolini who was slung up dead by the legs with shirt tails dropped
off his naked belly, and the flies, on whom he had also declared war,
walked on his empty face relaxed of its wide-jawed grimace, upside down"
(345). The war on flies is later dramatized in Robey's assault on the
cockroaches—surely a losing battle. Mussolini would have done better,
in the long run, to keep his feet on the ground. His end is at once ironically suggestive of the high flying aspirations of the superman, the stockyards of Augie's home town, and the Nazi concentration camps.

Meanwhile in the lifeboat, Basteshaw propounds his theory that man's
greatest problem, boredom, can be overcome in a test tube. His optimism about this project is based on his discovery that "simple cells wish
for immortality whereas the complex organisms get bored" (505). The
trick, then, is to synthesize a creature that is both complex, unlike sterile
simple cells, and immune, unlike man, to boredom. Basteshaw's description of the new breed of man envisioned in his utopia is rousing; Augie
has, however, met a number of people whose schemes seem to provide
simple answers for what is obviously a complex human condition. More
specifically revealing are Augie's remarks on Rousseau-the-Utopianist,
"this sheer horse's ass of a Jean-Jacques who couldn't get on with a single human being, [who] goes away to the woods of Montmorency in order
to think and write about the *best* government or the *best* system of education" (328–29). Augie's pummeling Basteshaw for not helping him into
the lifeboat and Basteshaw's later attack on Augie with an oath are more
dramatically indicative of the great distance man must travel before
reaching even the most modest of utopias. Thus, we learn that Basteshaw-
the-scientist, so positive of their proximity in the lifeboat to the Canary
Islands, "those happy isles" (511), as Augie describes them in an ironic
reference to Basteshaw's utopian dreams, is wildly mistaken as to their
location. Like all of Bellow's would-be-supermen, Basteshaw is lost insofar as he has no idea where he is on the spectrum of possibilities that
run from the less-to-the-more-than-human.

Basteshaw's willingness to tamper with the "secrets of life" (505) is
the outcome of his horror at the insignificance of individual lives—
especially of course his life—in the face of nature's staggering multiplicity. And how, Basteshaw rhetorically asks, does this desire to be "the most
desirable kind of man" (503) start?: "Well, go back to when I was a kid
in the municipal swimming pool. A thousand naked little bastards
screaming, punching, pushing, kicking . . . the shoving multitude bears
down and you're nothing" (503). The flaw, as Augie points out, in trying

to escape this feeling through utopian schemes is the tendency to "overlook the part of nature" (359), which is, of course, precisely the condition Basteshaw has described. Basteshaw's horror at the profligate
fecundity of nature is in a sense the obverse of Thea's and Robey's tendency to confuse quantitative increase with qualitative enhancement.
While Thea sees more meaning in more animals, Bateshaw sees less personal significance in more human beings. They are, of course, equally
mistaken. The antidote for Basteshaw's despair is implicit in one of
Henderson's more perceptive insights. What really counts is not absolute numbers, but how man interprets them:

> Being in point of size precisely halfway between suns and the atoms,
> living among astronomical conceptions, with every thumb and fin-
> gerprint a mystery, we should get used to living with huge numbers.
> In the history of the world many souls have been, are, and will be,
> and with a little reflection this is marvelous and not depressing. Many
> jerks [like Basteshaw] are made gloomy by it, for they think quantity
> buries them alive. That's just crazy. Numbers are very dangerous,
> but the main thing about them is that they humble your pride. And
> that's good. But I used to have great confidence in understanding.
> (137)

Basteshaw reacts to this same enormity by trying to conquer it with
scientific abstraction. In this context, Augie's identification of Basteshaw
with the horse—he is even described as "neighing and plunging" (503)
in the boat—alludes to Swift's famous "rational animals," the
Houyhnhnms. Correlative with the tendency of abstraction to rarefy consciousness are "utopian" schemes that have thinned out the human population. Basteshaw's horror of the "shoving multitude" is an imagistic pun
on the piles of corpses that came out of Nazi attempts to "improve" the
human race by eliminating what they considered the undesirable strains.
Basteshaw's father's nickname in Chicago business circles, "Butcher
Paper" (497), again points to the relationship between Basteshaw's ideal
and the Chicago stockyards and the concentration camps of Eastern
Europe.

The humiliating outcome of Basteshaw's attempt to achieve a sort of
apotheosis through scientific mastery of nature is but one of the many
episodes in *Augie March* that is echoed in *Henderson the Rain King*. The
Arnewi, the first of two tribes that Henderson visits in Africa, are ex-
periencing a plague of frogs that has infested the cows' drinking water.
Henderson, a Connecticut Yankee, destroys the frogs, but in so doing,
also blows the cistern sky-high. When the water (and frog parts) descend,

Henderson becomes, for the first time, and for the first tribe, a rain king. Despite his genuine insight into the "humane side of" (77) the cows' dilemma, his hubris is clearly evident in his casting himself in the role of Messiah; he even sings a bit of Handel's famous oratorio while he plans and executes the demolition. His unusually sensitive insight that "the life of those frogs must have been beautiful, and they fulfilled their ideal" (77) is especially incriminating in view of his equally insensitive desire "to let fall the ultimate violence on these creatures in the cistern" (77). Henderson's murderous assault upon the frogs is representative of a profound, instinctual resentment of life. His own description of the polliwogs "with full tails like giant sperm" (53) is suggestive of the direct attack upon nature that his technological feat represents. Little wonder that Henderson, incessantly in a state of agitation, is envious of the frogs:

> And I stared in [to the cistern] and realized for myself that there was considerable activity just below the surface. Through the webbing of light I first saw polliwogs with huge heads, at all stages of development, with full tails like giant sperm, and with budding feet. And then great powerful frogs, spotted, swimming by with their neckless thick heads and long white legs, the short forepaws expressive of astonishment. And of all the creatures in the vicinity, bar none, it seemed to me they had it best, and I envied them myself. (53)

There are two seemingly contradictory tendencies in this passage which are of equal importance in Bellow's bestiaries. On the one hand, Henderson empathizes with the frogs, however temporarily, by humanizing them, seeing them as expressing "astonishment." It is just as important, on the other hand, to note the way the frogs are different from man: frogs are self-coincident in that they are able to "fulfill their ideal" (77). Without the self-thwarting tendencies of man's unique soul/body division, the frogs simply "are." "Neckless," they never experience any distance between the mind's aspirations and the body's desires.

The implicit allusion to the mind/body split which the frogs do not experience is one of the subtler examples of Bellow's preoccupation with dualism throughout this novel. Perhaps the most obvious of these references to dualism is implicit in the antagonism between Henderson's two African tribes, one a "soft" cow culture, the other a "hard" lion one. As with Thea's bird-reptile construct, there was an original state of unity: the tribes "were once the same and one, single tribe" (141). Of similar thematic significance is Henderson's attempt to, as he puts it, "reach my father by playing on his violin" (30), at the same time that he raises pigs on his Connecticut farm. Henderson's striving to make "the voice of angels . . . come out" (29) of his father's violin is the "more" of the spirit's aspiration; in counterpoint is his sacrilegious pig farm, an attempt to debase himself by nurturing swine flesh. In the same thematic vein, Henderson's father was himself the famous author of "that book on the Albigensians" (10), a sect of Manichean dualists whose heresy flourished in Southern France in the Middle Ages. Henderson's return to Albi and his emphasis on the Continental cathedrals are symbolic of his need to unify his sensibility in much the same manner as the medieval crafts-men managed to integrate the grotesque and the celestial in their tem-ples to the Virgin Mary.

The enormous spectrum of creatures, both imaginary and real, represented in cathedral art is indicative of the most general significance of Bellow's bestiaries: what Herzog calls "the mixed condition of life."[5] The sprawling, heterogeneous mixture of cathedral art is also appropri-ate for describing Bellow's own unique style. The all-inclusive scope of *Augie March* is a result of the startling range of its narrator's concerns: Augie is at once a picaro on the make, and an introspective thinker in search of the meaning of life. *Henderson the Rain King* is similarly defined by the startling multiplicity of its narrator's concerns. Henderson's tor-rential style is but an older, gargantuan version of Augie's comparatively modest, but similarly energetic, voice. Henderson is merely more insis-tent and more explicit about what he calls, in describing his emotions in the lion's den, the "richness of the mixture" (191). Bellow's rich mix-ture of narrative episodes and stylistic modes is everywhere indicative of his belief in the inadequacy of reductive "more or less"/"either-or" descriptions of situations that require "both-and"/"more and more" formulations in order to be appreciated.

The unique melange of incident and style in Bellow's mature novels— by which I mean all his novels except *Seize the Day* (1956) and his first two—also directs us to his essentially comic vision. In this context, the *"animal ridens"* (536) at the finale of *Augie March* announces Bellow's shift from the existential perspective of *Dangling Man* (1944) and *The Victim* to a broader description of the human condition. Appropriate for this new comic willingness to accommodate to things as they are—to nature, in other words—is man the laughing animal, not just another animal, but the animal that laughs. The message of man's immanence in nature is implicit in the mixed condition of the human situation, or as Henderson says, remembering a previous experience with an old broken-down dancing bear, nothing, not even pigs, comes to us as a "tabula rasa." Ironically, if we recall Augie's remark about Thea's disappointment at the failure of their Mexican venture, even man's relationship with pigs is more complicated than Henderson would have it: "wild nature . . . [has]

humanity mixed with it; such as there was in the beasts that embraced Odysseus and his men and wept on them in Circe's yard" (355). The episode with the bear is worth citing at length not only as the culmination of Bellow's novel, but also because it is, significantly enough, the most explicit and moving of his scenes in which human beings and animals share a moment of creaturehood. This recollection is the till-now-forgotten "shot in the arm from animal nature" (212) that originally prompted Henderson's trip to Africa:

> I worked with Smolak [in a circus]. I almost had forgotten this animal, Smolak, an old brown bear . . . . This ditched old creature was almost green with time and down to his last teeth, like the pits of dates. For this shabby animal Hanson had thought up a use. He had been trained to ride a bike, but now he was too old. Now he could feed from a dish with a rabbit; after which, in a cap and bib, he drank from a baby bottle while he stood on his hind legs. But there was one more thing, and this was where I came in . . . . Smolak and I rode on a roller coaster together before large crowds. This poor broken ruined creature and I, alone, took the high rides twice a day. And while we climbed and dipped and swooped and swerved and rose again higher than the Ferris wheels and fell, we held on to each other. By a common bond of despair we embraced, cheek to cheek, as all support seemed to leave us and we started down the perpendicular drop . . . . I said to Hanson, as I recall, "We're two of a kind. Smolak was cast off and I am Ishmael, too . . . ." So if corporeal things are an image of the spiritual and visible objects are renderings on invisible ones, and if Smolak and I were outcasts together, two humorists before the crowd, but brothers in our souls—I enbeared by him, and he probably humanized by me—I didn't come to the pigs as a tabula rasa . . . . Once more. Whatever gains I ever made were always due to love and nothing else . . . . He held me in his arms and gave me comfort. And the great thing is that he didn't blame me. He had seen too much of life, and somewhere in his huge head he had worked it out that for creatures there is nothing that ever runs unmingled. (283–84)

The relationship between this sort of epiphany and Bellow's comedy is perhaps best illustrated by seeing it in the context of his attitude toward tragedy. In *Herzog* Bellow refers to *amor fati*, the essential element in Nietzsche's writings on tragedy. According to Herzog, the problem with transcendence through *amor fati* is that people don't often survive long enough to experience the luxury of such heady emotions: "No survival. No *amor fati*" (389). Even more debunking is Henderson's interpretation of eternal recurrence, the corollary of *amor fati*. In Henderson's

estimation, eternal recurrence is apparent, less in Nietzsche's description of the *Ubermensch*'s dramatic defiance of an absurd cosmos than in
the depressing round of man's pathetic tendency to repeat himself because of his fear of death:

> No, graves are not deep but insignificant, a mere few feet from the
> surface and not far from fearing and desiring. *More or less* the same
> fear, *more or less* the same desire for thousands of generations. Child,
> father, father, child doing the same. Fear the same. Desire the same.
> Upon the crust, beneath the crust, again and again and again. Well,
> Henderson, what are the generations for, please explain to me? Only
> to repeat fear and desire without a change? This cannot be what the
> thing is for, over and over and over. Any good man will try to break
> the cycle. There is no issue from that cycle for a man who does not
> take things into his hands. (249, emphasis mine)

"More or less" is not here indicative of transcendence through the degradation of "less" to the level of "more," but of the "more or less" equiva-
lence of the succeeding generations of mediocrity.

We have seen Augie in Mexico and Henderson in the lion's den try
to break the cycle of eternal recurrence by identifying with nature's
nobler, more courageous beasts. This is the attitude that would go, in
effect, through nature to transcend the human condition. The verdict
of both books is that this endeavor, however admirable its intent, inevitably fails. The last word is clearly reserved for humbler creatures, for the
animal ridens, the humorist, not the soaring tragedian, before the carnival
crowds. Death becomes in this context, not something which man can
transcend through the defiance of *amor fati,* but rather a grim fact of
life most squarely faced, as it happens, in the arms of another creature.
This humble realization is the meaning of the final epiphany of *Henderson
the Rain King* when two creatures mingle together—enbeared and
humanized—by sharing a moment of love as they plunge together down
the roller coaster toward ineluctable death.[6]

Notes

1. Saul Bellow, *The Victim* (Harmondsworth: Penguin, 1947), 112–13.
2. Saul Bellow, *Henderson the Rain King* (Greenwich, Conn.: Fawcett Crest, 1958),
   212. Subsequent quotations are from this edition.
3. Saul Bellow, *The Adventures of Augie March* (New York: Viking, 1949), 358. Subsequent quotations are from this edition.
4. Walter Kaufmann, ed., *The Portable Nietzsche* (New York: Viking, 1954), 121.
5. Saul Bellow, *Herzog* (Greenwich, Conn.: Fawcett Crest, 1961), 166.
6. The circus setting of Henderson's and Smolak's art recalls the section on the

tightrope walker in *Zarathustra*. As always in *Augie March* and *Henderson,* the allusion to Nietzsche establishes Bellow's antithetical position. Nietzsche's tightrope walker's performance is a gratuitous flirtation with death. Augie and Smolak are, on the other hand, merely two creatures down on their luck.

Henderson the Rain King: A Parodic Exposé of the Modern Novel

Gloria L. Cronin

Responses of postwar novelists to the monumental achievements of the moderns have been uniformly troubled. Critic Nathan A. Scott speaks of their various forms of philosophical recoil—into the ivory tower, into sensibility, into disgust, into nightmare, or into tragic catharsis.[1] The problem for the contemporary novelist has been and is still the formidable task of deciding what fiction might yet say or be after the modern period of radical experimentation ended with the virtual rejection of language and literature itself. Feeling this strain, the graduate student hero of a Richard Chase dialogue speaks for the whole postmodern generation of literati when he comments, in awe and puzzlement, that "the greatest writers of the first half of the twentieth century lived in a high, tense world of strenuous and difficult metaphysics, moral doctrine, political ideology, and religious feeling."[2] Saul Bellow is perhaps the foremost among a handful of postwar novelists to have successfully thrown over the preoccupation of the moderns with cultural and religious dissolution, metaphysical loneliness, romantic agony, and estrangement. And he has been the foremost enemy of those derivative postwar novelists who, unable or unwilling to question the existentialist foundations of the modernist orthodoxy they inherited, have found a permanent home in the wasteland or its neighboring ghettos. Likewise, he has condemned the other popular literary alternatives to modernism—the clever but shallow comic celebration of absurdism, the naiveté of a shaky, hastily refurbished neohumanism, or the pseudoliterary muckraking naturalism of yet another group.

Instead he has sought to steer a moderate course between the excesses of disappointed idealism and nihilistic rage characteristic of much modern literature. Through the antiseptic and corrective device of

First printed in *Arizona Quarterly* 39, no. 3 (Autumn 1983): 266–276.

191

parody, he has held up for our scrutiny the false intellectual assumptions behind modernist ideologies concerning death, absurdity, mass society, estrangement, and stoicism, while at the same time he has turned upside down the reasoning of the wasteland ideologists, the Lawrentian primitivists, the Freudian psychoanalysts, the Camus stoics, and the logical positivists. Hopefully, *Henderson the Rain King* has helped liberate postwar fiction from the self-pity of modernism as successfully as Thomas Love Peacock's *Nightmare Abbey* helped liberate late nineteenth-century realistic fiction from the pathological excesses of Gothic horror and romance.

Bellow's critical stance in this novel was formulated in a series of seminal critical essays on modernism, many of which were developed before and during the writing of the novel. Three basic ideas emerge from these essays. First, there is his oft-repeated lament that thanks to Darwin and his theories of obsolescence, the modern movement to obliterate the "unity" of the nineteenth-century self was launched. The result of such thinking, says Bellow, is the creation in modern literature of a creature whose outlines are uncertain, and whose sense of self is all but destroyed.[3] Such a creature is haunted by reductive Freudian mythology concerning his nature and convinced that his likelihood of survival in mass society is very slender. Estranged from the corrective experience of everyday life, this underworld quester becomes "precious" in his responses and all but drowns in cultural self-pity as he attempts to flee the contaminated sewer of Western culture.

Second, there is his angry denunciation of those postwar novelists who ape the nihilism of the moderns, fail to question the accuracy of this *Weltanschauung* in the postwar world, and continue to write increasingly derivative and inartistic works.[4]

Third is the observation that the postwar novelists have done little to rescue literature from the unresolved modernist dichotomy which derived from the warring impulses of a defeated romantic idealism and a subsequent nihilistic rage, an impasse from which, he claims, it has barely moved in forty years.[5]

Henderson the Rain King, though a parody, is Bellow's serious attempt to restore faith in the self and existence by rending laughable and passé the absurdities of absurdism, the banalities of historicist thinking, and the ignominy of postmodern sewer searching. By satirizing the foolish excesses which have produced both rampant individualism and excessive disappointment with "self" and "civilization," Bellow presents Eugene Henderson, a burlesque of the absurd, victimized artist-hero. Violinist and pig farmer Henderson is a middle-aged, menopausal social outcast. A direct parody of the Hemingway stoic or narcissist, he is a metaphysically earnest, introspective, solipsistic, bumbling egocentric. Alienated from his wife, family, and society, Henderson has a neurotic preoccupation with death and a comical self-hatred. Believing with his prototypes that "there is a curse on this land,"[6] he laments his gross physical bulk, his horselike nose, his dirty underwear, and his precious bridgework with a self-devotion that is adolescent in its proportions. He is, in this respect, Bellow's explanation of what happened to the hero, or the self, when a generation of modern writers reacted with disappointment to the failed promises of Rousseauistic romanticism. With his initials E. H., his drinking, his .357 magnum rifle, private firing range, participation in a foreign war, and his fascination with African safaris, Henderson is more accurately a parody of the Hemingway hero, Bellow's example par excellence of the egocentric and ridiculous modern hero.

Such intense egomania on the part of this late modern hero receives particular exposure in the opening lines of the novel, which parody Italo Svevo and Proust: "My parents, my wives, my girls, my children, my farm, my animals, my habits, ... my prejudices ... " (3), Henderson cries out.[7] He is a parody of the Hemingway hero, who, says Bellow, "tests and examines himself ... [with] desperate self-devotion." Such a hero, Bellow accuses, is "isolated, self-absorbed and effortful" in his attempts to escape the dominance of mind.[8]

Also parodied is Henderson's Camus-like program of stoicism in face of the absurd. His violent attempts at self-flagellation provide much comedy as he describes himself stripped naked, shaved bald, and abandoned to the incoming American troops on the waterfront at Salerno. Then there is a Robert Jordan-like attempt at holding up the damaged bridge until the engineers' corps arrives. This, added to his monumental attempt to rack up five thousand sets of tennis in one season or his sleeping in sub-zero weather in his self-made igloo, makes for a humorous exposé of existentialist stoicism typical of the modern novel of the 1930s and 1940s.

But more laughable still is Henderson's capacity for farcical self-dramatization. With a typically modern metaphysical grandiosity and philosophical self-pity, Henderson introduces himself to Itelo with the words: "Who—who was I? ... A brutal and violent man driven into the world. A man who has fled his own country, settled by his forefathers" (76). The tone becomes even more melodramatic after the hilarious destruction of the Arnewi frog pond. Prostrating himself before Romilayu with a speech which is delightfully ridiculous, Henderson cries out: "Stab me .... Stab, I say ... don't forgive me. I couldn't stand it. I'd rather be dead" (109). The origin of his stance and that of the modern quester is slyly suggested by Bellow when, after the twin debacles of the burning bush and the frog pond, Henderson declares his desire to be-smear himself with sackcloth and ashes like an Old Testament prophet or in the style of John the Baptist cast himself out into the desert to live on locusts. Such exquisite romantic agony so prevalent in the modern novel is irresistible to a parodist like Bellow.

But perhaps of more serious note than this aspect of the modern novel is Bellow's concern over what he considers to be its neurotic existen-tialist preoccupation with death. As Henderson goes through a progres-sively intense series of experiences with death, Bellow discloses the sad failure of the existential hero to react with dignity and composure in the face of death. When his brother dies, Henderson runs away from home and casts himself into the arms of Smolak, a moth-eaten old cir-cus bear, reminiscent of a giant and much-worn child's toy. In addition, we find him at 56 playing violin pieces dedicated to his dead parents as he attempts to transcend the finality of death and the grave through the intensity of art. His total failure to react maturely to death is demon-strated when, after shouting his spinster housekeeper to death one morn-ing, he pins a note "DO NOT DISTURB" on her and runs away to Africa. Once there, however, he is finally forced to confront death in a variety of ways. There is the constant reminder of death in all the skulls hang-ing within the Wariri village. Then there is Henderson's symbolic ex-perience of toting the dead Sungo on his back. But above all is his death therapy with Atti the lioness in the rank, terrifying lion's den beneath the royal palace. Through these hilarious therapy sessions comes Bellow's ultimate comic comment on the castrating effect of the modernist preoc-cupation with death. Recall the marvelous picture of Henderson, geni-tals shriveled in fright, loping around the pungent-smelling dungeon with Atti the lioness lapping him frequently from behind and continuing her terrifying investigative sniffing. The existentialist hero, Bellow is saying, seems ill-equipped by his inadequate philosophy to handle the phenome-non of death and is therefore rendered impotent to the full potentiali-ties of life.

Yet Henderson is more than just a parody on the modern hero. Henderson is a parody of the qualities of solipsism, morbidity, self-abasement, and self-aggrandizement wherever they appear in literature. Within Henderson are subsumed all the great questing heroes of Western literature: Moses, whose burning bush miracle Henderson can't quite duplicate; Daniel, who flirted even more heroically with lions; John the Baptist, who also had a romantic predilection for desert places; Atlas, who supported an entire globe, not just a mere bridge; Don Quixote, whose windmills remind us of Henderson's quest for transcendence; Hemingway, who faced lions and death in Africa; Oedipus, who was rejected by his father and expelled from society; Tristram Shandy, the egocentrist who lost himself in flashbacks and nose problems; and, finally Ahab, the ultimate existentialist, who was also hypnotized by fear of death.

And while he is exposing the absurdities of the "absurd" hero, Bellow also parodies the major stylistic clichés of the modern novel. The book is in fact a Joycean-type museum of all the artillery pieces of modern literature—consider its reliance on anthropological materials like the ancient fertility rituals lifted straight out of Eliot's favorite source, Jesse L. Weston; dense patterns of symbol and allusion; heavy-handed wasteland imagery; Freudian personality theory; the ironic hero-flight from civilization; and the intermingling of underworld nightmare and surface realism.

Bellow's disapproval of the intense allusiveness, re-created mythologies, and mazelike symbolism of the modern novel is also manifest in *Henderson the Rain King*. In "Deep Readers of the World, Beware!" published the same year as the novel, he complains that "the best novelists and poets of the century" educated a whole generation of teachers and students to turn all butterflies into symbols of metamorphosis and all references to bread into sacrament symbols, until the process of "culture-idolatory, sophistication and snobbery" caused modern reader and writer alike to elevate meaning above feeling.[9] In *Henderson*, Bellow parodies this kind of intellectual sophistication and allusiveness in delightful ways. Mimicking the pretentiousness of Eliot and Joyce, who tried to combine in individual works the whole Western literary heritage, he throws in large doses of archetypal symbology borrowed right out of Fraser, misquotes liberally from the Bible, refers to Jung, Freud, Sartre, and Wordsworth, offers tidbits from obscure quack psychologists, and makes numerous references to Whitman and William James. The "deep reader" might indeed beware of taking all of these red herrings seriously.

Even Bellow's use of the journey "to the heart of darkness" and its African setting is an attempt at mocking the inward psychic journeys of a generation of modern questers. But instead of the deadly earnestness of the quests in earlier works we get Henderson's comic bungling ironically couched in imagery and symbol drawn straight from Eliot and Joyce's favorite sources. Bellow even sifted the thesis written by his anthropology teacher, the famous ethnologist Melville J. Herskovits, in order to construct the myth of the dying king, and the Wariri ceremonies and customs.[10]

But most obvious is his deliberate parody of the Fisher King-Grail legend. Fusing this in typical modernist fashion with the old Grail legend and the underworld journey, Bellow nevertheless effects a neat anti-modernist reversal of the journey. Henderson emerges renewed in body and spirit rather than mutilated and impotent like Eliot's Fisher King, or consumed by savagery like Conrad's Mr. Kurtz. Using the main elements of the original myth, Bellow produces a restored version of it. Henderson is the buffoonish American Purple Heart recipient rather than the Holy Grail knight. Instead of the injunction to ask all he meets the whereabouts of the Holy Grail, this knight is impelled to ask a fat black African woman the meaning of life. In place of the Chapel Perilous where the Grail knight meets the temptress, Henderson ends up in a ramshackle native hut where he is awakened in the middle of the night by a giggling, fat black woman bringing the bride price. As for the encounter with the dead brother knight, Henderson has to carry the dead body of the previous Sungo on his back.

Also parodied is the preoccupation of the late modern novel with Freudian personality theory. A deliberately implanted set of clues identifies Henderson in Freudian terms as an oral dependent or passive anal type personality, an observation amply developed by a previous critic.[11] Yet not identified by the critic is the comic satiric intent of such Freudian psychological concepts. Bellow has made many attempts at overthrowing the reductive mythology of Freudianism in previous novels and in a full-length play entirely devoted to the topic.[12] Therefore it is not surprising to find this kind of satirical thrust in *Henderson*.

Associated with his attack on modern psychology is a clever and less obvious attack on naturalistic sociology with its theories of anomie, alienation, and mass society. Henderson discovers to his amazement that far from being daunting and alienating, sheer numbers of individuals do in fact testify to the infinite variety and mystery of the universe. He decides "we ... should be more accepting of multitudes than we are.... This is marvelous, not depressing" (161–62). And instead of Henderson degenerating to the level of his pigs they, being "career animals" (56), respond most readily to human models for transcendence, Bellow's clever reminder of the faulty logic behind naturalistic philosophy of nature of the self.

But more important than this rattling of the foundations of modern social sciences is Bellow's attack on the Rousseauistic aggrandizement of the powers of the individual, the extremist romantic impulse which Bellow believes to lie behind much of the disappointment and anger in the modern novel. Representing this mode of thought is Dahfu, the African philosopher whom Bellow intends to be a parody on the American quack transcendentalist Wilhelm Reich. Dahfu, like Reich, preaches to Henderson of the absolute ability of the human imagination to transform man and the world. Even the transcendentally inclined Henderson spots the danger of this extremist philosophy. He concludes of Dahfu, "When I say that he lost his head, what I mean is not that his judgment abandoned him but that his enthusiasms and visions swept him far out" (235). Bellow, however, does not let Henderson off so lightly. He depicts him as the comic victim of a mystic vision, or at least a farcical version thereof. Initially swept away by Dahfu's philosophy, Henderson admits, "I was blazing with . . . the loftiness of our conversation and I saw things not double or triple merely, but in countless outlines of wavering color, gold, red, green, umber, and so on, all flowering concentrically around each object. Sometimes Dahfu seemed to be three times his size, with the spectrum around him" (215). So much for unalloyed transcendentalism and its consequences for the modern novel and its hero.

However, Bellow's attempt at parody of the worst excesses of the modern novel and its hero is not the act of a light-minded humorist. If he debunks the excesses of modernist self-pity and the stylistic formulas of the modern novel, it is in order to restore to the Anglo-American novel a measure of health, sanity, and truth about human existence. Though the stylistic formulas and metaphysical assumptions of the modern novel are made fun of, the viewpoints are nevertheless retained and refurbished for further use by the surgery of Bellow's moderating and analytical intelligence. It is not the anthropological search through primitive cultures for truths lost to Western civilization that Bellow deplores, only the naive assumption that truth is to be found by aping the sexual mores and lifestyle of a primitive people. And neither does he dismiss the ancient Grail legend. Rather, he assumes the truthfulness of its original bright promise of apotheosis for the questing knight by depicting Henderson dancing for joy against the arctic wastes of the polar ice cap with the Persian orphan boy (symbol perhaps of his restored soul) clasped in his arms. In other words, the parody in *Henderson the Rain King* functions to restore moderation and good sense to the twentieth-century novel which Bellow has diagnosed as having lost its ability to assess truthfully the possibilities of life. And if he appears to be making fun of Dahfu and Reich with their unbounded transcendentalist belief in the power of the imagination to transform man and the universe, it is because he believes that irresponsible unbounded romantic individualism lies at the heart of the pain and disappointment in life itself which scar modern literature.

Beneath all the mockery and intellectual sifting, Bellow steadily develops the story of a wounded sensibility healed and restored to everyday life, of a world purged of octopuslike cosmic coldness and reinvested with calm stars, simplicity, freshness, and mystery. All of Henderson's observations of nature assure him of beauty, design, and grandeur of the universe. Beneath the evidences of death, despair, sterility, pestilence, and madness in the novel lies that ancient resurrection myth, the Grail legend, unearthed by Bellow from the junkpile of wasteland ideology and polished anew through the burnishing away of nihilistic despair. With lyrical tenderness and high seriousness, Bellow attempts to resolve the central dichotomy of the modern novel by having his hero move from personal chaos to spiritual reintegration, from Africa to the USA, from ignorance to knowledge, from absurdism to belief. Against the Hobbesian fear that life might only be a "sick and hasty ride, helpless through a dream into oblivion," Henderson offers his prayer to an unknown God: "Oh, you . . . . Something . . . you Something because of whom there is not Nothing. Help me to do thy will . . . . Oh, Thou who tookest me from pigs, let me not be killed over lions. And forgive my crimes and non-sense and let me return to Lily and the kids" (253). It is the prayer of a reformed modern hero, sobered by his previous excesses and confirmed in his hard-won belief in the possibilities of human existence.

Notes

1. Nathan A. Scott, Jr., *The Broken Center: Studies in the Theological Horizon of Modern Literature* (New Haven: Yale University Press, 1966).
2. Richard Chase, *The Democratic Vista: A Dialogue on Life and Letters in Contemporary America* (Garden City, N.Y.: Doubleday and Company, Inc., 1958), 16.
3. Saul Bellow, "Distractions of a Fiction Writer," in *The Living Novel: A Symposium,* ed. Granville Hicks (New York: The Macmillan Company, 1957), 18–19. See also Bellow's "Literature" in *The Great Ideas Today 1963,* ed. Robert M. Hutchins and Mortimer J. Adler (Chicago: Encyclopedia Britannica, Inc., 1963), 135–79, and his "The Sealed Treasure," *Times Literary Supplement,* 3, (1 July 1960): 414.
4. Saul Bellow, "Cloister Culture," in *Page 2: The Best of "Speaking of Books"* from the *New York Times Book Review,* ed. Francis Brown (New York: Holt, Rinehart and Winston, 1969), 3–9.
5. Saul Bellow, "Some Notes on Recent American Fiction," *Encounter* 21, no. 5 (November 1963): 22–29.
6. Saul Bellow, *Henderson the Rain King* (New York: The Viking Press, 1959), 38. Further quotations are from this edition and are cited parenthetically in the text.
7. Bellow discusses Svevo's *The Confessions of Zeno* in his "Literature," in *The Great Ideas Today 1963,* 164.
8. Saul Bellow, "Hemingway and the Image of Man," *Partisan Review* 20 (1953): 338–42.
9. Saul Bellow, "Deep Readers of the World, Beware!" *New York Times Book Review,* 15 February 1959, 1.
10. Melville J. Herskovits, *The Cattle Complex in East Africa* (Menasha, Wisc., 1926). This book reprints Herskovits's doctoral thesis (Columbia University), which

first appeared in *American Anthropologist,* n.s. 28 (1926): 230–72; 361–88; 494–528; 633–64.

11. Judith Moss, "The Body as Symbol in Saul Bellow's *Henderson the Rain King,*" *Literature and Psychology* 20 (1970): 51–61.

12. Much has been written on the influence of Wilhelm Reich on Saul Bellow, but few other critics have indicated just what Bellow's particular interest in Reich was. Eusebio L. Rodrigues's essay "Reichianism in *Henderson the Rain King,*' " *Criticism* 15 (1973): 212–33, provides the best background information.

White Man's Black Man: Three Views

Mariann Russell

In 1959 Rabbit Angstrom, hero of Updike's *Rabbit Run*, lived in a small Pennsylvania town which was almost empty of "black folk." The only black given more than cursory attention was a waitress in a bar that Rabbit visited. She was of no importance to the plot of the novel; she represented merely a narrative detail. Ten years later in the sequel to *Rabbit Run*, Rabbit's small town is virtually alive with blacks: they ride on the bus, they appear on the streets, they work in the print shop where Rabbit and his father work, and one of them is a major figure in the plot. Either the town has suffered a mass migration up North, or there has been a change in Rabbit's consciousness, or there has been a change in the imaginative concern of Rabbit's creator.

Saul Bellow in *Mr. Sammler's Planet* (1969), John Updike in *Rabbit Redux* (1971), and Bernard Malamud in *The Tenants* (1971) have all included blacks in their latest novels. These novelists, dealing primarily with the developing consciousness of their protagonists, also treat the public world of the sixties and seventies. One of the elements of that American scene was a new intrusion of blacks upon the white consciousness. What is proposed here is to examine the roles played by Northern urban blacks appearing in these recent novels in order to see what the white authors have made of their black characters.

It will be seen that these blacks are less than fully imagined characters who play the role of the "other." They embody anarchic elements appearing in society as a whole and within the personalities of the white protagonists. These elements, felt to be threatening and destructive, are imagined as alien or "other." The black man becomes a convenient metaphor for the disturbing elements in white society and is, in the last

First printed in *College Language Association Journal* 17 (1973): 93–100.

201

analysis, not an image of black culture, but a mirror image of the prevailing white culture.

Mr. Sammler's Planet opens with the protagonist's involvement with a
black character, a pickpocket whom he observes working on the Broadway bus. What can be said about the black as he impinges on Sammler's
consciousness? First of all, the physical description indicates that he is
black, muscular, and splendidly dressed. His dark glasses (Chistian Dior
design?), tab collar, cherry silk necktie, camel's hair coat, and French perfume mark the pickpocket as a New York City mod barbarian. Sammler
refers to him as some "large beast," "puma-like," and later posits a "certain majesty" to this representative of "the barbarous world of color"[1]
that lurks beneath New York's "hypercivilized" exterior. Secondly, the
black is a thief, a criminal. As observed by Sammler, he makes his living
through preying on the careless and the weak. Thirdly, this black is sexually aggressive. In a scene that is referred to again and again, the black's
aggressiveness, muscularity, and criminality are fixed in an act of sexual display, imaging what Sammler later calls "sexual niggerhood."[2]

Thus far, this splendidly dressed, new barbarian seems very like a
stereotype of the black as primitive. Dressed like a dandy, a thief who
expresses himself through sexual display rather than through words, he
seems to become in Sammler's consciousness an analogy for the forces
which the old man in his civilized, Polish-Oxonian way is trying, however
feebly, to combat. It would seem that the Negro pickpocket, placed at
the beginning of the novel, becomes an image of the forces at work in
the book. Shula is a thief like this criminal; Angela is flamboyantly sexual like this exposer; Wallace, like the black, is completely undisciplined;
and, like the stylishly dressed pickpocket, the modishly dressed Eisen
has a kind of innocent savagery. Only one of these connections is made
explicit by Sammler, but the old man's consciousness returns to the thief
like a tongue searching for a missing tooth. Sammler's comparison of
his daughter Shula's theft of a manuscript to the thief's activities may
seem somewhat strained (the theft of a manuscript by an eccentric daughter does not usually invite comparison with a sinister black pickpocket),
but it indicates what the pickpocket becomes in the mind of Sammler.
He becomes an analogy for those "dark" forces of limitlessness, lawlessness, madness, and chaos that threaten to overcome the discipline and
civility to which Sammler pays hard won tribute.

Sammler himself when talking about these forces links them to "sexual niggerhood" (Bellow, 149), the "black side of life" (149), "dark romanticism" (34), and "the healing power of black" (34). "Millions of civilized
people wanted oceanic, boundless, primitive, neckfree nobility . . . " (149).

Quite obviously, on this level the black is an analogy for threatening disorder. Reviewers in describing the confrontation between Sammler and the pickpocket do not fail to point this out. The thief represents the "limitless" to one reviewer, "chaos and dark night" and "the imperious ego" identified with "sex and crime" to another, "raw lawless primordial threat" to another, and "lawlessness, sexual potency, self-delight" to still another.[3]

However, Bellow is far from simplistic in his treatment of the conflict between typical black primitive and civilized white protagonist. The black exercises a kind of fascination for the Jewish survivor of wartime horror. Sammler admits that he had sought occasions to ride the bus in order to view the thief at work. Why the attraction? It is somehow obscurely linked to the motive that had led the elderly Sammler to cover the Six-Day War as a correspondent. And, still more obscurely, it is linked to that motive that had led the wartime partisan Sammler to kill—with joy. In mentally returning again and again to the pickpocket, Sammler is dealing not only with a practical dilemma about riding the bus or the subway, not only with a representative of the "masquerade" of mythomania that he finds enacted on New York's upper West Side, but also with his own reaction to the "madness" represented by the pickpocket.

It is significant that the black is finally defeated by another survivor, Eisen, who beats the black unmercifully with homemade art objects. The grotesquerie of the scene does not obscure the fact that the primitive violence of the thief is overcome only by the mindless violence of the survivor. The pickpocket is no match for this product of European civilization. The undercurrent that had first attracted Sammler to the pickpocket's activities has surfaced in Eisen's battering the pickpocket with Jewish medallions. The civilized Mr. Sammler, carrying within himself the seeds of counterviolence, unwittingly leads the pickpocket to a retribution more savage than his own activities. The black pickpocket can be seen as the manipulation of one set of stereotypical feelings, but, more meaningfully, he represents one aspect of Mr. Sammler's humanity.

While Saul Bellow's black remains chiefly an image, John Updike's black is a compound of novelistic role playing and the kind of surface verisimilitude for which Updike is justly praised. In earlier sections of the book, Updike creates the texture of white-black relations (from the white perspective) through his protagonist's comments about blacks, the encounter with the black on the job, and the scene in the black bar. He shows the same kind of verisimilitude in portraying his chief black character, Skeeter. The details of Skeeter's language and his physical characteristics (5′ 6″, 125 pounds, large Afro, goatee, and glasses) are presented with those novelistic brush strokes that readily suggest a type. Skeeter's character is a mix of black types familiar from newspaper and television images. He is a sexist black Vietnam veteran, pusher, nationalist, and preacher of doom.

However, Skeeter's character does not hold to a center. This small-time pusher, projected into the role of a major character, quickly assumes almost fantastic qualities, at least partly because of the role he is asked to play. "He is poison, he is murder, he is black!"[4] Skeeter proclaims himself to be a black Jesus looking calmly beyond impending destruction to his triumphant reign. He describes his God: "Chaos is His holy face." (Updike, 291). Plainly irrational ("religious-crazy"), this black angel of destruction and death destroys the messenger of love, Jill, first with dope and then inadvertently through fire as white middle-class neighbors react to the black-white sexual drama being enacted before them by burning both house and girl.

A deep and corrosive hatred of whites would be an obvious explanation of Skeeter's lifestyle and such actions as his taunting of Rabbit before his child and his rape of Jill while Frederick Douglass's autobiography is being read aloud. Updike alludes to such hatred ("There seems to be not only a history but theology behind his anger" [122]), but nowhere adequately explores it. Although less than a whole character, Skeeter remains to play the role Updike has assigned to him: to be quite literally a black messiah to the book's protagonist, Rabbit Angstrom.

Rabbit's story is figured by the controlling image of the lunar voyage. Rabbit (Harry), a conservative suburbanite is jerked out of his own dullness, rages, and frustration by his wife's leaving him for another man. Harry ventures out in a voyage into the other worlds of flower children and blacks, and finally returns safely to his planet, his once-strayed wife. The nature of Rabbit's venture into space is strangely passive. Just as Jill, the flower child in the soiled white dress, happens into Rabbit's life and introduces him to the alternative culture of youth, Skeeter happens into Rabbit's life and introduces him to the alternative culture of blacks. In both cases, the introduction leads to mere acquaintanceships with these cultures.

Yet, somehow, a change is effected. Rabbit learns to smoke pot and watch black-white sex relations. He is somehow liberated, "not so up-tight." Skeeter even calls him a "nigger," and Rabbit Angstrom has become a "white-nigger" of sorts. Skeeter and Rabbit share Jill's body. When he expresses hatred of his upper-class Penn Park neighbors, Harry comes near to sharing Skeeter's feelings. This middle-class Pennsylvanian winds up running "some kind of commune" where sex, drugs, and seminars on Afro-American history are the order of the night. Peter Rabbit becomes B'rer Rabbit before this trip to other worlds is cut short by the death of Jill.

Thus, in Skeeter, Rabbit finds his other self, the living embodiment of the disturbing elements in his public and private life. Vietnam, student protest, and ghetto riots arouse Rabbit's hatred and resentment. In confronting Skeeter, Rabbit is to some extent confronting the supposedly alien forces in his public world: "Rot and black madness creeping in" (167). Furthermore, Rabbit's hatred and resentment have their origins in his inner world. Here Skeeter acts as a kind of exorcist as he somehow helps to rid Rabbit of hatred and fear by personifying them. Through confrontation with this ill-defined black hatred and rage, Rabbit's own rage and frustration are partly healed. Again, in this novel, the black character becomes the reflex of the emotion of the white protagonist.

In *The Tenants* the black-white confrontation has no optimistic outcome. This novel, like the other two, involves a black-white confrontation in which the white character embodies the more "civilized" qualities while the black character embodies anti-social tendencies. There is, on the one hand, Harry Lesser, author of one good and one bad novel, who is trying to finish his current ten-year-old novel, "The Promised End." In the same decaying tenement is the black artist, Willie Spearmint, working on his first novel, variously entitled "A Nigger Ain't Shit," "Missing Life," and "Black Writer." Lesser's novel is about "'love, I guess'" and represents his attempt to achieve love by defining it in a novel. Willie's novel, containing autobiographical material and scenes from black life, is really about the searing effects of hatred, violence, and oppression ("Five stories, five deaths . . . ").[5] Willie's novel is all corrosive substance with little or no form. Lesser's novel, with its formalistic device of novel writing within the novel, lacks a successful conclusion because Lesser knows nothing about love in real life.

As the novels contrast, so do the authors. Willie is "crude, coarse, insulting—one whose dedication to the Black revolution is confused by his association with his white mistress."[6] Willie, essentially a man of violence, has to work out the conflict between writing and revolution. Lesser, a once-successful author, is essentially nonviolent and apolitical, and completely dedicated to his writing.

But there is more than simple confrontation here. There is again the white's attraction to the black who represents the outlawed life. The black writer becomes a kind of alter ego to Lesser. Irene remarks, "You're both alike'" (Malamud, 140), when commenting on the two authors' putting writing before love. There is the recurring image of the white novelist, trying to forge and reforge his book in the solitude of his own apartment, while he knows that in the same building working at a similar task is the black "other." The two characters come to a kind of substitution of lifestyles as Willie adopts Lesser's more stringent routine and Lesser takes over Willie's girlfriend. Finally, after Willie burns Lesser's manuscript, the essentially non-violent Lesser explodes into violence and destroys Willie's typewriter ("It bled black ink," 227), as each writer tries to destroy the inner life of the other. Willie has caused Lesser to find seeds of violence within himself.

The presence of the black alter ego in the novel does not lead to the kind of salvific ending that can be read into *Rabbit Redux*. The last scene shows what the confrontation of black and white has unleashed. In a jungle setting the two authors cut at each other, Lesser striking at Willie's head and Willie castrating Lesser. Behind the obvious symbolism lies the simple conclusion Malamud states: the mutual exchange is one of anguish as each is made to feel the other's pain. Substitution and the presence of the alter ego do not bring healing but rather a plunge into inner depths. Willie is confirmed in hatred; Lesser is confirmed in lovelessness.

Malamud has attempted to make of his black-white confrontation something more than another stab at presenting the topical theme of black-in-white-culture-of-the-sixties. Malamud may see *himself* as moving beyond stereotype "to make black more than color or culture and outrage larger than protest or ideology" (67). He is surely attempting to show the struggle of two characters for a salvation which each could give the other. *"Hab rachmones,"* but the compassion necessary to complete the inner life of each character is seen chiefly through its absence in the failed relationship of Willie and Harry. Ultimately, the story contains neither exploration nor transcendence of the Jewish-black hostility Malamud presents.

So, Willie remains the "other." His character, like his name, depends on the role he must play in the novel. The black is never more than Lesser's alter-ego. Willie's speech, dress, drug-taking, and sex life form the attraction of a lifestyle that is a mask for qualities that the white protagonist discovers within himself.

There is a curiously unreal quality about these three black characters. Wearing mod clothes, or taking drugs, or using street dialect, each one intrudes into the lives of the white characters. Apparently colorful, the blacks are really shadows projected by the protagonists as the black figures tend to become analogues for the protagonists' states of feeling. However interesting these authors' characterizations may be, they do not go beyond the portrayal of the black man as the "other."

Notes

1. Saul Bellow, *Mr. Sammler's Planet* (Greenwich, Conn.: Fawcett Publications, Inc., 1970), 8. Further references are in the text.
2. An adequate discussion of the treatment of sexuality and blackness in these novels would require a separate article. Here the matter is subsumed in the general discussion.
3. The reviewers in the order named are Keith Opdahl, "Bellow's Planet," *Commonweal* 91 (13 February 1970): 535; Charles Thomas Samuels, "Bellow on Modernism," *The New Republic* 162 (7 February 1970): 28; Beverly Gross, "Dark Side of the Moon," *The Nation* 210 (9 February 1970); Irwin Stock, "Man in Culture," *Commentary* 49 (May 1970): 92.
4. John Updike, *Rabbit Redux* (New York: Alfred A. Knopf, 1971), 208. Further references in the text.
5. Bernard Malamud, *The Tenants* (New York: Farrar, Straus and Giroux, 1971), 66. Further references in the text
6. Addison Gayle, Jr., "Controlling Black Images," *New York Amsterdam News*, 1 January 1972, D5, discusses the role of the black messiah in *The Tenants* and *Rabbit Redux:* "Like Willie Spearmint, Skeeter is the messiah of sin and degeneracy, destined to save America by injecting into her veins, not black pride, black awareness, or black beauty, but jazz, sex, and heroin" (D5).

The World as Will and Idea:
A Comparative Study of *An American Dream* and *Mr. Sammler's Planet*

Susan Glickman

In his study *Four Postwar American Novelists*, Frank D. McConnell remarks that Saul Bellow's literary preeminence was consolidated in the fifties, only to be challenged in the sixties by writers more radical, both in sentiment and style, than himself. Bellow seemed to have created a normative voice and vision against which others could measure themselves and against which they rebelled. McConnell suggests that

> *Mr. Sammler's Planet* is Bellow's own recognition and ironic statement upon this emeritus status. Artur Sammler, his septuagenarian European hero living through the manic sixties in the heart of New York City, is unmistakably a vision of his own fictive career, ignored or (worse) pensioned off by the very writing it has generated .... In [Sammler's] question "Who had made shit a sacrament?" we can hear Bellow's own cultured, traditional revulsion against the scatological metaphysics of Mailer's *An American Dream*, Barth's *Giles Goat Boy* and Pynchon's *V.*[1]

McConnell's reading may seem mischievous, but it is persuasive, as long as one emphasizes the ironic distance apparent not only in the characterization but also in the omniscient narration. Sammler is shown up from the start as a posturing and self-righteous figure:

> He, personally, stood apart from all developments. From a sense of deference, from age, from good manners, he sometimes affirmed himself to be out of it, *hors d'usage*, not a man of the times. No force of nature, nothing paradoxical or demonic, he had no drive for smashing through the masks of appearances. Not "Me and the Universe."[2]

First printed in *Modern Fiction Studies* 28, no. 4 (Winter 1982–83): 569–82.

This passage, in the characteristic rhetoric of the book which at once captures Sammler's personal syntax and points up his pretensions, is revelatory both of his pride and of his self-deception. This is his avuncular role, the "age" and "good manners" subtly conveyed by the slight emphasis given to both the popular American slang and the familiar French expression to remind us that, just as their meanings are identical, so is there nothing new in the apocalyptic pretensions of the sixties generation. Mr. Sammler's been around; he's seen it all before. But at the same time the entire book is a testament to Sammler's unwearying preoccupation with "Me and the Universe" (the principle study of his old age being the mystical texts of Meister Eckhart) and to his grim fascination with "smashing through the masks of appearances." He is unrelentingly harsh in his analysis of other people and of the social games they play. To give him his due, he is quite aware of his own role as the prophet from the past, and, indeed, the fierceness of his scrutiny derives in part from a desire to discern some common humanity, some shared principles of being, which can join him to the human race from which he declares his independence. That he only has one eye has a double significance; it implies a lack of perspective in how he views external reality (a roomful of ordinary college students in "his obstructed vision" becomes "a large, spreading, shaggy, composite human bloom" [*MSP*, 40]), but it also implies the ability to connect simultaneously with an inner reality. ("The damaged left eye seemed to turn in another direction, to be preoccupied separately with different matters" [*MSP*, 32].)

Mr. Sammler starts out alienated—as a survivor of the death camps, as a widower, as an old European afloat in the American cult of youth. But he doesn't *believe* in alienation. There is a plaintiveness, an elegiac tone in *Mr. Sammler's Planet,* that cuts through the satire and reminds us that through the reveries of this pompous old man Bellow is concerned about examining very real questions of human survival in this century. More particularly, though Mr. Sammler's "planet" is earth, because he is also known as Uncle Sam(mler), it is really America that we are talking about, the same country Norman Mailer investigates in *An American Dream.*

Norman Mailer would seem to be one of those proponents of shit as a sacrament, one of those apologists for despair whom Mr. Sammler derogates. In *An American Dream*, however, Mailer seems to be doing the same thing as Bellow: acknowledging and satirizing his own popular image by creating a protagonist who is something of a caricature of himself and endowing him with those attitudes and beliefs most likely to enrage his critics. Stephen Rojack (the name "Stephen" may signal that this book is to be a portrait of the artist) has served in World War II, been involved in politics, been prominent on television, and "professes" existential psychology—all well-known aspects of the Mailer myth. These accomplishments are all heightened in the novel, where Rojack gains the Distinguished Service Cross, is elected to Congress, has his own television show and a tenured teaching post, and actually succeeds in killing his wife and getting away with it. (Mailer is most notorious for having stabbed *his* wife after a party.)

Not only does Mailer flaunt the excesses of his public persona in this novel; he also defies the critics by flaunting the excesses of his style, writing in magazine installments at a time when he might have been expected to settle down and write a "well-made novel." In fact, *An American Dream* is extremely well made as the fantasia it is, but nothing could be further from the deliberately high style of a writer like Bellow. What is most striking is that, despite their utter distinctness *in* style, *An American Dream* and *Mr. Sammler's Planet* have very similar narrative strategies, and very similar thematic concerns.

In both books a secular Jewish intellectual spends a couple of wild days in New York City (2½ days for Sammler, 1½ for Rojack) confronting a series of bizarre characters involved in violent and/or sexual activities, while simultaneously dealing with the death of a loved one—*the* loved one who had made "the American Dream" possible for that hero (Elya Gruner for Sammler, Deborah Kelly for Rojack). Both books modulate constantly between naturalistic narrative, social satire, wild fantasy, and intensely private meditation. Both heroes undergo a kind of religious pilgrimage that ends with them considering the body of a dead man on an autopsy table. Both stories include an heiress (Angela Gruner; Deborah Kelly), a "blond bombshell" (Angela again; Cherry Melanie), a black "Prince of Harlem" (the pickpocket; Shago Martin), and sexual perverts (Walter Bruch; Barney Kelly and Bess Trelawne). The action of each includes the hero's relationship to his daughter, his feelings about sex, his brushes with the police, the university, business, and crime. Both books even end with the hero coming into money.

Of course to relate the two novels in this way is to give nothing of the flavor of either and to distort the meanings of both. But it is interesting how many details overlap. Perhaps this is because so many of them come out of popular American iconography and represent the common wisdom about the state of the Union. It is also possible that Bellow deliberately raided Mailer's novel (*Mr. Sammler's Planet* came out in 1970, *An American Dream* in 1965) in order to make his critique of his rival's viewpoint more witty and more comprehensive.

The moon is the central symbol in both these novels, maintaining its traditional value as the borderline between time and eternity, the emblem of the realm of mortality and change, the seasons, the tides, and man's inner life. It also accrues particular resonances in each work. The moon is full throughout *An American Dream*, and the story begins with Rojack's being tempted by her spectral voice to commit suicide. He also remembers that the moon was full the night he killed four Nazis during the war, a turning point in his life wherein he gained personal insight into magic and instinct, and public acclaim as a war hero.

Mr. Sammler emphasizes the traditional associations of the moon by quoting Milton and Shakespeare, the first from *Comus* (*MSP*, 91), a work in defense of chastity, and the second from *Antony and Cleopatra* (*MSP*, 180), a work in defense of erotic love. He has plenty of reason to be preoccupied with the moon because his daughter Shula has stolen an Indian scientist's manuscript on the subject, in memory of her father's former friendship with H. G. Wells. A good part of the plot is taken up by Sammler's attempts to retrieve and return this work because the scientist, Govinda Lal, had hoped to publish it "by the time of the first moon landing" (*MSP*, 161). Moreover, all of Sammler's friends and relations are lunatic; Shula is described as "loony" (24, 107), as is Wallace (82; Sammler also calls him "Dans la lune" at 88). The condition is epidemic—Sammler's acquaintance Feffer remarks upon "all those guys running for mayor like a bunch of lunatics" (*MSP*, 113; one of those guys of course was Norman Mailer.) But though the moon's effect on susceptible humanity is chaotic, in itself it stands for purity and containment. Thus Sammler, perplexed by his niece Angela's promiscuity, is "pleasantly haunted by moon visions. Artemis—lunar chastity" (64). He compares the old myths to Lal's new utopian fantasy of an ascetic lunar colony.

> The moon serves in the novel as the central symbol for both the goal of advanced technology and the future of man. But, in Sammler's view, the technological advances appear to be occurring in a moral void and thus the future of man is uncertain.[3]

Rojack too connects the moon with the future of man and imagines that in the moonlit deserts of the west a "new breed of a man" is being born.[4] But the moon for him is a symbol of sterility and waste, associated with the false paradise that is Las Vegas and with charnel houses (*AAD*, 153). The "platinum lady" of the moon (19) seems to be a personification of Rojack's death wish, just as the other blond, Cherry, whom he immediately impregnates, is a manifestation of the life force. Right after a vision of Deborah's "lone green eye" while walking the parapet, he looks up at the moon—"princess of the dead, I would never be free of her" (242)—and it is impossible to tell whether "her" in this context is the moon, Deborah, or both. *An American Dream* invests the moon with the same qualities of madness and murder as its human characters and so attributes these qualities directly to lunar influence. In *Mr. Sammler's Planet*, however, the term "lunacy" is used ironically, with a clear recognition that all the mythology about the moon is anthropomorphic and stems from man's ignorance about himself and his universe. Hence the insistence on the moon as a scientific phenomenon in Lal's manuscript. For Lal, the moon symbolizes the salvation of man by science rather than his damnation by passion. This is perfectly in accord with Mr. Sammler's statement that "visions or nightmares for others [are] but for him daylight events, in full consciousness" (*MSP*, 126).

Sammler makes this observation when he finally gives in to the suppressed memory of having killed a Nazi soldier. His wartime experience was the complete inversion of Rojack's and reveals the other side of war. Whereas Rojack experienced in battle a perfect coordination of instinct and intelligence, a moment of total personal integration that he remembers with almost sexual satisfaction, Sammler killed his Nazi in a state of complete brutalization and lack of control. He shot a naked and defenseless man after he had stripped him of the clothes and food that were all he really wanted. What is grand and visionary for Rojack is reduced to something mean and nasty by Mr. Sammler, a strategy in operation throughout Bellow's book.

> The evident fact is that Mr. Sammler is the Jew who, after Hitler, cannot forgive the world, for he recognizes that its exterminations may be more pleasurable than its lusts. He has decided, not as the rabbis have decided but as Jewish novelists have decided in this first era of fiction by many Jews, that the "world" is a very bad place indeed. In God's absence human consciousness becomes the world.[5]

The events of World War II—especially the concentration camps and the genocide—are an essential proof of human evil for both Bellow and Mailer. They each began their literary careers confronting that war, Bellow in *Dangling Man* (1944) and Mailer in *The Naked and the Dead* (1948), and both come back to it as a metaphor for the existential condition of man. Their characters are usually offered the alternatives of total abdication of selfhood through regimentation, or resistance to conformity—and resulting alienation. The relationship of war to peacetime totalitarianism is made clear in Sammler's meditation on how Germany eliminated the Jews by institutionalizing murder:

> Man is a killer. Man has a moral nature. The anomaly can be resolved
> by insanity only, by insane dreams in which delusions of conscious-
> ness are maintained by organization, in states of mad perdition cling-
> ing to forms of business administration. Making it government work.
> (*MSP*, 180–81)

The same association of Nazis, business, and government is apparent
in *An American Dream* in the relationship between Ruta and Kelly, and
in this regard it is significant that Kelly's fortune began in Army Surplus
(*AAD*, 223).

The same association of Nazis, business, and government is apparent
However, despite his analysis of the holocaust, Sammler is skeptical
of blaming institutions for madness and murder and insists that people
recognize their *individual*, as well as their collective, responsibility.
Although institutions can be and are built to exploit people's weaknesses,
"madness is the attempted liberty of people who feel themselves overwhelmed by giant forces of organized control. Seeking the magic of extremes" (*MSP*, 134). "The magic of extremes" is exactly the route to
salvation proposed by *An American Dream*. Certainly paranoia about public institutions can't go much further than it does in Mailer's fable, where
the hero, having passed through the Military and the Government before the action starts, proceeds to break off with High Society, Academia,
and the Media, while opposing the Police, the Mafia, Big Business, and
the Underworld. Mr. Sammler is as disillusioned about powerful organi-
zations as Rojack is, but his greatest terror is not of authority but of anarchy, not of external forces but of internal emotional chaos.

Although both Sammler and Rojack may be said to be alienated from
the emptiness of modern life and so on, they attribute that emptiness
to entirely different things. Sammler is concerned with the loss of
civilized graces and of belief in human community that he sees in postwar society. He is enraged by the cult of primitivism, and his world is
full of people degraded to the status of animals. Bruch is "apelike" (*MSP*,
58), Lal a "birdy man" (186), Wallace "a kinky cat" (83), and Sammler
himself "cat-whiskered" (72), sporting overhanging brows "as in some
breeds of dog" (8). Angela calls herself "a skunk" (61), but to her father
she is a "cow" (74) and to her brother a "swine" (171). The rather mild,
domestic quality of much of this imagery suggests how *ordinary* man's
bestiality is—how inescapable a fact of everyday life. It is petty and utterly without glamor, but pervasive. And it is this that terrifies Sammler.

Mailer uses as much animal imagery as Bellow does, but whereas
Bellow's is mostly of the barnyard sort, reducing human behavior to a
squabble in a henhouse, Mailer's focus is on the wild carnivores of jungle
and desert and elevates human wickedness to something spectacular. To

Rojack, Deborah is a "lioness" (*AAD*, 16) whose apartment is a "padded jungle" (44); her cruelty is like "sucking the marrow from a broken bone" (22), and Shago also experiences her as a "cannibal" (179). Cherry is "pure cat" (105), and when she and Rojack first make love it is "like animals . . . across a track of jungle" (120). Indeed, all Rojack's meetings with others are described in such terms. It is mostly his nose that conveys such images to him, that tells him that Ruta is an "alley rat" (46), Deborah a "wild boar full of rut" (38), Kelly "a big foul cat" (203), and Shago in a "poisonous snake of a mood" (173).

Sammler's nose is equally active, noting the French perfume of the pickpocket (*MSP*, 13) as well as the slight "fecal carelessness" of Wallace (82). The significance of the sense of smell for both writers is that it "suggests a regression to a more primitive mode of perception and orientation. Language is efficient only on one level, elsewhere it is often safer to follow your nose."[6] As cerebral as these men are, both are ultimately searching for some truth about human nature than can be felt instinctively rather than reasoned out. Rojack, with his "not inconsiderable thesis that magic, dread and the fear of death are the roots of motivation" (*AAD*, 15), is particularly inclined to trust his nose as the organ of truth. Part of his lecture "On the Primitive View of Mystery" is quoted midway through the novel, and it elucidates this point.

> In contrast to the civilized view which elevates man above the animals, the primitive had an instinctive belief that he was subservient to the beasts of the jungle and the beasts of mystery.
>
> To the savage, dread was the natural result of any invasion of the supernatural: if man wished to steal the secrets of the gods, it was only to be supposed that the gods would defend themselves and destroy whichever man came too close. By this logic, civilization is the successful if imperfect theft of some cluster of these secrets, and the price we have paid is to accelerate our private sense of some enormous if not quite definable disaster which awaits us. (*AAD*, 150)

The evidence of the novel demonstrates that Rojack subscribes to this "primitive" view. In contrast, Sammler holds to the "civilized view" which maintains that, far from being hostile to man's mastery of his environment, the powers of the universe support and encourage it. "Dread" for Sammler is not the apprehension of divine retribution but the glum expectation of human failure. Civilization will fail *because* of that in man which is still primitive.

Like Freud in *Civilization and Its Discontents,* like Marx, like most Western humanists, Sammler believes in the deferral of personal gratification for long-term moral pleasure. He believes, that is, in the worth of the "social contract" and in the existence of the common good, and is devoted to the Aristotelian ideal of the "Polis." Appropriately enough, in his youth he was associated with the "Cosmopolis Project for a World State," which he describes as "a service society based on a rational scientific attitude towards life" (*MSP*, 41). He is now disenchanted with science, as his conversations with the Utopian theorist Govinda Lal make clear, but unlike Lal he has not given up on the possibility of creating a better world for man here on earth. (Perhaps it is worth noting here that Dr. Gruner's fortune, which enabled him to support Sammler, was derived from real estate. See 72.) Indeed, it is because he no longer believes in science that he cannot imagine Lal's lunar colony redeeming mankind.

> His personal idea was one of human beings conditioned by other human beings, and knowing that present arrangements were not, *sub specie aeternatis, the* truth, but that one should be satisfied with such truth as one could get by approximation. Trying to live with a civil heart. With disinterested charity. With a sense of the mystic potency of mankind. (*MSP*, 125–26)

Even the title of Bellow's book, *Mr. Sammler's Planet,* suggests that the work will be concerned with universal issues and that in it the individual will be related to the world of which he is a part. It is appropriately narrated in the third person. On the other hand, *An American Dream,* as *its* title makes clear—*a* version of the dream, not the popular one—is a much more private vision and hence told in the first-person voice. Mailer has, in all his works, "made some drastic disavowal of the *Polis* as the scene and setting of human existence;" he insists instead "on the politics of social reconstruction being superceded by a politics of salvation."[7] This politics of salvation is dramatized in an exaggerated form in the novel: the secular intellectual, bogged down in inauthentic social roles, undergoes a redemption by fantasy and instinct. The same thesis is explicated at length in Mailer's famous essay of 1957, "The White Negro," which elevates the hipster to the status of existential hero and superman.

The hipster's search for an authentic, better, or transcendent self is primarily by way of sex, the Reichian path to the instinctual unconscious. In this regard Mr. Sammler's reminiscence of Schopenhauer—after whom he was named "Artur"—is instructive. According to Schopenhauer in *The World as Will and Idea:*

> Only ideas are not overpowered by the Will—the cosmic force, the
> Will, which drives all things. A blinding passion. The inner creative
> fury of the world. (*MSP,* 191)

This is the power that Mailer worships, recognizing like Schopenhauer
that "the organs of sex are the seat of the Will" (*MSP,* 191). Thus Mailer
declares that

> to be with it is to have grace, is to be closer to the secrets of that
> inner unconscious life which will nourish you if you can know it,
> for you are then nearer to that God which every hipster believes is
> located in the senses of his body . . . God; not the God of the churches
> but the unachievable whisper of mystery within the sex. The para-
> dise of limitless energy and perception just beyond the next wave
> of the next orgasm.[8]

For Mailer, the pursuit of spiritual fulfillment is best expressed by a
sexual metaphor; he is not just using sexual *language* metaphorically
but imagining that sex itself is something of a physical analogue for a
spiritual reality. He holds that the only experience of eternity accessible
to man is the suspension of time and loss of personality one has in
orgasm.

The problem with the pursuit of God "beyond the next wave of the
next orgasm" is that such a quest is radically private, and for Bellow the
truly religious goal is somehow to integrate this ecstatic private self with
the suffering public self. The only way to do this, to transcend the insatiable "Will," is by means of "Ideas." Ideas can accommodate the dialectic of instinct and ethic; the will can tolerate no compromise. Thus
if Mailer's God is energy and his experience of God orgasm, Bellow's
divinity is Mind, and *his* experience of it thought.

These fairly serious propositions are the foundation for the fantasy
and satire in both novels; neither author appears to want to be taken
too seriously. So Bellow's intensely sincere refutation of Mailer's ethic
in *The White Negro* is put into the mouth of a testy, one-eyed old refugee,
who seems to have racist tendencies and has just been sexually harassed
by a black pickpocket.[9] It is possible that Feffer points us in the direction of Mailer's essay when he tells Sammler, "You're wise but not hip"
(*MSP,* 111), and Sammler seems to be referring to it when he complains
that "the mental masses" "inheriting everything in a debased state had
formed an idea of the corrupting disease of being white and the healing

power of black" (34). Sammler is particularly disturbed by "the peculiar aim of sexual niggerhood for everyone" (149).

Leslie Fiedler holds that "the negro is the Jew's archetypal opposite, representative of the impulsive life even as the Jew is the symbol of the intellectual."[10] This observation applies to Mailer's and Bellow's novels, in both of which a Jewish intellectual is threatened by a sexually powerful Negro, and in both of which the Negro is severely beaten in retaliation. Both the pickpocket in *Mr. Sammler's Planet* and Shago Martin in *An American Dream* are ambivalently seen as "African Prince or great black beast" (*MSP*, 77). Both are exquisitely dressed; both are members of the underworld (the pickpocket through crime, Shago by his profession as jazz musician); and both are cut off from white society by their speech habits as well as their color (the pickpocket doesn't speak at all; Shago spouts a weird hipsterese). The presence of both men is experienced as irresistably sexual; Sammler is fascinated by the pickpocket and goes to Columbus Circle a dozen times to seek him out. He notes every detail of the man's clothing, his body contours, even his smell, and, when the man retaliates for Sammler's spying, the sexual connotations are unmistakeable. The pickpocket propels the old man through the lobby of his apartment building, "pressing him bodily, belly to back. He did not lift his hands to Sammler but pushed" (*MSP*, 48) before defiantly exposing his penis to Sammler.

The intimacy of this encounter parallels that between Shago in *An American Dream*, where sexual rivalry over Cherry gets transformed into a suppressed homosexual encounter. Rojack takes Shago "from behind" (*AAD*, 181) to fight with him and then smashes him up and down on the floor before throwing him out the door, "getting a smell of full nearness, as if we'd been in bed an hour" (182). His symbolic emasculation of Shago is complete when he retains the black man's umbrella as a talisman, appropriating some of Shago's powers with it.

Rojack stops himself from killing Shago, but his rage is enacted fatally upon the singer through a third party who beats his head in with an iron bar. This incident is mirrored in *Mr. Sammler's Planet* when Sammler begs Eisen to intervene in the scuffle between Feffer and the pickpocket, and Eisen proceeds to smash the Negro's face with a bag full of *iron* medallions. Sammler succeeds in preventing Eisen from killing the man, but he is unable to argue with his son-in-law about the necessity for such violence because, as Eisen reminds him,

> you can't hit a man like this just once. When you hit him you must really hit him. Otherwise he'll kill you. You know. We both fought in the war. You were a Partisan. You had a gun. So don't you know? (*MSP*, 266)

This alludes to Sammler's own cold-blooded murder of the German soldier in Zamosht forest and is a reminder that he has enacted his own
violence vicariously through Eisen. The vicious stupidity of Eisen is im-
mensely depressing to Sammler because he has no antidote for it and
because he knows where it comes from, having been once equally brutal-
ized himself. The pathetic aspect of the whole encounter—after all, the
man was only a pickpocket and not a killer—is pointed up by its echo
in one of the other plots. Shula's stealing of Lal's manuscript and her
attempt to seduce him by dressing up in a sari represent a comic and
feminine version of the pickpocket exposing first his theft and then his
genitals to Sammler. When associated with the eroticism of Angela and
the shady deals of Wallace and Feffer, the implication seems to be that
sex and violence have become means of "expressing oneself" in this
society.

Though Rojack boasts that he feels good about having beaten Shago
(*AAD,* 184), he knows that his actions have been cowardly and demean-
ing and that he has not fought fair. There is a further suggestion that
this fight is a turning point for Rojack: the point at which his luck goes
bad.

> It had all gone wrong again. I could feel the break in the heavens.
> If I could have taken some of it back, I would have returned to that
> moment when I began to beat Shago to the floor and he dared me
> to let him go. (*AAD,* 184)

The later murder of Shago—which seems to have been inspired in part
by Rojack's "evil eye" and which Rojack witnesses telepathically through
the umbrella—results in Cherry's death, a mistaken retaliation by Shago's
friends. Furthermore, Rojack feels a voice telling him all night to go to
Harlem if he wants Cherry to live, but he resists it, the implication being that he could have prevented Shago's death, and thus Cherry's, had
he been there. So by refusing to confront Shago honorably, and with
him "some hard-lodged boulder of fear [he] had always felt with Negroes"
(182), Rojack loses Cherry and his chance for real love.

The beating of the black man is something of a climax in *Mr. Sammler's
Planet* also. Not only is it the culmination of an action begun in the opening moments of the book, but it is one of a series of events that waylay
Sammler when he is desperately trying to get to the deathbed of his
nephew Elya Gruner. Because Gruner's doctor is a little vague about the
actual time of death (*MSP,* 283), there is the possibility that it took place
while the beating was occurring, the explosion of violence on the street
paralleling the hemorrhage in Elya's brain.

If Elya Gruner's aneurysm is a metaphor for the hidden violence Sammler fears in American life, cancer is the explicit metaphor for Rojack's perception of his country's sickness. In fact, violence is seen by Rojack as the *antidote* to the cancer of conformity: in the first scene, when he decides not to commit suicide, he thinks, "If I died from a revolt of the cells, a growth against the design of my organs, . . . this was the moment it all began; this was the hour when the cells took their leap." (*AAD,* 20). Cancer is everywhere in this novel. Rojack's spontaneous lie that Deborah had cancer turns out to be true; Eddie Gannuci is riddled with it, and after leaving New York Rojack ends up at the autopsy of a cancerous man in Missouri. The stench of putrifying flesh stays with him for the rest of his trip out west, and one can't help but feel that the dead man represents the corpse of the American Dream.

Both Rojack and Sammler are themselves twice-born, brought back from the dead. Sammler literally crawled out of a mass grave in Poland; Rojack undergoes a kind of metaphysical rebirth after murdering his wife. Killing Deborah is symbolic of killing the evil in himself. From their rebirths the two men go on opposite routes to salvation—Sammler has to strive to reconnect himself to mankind and Rojack to disconnect himself from it. If Sammler is trapped inside himself, Rojack has no "self" at all, only a series of social roles to be divested.

Rojack's predicament is that he has accepted "The American Dream" at face value; the novel shows how this fantasy of wealth and power is in fact a nightmare. Deborah personified this dream for her husband. "With her beside me, I had leverage . . . . I was one of the more active figures in the city—no one could be certain finally that nothing large would come of me" (*AAD,* 24). However, what Deborah really turns out to be for Rojack is a succubus, the nightmare who comes to men in sleep.

> More than once had I sat up in a strange woman's bed feeling claws on my chest, a familiar bad odor above the liquor on my tongue and Deborah's green eyes staring at me in the dark, an oppression close to strangling on my throat. (*AAD,* 40)

Through her Rojack has sold his soul to the devil, represented in America by her father, Barney Kelly, the control center for institutional evil in finance, politics, and crime. In the final scenes of the novel, Kelly is revealed as the "adversary" (the literal translation of "Satan") with whom Rojack must fight to redeem himself. In fact, there are traces of the traditional Christian tripartite scheme of temptation in *An American Dream,* with Deborah representing "The World," Ruta—in whose body the war between God and the devil is symbolically waged—"The Flesh," and Kelly

"The Devil." That Rojack succeeds in opposing all three powers and in appropriating their various talents indicates his new mastery over himself. Nonetheless he is unable to preserve the life of the woman he loves because it is impossible for even the pure in heart to combat all the evils in America at once; he cannot be at the Waldorf and down in Harlem at the same time. So at the end of the book he leaves America, having travelled to Las Vegas, the false paradise glimpsed during intercourse with Ruta (49) rather than having attained the heavenly city envisioned when he kills Deborah (35) and makes love to Cherry (122).

Because of its purgatorial motif, *An American Dream* has been compared by several critics to Bunyan's *Pilgrim's Progress*.[11] Similarly, Robert Dutton notes in *Mr. Sammler's Planet* the many "Vanity Fairs" and "Sloughs of Despond" that "the Pilgrim Sammler encounters on his progress toward Elya Gruner and religious affirmation."[12] The religious strain in *Mr. Sammler's Planet* is not as overtly allegorical as that of Mailer's novel, but nonetheless Sammler is a devotee of Meister Eckhart, is preoccupied with religious questions throughout the book, and concludes it in prayer. Sammler's prayer insists that deep down we all know "the terms of our contract," that there does exist a foundation of truth and permanence in human life and it is to be found in fulfilling our bond toward others. There is a curious parallel to this longing for normalcy and certitude in *An American Dream* when Rojack imagines himself praying to be rid of magic. "'God,' I wanted to pray, 'Let me love that girl and become a father, and try to be a good man, and do some decent work'" (*AAD*, 153). Richard Poirier wryly observes "the nearly hippie simplicity with which he would replace his hip embattlement."[13] Even Cherry, the tough nightclub singer, reveals that deep down she wants to have a baby and "be a lady" (187). There is a certain pathos to these confessions of ordinary human expectations within the context of the novel, but they should remind us that it is, after all, a surreal *dream* vision and not an alternative reality.

The major difference in the religious pattern in the novels resides in the different conceptions the two novelists have of God. For Bellow, God is the realm of "Ideas" that Schopenhauer suggested transcends the brute generative energy of the "Will." He seems to posit enduring and absolute values as innate in human consciousness. Mailer, on the other hand, sees God as a vulnerable figure and the universe as the battleground of good and evil. In the *Paris Review* interview of Winter 1964, Mailer was asked if there was "a hidden pattern being worked out in [his] books." He replied, "I have some obsession with how God exists. Is he an essential God or an existential God; is he all powerful or is he too an embattled existential creature who may succeed or fail in his vision."[14] *An American Dream* is shaped according to the existential premise, whereas Bellow's novel takes the essentialist view. What this also seems to involve is Mailer's insistence that in order to combat the Devil, man must not only acknowledge but exploit and *express* the evil in himself, whereas Bellow remains firm that humanity must learn somehow to *overcome* that evil without acting it out.

The radically different, even opposite, stances Mailer and Bellow take on the issues of man's place in nature and society, the character of the religious quest, the function of evil, and the roles of will and intellect make them the Blake and Wordsworth of modern American letters. Bellow's novels in great detail and at great length map "the growth of a poet's mind," whereas Mailer's intention seems to be to write, like Blake, a Bible of hell. Bellow always makes clear the isolation of the individual and the privateness of his imaginative life—and then tries to find in that private imagination proof of the essential unity of mankind. This pattern is very similar to that charted by Geoffrey Hartman with reference to Wordsworth: the conversion of "apocalypse," or the utter separation of man from nature, into *akedah,* or the *binding down* of man *into* nature.[15] But Mailer is emphatically a prophet of apocalypse, like Blake demanding that the current civilization fall and cease and that the world be remade in the image of the Human Form Divine.

Notes

1. Frank D. McConnell, *Four Postwar American Novelists* (Chicago: University of Chicago Press, 1977), 3–4.
2. Saul Bellow, *Mr. Sammler's Planet* (Greenwich, Conn.: Fawcett Books, 1970), 125. Subsequent references to this edition will be made parenthetically in the text as *MSP*.
3. M. Gilbert Porter, *Whence the Power?* (Columbia: University of Missouri Press, 1974), 172.
4. Norman Mailer, *An American Dream* (New York: Dell, 1965), 251. Subsequent references to this edition will be made parenthetically in the text as *AAD*.
5. Alfred Kazin, "The Earthly City of the Jews," in *Bright Book of Life* (Boston: Little, Brown, and Co., 1971), 137.
6. Tony Tanner, "On the Parapet," in *Will the Real Norman Mailer Please Stand Up?* ed. Laura Adams (Port Washington: Kennikat Press, 1974), 132.
7. Nathan A. Scott, *Three American Moralists* (Notre Dame: University of Notre Dame Press, 1973), 94.
8. Norman Mailer, *The White Negro* (San Francisco: City Lights, 1957), 12.
9. Indications of a rather trivial racism on Sammler's part are his scorn of Angela for contributing to "defense funds for Black murderers and rapists" (14) and of Wallace for wishing "to be of use to little black children, to be a basketball coach in playgrounds" (89). In the light of these remarks it is amusing

that Sammler himself is persuaded into giving a talk at Columbia "for a student project to help backward black pupils with their reading problems" (38).

10. Leslie Fiedler, *Waiting for the End* (Harmondsworth: Penguin Books, 1964), 107.

11. The critics who have argued most persuasively for this analogy are Barry Leeds in *The Structured Vision of Normal Mailer* (New York: New York University Press, 1969), and Jean Radford in *Norman Mailer: A Critical Study* (New York: Harper and Row, 1975).

12. Robert R. Dutton, *Saul Bellow* (Boston: Twayne, 1971), 162.

13. Richard Poirier, *Mailer* (London: Wm. Collins Sons, 1972), 129.

14. Quoted by Helen Weinburg in *The New Novel in America: The Kafkan Mode in Contemporary Fiction* (Ithaca: Cornell University Press, 1970), 127.

15. Geoffrey Hartman, *Wordsworth's Poetry 1787–1814* (New Haven: Yale University Press, 1964). Nathan Scott makes a similar observation in *Three American Moralists* about Bellow's insistence on the need for "transcendence downward"—not out of but *into* the heart of the human situation. He refers us to Heidegger's concept of "Gelassenheit," which he defines as "a quiescent submission to the multileveled and radical mystery of existence, the way of *falling* into peace" (134).

"Two Different Speeches": Mystery and Knowledge in *Mr. Sammler's Planet*

Ellen Pifer

From his first novel, *Dangling Man* (1944), to his most recent fiction, Saul Bellow has created an almost unbroken series of protagonists doing mental battle with themselves and the world. Riddled with contrary emotions, Bellow's main characters waver uneasily between alternate commitments—to action, fellowship, and worldly self-assertion, on the one hand, and to stillness, contemplation, and solitude, on the other. While the outward manifestations of psychic stress are readily observable in Bellow's characters, the deeper sources of this conflict prove to be less apparent. Of all Bellow's novels, *Mr. Sammler's Planet* has particularly baffled, even repelled, those readers unaware of the protagonist's rift in consciousness. Bellow's seventh novel has received a markedly disproportionate amount of hostile criticism largely because critics have assumed that the protagonist, Artur Sammler, is devoid of psychological conflict. They admonish Bellow for creating a static or "dead" character, who, as Alfred Kazin remarks, "has to be right all the time."[1] Sammler's obsession with knowing, says John J. Clayton, evinces a man who has "buried his passionate, modern, conflicted self."[2]

As these remarks suggest, the critics' failure to detect vital signs of life in Sammler may proceed from their tendency to regard his active consciousness—and even his passion for thinking—as solely or narrowly intellectual. To the contrary, I shall argue that the ceaseless dialectic of Sammler's consciousness, the urgent unfolding of his internal self-argument, is profoundly psychological in the root sense of the term. It is his psyche, not just his mind, that is divided on most issues; nor are these issues mere abstractions. The rift in Sammler's psyche is dramatically manifested in his emotional relationships with others, in the things that happen to him and in the actions he takes. As I hope to show,

First printed in *Mosaic* 18, no. 2 (Spring 1985): 17–32.

Sammler's passion for thinking does not render him superfluous or irrelevant to the concerns of contemporary humanity. Superannuated,
world-weary, and aloof as he is, Sammler nonetheless embodies the epitome of the "passionate, conflicted, modern self." Through the dynamics
of his character's consciousness, forever troubled by and in confrontation with the world, Bellow articulates the divided consciousness which
is, in his view, the marked characteristic of contemporary "intellectual
man."

The rift in Sammler's psyche may be initially identified as the polari-
zation of two modes of consciousness, the analytic and the intuitive. Psy-
chically alternating between these poles, Sammler perceives reality in
radically opposing terms. Through analysis, moreover, he attempts psychologically to disengage himself from the world—and from the claims
he *intuitively* knows it has upon him. The impetus of the novel's unfolding action succeeds, however, in drawing him more and more deeply
into its dynamic. The conditions of mortal existence, as Bellow demonstrates, demand more from the individual than analytic solutions. As
Sammler comes to recognize, the individual is himself part of the existential "problem." He must appropriate (in the Kierkegaardian sense)
and be reconciled to the very reality he seeks to analyze and explain.
For Bellow as for Kierkegaard, reconciliation to existence springs from
acknowledging the source of mystery in human life. That is why
Kierkegaard and other modern Christian thinkers, such as Étienne Gilson
and Gabriel Marcel, help to elucidate both the conflict and the mystery
operating at the heart of Bellow's novel. Rallying Christian thinkers to
illuminate the fiction of a Jewish novelist writing about Jewish characters may strike some readers as strange, indeed. Certainly Sammler, a
Polish survivor of the Holocaust, shares with his author a strong ethnic
and cultural identity as a Jew. Yet as Sammler avidly studies a medieval
German mystic, Meister Eckhart, and ponders the meaning of
Kierkegaard's "Knight of Faith," he also evinces a powerful attraction
to the Christian mysteries.

Openly avowing this affinity with Christian mystery, Bellow has said:
"In *Herzog* and *Henderson the Rain King* I was kidding my way to Jesus,
but here [in *Mr. Sammler's Planet*] I'm baring myself nakedly." Questioned,
in a later interview, about the credibilty of the novel's ending—when
Sammler "speaks of what each man knows in his heart"—Bellow says:
"You're to believe in it as much as you can believe in the New Testament . . . . Look, you meet someone on the street and he says, give all
you have and follow me—on what does he base his injunction? He bases
it on the assumption that the truth is known."[3] Such statements,

challenging what Bellow calls contemporary "head culture," suggest that critics may have been too conservative in their assessment of the dichotomies underlying this author's fiction. Drawing on Western rationalist traditions, most of Bellow's commentators perceive in his novels a conflict between the self and the world, between the individual's needs and society's demands. Or, pressing a little further, they point to the novelist's occasionally "Platonic" suggestion of a world of truth and value persisting beyond the ephemeral reality of appearances.[4]

Bellow's own argument appears, more radically, to be with reason itself—or at least with the current hegemony of scientific rationalism that has driven religious modes of perception underground. Distinguishing between the dominant influence of contemporary "head culture" and the individual's persistent "internal beliefs," Bellow says: "You can depend upon educated people to tell you that of course they are agnostic rationalists, but what they really are is their very own well kept secret.... Of course there are two different speeches, and everybody knows that by now. There are things you say, civilly, in polite society; and there are things you say to yourself before you fall asleep."[5] Because this code of "internal beliefs" has virtually been banished from the "polite society" of educated exchange, Bellow finds that "there's really no language" at the present moment by which to convey the "secrets" of the spirit. In *Mr. Sammler's Planet*, nevertheless, he supplies his own articulate version of the "two different speeches" by which contemporary "intellectual man" registers and orders experience—giving voice to the polarities of modern consciousness.

Because Artur Sammler is perhaps the most private of Bellow's protagonists, because he is a man who speaks largely and continually to himself, Bellow's distinction between private and public "speech" may be understood in its deeper implications. In Sammler's consciousness there is a rift not only between "received opinions" and privately held beliefs but between two fundamental operations of the psyche as it engages or confronts the world. Employing a distinction Pascal made centuries ago in his *Pensées,* one may say that two modes or processes of thought, the analytic and the intuitive, draw Sammler's mind in opposing directions, toward meanings that contradict and conflict. Because the principles of intuitive understanding "are felt rather than seen," said Pascal, "there is the greatest difficulty in making them felt by those who do not of themselves perceive them."[6] In a more acutely analytic age than Pascal's, the "difficulty" may arise not only from a "mathematical" or logical mind confronting an intuitive one but from within a single, "conflicted" psyche. In this sense Sammler proves the very epitome of Clayton's "conflicted, modern self," because Sammler's formidable powers of ratiocination and analysis make him doubt the validity of his own "felt" knowledge and beliefs.

The shifting modes of Sammler's perception unfold a continuous dialectic between the "two different speeches" of his consciousness. Two different modes of reading reality, as well as speaking or articulating reality, may be said, furthermore, to characterize his internal discourse. The special urgency with which Sammler devotes himself to observing phenomena derives from his crucial experiences during the Second World War. A fugitive first from the Germans and then from anti-Semitic Poles, Sammler spends several months hiding out in a mausoleum. There, cut off from human society and the sweep of current events, he turns his attention to local phenomena, finding "curious ciphers and portents" in the tiny movements of an insect or a drop of water. In the mausoleum he finds "symbols everywhere, and metaphysical messages." For a Jew hiding out, the disturbance of a straw or the movement of a sparrow is a minute, but by no means trivial, bit of empirical data that might spell the difference between survival or disaster, security or exposure. But it is not simply personal survival that spurs Sammler to decipher the messages relayed by phenomena. For him they also bring pressing news concerning the fate of Western civilization and, possibly, the human race itself. Not only the German nation but "all of civilized society" seems caught up in a "state of madness." From that summer in the mausoleum, when he finds portents of disaster in the webs traced by solitary spiders, Mr. Sammler continues to read, with prophetic intuition, history's apocalyptic message: its "bad news for humankind, bad information about the very essence of being."[7] Probing the mystery of human fate in this way, Sammler implicitly acknowledges his own participatory role in the symbolic drama being enacted: "It was the Sammlers," he thinks, "who kept on vainly trying to perform some kind of symbolic task. The main result of which was unrest, exposure to trouble. Mr. Sammler had a symbolic character. He, personally, was a symbol . . . . And of what was he a symbol? He didn't even know" (91). What the diviner or seer does know, however, is that his own life is subject to whatever "symbolic" truth or meaning he unveils.

While engaged in this essentially intuitive mode of registering reality, Mr. Sammler is also an avid "reader" of a markedly different order. As a representative of modern "intellectual man," he seeks to know in ways and according to principles that are, in contemporary Western "head culture," more widely practiced and respected. Through the "strain of unrelenting analytical effort," vast accumulations of data and facts are formulated into laws and theories that explain, rather than embody, reality (21). In the novel's opening paragraph, Mr. Sammler is already tackling these "superstructures of explanation." Awaking "shortly before dawn" in his West Side bedroom, he immediately resumes the inner dialogue that fills his waking hours:

> Intellectual man had become an explaining creature. Fathers to children, wives to husbands, lecturers to listeners . . . . The roots of this, the causes of the other . . . the history, the structure, the reasons why. For the most part, in one ear out the other. The soul wanted what it wanted. It had its own natural knowledge. It sat unhappily on superstructures of explanation, poor bird, not knowing which way to fly. (3)

Uneasy and unhappy, the soul perches, "poor bird," on comfortless "superstructures" that are satisfactory only to the intellect. As the world of "objective" facts and public events grows daily more accessible to him, contemporary "intellectual man" is ever more caught up in the endless relay and exchange of information, opinion, and idea. He must analyze and explain the voluminous data at hand in order to understand how it affects and alters the body of information which previous analyses and explanations have erected. "All will explain everything to all, until the next, the new common version is ready," thinks Sammler (19). But meanwhile that inner world of truth and value—eternally revealed to the soul and forming its own "natural knowledge"—tends to be swept aside by the tide of technical data and media "input." By "natural knowledge," Bellow is not, of course, referring to biological instinct but to innate faculties of intuitive understanding. In the cited passage, he suggests that where the authority of "natural knowledge," and the source of an individual's humanity, was once located, there now appears only a void. Because human beings cannot arrive at moral values by determining and analyzing a set of facts, knowledge of these values has come to be doubted, devalued, or debunked. The point is implicitly illustrated by Robert Boyers, who challenges Sammler's affirmation of knowledge at the end of the novel because "it is not exercised by specific phenomena, by the accumulation of sensible experience."[8] I shall argue later in this essay that Sammler does indeed undergo crucial, "sensible experience"; but what Boyers may be objecting to is that the basis of Sammler's knowledge remains, as Pascal says, "felt rather than seen." Not phenomena but the mode in which they are apprehended, or intuited, is the only real basis for such understanding. (To the scientific observer, this point may appear merely tautological.)

Criticizing the tenets of scientific rationalism, Bellow invokes, in the novel's opening paragraph, the ancient truths of the soul, possessed of its own needs—"want[ing] what it wanted"—and "its own natural knowledge." In Western thought, says the French philosopher Étienne Gilson, the soul has traditionally been regarded as "a spiritual principle substantially united to a body": "mind," on the other hand, has been regarded ever since Descartes as "a thinking substance distinct from, and exclusive of, the body." As Gilson demonstrates, the Cartesian separation of mind from matter led inevitably to the disintegration of the concept of man's "substantial unity." Faced with questions concerning human existence or, for that matter, the existence of the world, the Cartesian mind—having effected its separation from the body—set itself the task of proving (or disproving) a reality that, says Gilson, "could not be proved, not because it is not true, but on the contrary, because it is evident... to a soul, not to a mind."[9] Things evident to a soul, in other words, are not necessarily evident to a mind. Although such brief remarks cannot possibly rehearse the argument in sufficient detail, they should serve to recall the philosophical context from which arise Bellow's assertions concerning the "two different speeches" of modern consciousness: the socially acceptable discourse of the "educated," or Cartesian, mind and the persistent murmurings of the more ancient soul—once "substantially united" to the body, of both humankind and the world, but currently in hiding.

Artur Sammler has inherited from Descartes's mathematical account of reality that modern habit of severing mind from matter, the operations of "pure" intellect from the soul's "natural knowledge." Bellow provides an objective correlative for this rift in Sammler's vision by drawing attention to his impaired eyesight.[10] Blind in one eye, the old man sees only "partially," his left eye having been damaged during the war by a Nazi guard's rifle-butt (184). In the Holocaust he "lost his wife, lost an eye" and the underlying sense, as well, of being grounded in human existence. He tends to regard his "onetime human" life as having been "burnt away" by this century's conflagrations (15–16, 224). In his view, he is "human, in some altered way. The human being at the point where he attempted to obtain his release from being human" (251). Sammler's sense of personal devastation, loss, and detachment thus dramatizes in extreme terms the rift dividing modern consciousness into Bellow's "two different speeches." In the novel, these two modes are evinced by the disjunctive operations of Sammler's "two different-looking eyes" (72).

It is from the "blind side" of Sammler's skull that certain "inward" and "uncommunicative" processes tellingly originate (18, 259). In that blindness, as though shunning "the things met with in this world," Sammler's distressed and hampered soul longs for liberation from this "prison" formed by his "perceptions in space and time" (57). Sammler's intellect, on the other hand, remains alert and attentive to the phenomena registered by his operative right eye and the impressions transmitted to his brain by the "sightful side" of his skull (86). A passage describing Sammler in the act of reading a book highlights this point: "Careful to guard his eyesight, he passed pages rapidly back and forth before his [right] eye, the large forehead registering the stimulus to his mind. The damaged left eye seemed to turn in another direction, to be preoccupied separately with different matters" (31). While Sammler's right eye registers phenomena that provide "stimulus to his mind," the blind eye is "separately" engaged—seeking detachment from those "perceptions in space and time."

From this disjunction in perception there arises, furthermore, a dichotomy in the way Sammler responds not only to the "things met with in this world" but also to other people. It accounts for the "look of rebuke as well as the look of receptivity" that registers in Sammler's response to the claims of existence (72). His "receptivity," I would suggest, is largely mental; that is, he freely opens his mind, or analytic faculties, to stimuli from which he ultimately tries to remain detached. As a "thinking substance distinct from the body," to repeat Gilson, Sammler can glory in the operations of sight: "To see was delicious. Oh, of course! An extreme pleasure!" At the same time, "the vividness of everything" to which his right eye is exposed "also dismayed him" (298). With this sense of dismay at the human condition, he "rebukes" the world, turning his blind eye "in another direction." He would deny the essential bond uniting his weary spirit to the world's—and his own—body. In "contraction from life," therefore, Sammler's "dead eye" blindly seeks guidance from those who counsel divestment of worldly distractions (137–38).

Here Sammler's most prominent guide is Meister Eckhart, the medieval German mystic who preached detachment from earthly and human matters as the means to finding God: "See that you are stripped of all creatures, of all consolation from creatures. For certainly as long as creatures comfort and are able to comfort you, you will never find true comfort. But if nothing can comfort you save God, truly God will console you." Having read this passage from Eckhart, "Mr. Sammler could not say that he literally believed what he was reading. He could, however, say that he cared to read nothing but this" (253–54). Sammler's affinity for Eckhart would appear to be further evidence of what most critics deem his hostility to life and other people—"his attempt to turn the world into thought in order to stay aloof and safe."[11] What tends to go unnoticed, however, is that Bellow arranges things in the novel so that Sammler, who becomes increasingly entangled in worldly affairs and in the lives of others, ultimately recognizes that such earthly divestment is both impossible for him and, in any case, a humanly insufficient alternative. As the novel develops, Sammler gradually acknowledges the bonds—indissoluble for the mortal duration—that unite soul and body and bind him to quotidian existence.

The detachment with which Sammler endeavors to view reality, the estrangement of mind from body, may account for the void he himself contemplates at the novel's opening—the void yawning between the soul's "natural knowledge" and the inadequate but elaborate "superstructures" of "intellectual man." Yet he also senses "that the way he saw things could not be right," that "life was not and could not be what he was seeing" (110). The clue to his error lies in the very formulation of this sentence, because to human beings real "life" is not merely an object to be "seen" from the outside. Nor can it truly be understood without the participation of the would-be observer in its processes. Although he intermittently registers this awareness, it takes the duration of the novel for Sammler to accept, over the reluctance of extreme age and fatigue, his full initiation into the mysteries of the living.

The existence of mystery, to which Bellow repeatedly returns in his fiction, underlies his vision of reality. To apprehend mystery is, in the novelist's own words, to ascribe to "what we don't know" a "metaphysical character," not a "naturalistic" one.[12] In his *Metaphysical Journal*, Gabriel Marcel makes a similar distinction between empirical and spiritual apprehension of the unknown:

> What is unknown and does not know is merely ignored. What knows and does not wish to be known, and proceeds in such a way as not to be known, is mysterious (there is also the category of that which is powerless to make itself known—this, too, belongs to the order of the ignored). The idea of mystery thus implies the idea of power and it is bound up with the very idea of God.[13]

The paradox, from a strictly logical viewpoint, of all religious belief stems from the fact that spiritual knowledge, unlike scientific knowledge, is grounded in this essential mystery. While the laws of a divinity may be revealed to human beings, the nature of that divinity remains hidden. Knowledge based upon acceptance of mystery implies the discovery not of physical laws governing nature but of moral imperatives governing human life. Despite his self-consciously modern "wish that it did not persist," Sammler acknowledges his intuition of mystery and of moral absolutes (236). He affirms that "life is sacred" and murder absolute evil—despite all the practical evidence, accumulated with such ferocious intensity during this century, that human nature is destructive and even murderous. "Everybody," he says, "knows what murder is. That is very old human knowledge. The best and purest human beings, from the beginning of time, have understood that life is sacred" (18).

The belief that "life is sacred" is rooted in a fertile mystery, whether theologically formulated or not, which precedes or transcends the ability to explain and verify "facts." It is not a problem human beings are capable of solving but a condition in which they exist. A problem, by contrast, holds out the promise of solution if the proper data and methods of analysis can be applied. As Marcel points out, "a genuine problem is subject to an appropriate technique by the exercise of which it is defined; whereas a mystery, by definition, transcends every conceivable technique. It is, no doubt, always possible (logically and psychologically) to degrade a mystery so as to turn it into a problem."[14] The existence of evil may serve as a case in point. From time immemorial, human beings have sought to "degrade" the mystery of evil into a problem. By objectifying evil, that is, the observer seeks to locate it outside himself, in a source or a cause rather than a condition in which he participates.[15] To exempt oneself from the conditions either of evil or of existence may prove, in Marcel's words, "a fundamentally vicious proceeding, whose springs might perhaps be discovered in a kind of corruption of the intelligence."[16]

In this century such "corruption of the intelligence" has proliferated in countless forms, most especially in the virulent formulations of ideologues. Bellow's Sammler, witness of two world wars and survivor of the Holocaust, has experienced firsthand the wholesale devastation that can ensue from such "corruption of the intelligence": he has been the victim of would-be ideological "supermen" who, exempting themselves from moral law, attempted to treat "the problem of evil" by locating its source outside themselves. Yet Sammler, although no ideologue, is also attracted to final solutions. As an intellectual and "explainer," he critically analyzes the "problem" of existence and of evil. That he mentally seeks solutions to such problems while he simultaneously seeks refuge from the demands of actual existence is both ironic and revealing. Perhaps that is the temptation, always, for the Cartesian mind grappling with the insoluble "mysteries of inhuman power" (26). There is heady freedom in thinking one has found a solution to the problem, as though the thinker were extricating himself from the binding and at times unbearable conditions of earthly existence. The acrobatic mind would soar free of telluric conditions and the tyranny of gravity, to which matter is subject.

The intellectual's attempt to treat existence "as a problem with a ready answer" has been openly dismissed by Bellow in a playful but astute metaphor. Discussing the rationalists' compulsion to debate, explain, justify, or deny the value of life, he says: "The mystery is too great. So when they knock at the door of mystery with the knuckles of cognition it is quite right that the door should open and some mysterious power should squirt them in the eye."[17] In *Mr. Sammler's Planet,* the power of mystery similarly exposes the absurdity of Sammler's efforts to detach himself from the conditions of mortal existence—to think of himself as "a visiting consciousness which happened to reside in a West Side bedroom" (73).

Paradoxically, it is Sammler's habit of minute observation that draws him into the vortex of human actions from which he keeps hoping to detach himself. His good right eye, "full of observation," inevitably pro-vokes or stimulates those "inward processes" he would rather hold aloof from the world. At the novel's opening, Sammler has already been ob-serving for some time a pickpocket deftly plying his trade on a New York City bus (4). Rapt with attention, he watches the thief unclasp his vic-tim's pocketbook like a doctor lightly touching a patient's belly. To Sammler, this dark action, like all "horror, crime, murder," seems to "viv-ify all the phenomena, the most ordinary details of experience. In evil as in art there was illumination." Thus the world is suddenly and "wick-edly lighted up. Wicked because the clear light made all objects so ex-plicit, and this explicitness taunted Mr. Minutely-Observant Artur Sammler. All metaphysicians please note. Here is how it is. You will never see more clearly. And what do you make of it?" Something about "the essence of being" is thus revealed to Sammler; he has "received from the crime the benefit of an enlarged vision" (11–12). Yet this illumina-tion does not, like the rays of a microscope, light up phenomena that can be objectively measured. Sammler believes he "will never see more clearly," and yet he is left with the still unanswered question: "And what do you make of it?"

The question unanswered, the "problem" unsolved, Sammler neverthe-less craves a repetition of the experience, a revelation of its essential mystery. "Four fascinating times" he watches the skillful performance repeated, until the pickpocket, inadvertently alerted, quietly follows Sammler back to his apartment (10). There, in the empty lobby, he delivers a wordless message, a sure sign of warning, to the startled old man. The man unzips his fly and boldly exposes himself to Sammler: "The man's expression was not directly menacing but oddly, serenely masterful. The thing was shown with mystifying certitude. Lordliness. Then it was returned to the trousers. *Quod erat demonstrandum.* Sammler was released. The fly was closed" (49–50). Like a philosophical proof—*quod erat demonstrandum*—the authority of power is graphically demonstrated. Later in the novel, the pickpocket again serves to open Sammler's eyes to reality. Although occurring under very different circumstances, the scene again focuses on Sammler's intent absorption of visual details—bringing revelation in a rather exact sense of the term, as visually *revealed* truth. As he stands on the sidewalk, watching the pickpocket and Lionel Feffer struggle for possession of a camera, Sammler becomes acutely aware of his role as observer. Shifting his attention to the assembled onlookers and "staring hard," he examines their "faces, passing from face to face among the people along the curb . . . . Then it struck him that what united everybody was a beatitude of presence. As if it were—yes—blessed are the present" (288–89). Then, however, a dreadful feeling steals over Sammler, the suspicion that he is no longer a member of this "blessed" human community. "And suddenly he saw himself not so much standing as strangely leaning, as reclining, and peculiarly in profile, and as a *past* person" (289–90).

The reclining figure of a corpse, here graphically rendered, literally signifies the detachment from life Sammler has been seeking. Now, with this sudden vision of himself as a corpse, he perceives that he has elevated death over life and recognizes that, though physically weak, he is still very much alive, here and now, on this planet. Standing in the midst of chaos, cruelty, and violence, Artur Sammler tacitly affirms life by rejecting that shadowy "past person":

> That was not himself. It was someone—and this struck him—poor in spirit. Someone between the human and not-human states, between content and emptiness, between full and void, meaning and not-meaning, between this world and no world. Flying, freed from gravitation, light with release and dread, doubting his destination, fearing there was nothing to receive him. (290)

Spurred by this sudden recognition, Sammler rushes to engage with existence, attempting to break up the fight; his efforts to halt the struggle backfire, however. His son-in-law, Eisen, whose help he has sought, viciously attacks the black man. In response to Sammler's horrified protests, Eisen reminds the old man that he has known violence before: "You know. We both fought in the war. You were a Partisan. You had a gun" (291). This association between Eisen's murderousness and Sammler's wartime experience is highly significant, and Bellow has carefully prepared for its development in the novel. In an earlier scene, Sammler recalls how, in the dead of winter and on the verge of starvation, he had ambushed a German soldier in the Zamosht Forest. Forced to disarm and surrender his clothes and supplies, the German, standing naked in the snow, had pleaded with Sammler not to shoot. "Don't kill me. Take the things," he had said, "I have children." Sammler had answered by pulling the trigger (138–39). Recalling that perverse pleasure, Sammler asks himself:

> Was it only pleasure? It was more. It was joy. You would call it a dark action? On the contrary, it was also a bright one .... When he fired his gun, Sammler, himself nearly a corpse, burst into life .... When he shot again it was less to make sure of the man than to try again for that bliss. To drink more flames. (140–41)

Here is another illumination from evil, the world "wickedly lighted up" as it is by the pickpocket on the bus. From both illuminations, the "mystery" of evil emerges in a "clear light," vivifying "the most ordinary details of experience."

When the pickpocket exposed himself in the lobby, Sammler perceived the black man's member as a "symbol of superlegitimacy or sovereignty. It was a mystery. It was unanswerable" (55). In this "mystery," however unlikely it may seem, the old man is now shown to participate. In the Zamosht Forest Sammler had wielded the cruel sovereignty of brute force. He had released the trigger not to save his own life but to give vent to his power, to experience the animal ecstasy of conquest. Although Sammler initially perceives the pickpocket's "assertion of power" as a sign of Western culture's general "madness," the black man's ultimate function is to illuminate the *specific* existence of Mr. Sammler (55). Through this encounter with his apparent opposite, Sammler is led to confront, unexpectedly, himself—a part of the very "problem" he is attempting to analyze.

Most often described as a symbol of evil, urban violence or Sammler's own repressed sexuality, the pickpocket's function as a catalyst for Sammler's revelation appears thus far to have been overlooked.[18] Unlikely as the comparison between this "African prince or great black beast" and the aged European intellectual might at first seem, the pickpocket clearly serves to implicate Sammler in his condition (14). That Sammler acts to save the thief's life after having been mortally threatened by him is itself highly suggestive.[19] Bellow draws the reader's attention to the doubling theme in more apparent ways as well: both men, for example, gaze at the world through tinted glasses. While the pickpocket sports fashionable "gentian violet" glasses expensively ringed with "Dior gold," Sammler wears plainer "colored specs" to hide his disfigured left eye (50, 87). His most dominant features are, in fact, those "pale-tufted eyes shaded by tinted glasses" (16). Sammler's spectacles are clearly linked to his role and identity as observer. But when, on the bus, Sammler suddenly realizes that the pickpocket has spotted him watching the thief's dark actions, the old man has an uncanny sense of their roles being reversed, as in a mirror: "Mr. Sammler in his goggles was troubled in focusing. Too much adrenalin was passing .... It was at this moment that, in a quick turn of his head, [the pickpocket] saw Mr. Sammler. Mr. Sammler seen seeing was still in rapid currents with his heart" (46–47). The observer, "seen seeing," abruptly becomes the object of observation—and the initial object, the pickpocket, now assumes the role of observer himself. Later, when the pickpocket proceeds with his graphic "lesson" in the lobby, he begins, significantly, by removing Sammler's (the observer's) spectacles. Delivering his "message," the black man will not allow Sammler to maintain his detached vantage: "Then the smoked glasses were removed from Sammler's face and dropped on the table. He was directed, silently, to look downward" (49). At the lesson's conclusion, the black man "picked up Sammler's dark glasses and returned them to his nose. He then unfolded and mounted his own, circular, ... gently banded with the lovely Dior gold" (50). Still later, when Sammler recalls their strange and wordless encounter, their "two pairs of dark glasses" form twinned images in his memory (65).

At this point in the novel Sammler already makes a telling, though indirect, comparison between the black man's "creatureliness" and his own: "In the past, Mr. Sammler had thought that in this same biological respect he was comely enough, in his own Jewish way" (66). Though such biological "comeliness" matters little to Sammler "now, in the seventies," he implicitly regards the pickpocket's exposed member as a dark reflection of his own. Sammler's "descent" to recognized creatureliness appears to be an essential aspect of his gradual and acknowledged reappropriation of earthly existence. Indeed, when Sammler first involuntarily recognizes the thief, as the pickpocket corners another victim on another bus, Sammler has the intense sensation of "immediate descent," both physical and emotional: that of "a stone falling" and "his heart sinking" (45). This sudden assertion by the forces of gravity of "a law of nature" already foreshadows Sammler's ultimate return, emotionally and spiritually, to his "planet" earth.

Later in the novel Sammler comments on the effects of his encounter with the pickpocket: "Objectively I have little use for such experiences, but there is such an absurd craving for actions that connect with other actions, for coherency, for forms, for mysteries or fables. I may have thought that I had no more ordinary human curiosity left, but I was surprisingly wrong" (120). Sammler makes a telling distinction here between the "objective" vantage he customarily adopts as a detached observer

and his "ordinary human curiosity." Attachment to life, recognition of
one's participation in the world, is identified in Sammler's mind with
a kind of knowledge more "human" than that which his own "objective"
analysis yields. "The objective tendency," as Kierkegaard says, "proposes
to make everyone an observer, and in its maximum to transform him
into so objective an observer that he becomes almost a ghost."[20] Where
matters of existence are concerned, the objective vantage may not be
assumed, as in science, to be superior to subjective forms of knowledge.
That is why Sammler, in his ultimate encounter with the pickpocket, perceives detachment as the condition of one "poor in spirit"—a "past person" caught "between human and non-human states." This is the ghostly
existence Sammler rejects; it is false, "not himself."

The analogy between Sammler's and Kierkegaard's ghostly metaphors
is hardly accidental. Underlying Sammler's ceaseless internal dialogue
is the tension between perceived categories of subjective and objective
knowledge, categories to which Kierkegaard devoted hundreds of pages
in his *Concluding Unscientific Postscript*. In acquiring objective knowledge,
of mathematical or physical laws, for example, one does not have to become subjectively involved. Their acquisition, as Gilson says, "is wholly
unrelated to [one's] own *Ego*."[21] Objective knowledge of love or of God,
on the other hand, is impossible, because the "object" to be known—
God or the beloved—affects and is actively appropriated by the knowing subject.

In counterpoint to Sammler's subjective appropriation of existence
is his intermittent longing for "release from Nature"; he is drawn to Dr.
Lal's scientific treatise on future moon-colonies because it suggests to
him technological possibilities for divestment. On the moon, "conditions
altogether different" in the psychological as well as the physical sense
might obtain. "Austere technicians—almost a priesthood" might succeed
in creating an environment of "lunar chastity." In so rationally austere
a world there might be no lovers, no mystery, no participation in the
sublunar "madness" of irrational existence. Everything in Sammler's own
existence, however, conspires against the credibility, let alone the fulfillment, of such "moon-visions" (67). The claims of existence, like the
physical laws of Nature and gravity to which they are wedded, are shown
to hold sway over every human being. As Sammler comes to realize, death
offers the only possible release from these human laws. The pickpocket,
as I have suggested, is the catalyst for Sammler's gradual coming to terms
with gravity and his conscious re-entry into "the bondage of the ordinary and the finite" (117–18).

Just as Sammler's powers of minute and exacting observation paradoxically implicate him, through his encounter with the criminal, in both

the "creatureliness" and the "murderousness" of his species—and in the mystery of evil—so does his propensity for "moon-visions" paradoxically draw him deeper into the labyrinth of human relationships. Learning that his daughter Shula has actually stolen Professor Lal's scientific treatise, Sammler awakens to a renewed sense of responsibility not only to Lal but to his own flesh and blood as well. He immediately becomes involved in a complicated series of events that strengthen his bonds with others. He discovers, moreover, that his nephew, Elya Gruner, on whom he has been financially dependent for years, had received payment from the Mafia for illicit medical "favors." Through Gruner, he is further implicated in the flawed existence of imperfect humanity. There is nothing "pure," in the Cartesian sense, about the mixed conditions of creaturely existence. Sammler inwardly avows, however, that for all his human imperfections, Elya Gruner, who dies at the novel's end, was not only a good man but a better person than Sammler himself: "At his best this man was much kinder than at my very best I have ever been or could ever be" (313). In life Elya Gruner was able "to do what was required of him"; by the end of the novel Sammler knows that, until his own release from the "bondage" of the finite, he too must carry out the terms of the "contract" binding him, like every other human being, to existence.

At every turn in this novel, try as he may to remain a detached observer, Sammler is caught up in the web of existence; he can no more break the bonds that tie him to others than he can defy gravity itself. For Sammler is bound to humankind not just by nature, or evil, but by love. His exasperation with his crazy daughter Shula may be profound, but his love for her is far more profound: "He cared too much for her. He cherished her. And really, his only contribution to the continuation of the species!" (116). If one is not yet a "past person," objective analysis of the terms of existence will take second place to that subjective process by which the lover, of God or of other human beings, actively appropriates what he knows. For the living, existence cannot be solved by a philosophical, social, or scientific system. The "knuckles of cognition," in Bellow's phrase, cannot open the "door of mystery." Not until he has endured yet another mortal loss, the death of Elya Gruner, does Sammler fully embrace the "mystery of dying" and of life itself (273). Only at the novel's close does he remove the tinted glasses shielding his "two different-looking eyes." In a "level" gaze uniting the operative right eye with the left one's "sightless bubble," Sammler's divided vision appears, for the first time, to become whole (311–12).

Bellow's affinity for Kierkegaard's existential viewpoint should by now be obvious. Not only do relevant passages from Kierkegaard's writings illuminate Sammler's situation but Sammler is also shown to be conscious of such analogies: "Able to carry the jewel of faith, making the motions of the infinite, and as a result needing nothing but the finite and the usual"—this is Sammler's understanding of Kierkegaard's "Knight of Faith," as he recalls to himself a passage from *Fear and Trembling*. To arrive at a true sense of the eternal within existence is, Sammler perceives, the task of "the real prodigy" of contemporary culture (62). Rather than seek release from the bondage of the finite, this modern champion would evince his faith by participating fully in the most mundane duties and tasks of finite existence. Sammler's psychological re-entry into his "planet" at the end of the novel, his renewed recognition of the earthly obligations assumed through such a "homecoming," suggest that he may have fulfilled a quest comparable in some ways, at least, to that of Kierkegaard's Knight. In the philosopher's words, Sammler has been "reconciled with existence" while having forgotten none of its cruelty and pain.[22]

That essential forms of knowledge are both subjective and rooted in the everyday is the Kierkegaardian paradox underlying Sammler's gradual reconciliation to existence. As a *speculative* possibility, this celebration of the ordinary occurs to him rather early in the novel. "What if," he thinks, "some genius were to do with 'common life' what Einstein did with 'matter'? Finding its energetics, uncovering its radiance" (147). The source of radiance in the common life of human beings is not, of course, physical light traveling at measurable speed through the universe but the soul's illumination of truth. This light does not emanate from the multifarious data of existence but from the mind that irradiates phenomena with understanding. Because, as I have tried to show, the "light" of Sammler's own understanding tends to fluctuate between the poles of analysis and intuition, or between modes of subjective (or "natural") and objective knowing, the phenomena he observes are irradiated by contrary shades of meaning. For Sammler, the same phenomena that evince the disorder and "madness" sweeping Western culture also yield, when seen in another "light," evidence of humanity's extraordinary and consistent "regard for order":

> But wait—Sammler [thought] cautioning himself. Even this madness is also to a considerable extent a matter of performance, of enactment. Underneath there persists, powerfully too, a thick sense of what is normal for human life. Duties are observed. Attachments are preserved. There is work. People show up for jobs. It is extraordinary .... For such a volatile and restless animal, such a high-strung, curious animal, an ape subject to so many diseases, to anguish, boredom, such discipline, such drill, such strength for regularity, such

> assumption of responsibility, such regard for order (even in disorder)
> is a great mystery, too. Oh, it is a mystery. (146–47)

Within the compass of this passage Sammler moves from contemplation
of the human being as problem to the mystery of being. The biological
factors invoked by the analyst to account for the limited nature of man—
this volatile, restless, and disease-ridden ape—also testify, when irradiated in a different light, to the mysterious power of the human being
to transcend those limits outlined, and apparently verified, by the data.

In passages such as this one, Bellow traces the movement of a soul
not turning away from reality but engaged with it, articulating what it
knows. To hearken to that inner speech, that "different speech" affirm-
ing the soul's "natural knowledge," one does not reject concrete
phenomena or the claims of existence, as Meister Eckhart counsels.
Rather, by participating in the ordinary and the finite one may
discover—beneath the confusing surface and overlapping "superstructures of explanation"—life's radiant source. These "energetics" cannot
be uncovered by an Einstein, however; rapping with the "knuckles of
cognition" will not open the door. A mystery that draws the observer
into its reality, the "radiance" of common life may be penetrated only
from within. The knowledge Sammler had sought in detachment he discovers, instead, through his love for others and his acknowledged participation in the conditions of mortality. This is the knowledge of which
Sammler speaks, in a "mental whisper," at the end of the novel.

These final lines are often misread, I believe, because the rift in
Sammler's consciousness has heretofore received inadequate attention.
Most of Bellow's critics find the novel's concluding lines unconvincing;
some detect a note of "emotional withdrawal" or even of "self-reproach"
on Sammler's part.[23] Yet the very form of Sammler's final utterance signals, as it brings to rest, the conflict between the "two different speeches"
of his divided consciousness. Contrary to Kazin's assumption, for example, that the closing lines reiterate Sammler's "Jewish passion" for
"ratiocination as the only passion that doesn't wear out," the mode of
Sammler's address appeals neither to reason nor to scientific objectivity.[24]
He speaks, after all, in a medium that is the soul's acknowledged mode
of discourse—the language of prayer itself: "For that is the truth of it—
that we all know, God, that we know, that we know, we know, we know"
(313). Here the knowledge Sammler affirms, as Gilson says, is "evident
to a soul, not to a mind," and is most appropriately articulated in the
cadences of prayer. Throughout the novel, however, Bellow has employed
the contemporary language of fiction to distinguish the "two different
speeches" of Sammler's divided psyche. Thus the novel, by voicing

modern "intellectual man's" conflict, retrieves, to some extent, the ancient knowledge of which he has dispossessed himself.

Notes

1. Alfred Kazin, *Bright Book of Life: American Novelists and Storytellers from Hemingway to Mailer* (Boston: Little, Brown, and Co., 1973), 134, 136–37.
2. John J. Clayton, *Saul Bellow: In Defense of Man,* 2nd ed. (Bloomington: Indiana University Press, 1979), 234–36; also see Mark Schechner, "Down in the Mouth with Saul Bellow," *American Review* 23 (1975): 64, 67; cited in Clayton, 235; David Galloway, "*Mr. Sammler's Planet:* Bellow's Failure of Nerve," *Modern Fiction Studies* 19, no. 1 (Spring 1973): 23–24.
3. Jane Howard, "Mr. Bellow Considers His Planet," *Life,* 3 April 1970, 59; Robert Boyers, "Literature and Culture: An Interview with Saul Bellow," *Salmagundi* 30 (Summer 1975): 23.
4. See, for example, Malcolm Bradbury, "'The Nightmare in Which I'm Trying to Get a Good Night's Rest': Saul Bellow and Changing History," in *Saul Bellow and His Work,* ed. Edmond Schraepen (Brussels: Free University of Brussels, 1978), 28; also see, in Schraepen's volume, Brigitte Scheer-Schäzler, "Epistemology as Narrative Device in the Work of Saul Bellow," 105, 109; M. Gilbert Porter, "Hitch Your Agony to a Star: Bellow's Transcendent Vision," 80, 87; Tony Tanner, "Afterword," 143; also see Clayton, 262.
5. Boyers, "Interview with Bellow," 8.
6. *Pascal's Thoughts,* trans. W. F. Trotter, in Blaise Pascal, *Thoughts, Letters, Minor Works,* ed. Charles W. Eliot, *The Harvard Classics* 48 (New York: Collier, 1910), 9–10.
7. Saul Bellow, *Mr. Sammler's Planet* (New York: Viking, 1970), 90.
8. Robert Boyers, "Nature and Social Reality in Bellow's *Sammler,*" *Critical Quarterly* 15 (Autumn 1973): 44.
9. Étienne Gilson, *The Unity of Philosophical Experience* (New York: Scribner's, 1937), 173, 184.
10. See M. Gilbert Porter, *Whence the Power: The Artistry and Humanity of Saul Bellow* (Columbia: University of Missouri Press, 1974), 161–62.
11. Clayton, 245, 249–50, 260; also see Bradbury, 23; Sarah Blacher Cohen, *Saul Bellow's Enigmatic Laughter* (Urbana: University of Illinois Press, 1974), 184–85, 209; Galloway, "Culture-Making: The Recent Works of Bellow," in Schraepen, ed. *Saul Bellow and His Work,* 59.
12. Boyers, "Interview with Bellow," 19.
13. Gabriel Marcel, *Metaphysical Journal,* trans. Bernard Wall (Chicago: Henry Regnery, 1952), 160–61.
14. Marcel, *The Mystery of Being I,* trans. G. S. Fraser (Chicago: Henry Regnery, 1950), 211–12. Marcel is quoting himself here; the passage is taken from the English translation of *Being and Having.*
15. I am indebted to Richmond Hathorn, who discusses Marcel's meditations on evil in his study, *Tragedy, Myth and Mystery* (Bloomington: Indiana University Press, 1962), 17.

16. Marcel, *The Mystery of Being* I, 212.
17. Gordon Lloyd Harper, "Saul Bellow: An Interview," *Paris Review* 37 (Winter 1965); rpt. in *Saul Bellow: A Collection of Critical Essays,* ed. Earl Rovit (Englewood Cliffs, N.J.: Prentice-Hall, 1975), 14.
18. See, for example, Clayton's psychoanalytic interpretation, 238.
19. Cf. Galloway, 55.
20. Soren Kierkegaard, *Concluding Unscientific Postscript,* trans. David F. Swenson and Walter Lowrie (Princeton: Princeton University Press, 1968), 118.
21. Étienne Gilson, *Being and Some Philosophers* (Toronto: Political Institute of Medieval Studies, 1949), 143–44.
22. Soren Kierkegaard, *Fear and Trembling,* trans. Walter Lowrie, in *A Kierkegaard Anthology,* ed. Robert Bretall (Princeton: Princeton University Press, 1947), 123.
23. See, for example, Clayton, 246; Cohen, 193; and Porter, *Whence the Power?* 180.
24. Kazin, 137.

Cri de Coeur: The Inner Reality of Saul Bellow's The Dean's December

Matthew C. Roudané

[The Dean's December] *was a* cri de coeur. *I just could no longer stand the fact that the city and the country were in decay under our very eyes and people would not talk about the facts. They might talk about money to change things, but never about what was actually happening. No one levels any more. So it was a cry. But I don't know whether anyone heard it.*[1]

Saul Bellow

Much of the critical reception to and apparent dissatisfaction with Saul Bellow's *The Dean's December* centers on the mimetic fallacy and narrative inertia to which the novelist falls prey. Largely a novel of ideas, its detractors claim, *The Dean's December* tediously plods along with its thinly sketched characters.[2] Perhaps the novel lacks the vitality of *Henderson the Rain King*, the technical virtuosity of *Seize the Day*, the aesthetic richness of *Humboldt's Gift*, and the lightheartedness of selected pieces in *Him with His Foot in His Mouth and Other Stories*, but *The Dean's December* ultimately embodies an engaging tale, one as complex and multivalent as any Bellow fiction to date.[3] A careful examination of Bellow's ninth novel reveals a successful fusion, in the Coleridgean sense, of idea and image. This fusion accounts for a novel that extends Bellow's philosophical absorption with the individual's struggle with the complex business of living. In the study that follows, I hope to demonstrate that *The Dean's December* forms a coherent whole through the objectification of Albert Corde's inner reality, a reality that mirrors far too accurately, Bellow suggests, our contemporary world.

During an interview, Bellow clarified what were his central thematic concerns within *The Dean's December*:

First printed in *Studies in the Humanities* 11, no. 2 (December 1984): 5–17.

> I wanted to write a book about Chicago, and I went out to look at
> the town again. This new inspection didn't inspire humor. The facts
> were dreadful. What were my thematic concerns, you ask? One of
> my themes is the American denial of real reality, our devices for evad-
> ing it, our refusal to face what is all too obvious and palpable. The
> book is filled with protest against this evasion, against the techniques
> of illusion and the submission to taboos by means of which this is
> accomplished. Corde thinks that we are becoming wraiths, spooks.
> It seems to him that we have lost all capacity for dealing with
> experience—no capacity to think about it, no language for it, no real
> words.[4]

The present study, then, investigates what precisely motivates Corde. Surrounded by a world which seems incapable of "dealing with experience,"
Corde is at once attracted to and repulsed by, in terms of his public and
private self, those in Bucharest and Chicago whose "denial of real reality" obfuscates their political, aesthetic, and moral faculties. Bellow
summed up the effect of this condition on the individual as "the slum"
of the psyche.[5]

Bellow's narrative technique shows the world as filtered through the
consciousness of Corde. Bellow's strategy is to use the inner meditative
perceptions of Corde's mind as the shaping principle of the novel. Within
this context, critical objections to the novel's inertia, to the actionless-
ness of the plot, seem questionable. As Allan Chavkin convincingly argues, "The style of the novel is in accord with the meditative form. Bellow
has created a language that captures the process of Corde's mind as it
explores its problems."[6]

What strikes us most forcibly in *The Dean's December* is not the external environment—the enameled bureaucrats in Bucharest, the rape and
murder victims in Chicago—but the image of the protagonist, Corde.
As Stanley Trachtenberg, in writing about Bellow's heroes in general,
observes: "Environment has functioned less as an influence on events
and characters than as a projection of their inner conflict, a symbol as
well as an agent of inhuman darkness. Bellow's protagonists are thus
placed in a social environment but oppressed by personal natural forces
that obscure the resulting tensions by developing them in oblique relation to their framing situations."[7] Trachtenberg's remarks apply to Corde
precisely. To be sure, the narrative line of the novel, with its graphic
depiction of "social environment," interests us; but what engages Bellow's imagination is Corde's ongoing struggle to evaluate *internally* his
self, and that way in which that self responds to the other. It is a disarming

correlation. Within *The Dean's December*, Bellow thus presents the inner reality of Corde, a consciousness which is in crisis with the external world. As cosmic observer, Corde discovers "the slum" of the psyche, a corrosive force which, for Bellow, devitalizes contemporary civilization in general and its denizens in particular. Bellow, himself, clarifies this point in his remarks on the novel:

> What I meant was there is a correspondence between outer and inner, between the brutalized city and the psyche of its citizens. Given their human resources I don't see how people today can experience life at all. Politicians, public figures, professors address "modern problems" solely in terms of employment. They assume that unemployment causes incoherence, sexual disorder, the abandonment of children, robbery, rape, and murder. Plainly, they have no imagination of these evils. They don't even see them. And in *The Dean's December* what I did was to say, "Look!" The first step is to display the facts. But the facts, unless the imagination perceives them, are *not* facts. Perhaps I shouldn't say "perceives"—I should say "passionately takes hold." As an artist does. Mr. Corde, the Dean, passionately takes hold of Chicago and writes his articles like an artist rather than a journalist. He's an in-between type, perhaps like the Orwell who wrote *Down and Out,* or the *Wigan Pier* book.[8]

Corde's compassionate (and at times misplaced) assault against such a corrosive force motivates his responses throughout the novel. As Corde reflects: "But I (damn!), starting to collect material for a review of life in my native city, and finding at once wounds, lesions, cancers, destructive fury, death, felt (and how quirkily) called upon for a special exertion—to interpret, to pity, to save!" (201). We sense in the preceding passage Corde's optimism, and Bellow scholars will quickly note that such an attitude is characteristic of the Bellow hero. What confirms our sense, however, is Corde's qualifying reflection which immediately follows: "This was stupid. It was insane. But now the process was begun, how was I to stop it? I couldn't stop it" (201). Corde's "review" of Chicago led to a discovery of a more unnerving fact—that the "lesions" and "cancers" were only surface manifestations of a deeper condition: "It was not so much the inner city slum that threatened us as the slum of the innermost being, of which the inner city was perhaps a material representation" (201). Reflecting on the rootedness of such a condition generates much anxiety in Corde, an anguish that reveals more about the quality of his sensibility and values than Chicago's slums: "As I spelled this out I felt that I looked ailing and sick. A kind of hot haze came over me. I felt my weakness as I approached the business of the soul—its true business in this age" (201).

As one approaching "the business of the soul," Corde extends the tradition of the Bellow hero. Like Artur Sammler in *Mr. Sammler's Planet,* Charlie Citrine in *Humboldt's Gift,* and Herschel Shawmut in "Him with His Foot in His Mouth," Corde appears overly sensitive, highminded, shrewd, contradictory, a man "subject to fits of vividness" (151). That is, Corde wrestles with the same psychological conflicts that weigh so heavily on the Bellow protagonist. He inherits many of the traits which M. A. Klug defines in Bellow's central figures: "Bellow's heroes contain both the heroic self and the ordinary self. . . . His heroes are driven in pursuit of self-perfection and at the same time paralyzed by immersion in a hostile environment of death."[9] Corde finds himself caught in such a conflict.

A Dartmouth graduate, World War II veteran, and formerly talented journalist, Corde now holds a deanship at a Chicago university. Disheartened by the media's inability to report honestly and adequately about human intercourse, Corde recently published, in his "pursuit of self-perfection," a highly controversial series of articles in *Harper's,* an exposé chronicling the human wasteland of his native city. Corde explains his motives for writing the articles to childhood cohort and now-prominent journalist Dewey Spangler, pinpointing the source of his lover's quarrel with the world:

> I meant that we'd better deal with whatever it is that's in us by na-
> ture, and I don't see people being willing to do that. What I mainly
> see is the evasion. But this is a thing that works on the substance
> of the soul—the spirit of the time, in us by nature, working on every
> soul. We prefer to have such things served up to us as concepts. We'd
> rather have them abstract, stillborn, dead. But as long as they don't
> come to us with some kind of reality, as facts of experience, then
> all we can have instead of good and evil is . . . well, concepts. Then
> we'll never learn how the soul is worked on. (243)

We learn much about Corde's sensibility as well as Bellow's moral seriousness in the above passage. To learn about the human soulscape, Corde feels a moral imperative to rediscover, ontologically, the nature of human communication and objective reality. Bellow establishes this point emphatically while presenting one of Corde's inner reflections: "Therefore the first act of morality was to disinter the reality, retrieve reality, dig it out from the trash, represent it anew as art would represent it" (123). This is why Corde's directing force in life centers on the impulse "to recover the world that is buried under the debris of false description or nonexperience'" (243). In Bellow's presentation, Corde believes that our reliance on abstractions denatures the vitality implicit in human interaction. Such a dependency, for Corde, blocks any real communication.

Corde accepts the Shelleyan injunction that art pleases, delights, and instructs—even in a business-as-sacrament world. Corde embraces the language of art because of a conviction that poetic discourse is a valid, felt symbolic formulation of human experience. Poetic discourse plays counterpoint to the "false consciousness" and "horrible distortions" to which the language of journalism gives rise. Poetry embodies, for Bellow, "real" experience, functioning to provide a more adequate account of human events, not when they are merely reported journalistically, but when they are experienced, according to T. S. Eliot, as felt thoughts. Discovering one's humanity is possible through art, Corde posited in *Harper's,* because "perhaps only poetry had the strength to rival the attractions of narcotics, the magnetism of TV, the excitements of sex, or the ecstacies of destruction'" (187).[10] Appalled by the falsification of experience implicit in a "modern public consciousness'" (122) that precludes the masses' "capacity to experience" events (123), Corde accepts his self-issued challenge to take a qualitative measurement of the world around:

> Thus he had taken it upon himself to pass Chicago through his own soul. A mass of data, terrible, murderous. It was no easy matter to put such things through. But there was no other way for reality to happen. Reality didn't exist "out there." It began to be real only when the soul found its underlying truth. (266)

We may gain deeper understanding of Bellow's protagonist by examining the way in which he responds to selected key figures within the novel. Corde finds himself in Bucharest, lending emotional assistance to his wife, Minna, who is attempting to visit her stricken mother, Valeria Raresh. Such visits seem impossible because of strict Communist Party Hospital rules.

The enforcer of the Hospital's rules is the Colonel, whose unyielding stance brings him and Corde into immediate conflict. Bellow wastes little time in establishing the differences between the two: "Where the Colonel was tight, Corde was inclined to be loose. The Colonel's sparse hair was

straight back, military style; Corde's baldness was more random, a broad
bay, a struggling growth of black hair" (2). In context, the physical
dissimilarities are emblematic of deeper differences, based on human
values, between the two. Bellow develops, for example, an image of the
Colonel as a man who appears detached from human suffering, but who,
like Nurse Ratchett in Ken Kesey's *One Flew Over the Cuckoo's Nest* or the
interrogators Zakarakis and Theophiloiannakos in Oriana Fallaci's *A
Man,* relishes doling out punishment:

> The Colonel, towards the end of the interview, put on a long, judi-
> cious look—cunning, twisting the knife—and said that if Valeria was
> removed from the intensive care unit, Minna might come as often
> as she liked. Unhooked from the machines, the old woman would
> die in fifteen minutes. This of course he did not spell out. But there
> was your choice, madam. This was the man's idea of a joke. You de-
> livered it at the point of a knife. (5–6)

The callousness of the Colonel counterbalances the sensitivity of Corde,
who appears overwhelmed by the sight of bedridden Valeria:

> Every bit of it moved him—more than that, it worked him up; more
> than that, it made him wild, drove him into savage fantasies. He
> wanted to cry, as his wife was doing. Tears did come, but also an
> eager violence, a kind of get-it-over ecstasy mingling pity and de-
> structiveness. (5)

The intensity of his response provides us with an early indication concerning the depth of Corde's capacity to feel.

That many of the characters in the novel are unwilling or unable to
match Corde's passionate immersion into daily and worldly encounters,
his capacity to feel, becomes obvious when, through the meditative consciousness of Corde, we are privy to their responses. One who plays a
pivotal role is Dewey Spangler.

Spangler's observations and criticisms of Corde further narrative development and increase our knowledge of what motivates Bellow's hero.
Fortuitously meeting in Bucharest, Spangler and Corde reminisce about
childhood predicaments and present achievements. As a child, for instance, Corde was drawn to Spangler for his interest in the humanities:
"'It was the poetry and the philosophy . . . . It was Spinoza and the Walt
Whitman. It was the William Blake. Nobody else was interested'" (116).
For Corde, Spangler stood as a rare individual: a high school peer who
also read and discussed Great Things (they co-authored a book at age

sixteen), and who dared to define himself through action, as seen when he takes on an infamous Bleacher Bum:

> Bossy, fussy little bastard, in spite of his world eminence he was still Screwy Dewey, the starved alleycat boy intellectual—the same Dewey who had fought a two-hundred pound Cubs fan in the Wrigley Field bleachers, hitting him with a book of poems. Spangler had been a frightful kid, but Corde had loved him. (110)

Bellow suggests that the unifying connection between Corde and Spangler as adolescents centered around their shared focus on liberal arts.

For Spangler, however, such study is best left for adolescents; it has no real place in a sophisticated world: "Spangler was marveling (teasing) that this juvenilia should still be so influential. Spangler had put it behind him; for some reason Corde had not" (120). Because he is still influenced by poets and poetry, reflects Spangler, "Albert had lost his grip" (120), not only with what it means to be a mature adult, but with objective reality as well.

Bellow heightens the spiritual gulf between the two by presenting a Spangler who has mastered his vocation well, who has become a force to be reckoned with in the professional world. And a clever, practical-minded Spangler has fortified himself within the Fourth Estate, embellishing reports with trendy allusions to the arts (120–21). Bellow, during an interview, discussed Corde and Spangler's relationship:

> Corde was educated in Lincoln Park together with Dewey Spangler. They read poetry together. Corde took poetry seriously, whereas Spangler did not. Corde makes real demands upon language. To Spangler, the columnist, words do not matter. Now how does Corde survive? Remember that he reads *The Chicago Tribune* every day. It is Corde's conviction that without art, it is impossible to interpret reality, and that the degeneration of art and language leads to the decay of judgment.[11]

However, from Corde's viewpoint, Spangler looms as a well-meaning yet lacking individual. This is not to suggest that Spangler assumes the charlatan role Dr. Tamkin does in *Seize the Day*, but we sense a scheming and selfish quality to Spangler that invites the comparison. Like Tamkin, Spangler "was suavely solicitous—oh, what a smoothie Dewey had become in the great world!" (233). And Spangler seems perceptive but, again like Tamkin, uses his knowledge to manipulate. Corde senses this—

"Corde wondered whether he wasn't being interviewed by Dewey" (244), an intuition which is confirmed when, near the end of the novel, Spangler publishes such disparaging remarks about his "friend" that Alec Witt, provost of the university, fires Corde.

Despite his weaknesses, however, Spangler provides the reader with more insight on the novel's central intelligence, Corde:

> In *Harper's* you crossed and offended just about everybody. You might have gotten away with it if you had adopted the good old Mencken *Boobus Americanus* approach. Humor would have made the difference. But you lambasted them all. Really—you gave 'em hard cuts, straight across the muzzle. The obscurity of your language may have protected you somewhat—all the theorizing and the poetry. Lots of people must have been mystified and bogged down by it, and just gave up. All the better for you if they didn't read your message clearly. They're all happy, of course, to see you get your lumps. (117–18)

But the nature of Spangler's remarks on his lifelong friend are throughout the novel double-edged: on the one hand they function to illustrate the shared perceptivity and reactions both men have towards certain American institutions; but Spangler's critical remarks of Corde, on the other hand, point towards a gulf in values that ultimately will sever their relationship.

Finally, Spangler emerges as a despicable figure. He appears as such a figure because of a lack of authentic sensitivity towards Corde's predicament. He knows that Corde is in the midst of an emotionally draining period with the death of Valeria and with the controversial Ricky Lester trial. And yet Spangler displays no real concern for Corde. Rather, he "interviews" Corde and proceeds to betray their sense of confidentiality, to violate the limits of friendship, using Corde to better his own career. While reading Spangler's article, Corde appears momentarily shattered: "As he read this, the Dean discovered that he almost stopped breathing. What a smart little monster Dewey was, and what a keen schemer, and how rivalrous. He disposed of the Dean by describing him as an unwitting alien" (300). And minutes later Corde reflects his innermost feelings about Spangler: "Oh, fuck you, Dewey, and your Julian Brenda! Corde, knuckling his eyes, smarting with sweat, read on. There wasn't much left, thank God" (302). Between Corde's reflections and the omniscient narrator's reports, we learn how insecure, opportunistic, and competitive Spangler turns out to be. Spangler's childhood insecurities apparently carry over into adulthood, for his responses seem calculated to belittle Corde emotionally, to show his nemesis who is "better." To be sure, the reader pities Spangler's pathetic physical condition, one that probably fuels his insecurities, but in the final analysis, he emerges as an egocentric "schemer" whose physical ailments provide no excuse for his verbal assault.

Throughout *The Dean's December*, Bellow presents Corde in several antagonistic relationships as seen, for example, in his encounters with the Colonel, Spangler, Sam Varennes, and Mason Zaehner, Jr. However, Bellow also shows Corde in sympathetic correspondence with several other characters—Sam Beech, Rufus Ridpath, and Toby Winthrop, for instance—and these positive relationships give us a fuller understanding of Corde. But a look at two other pivotal figures with whom Corde interacts best illustrates my point.

Corde's relationship with Valeria is thematically central to the novel. Their relationship reveals the depth of Corde's capacity to love. An early key scene demonstrates this point. In the opening chapter, we learn that while Minna read a paper at a scientific conference, Corde escorted Valeria for two days. It was an awkward time for Corde, presumably because his mother-in-law scrutinized his character and his worthiness during this time. Touring the Étoile, Corde realized the vacation was physically too demanding for the near-eighty-year-old Valeria: "He was upset for her. She couldn't keep her balance; she was tipping, listing, seemed unable to coordinate the movements of her feet" (15). Although she does not care to admit it because of her strong spirit, Valeria is extremely frail.

But what makes this scene thematically important is its suggestion that Corde appears intuitively in touch with Valeria: he is not only aware of her frailty but radiates a genuine concern for the old woman's predicament. Bellow elaborates this point later when Valeria is moments from death: "Corde thought of her with extraordinary respect. Her personal humanity came from the old sources" (105). It is her "personal humanity," of course, to which Corde responds; further, it is a response tempered not out of any sense of familial duty, but out of his authentic rapprochement with Valeria: he has discovered in Valeria "the feeling of human agreement" for which he constantly yearns (13).

Bellow further presents the nature of Corde and Valeria's relationship during a rare hospital visit. Verbal expression of their love surfaces for the first time within this scene:

> Consciousness was as clear as it had ever been. No, more acute than ever, for when Minna signaled that he should take her hand (again he noted the blue splayed knuckle, and the blue kink of the vein there), she pressed his fingers promptly. He said, "We came as soon

> as possible." Then as if he should not delay the essential message,
> he said in his deep voice, "I also love you, Valeria." (128)

Bellow then presents the impact of Corde's felt declaration, mixing the
tragic and the comic:

> This had a violent effect. One of her knees came up, her eyes, very
> full under the skin of the lids, moved back and forth. She made an
> effort to force them open. Her face was taken by a spasm. The moni-
> tors jumped simultaneously. All the numbers began to tumble and
> whirl. He might have killed her by saying that. Either because she
> believed him or because she did not. But she ought to have believed
> him. So far as he painfully knew, it was the truth. (128)

The significance of this passage lies in its presentation of a palpable
love between Corde and Valeria. And because Minna has been so preoccupied and, hence, detached from her husband, the shared love here
seem accentuated.

That Valeria reciprocates his love becomes evident for Corde when
he, to his astonishment, receives her gold watch as a gift. An emblematic
gift, the watch signifies to Corde that she fully accepts him. The import
of the gesture becomes clear when he recalls the Étoile scene noted
earlier:

> He reckoned that after London, and especially after the Rowlandson
> exhibition and dinner at the Étoile, Valeria had accepted him as a
> full member of the family. When he had tried to take her by the el-
> bow because she was listing, could no longer keep her balance, when
> she pulled her arm away, it had depressed him (something like the
> streak of a black grease pencil over his feelings); he felt that she was
> irritated with him. But that hadn't been what it meant. On the con-
> trary, it was then that his probation had ended. (183)

Bellow emphasizes the sympathetic correspondence between Corde
and Valeria a final time: during the funeral and crematorium scenes.
While the authorities politicize her death, Bellow suggests that Corde
humanizes the event, a point made clear when he evaluates the proceedings: "The speeches now began. Corde had lived long enough in Europe
to be familiar with the Communist oratory, the lame rhythms or rhetorical questions and answers. 'Who is this woman? She was . . . a comrade,
a militant . . .' Terrible stuff" (211). Although the ossified, politically correct speeches serve their purpose, they also negate, by implication for
Corde, the loss in human terms. The political speeches, what Sinclair

Lewis in *It Can't Happen Here* calls "orgasms of oratory,"[12] have the same anesthetizing influence that American journalism has on the public consciousness. Such an influence motivates Corde to reaffirm his humanity. In some of the strongest writing in the novel—the Dantean crematorium episodes—Bellow clearly presents the humanizing quality Corde interjects during Valeria's funeral.

Although Bellow devotes little time developing Albert's relationship with Minna, it is also thematically central to the novel. At the end of *The Dean's December*, in fact, their marriage represents the much-needed grounding force for each. On the surface, however, we find little evidence pointing towards a constructive relationship. Scenes between them often appear more tense and awkward than stable. During this bleak December, Minna's understandable obsession with her mother's predicament sparks her indifferent, and at times hostile, stance towards Albert. Although her indifference and hostility permeate much of the narrative, Minna's emotional response to her husband heightens when she necessarily confronts the loss of a mother:

> I wasn't old enough to feel it when my father died. I was sad because everybody else was. But my mother's death is really horrible—being a corpse, and cremated, and tomorrow the cemetery. I can't accept it. And it's even worse to be angry, it's horrible. Not like a grown woman. I feel vicious. (258)

Bellow here presents Minna's internalization of Valeria's death. Her mother's end concretizes the abstract notion of death, although at this point Minna still has not accepted the inevitable. But the impact of death clearly burdens Minna, as Albert observes: "He saw how it was, undisguised, when she looked at him—the blank death. Her mother's death had taught her death. Triviality was unsupportable to her. Her judgment was rigorous, angry" (288). Throughout much of the novel, in fact, Bellow uses deathlike imagery in describing Minna, thus carefully objectifying the enervating effect of her mother's death: "White, pinched, Minna was scarcely breathing . . ." (258); and in an earlier description, Minna's physical condition clearly mirrors her mother's: "He avoided looking too closely at his wife. The tubercular whiteness of her face upset him. Her big shocked eyes were immobile, her lower lip indrawn, and she was gaunt, stiff. In a single week even her fingers had lost flesh, so that the joints and the nails stood out" (80).

Their marriage, like so many other marriages in Bellow's earlier novels, seems earmarked for failure. For example, in addition to the tension generated by their death vigil, Minna confesses that her husband remains somewhat of a mystery to her: "You turned out to be a much more emotional and strange person than I ever expected'" (259). Minna accepts and loves Albert but with some voiced reservations.

And yet by the end of *The Dean's December* what emerges is not the dissolution of marriage, but the *unification* of man and woman. Upon returning to the States, the Cordes experience the return of their spiritual vitality. Albert senses the regeneration of spirit because he can once again focus on the particulars of the world around him:

> For some weeks it had been impossible to give the world his full attention—he had been too busy, absorbed, unsteady, unbalanced. But now, thanks be to God, the world began to edge back again, to reveal itself. On the plane when he held his wife's thin hand, she was too ill and bitter to be aware of his touch; she shut him out. But he was minutely aware of things, and the source of his awareness was in his equilibrium, a very extensive kind of composure. Not that this composure didn't have tight areas, crawl spaces, narrow and painful corners where longtime miseries rankled and to which there was not easy access, but this rankling—sometimes an electric prickling in a circle around his heart—couldn't be separated from his sense of improvement, of coming into his own. (282–83)

Corde's renewed "composure," his "coming into his own" again allows for a final reflection. To be sure, Corde's conclusion about the status of modern cities seems little changed by the novel's end; they remain "emotional conditions and great centers of delusion and bondage, death" (285). And Corde appears as baffled as ever with respect to his interpretation of city life.

But the Albert Corde at the end of the novel is different from the Albert Corde of the opening chapters. The difference lies in our understanding of two issues, the first being Corde's new-found acceptance of the givenness of the world around him. No longer will Corde myopically pursue his personal holy crusade; rather, he will continue to articulate his convictions, probably in the Beech articles, but the suggestion is that he will be better equipped to argue, i.e., he will still launch a verbal "bristling gunboat attack" (277), but with better, more thoughtful rhetorical strategy. By the novel's end, we witness the maturation of Corde. Upon hearing that Ricky Lester's murderers were convicted—thereby securing a legal victory for Lydia Lester and a moral victory for himself—Corde feels, as he did at the sight of a bedridden Valeria, "worked up" (279), but hardly celebrates. For now he appears more capable of objectively grounding his perceptions in a cause he championed:

"It's true nobody will change, the jails stink and nothing significant has been added. In jail, out of jail, Lucas Ebry and Reggie Hines are exactly the same. There are millions where they come from—not attached to life, and nobody can suggest how to attach them" (279–80). For Bellow, it matters little that Corde cannot change the social injustices significantly. But what concerns Bellow greatly is the qualitative effect the external experience has on Corde.

As the novel ends, then, Bellow presents a hero who once again can clearly attend to his surroundings and who accepts what seems like a naturalistic universe. That is, like Yakov Bok in Bernard Malamud's *The Fixer,* who can finally celebrate the particulars of his world upon his prison release, Corde can now celebrate his rediscovered capacity to focus on his world. His public self thwarted by a world inimical to his values, Corde at least can gain solace, and energy, from his private self. Bellow clearly illustrates this when Corde learns from the benevolent Dr. Tyche that Minna will, despite her trauma, be able to complete her research at the Mount Palomar observatory in California. In the following passage, Bellow underscores the sense of Corde's regeneration:

> Corde drove home, comforted. The weather was bright, keen blue, an afternoon of January thaw. His car had been parked in the sun, so he didn't need to turn the heater on. At home he set a kitchen chair out on the porch. It was mild enough to sit there, on the lee side of the flat. The light was the light of warmer seasons, not of deep winter. It came up from his own harmonies as well as down from above. The lake was steady, nothing but windless water before him. He had to look through the rods of his sixteenth story porch, an interference of no great importance. Whatever you desired would be measured out through human devices. Did the bars remind you of jail? They also kept you from falling to your death. Besides, he presently felt himself carried over the water and into the distant colors. Here in the midwest there sometimes occurred the blues of Italian landscapes and he passed through them, very close to the borders of sense, as if he could do perfectly well without the help of his eyes, seeing what you didn't need human organs to see but experiencing as freedom and also as joy what the mortal person, seated there in his coat and gloves, otherwise recorded as colors, spaces, weights. This was different. It was like being poured out to the horizon, like a great expansion. What if death should be like this, the soul finding an exit. The porch rail was his figure for the hither side. The rest, beyond it, drew you constantly as the completion of your reality. (289–90)

Whereas Corde viewed the Rumanian horizon as a larger, naturalistic
projection of a sometimes malevolent world—"That's right, blame nature" (3), here he recognizes both his own and nature's "harmonies."
Such "harmonies" signal recuperation for Corde.

Within this passage also lies a transcendental quality which Malcolm
Bradbury finds in the conclusion of several Bellow novels. "Such transcendental intentions," argues Bradbury, "are an essential direction of
his work, and part of his philosophy of the novel's power for us."[13] Bellow's transcendentalism in the above passage signifies, I think, Corde's
new-tempered acceptance of his predicament; even the tonal quality of
the language mirrors not only Corde's newly discovered calmness, but
his sharper, more mature perceptions of his surroundings. If the protective bars in his Chicago apartment windows remind him of prison,
they also serve, he sees, as a buffer against the kind of death Ricky Lester
suffered. Even Spangler's damning exposure of Corde in "The Tale of
Two Cities" column, although clearly upsetting, seems to help him clarify for himself the importance of persevering, if more tactfully, in his
social criticisms.

The second issue underscoring the change in Corde lies in the last
chapter, a chapter presenting for the first time husband and wife attend-
ing to the other with felt love and a sense of honest commitment. The
separateness of Albert and Minna that dominates the narrative gives way
in Chapter XIX to the togetherness they finally share. Bellow, himself,
confirmed this point during a discussion of the novel:

> It is real [the authentic love connecting the Cordes]. Why shouldn't
> it be? It is real, and therefore it is an achievement. The estrange-
> ment of human beings from one another is a fact of life, no longer
> a hypothetical matter. The price you pay for the development of con-
> sciousness is the withering of the heart. Therefore, one must *will* the
> recovery of feeling, and one must use one's intelligence, too; one
> must take private reckoning, at which we have become very skillful,
> and turn it around, force its reversal. *How* is one to educate oneself
> to feeling? I treated the subject comically in *Henderson the Rain King.*
> There I suggested that it might be done by imitating a noble beast,
> or by imitating an African king who has himself come under the in-
> fluence of a noble beast. *Henderson* is probably the better book be-
> cause its argument is less direct. *The Dean* is more important because
> it's closer to the actual truth as that truth is experienced by intelli-
> gent human beings. Corde recognizes the necessity of ennobling reck-
> oning. He comes to understand that we carry about, within, an
> iceberg which has to be melted. Intellect, itself a source of coldness,

must become involved in the melting project. To have intellect devoid of feeling is to be crippled. To recover the power to walk—in feeling—we begin by calling on the will. The return of love begins with the *study* of love, with discipline. If you wish Eros to return you must prepare a suitable place for him.[14]

In the last chapter, then, Corde attempts, successfully Bellow suggests, "to *will* to recovery" his feeling, not only for humanity but for Minna, for their marriage. The freezing temperature at the observatory generates, for Corde, an internal warmth—"the melting project"—that begins to dissolve the "iceberg" to which Bellow referred. Like the ending of an Albee play, the closing of *The Dean's December* offers no guarantee that the future will be secure: "It won't be a restful life," Minna accurately confides to her husband (307).

For Bellow, however, just the possibility of communicating and loving the other provides a necessary source of hope. It appears as if Corde regains a much-needed perspective on his public and private self by realizing and accepting what Henderson discovered in *Henderson the Rain King*: "It's too bad, but suffering is about the only reliable burster of the spirit's sleep. There is a rumor of long standing that love also does it."[15] In *The Dean's December*, Bellow suggests something of the unifying force of love, linking the three in this novel who experience it most intensely— Valeria, Minna, and Albert.

Rediscovering the sources of their love, Albert and Minna gain a kind of transcendental spiritual bonding. This is most evident when Minna shares her world with Albert during their ascent to the top of the observatory. It is Albert's first trek up in the dome, and the atmospheric conditions seem perfect for Minna's research: it is a Hemingwaylike clear, cold, and dry evening.

Bellow proceeds to develop the symbolic richness of the observatory setting. Although imagistically connecting the observatory's dome with the dome in Valeria's crematorium, Bellow emphasizes not decay, death, but the presence of life, living. The regenerative ambience enveloping the observatory dome stands in unmistakable contrast to the devitalizing aura of the crematorium dome. Symbolically, the death of Valeria now gives way to the rebirth of her daughter, whose research activities at the end of the novel assume a therapeutic role for her. As Corde reflects, "This Mount Palomar coldness was not to be compared to the cold of the death house [Valeria's crematorium]. Here the living heavens looked as if they would take you in" (311). For the first time in the entire novel Minna appears alive, and is one with "the living." Minna is "cheerful" (312), buoyed by three key points: her coming to terms with her mother's death; her return to her professional passion; and her renewed love for her husband. Bellow suggests that through literally surveying the cosmos, Minna symbolically becomes rooted in reality, fixed in the earth. Coupled with Albert, she regains her ability to observe the galaxy as well as, in context of Bellow's imagery, her own inner space, her soulscape. Bellow further implies that through Minna, Albert relocates some semblance of meaning and value in the complex business of living. As Bellow points out, Albert "seemed to be picking up signals from all over the universe, some from unseeable sources" (132), but it is only with Minna's support that, ultimately, he can interpret clearly these "signals."

In seeing the universe body forth above the telescope, Albert experiences what the existentialists call a sense of freedom. This sense of freedom appears during his reflective analogy of the water and its liberating effects on the soul to his Mount Palomar experience:

> Once, in the Mediterranean, coming topside from a C-class cabin, the uric smells and the breath of the bilges, every hellish little up-to-date convenience there below to mock your insomnia—then seeing the morning sun on the titled sea. Free! The grip of every sickness within you disengaged by this pouring out. You couldn't tell which was out of plumb, the ship, or yourself, or the sea aslant—but free! It didn't matter, since you were free! It was like that also when you approached the stars as steadily as this. (311)

Celebrating his freedom, Albert authentically feels his connection with Minna, who stands as his "representative among those bright things so thick and close" (312).

Considering the novel as a whole, it seems entirely fitting that Corde served for years as a college dean. That is, according to its discussion of the former uses of the word "dean," the *Oxford English Dictionary* reports that in both Greek and Latin, "the form of the word offers difficulties. In both languages, it also had an early astrological sense, the chief of ten parts, or of ten degrees, of a zodiacal sign." As cosmic interpreter, Corde assumes the position of a kind of poetic astrologer, one who "had been sent down to *mind* the outer world, on a mission of observation and notation" (210). But luckily for Albert, Minna is "a 'hard' scientist" (2), an astrophysicist, the one who ultimately is most capable of keeping the dean on "terra firma."

Notes

1. D. J. R. Bruckner, "A Candid Talk With Saul Bellow," *The New York Times Magazine*, 15 April 1984, 52.
2. Although Bellow "is often hailed as a novelist of ideas," writes James Wolcott, the "ideas seem to me to be his undoing"; accordingly, the novel "becomes little more than a think piece—("Dissecting Our Decline," *Esquire*, March 1982, 136). George Stade finds the novel lacking in mimetic energy because Corde "is only presented to us in silhouette" and that Bellow's work would be more compelling "if its ideas had been filtered through a character more capable of changing himself or of surprising us . . . " ("I, Me, Mine," *The Nation*, 30 January 1982, 118). For James Atlas, the plot seems "contrived," Corde's ruminations "static and belabored"; finally, "Even a novel of ideas has to have a plot" (*The Atlantic*, February 1982, 78). Diane Johnson argues that "most of the characters are not especially interesting" (*New York Review of Books*, 4 March 1982, 6), while Hugh Kenner contends that the dialogue at times appears implausible, sounding like "platitudes from Communication 1A" (*Harper's*, February 1982, 64). Similarly, Robert Towers notes that the novel suffers from "the problem [and lack] of narrative momentum" (*The New York Times Book Review*, 10 January 1982, 22). Helen Dudar finds it "an infuriatingly uneven book that veers, not without visible effort, from drear to dazzle" (*Saturday Review*, January 1982, 17). And William Harmon complains that "What *The Dean's December* lacks is an exact sense of Corde's aptitudes and capacities" (*Southern Humanities Review* 17 [Summer 1983]: 281). However, supporting Bellow's achievement in *The Dean's December* stands Allan Chavkin, "Recovering 'The World That is Buried Under the Debris of False Description,'" *Saul Bellow Journal* 1 (Spring/Summer 1982): 47–57; and Judie Newman, "Bellow and Nihilism: *The Dean's December*," *Studies in the Literary Imagination* 18 (Fall 1984): 111–22.
3. Bellow himself concedes that his latest novel is a different kind of work: see Eugene Kennedy, "A Different Saul Bellow," *Boston Globe Magazine*, 10 January 1982, 12.
4. Matthew C. Roudané, "An Interview With Saul Bellow," *Contemporary Literature* (Fall 1984): 270.
5. Saul Bellow, *The Dean's December* (New York: Harper and Row, 1982), 201. All subsequent page references appear in the text.
6. Chavkin, 52.
7. Stanley Trachtenberg, ed., "Introduction," *Critical Essays on Saul Bellow* (Boston: G. K. Hall, 1979), xiii.
8. Roudané, 273.
9. M. A. Klug, "Saul Bellow: The Hero in the Middle," in Stanley Trachtenberg, ed., *Critical Essays on Saul Bellow* (Boston: G. K. Hall, 1979), 183.
10. Bellow elaborates on this issue in Cathleen Medwick's useful "A Cry of Strength: The Unfashionably Uncynical Saul Bellow," *Vogue*, March 1982, 368–69, 426–27.

Toward a Language Irresistible: Saul Bellow and the Romance of Poetry

Michael G. Yetman

Natives of poverty, children of malheur,
The gaiety of language is our seigneur.
    —from "Esthétique du Mal," by Wallace Stevens

Could I revive within me
Her symphony and song,
To such a deep delight 'twould win me,
That with music loud and long,
I would build that dome in air,
That sunny dome! Those caves of ice!
    —from "Kubla Khan," by S. T. Coleridge

It is a supposition of Saul Bellow's *The Dean's December* that the reality of contemporary urban life is lost on most people because of the languages used by specialists to describe it. This may be true even to those who experience that reality firsthand, on their own pulses. Politicians, media people, sociologists, anthropologists, social engineers—these give us our official versions of things. What is bad about accepting these official views (signified by our adoption of their descriptive vocabularies) is that too often in doing so we nullify our own perceptions, dismissing them as eccentric and even delusive, whereas what is in fact distortive and delusive are the abstract conceptual models of the so-called experts. To assert the authority of personal as opposed to public or general experience is a major purpose of Bellow's 1981 novel. In a moment of heightened reflection the protagonist asks: Why does the contemporary *zeitgeist* "demand that one's own sense of existence (poetry, if you will) be dismissed with contempt?"[1] If ever a book did so, *The Dean's December*

First printed in *Papers on Language and Literature* 22, no. 4 (1986): 429–47.

constitutes a rejection, a dismissal "with contempt," of the non-poetic, objectivist biases of contemporary social thought.

In the sentence quoted above, "poetry" means, of course, personal vision, the unique product of that ongoing intercourse between the self and the world which characterizes healthy mental existence. A second meaning for poetry is the language used to describe and encapsulate personal vision. The two meanings obviously complement each other yet are different. All of us, by reacting imaginatively to experience, partake of the first kind of poetry; but only the artist, who combines imagination and experience through language, has the power amidst the welter of scientific jargon to "recover the world that is buried under the debris of false description or nonexperience" (243). Language, then, specifically poetic language, is the key which alone unlocks the human significance of things, events, perceptions. In its second, more formal sense, poetry is synonymous with the older meaning of philosophy; implicit in each is an extraordinary power of intellectual discernment and ethical judgment: a hint of, or at least a potential for the achievement of, human wisdom.

Bellow is an old-fashioned, conservative thinker. His view of language is similarly conservative and old-fashioned. Like those archlogocentrists before him, the English romantics, he believes that, properly used, words capture and preserve the truth or reality of human experience, including its moral dimension. Improperly used, however, words can obscure and distort "reality" out of recognition. In this latter regard, one is reminded, in reading *The Dean's December*, of George Orwell's classic "Politics and the English Language." According to both authors, the relation between the way things are said and the way we apprehend them is crucial. Bad language impounds the fullness of experience, edits it, enables the user consciously or unconsciously to see and depict only a limited, distorted version of it. Good language on the other hand gives a more honest view of things; if it edits experience it does so with the help of the moral sense, the imagination, compassion, and is therefore "truer" to perceptions, less likely to be narrowly self-serving.

Bellow's traditionalist, logocentric understanding of language as both the creator and the vehicle of personal vision needs no introduction to the student of modern letters or, for that matter, of contemporary literary theory. A majority of the significant literary works in English during the past two centuries has been written with the same presumptive view of the symbiotic relationship between language and experience. Despite the teachings to the contrary of nineteenth- and twentieth-century nonidealist language theorists, beginning with Peirce and culminating in Derrida, and notwithstanding the current practice in the academies of Derrida's often brilliant deconstructing progeny, who deauthorize language while simultaneously denying its referential function, Bellow's work reminds us that some of the best imaginative writing today continues implicitly to assert the Coleridgean belief that language is a conduit between mind and reality, that words reflect and at the same time interpret, humanize, even "save" through imagination the stuff of literal experience.[2] The persistence of logocentrism in modern letters is attributable in part to the persistence of the ideas of romanticism in the modern experience. The romantics were, of course, the first modern writers to insist upon the idealizing function of language: the power words possess to change, even transubstantiate, "reality" by reuniting, in the wake of the Cartesian split, subjectivity and objectivity in a third, seemingly *sui generis* order, the linguistic construct itself.[3]

With its romantic underpinnings, logocentrism is useful to an assessment of *The Dean's December* as a novel that dramatizes, among other things, some of the enduring tensions within modernism. The quarrels between the rational and the intuitive, the scientific and the subjective as sources of personal intellectual authority, moral guidance, and emotional allegiance are central thematic concerns of this book; and if he poses no definitive resolutions to these various contests, there can be little doubt as to which side of the question Bellow himself usually stands on. Perhaps the most disappointing feature of the novel is the main character's having no pointedly selfish goal or project, only a quixotic one of saving the world. There is too little emphasis on what Bellow does best—generating strategies of personal psychic and emotional survival in a wacky, devouring world and not enough of that marvelous plasticity and self-serving disengagement that we have come to expect from the Bellovian central consciousness at its most rambunctious.[4]

Still, whatever its faults, *The Dean's December* is both disturbing and brilliant: disturbing because it so flagrantly defies the reigning "correct" opinions on important racial, political, and moral questions; brilliant because even when we find ourselves in deepest disagreement with the author's ideas, we are obliged to credit him with having rendered them vividly, entertainingly, and with a candor that is both refreshing and deprecatory toward its own self-seriousness. The author is more of a crank than ever, but he can hardly be accused of not knowing it. One critic has complained about the novel's paucity of imaginative flourishes.[5] Nonsense. It fairly glows throughout with tiny verbal conflagrations in each of which the hero, Albert Corde, purifies his spirit by singeing his self-image in the fires of self-mockery. In the art of the self-reflexive putdown, Corde is anybody's equal.

In certain clear-cut ways the business of *The Dean's December* is continuous with that of all of Bellow's fiction since *Henderson the Rain King*. It chronicles the complex relationship of an intensely self-absorbed, intelligent, imaginative, ethical, humanly warm, funny, and eccentric protagonist and his many-peopled, many-evented, perplexing, dizzyingly changeable and, above all, uncontrollable life world. Bellow is past master at rendering the joys, tensions, sadnesses, splendors, excesses and frustrations of the contemporary scene. Moses Herzog, Eugene Henderson, and Charlie Citrine are preeminent achievements in the type of character-at-bay fiction which their author practically invented. *The Dean's December* is a shorter, leaner, though no less well-crafted work in the same manner. Like its length, the novel's comedy is more subdued, less well balanced with its main theme and plot. Given the ponderousness of these—respectively, the failure of human imagination to deal with contemporary urban problems, and the much more personal, impotent, and dreary vigil of Corde and his wife Minna at the lingering, month-long dying of Minna's mother—the less boisterous, less antic flavor of the book, especially when compared to that of its immediate predecessor, *Humboldt's Gift*, seems entirely appropriate. It is more like *Mr. Sammler's Planet* in its "last days" aura; things aren't as yet hopeless but, don't worry, they're getting worse each day.

The novel begins in Bucharest, Rumania, during the month of December in an unspecified recent year. The narrative focuses on the thoughts, observations, and reflections of the American Albert Corde, in his mid-fifties, a former Paris correspondent for the international *Herald Tribune*, and for the last ten years a professor of journalism and dean of students at a large Chicago university. Corde has a great deal of free time in Rumania because there isn't very much he can do for his wife or his mother-in-law, Valeria Raresh, who has suffered a heart attack and a stroke and who can move only her fingers to signal consciousness. Life in Bucharest, like the prognosis for the sick old woman, is hopelessly dreary. The hospital where Valeria lies dying is run by a spiteful petty bureaucrat, a Secret Police colonel who, miffed at a rule-breaking unoffical visitation of Valeria by Corde and Minna soon after they arrive in the country, will allow but one more visit before the end. Sadistically, he requires the daughter to decide when this will occur, thereby forcing her to gamble on how long the old lady might last, and even, perhaps, to miss out on the final farewell should she go into rapid decline. Through all of this emotional pain for mother and daughter, Corde, who is used to being the master of situations for his younger, somewhat abstracted astronomer wife, finds himself unsettlingly useless, even unwanted. So he sits in the dimly lit, cold apartment where Minna grew up and broods, day after day, an eager (if aging) Achilles-of-officiousness with no Troy on which to prove his mettle.

Corde muses compassionately on the plight of the sweet old lady and defrocked Party member who, in having to face death alone, has been denied one of the basic human decencies. Ironically, the hospital where she is imprisoned is one Valeria herself founded thirty years earlier, before falling out of favor with the authorities because of her professional affiliation with psychiatry. Bellow's critique of Rumania, what Corde calls a "socialist wonderland" (53) and a "bughouse country" (78) is, like the place itself, unsparingly harsh. Encountering one afternoon a particularly dismal Bucharest street scene, his sense of the dessicated, narcoleptic spiritual condition of the citizens as reflected in their dilapidated physical surroundings, is unmistakable. Earthquake rubble strewn all about has never been removed; rat skeletons are flattened out on the streets. Corde observes some commuters, then interprets: "Coupled rusty-orange tramcars ran with a slither of cables. Pale proletarian passengers looked out . . . . Together with cast-iron sinks and croaking pull-chain toilets, these tramcars belonged to the old days. It was all like looking backwards. You saw the decades in reverse. Even the emotions belonged to an earlier time" (107).

When he isn't dwelling upon the doleful present Corde thinks about the recent past and, through two meetings with his old friend Dewey Spangler, a world-renowned syndicated newspaper columnist in Rumania to interview important people in the government, a good deal about the distant past as well. Spangler is a career rival of sorts who, though he may appear from Corde's descriptions more to resemble Art Buchwald than Walter Lippmann, is actually the latter's heir apparent, with ambitions to go even higher and claim the perch vacated recently by Malraux. Through Dewey's and his two afternoons of guarded reminiscences in the bar of the Intercontinental Hotel in Bucharest, Corde's long relationship with Chicago, the city of his birth and his later-years adopted town, is laid out for the reader from early times to the present.

From the recent past, Corde rehearses the history of his improbable involvement in a murder trial going on at the moment in Chicago. A white student of his college had died by defenestration the previous August and Corde has been instrumental in the indictment of two blacks—Lucas Ebry, a dishwasher, and Riggie Hines, a prostitute—arrested for the crime. He reflects, too, on his only sister Elfrida's son, Mason Zaehner, Jr., a personal friend of Ebry's, who led an unsuccessful campaign to get Uncle Albert's case against the alleged murderers quashed before it came to trial. He thinks of Mason Sr., dead three years of a heart attack, a La Salle Street lawyer and "highly intelligent top-grade barbarian" (231) in life; in death, one of the smoldering contributary causes of Corde's having been hurt into poetry in the form of two articles he published in *Harper's* magazine just before he left the U.S. These articles were originally intended to be a "mere review of life in [his] native city" (201), but then "something had come over him" (163); instead they became exposés: Corde's personal state-of-the-city accounts of political corruption, inadequate social service, cold turkey drug detoxification centers, murderous housing projects. The articles function as a subtext in the novel. Much more thought of and spoken about than actually quoted, they are but one of several, major, recurrent subjects of Corde's meditations.

Back home, the articles were met with perplexity, outrage, dismay, but mostly embarrassment for their author's sake, especially for his eccentric focus and sometimes apocalyptic language. What slowly emerges from Corde's month of musing in the Bucharest apartment of his dying mother-in-law is the central question of the novel: why did he write the Chicago articles in the first place? Corde surmises that the answer to this question may help solve the riddle of his entire life, whose mystery is inseparable from his deep yet ambivalent feelings toward his home town. Chicago is almost a separate character in *The Dean's December* and if we were to assign it a gender we would have to make it a female with strong, Oedipal blandishments for the protagonist. One reviewer complained about the absence in this book of the usual "willful, greedy dolls, broads and dames" who have drawn heavy flak from the feminists.[6] But if Corde, the uxurious husband, has in death a temporary rival for his wife's attentions, he finds in that toddling town an ample substitute for his imagination to fix upon: after all, he has carried on a love-hate relationship with the place for over fifty years.

The *Harper's* articles and Corde's personal *apologia* conflate in the handling of the theme of poetry in the novel. As defined earlier, poetry would describe the substance as well as the linguistic manner of the magazine pieces, their subject matter, and their style. It also signifies the passionate, uniquely personal style of the dean's entire life. Nobody has ever accused the Bellow protagonist of being a passive, unappreciative guest at life's banquet. Each attends the affair with a childlike wonder and a drooling appetency for every dish served up that rivals that of Browning's good Brother Lippi. Corde is no exception. Again and again he is described as a prodigious consumer: a great detail man (16), a "hungry observer" (8), an omnivorous reader, a gargantuan rememberer—in short, an alert, intensely sensitive, and outgoing human specimen. But what do other people care about this rich innerness of Corde's, the Keatsian gusto he consistently displays in his intercourse with the world?

Corde's contemporaries respect many kinds of skills and power, but that of being able to find the poetry in experience is not one of them.

Not only is imagination personal and celebratory, it has its social, declamatory uses too; clearly one of these, as *The Dean's December* reminds us, is to lay bare our habitual, even institutional inhumanity, our obliviousness to the squalor and cruelty in the world. Poetry alone demonstrates the existence of what Corde calls the "slum of innermost being" (201), of which the ghettos at the hearts of our great cities are but so many metonymic symptoms. The absence of imagination in assessments of contemporary life is ultimately, of course, a problem of perception; but, since our perceptions quickly become indistinguishable from the words used to describe them, it makes for special problems of language as well. The health of one is a measure of the health of the other. Much that is wrong with us, according to Bellow, is the result of our having foresworn the poetic and individual for the conceptual, mass media-induced, trend thinking of the day. Presumably, even the honorific status granted such words as "brain trust," "consensus thinking," "informed public opinion," as well as the deference paid by the modern world to statistical data, polls, and the "findings" of so-called specialists, support the author's view. What is most grievously wrong with our readings of the world is that they are descriptive, abstracted, not evaluative and corrective.

Since we are in the present predicament through a capitulation of individual to group thinking, it follows that the only way out is through a reversal of the process. We must learn once again to see the world as through the eyes of a Blake child, a Rilke, a Yeats, or a Plato, instead of those of the statistician, the bureaucrat, the social analyst. Only when such a radical reversion of seeing is accomplished will we once again apprehend the world imaginatively, not only as it is but also as it might be. The languages of contemporary discourse, of the intellectuals, the behaviorists, even the "event-glamour" (122) style of journalists like Corde's pal Spangler—all preclude fresh human assessments and reactions. When we view the world through these people's eyes, through their "dead categories" (90) and "corrupted" forms (122), what we apprehend is not events themselves but "real sounding" discussions of events, which, however "mutually comforting" (199), are nonetheless illusory, chimerical.

What does one see when he/she looks at contemporary urban America through the eyes of the vatic poet, the type Bellow clearly has in mind when he speaks of poetry? As was the case earlier with Bucharest, there is little that is either fanciful or pretty in Corde's account of Chicago and the lives of its people. Conditions are more reminiscent of Kurtz's

"horror" than Sandburg's hog butcher. In fact, a muted allusion to the
Sandburg poem becomes heavily ironic when Corde quotes from his articles an incident in which a man living in Cabrini Green had slaugh-
tered a pig in his apartment and thrown the guts on the staircase outside
where another tenant slipped on them and broke her arm. There's a lot
of slaughter still going on where the stockyards used to be, but most of
it is of a strictly human variety. Perhaps not surprisingly, images of
detachment, free-floating, untethered, disjunctive states abound in
Corde's descriptions of the criminal types, social rejects, the "doomed
people" (206) of the city's black underclass. These, we are told, in a
metaphoric language that, whatever their actual condition, succeeds at
raising them to the very condition of surreality it purports to describe,
"whirl," turbulent in "terrible wildness" (202). The best that can be said
of them is that they "kill some of us. Mostly they kill themselves" (207).

One of these citizens is Spofford Mitchell, an accused rapist-murderer
whose cultured, white public defender lawyer Corde interviews. Corde's
commentary, which constitutes the longest sustained quotation from the
Harper's articles in the text of the novel, stresses two points: first, the seeming indifference of Mitchell to the emotional torture he must have inflicted on his victim before killing her (it is a case of multiple rape over
a period of several days, the woman having been kept between times
locked in the trunk of Mitchell's car); and second, the way the lawyer's
defensive attitude during the interview protects him from having to confront with an adequate moral imagination the heinousness of his client's
crime. Disturbed almost as much by the lawyer's unwillingness to deal
with the victim's emotional trauma as he (Corde) imagines it for him
as by Mitchell's hardness of heart, Corde adroitly finesses the former
into listening to his explanation of the killer's probable psychosexual
nature. Corde hypothesizes that Mitchell must perceive "genital literalness" (204)—the forced momentary connections of his body with that
of another (any other?)—as the only means of expression available to
him, so many brief, violent, yet paradoxically human punctuations in
an otherwise unintelligible, manifestly inhuman, syntax of consciousness.

Despite his aim of sensitizing him to the horrors of Mitchell's acts,
Corde does not except himself from the nonpoetic (i.e., obscurantist)
tendencies of language that he associates with Varennes, the lawyer.
Somewhat surprisingly, he sums up their interview in a way that impli-
cates himself as a co-conspirator in soft-pedaling the facts:

> We sat there explaining evils to each other, to pass them off some-
> how, redistribute the various monstrous elements, and compose
> something the well-disposed liberal democratic temperament could

live with. Nobody actually said, "An evil has been done." No, it was rather, "An unfortunate crazed man destroyed a woman, true enough, but it would be wrong of us to constitute ourselves judges of this crime since its causes lie in certain human and social failures." A fine, broad-minded conclusion, and does us credit. (202)

The tone of self-accusation here suggests Corde's recognition of an occasional lapse in his personal quest after the fullness of truth. It also represents an implicit admission that the language of his magazine articles is not that different from the language of so many of his antagonists in the book, and tells us that what really sets him apart from them is the purity of his intentions or the tenacity with which he pursues them. (After all, Corde isn't a poet by profession; he's a dean with a special susceptibility to poetry and, of course, the kind of intense subjective response to experience that both he and Bellow associate with true poets.) In either case, what is important to my reading is Corde's insistence on the tendency of humans including, obviously, himself to distort what they see, and the way that such distortions are invariably mirrored in their words.

Another lost citizen in Corde's midwestern Inferno is Gene Lewis, whose girlfriend hollows out a boy's edition of *Ivanhoe* in order to hide a magnum revolver. This she gives to him before his sentencing for murder. Lewis disarms the courtroom guards, fires a round into the floor to show the judge he means business, and runs out, but in attempting to escape takes the wrong elevator which, when the doors open, confronts him with a group of alerted detectives who shoot him ten times in the head. There is a certain pre-verbal literalness here too, a rule-of-apocalypse that preempts the most basic communicative functions of language, to say nothing of the redemptive possibilities of traditional poetry. Both Mitchell and Lewis live by the law of sudden spontaneous violence. They kill and/or are killed willy-nilly. But Lewis, in particular, embodies all the self-destructive urges of the black underclass; and his life story, according to Corde, is but a hopped up, faster version of the slow attrition that characterizes the lives of many inner city people.

Then there are those Chicagoans, mostly white, who comprise the rest of the city's population: the middle-class "business" people. "Business," we are told, "means law, engineering, advertising, insurance, banking, merchandising, stockbrokering, politicking" (264). Obviously, these are the people who control things, the power people. While not untethered in the same way as the members of the ghetto communities, the middle classes too are dissociative in their thinking. Though by no means morally superior to them, they are better circumstanced, better educated, better heeled than their inner city counterparts; still, they seem even harder of heart, as deaf to the allurements of a civilizing poetry as the already damned. Dewey Spangler, for all of his analytic brilliance, belongs to this group, as do Elfrida, Corde's sister and, presumably, most of the readers for whom Corde wrote his *Harper's* articles. But the type is perhaps best represented in the novel by Elfrida's new husband's brother and his wife who live on the fortieth floor of a luxurious, well-guarded condominium from which the black slums can be viewed. This couple gives a birthday party (which Corde attends) for their pet Great Dane, believing in their "cheerful American" hearts that "all living creatures—all!—were equal" (294).

Worse than being simply deaf to poetry, many of Corde's fellow Chicagoans are, in addition, either the active agents or the consumers of the antipoetic, abstractionist tendencies of the day. Whether as generators or mere users of mass discourse, they traffic heavily in concepts, not facts, collectively constituting the "generality mind, the habit of mind that governs the world" (266). But it is the power people especially who, by controlling the communications sources, purvey and disseminate the distortions of public rhetoric; these Corde singles out as the greatest enemies of poetry.

At this point it might be well to acknowledge the dubiousness of Bellow's larger ideological ambitions in *The Dean's December*: his apparent desire to establish through Corde, beginning with his *Harper's* articles and culminating in the monomachy with the world that constitutes the novel itself, an Arnoldian reverence for ideas, taste, poetry—in short, an upper-case Culture to fend off all that devouring Anarchy. We might also wonder about the dangers of self-parody lurking in Bellow's use of his quixotic subtext, or quest-romance backgrounding plot. To put the latter problem in the form of a question, we can ask: does the Cervantine model, so useful for the sake of comedy, preserve a sufficient degree of dignity for both character and project (and the novelist's clear investment in each) to protect them from being dismissed as mere burlesques? Regard, for a moment, the bare "facts" of what I have been calling the novel's backgrounding plot. Stirred by a long-time revulsion to the deterioration of language in the world, our December hero has some months earlier finally taken arms against the windmills of Mediatalk and Specialistspeak, the standard of Dame Poesy (we imagine) fluttering from the tip of his poised-at-the-ready lance, or better, wrapped mummylike about the unwieldy volumes of Great Books he grips stoutly under either arm as he rides off into battle.

Of course I exaggerate tropologically in order to make my point. But more important, as we have seen the novel does not, except in teasing snippets, foreground these *Harper's* skirmishes, only Corde's more or less tranquil recollection and justifications of them. And even if Bellow had actually provided (instead of only hinting at) the kind of Marx Brothers scenario outlined in the last paragraph, such is the resiliency of his literary model that it is likely we would still be drawn to Corde, as we are to his prototype Quixote, because of the purity of his impulse and despite both the inadequacy of his weaponry (i.e., language) or the outcome of his mission. Thus Bellow manages not only to avoid offense by these hinted-at Cordean shenanigans but also to convince us that his choice of the Quixote model for his character was a masterful novelistic stroke. For the conventions of the quest-romance, combined as they are in *The Dean's December* with a comic-post-romantic-absurdist world view necessitate the establishment of an impeccable integrity of intention for the hero even while simultaneously calling for the thwarting of his design.

The difference between Corde and Eugene Henderson in this respect is instructive. Humor aside, that difference is not one of will or resolve but of the type of world each is granted to operate in. Henderson's world, being mythic, still allows for heroic accomplishments of the self; Corde's being realist-absurdist, resists, indeed mocks, any would-be savior's manipulations.

Apropos of the establishment of his role as would-be savior in the *Harper's* articles, Corde's fulminations against the way we speak (and hence see and think) now are based on the premise that a firm persuasion that a thing is so makes it so. As such, they call attention to rather than hide their author's quirks, enthusiasms, eccentricities—above all, as we have seen, his stunned social conscience. Yet his fiercely personal tone presumably gains for the documents their peculiar moral authority as well, for it demonstrates the practice of a concept very dear to both him and his inventor, the Hegelian imperative that one experience the world each day *engagée,* as one's direct personal fate. According to Hegel, without such an ongoing interpenetration of the self and the real there can be no sense of good and evil, no apprehension even of what is "real." This dictum is *the* central element of Corde's ethical code. In one of the superb lyrical/expository passages of *The Dean's December* the narrator explains the character's thinking:

> His own sense of the way things were had a strong claim on him and he thought that if he sacrificed that sense—its truth—he sacrificed himself. Chicago was the material habitat of this sense of his, which was, in turn, the source of his description of Chicago . . . . He wondered what reality was if it wasn't this, or what you were "losing" by death, if not this. If it was only the literal world that was taken

> from you the loss was not great. Literal! What you didn't pass through
> your soul didn't even exist, that was what made the literal literal.
> Thus he had taken it upon himself to pass Chicago through his own
> soul. A mass of data, terrible, murderous. It was no easy matter to
> put such things through. But there was no other way for reality to
> happen. Reality didn't exist "out there." It began to be real only when
> the soul found its underlying truth. (264–66)

Mostly what Corde finds missing in public discourse is this "truth," the
human fact about which all language purports to be commenting but
which, astonishingly, seems to be missing from it entirely at the present
time. Hence he styles himself a "moralist of seeing" (123) in what he takes
to be a world of blind men. His self-declared aim, once he warms to the
task, is nothing less than "to disinter reality" and "represent it anew as
art would represent it" (123).

Alas, the task of the artist, never easy even in the best of times, is dou-
bly difficult today. Not only must he discover a language capable of communicating irresistibly his program to a population whose sensibility
has been dulled to traditional poetic appeals, he must as well find one
that will correct faulty perception as it communicates its truth. But the
modernist suspicion of the language of personal vision is symptomatic
of a deep-seated suspicion of subjectivity itself. For nearly two hundred
years, in the West the language of authority has been that of the empirical sciences, not poetry. To Bellow, Western culture's choice of objectivity over subjectivity is not so much wrong as it is limiting, exclusionary.
The world needs both science and poetry. Indeed, it is possible for one
and the same person to embody both. The presence in the novel of Sam
Beech, an eminent geophysicist who has an intensely personal moral vision not unlike Corde's and who seeks to collaborate with Corde on a
series of laymen's articles to warn against the residual effects of dangerously high lead concentrations in some of the world's major cities, testifies to this. Beech, according to Corde, is a "man of feeling," a visionary
who perceives "earth's own poetry" (141). Clearly, when practiced at their
best, what is common to both poetry and science is the element of subjective, personal vision, which includes moral judgment. Beech's moral
attitudes are an inseparable part of Corde's assessment of him *as a scientist.*

Regarding his decision to make his own moral outrage public, Corde
had always thought he wasn't "advanced enough" (265) to be the artist
of the world as he saw it. Still, he feels compelled finally to try. Non-
scientist, nonpoet, he writes his essays in the only effective style he knows,
the romantic style of hortatory lyric subjectivity which has moved him
deeply ever since his undergraduate days at Dartmouth, where he read

many authors for the first time, and, even before that, in Chicago's Lincoln Park, on the green scrolled benches where, wide-eyed, he and his adolescent sidekick Dewey Spangler used to recite and discuss together the likes of Shelley, Nietzsche, Baudelaire, Wilde, Blake, and Whitman. To an audience conditioned to distrust such a premise, Corde asserts his unshakeable belief in the authority of precisely that type of inspired personal vision which the works of these authors represent. Not the nature of the contemporary experience but the unique experience of a contemporary is what *The Dean's December* offers us. Moreover, it affirms the superiority of such a vision to that of the jargon-riddled intellectuals on the one hand and the "jazzed-up fantasy" (243) of the mass media-controlled public on the other.

Corde's choice of the normative, boisterously self-expressive style of American letters since Whitman as his personal style of life reflects his author's understanding, at least since *The Adventures of Augie March,* of the freestyle male American character. Still, given its evident excesses, it is difficult to imagine that Bellow goes along wholly with this model for his character's literary style, Corde's written "poetry." Corde himself is healthily aware of and retrospectively embarrassed by his histrionic rhetoric, the tendencies to mysticism and self-heroizing, also what Dewey calles his end-of-the-line "abyssifying" (277). But it isn't simply an inept rhetoric or misapplied self-dramaturgy that does Corde in. Nor will it do to blame his failure of communication on Corde's borrowed language—presumably a linguistic and stylistic amalgam of all those moments of unaging intellect that shaped his imaginative and ethical responses years earlier—however valid, strictly speaking, that charge may be. For the simple fact is that the perfected vehicle for carrying Corde's message does not yet even exist. Until it does, Bellow seems to be saying, condemn if you will the character's outmoded bookish language as well as his unbalanced enthusiasm for the task; but don't, whatever you do, dismiss the impulse that prompted his efforts. There at least Corde was correct, unassailable. If ever the world is to be saved from its folly, it will be through some such impulse which has found the proper language to convert others to its author's views.

Will such a language ever be found, one so powerful of imagination, so persuasive of moral logic that it will galvanize the attention and win the respect of all prudent and conscientious men and women? This is of course the romantic rhetorical dream at its most ambitious, as found in the prophecies of William Blake or in the vision of the redeemed world of Shelley's *Prometheus Unbound,* where human speech and thought together are said to constitute nothing less than the "measure of the universe."[7] The hope that someday a language will be invented that might perform this prodigious alchemy dies anew with each writer who dreams, tries, and is baffled by the task. In certain ways the requisite subtleties of this hoped-for absolute *logos* increase with the passage of time and the proportionate growth in human problems and the new false and/or inadequate languages generated to describe and resolve these problems. Yet despite the failure of all previous attempts, the growing complexity of the enterprise, and the enduring deafness of moral man, such a be-lief in the redemption of human history through poetry persists from generation to generation. Perhaps the very capacity for this belief in a corrective vision housed in a language irresistible is what distinguishes, finally, the romantic from the tragic mind.

There have been at least three short studies of Bellow's indebtedness to that literary tradition which, in modern times, first propounded the hope of which we have been speaking.[8] If what has been hypothesized here about an idea of language in *The Dean's December* is correct, Bellow's affinity with the English poets who helped found that tradition is more ongoing, more intimate than that of many of his fellow modernists who, like him, have been strongly influenced in other ways by romantic ideas. Indeed, when we focus exclusively on the thematization of poetic lan-guage in this novel we cannot help concluding that Bellow is an anachronism of sorts, a direct throwback to the likes of Shelley, Blake, and the Coleridge of "Kubla Khan," and their belief that, at their most powerful, words can reshape, even rival in their "fullness" the substan-tiality of sensory experience.[9] For Yeats, Stevens (at least the esthete Stevens of the epigraph to this essay), Mallarmé, Joyce, and other later poets in the tradition, language came to be viewed more and more as an end in itself, a private affair, centrally important as a medium for art, but ultimately of little or no influence on the real nature of things.[10] As an informed, unusually well-read modern thinker, Bellow wouldn't disagree with any of this. Yet just as obviously, that side of Bellow which allows him to write without irony, admiringly, of Steinerian mysticism in *Humboldt's Gift*, or to be a lifelong praiser of the transcendental, bardic strain of American poetry, as embodied in Emerson and Whitman (and as an antidote to modernist pessimism), refuses to abandon the more radical romantic belief that the final goal of language is to embody the kingdom—or at the very least the literal pleasure dome and caves of ice of our second epigraph.

But why then, one inevitably asks, at this late date a novel that is so despairing of the very dream it champions? The answer is obvious: be-cause the chances of there actually occurring such a poetical coup against the existing order of things have never been more remote. The realist in Bellow knows this, has always known it. Perhaps this is why in his last two books Bellow has provided a *deus ex machina* of sorts, a have-one's-cake-and-eat-it option as a compensatory reward for the pertinacity with which his main characters have pursued the dream of imagination's ultimate triumph over facticity. In the face of a hopeless present and a presumed worsening of present conditions in the future, the protagonists discover a temporary escape from the dilemmas of history and aging existential personhood through a return to what as young men had made them hopeful in the first place, the idea of poetry, what Von Humboldt Fleisher calls the Ellis Island of the mind.[11] Thus Corde's conditioned recoiling from the depersonalization, the moral and aesthetic vacancy of the languages of contemporaneity, is usually attended by a simultaneous movement toward a language of supposed plenitude or presence—the same moral authorial presence of traditional verbal art which Derrida has been at such pains to teach us to recognize and repudiate.[12]

This habitual turn of Corde's mind back to poetry or, more accurately, the excitement of poetry as he first experienced it, may be taken as a linguistic symptom of that fuller process of romantic self-tropism which finds relief and distance from the irresolutions and impotencies of adulthood in the contemplation of the relative freedom and imaginative exuberances of childhood and adolescence. The source of this bent in the English tradition is Wordsworth's discovery of the profound imaginative resources of the writer's own childhood. But one need not be a writer to benefit from the personal past, and there are ample precedents for such restorative uses of the past in the American romantic tradition as well. F. Scott Fitzgerald, for example, more boldly than Wordsworth, locates the dream's source not alone in the personal past of his character but in the collective endeavor of those who have dreamt the American dream from the nation's earliest days, thereby enriching its content for later generations.

In any event, whatever form it takes and wherever it may be thought to be located, the need for something to fall back on, an imagined place to escape temporarily into, where the body is not bruised to pleasure soul, is as strong today as it was in Wordsworth's or Fitzgerald's time. Corde's reluctance to come back down to earth from the elevator car he accompanies his wife in as she swings out alone to study the stars on Mount Palomar at the very end of *The Dean's December* is understandable: the trip up was exhilarating, imaginatively liberating, a true mountain-moment of "poetry" brought about by modern science. But the reluctance may also be taken as symbolic of Corde's ambivalence throughout the novel of going once again face-to-face with a world toward whose quotidian woes increasingly, according to Bellow, the only sane human response seems to be one of self-closure: retreat or die of reality-blight.

"Miracles occur" Sylvia Plath doubtfully yet toughly asserts at the end of one of her poems, after the attempt to conjure a miracle has just failed miserably, and even as she steels herself for another long vigil before the next "random descent."[13] With the possible single exception of Jay Gatsby (whose inventor, we conclude, was no more willing than is Bellow to surrender the dream),[14] instances in modern and postmodern literature of a belief in the possibility of such divine visitations are about as rare as the visitations themselves. Yet Plath isn't the only hopeful despairer; nor among contemporary American novelists is Bellow. Will Barrett, the staunchly agnostic hero of Walker Percy's *The Second Coming,* suddenly concludes in the last paragraph of that book that God exists. This as a result of the dramatic entry into his empty middle age of the female partner he has searched for all his life and long ago given up hope of finding. In Percy's variation on the old-fashioned deathbed conversion scene, Barrett disingenuously asks, "Is she a gift and therefore a sign of a giver?"[15]

But in these instances, as of old, literature merely continues (some would say naively)[16] to imitate life. For we all dream. And wait. Whether like Gatsby, fully expecting or, like Plath and Barrett, doubtfully hoping, we too presume that one day soon—perhaps tomorrow—our dream will be within reach. As much as Gatsby's, what Corde's story teaches is that even as we thus look hopefully to the future for their consummations, the reason for our abiding thralldom to our dreams invariably lies behind, in our first encounters with them. Carraway was right: "So we beat on boats against the current, borne back ceaselessly into the past."[17]

Acknowledgments

This essay is a reworking of a talk first delivered before the English faculty of Nanjing University, Nanjing, P.R.C., and then to the members of the American Studies Institute, Shandong University, Jinan, P.R.C., in May and June of 1982. I wish to acknowledge the warm cordiality with which I was received by my Chinese hosts at both those institutions and to thank especially Diane Johnston, then second secretary-culture of the American Embassy, Beijing, both for her assistance in arranging this lecture tour during my tenure as Fulbright professor at Beijing University, 1981–82, and for obtaining the USICA travel monies that made the tour possible.

Notes

1. *The Dean's December* (New York: Harper and Row, 1981), 265. Page references are to this edition and are cited in the text.

2. A sketch of the influence of earlier, mostly twentieth-century, philosophers of language on Derrida's thought, from Peirce through Frege, Husserl, Austin, and especially Wittgenstein, is provided by Newton Garver in his Preface to Derrida's *Speech and Phenomena, and Other Essays on Husserl's Theory of Signs*, trans. and intro. David B. Allison (Evanston: Northwestern University Press, 1973), ix–xxix. A succinct statement of the contemporary attitude toward referentiality may be found in Edward W. Said's "Reflections on Recent 'American Left' Literary Criticism," in *The Question of Textuality*, ed. William V. Spanos, et al. (Bloomington: Indiana University Press, 1982). Said says: "Literature, in short, expresses only itself . . . : its world is a formal one, and its relationship to the quotidian can only be understood, as de Man implies, by means of negation or a radically ironic theory, as severe as it is consistent, whose workings depend on the equal and opposite propositions that if the world is not a book neither is the book the world" (16–17). For a fuller discussion of this subject see Study 7, "Metaphor and Reference," in Paul Ricoeur's *The Rule of Metaphor*, trans. Robert Czerny (Toronto: University of Toronto Press, 1977), 216–56.

3. See Isobel Armstrong, *Language as Living Form in Nineteenth-Century Poetry* (Totowa: Barnes and Noble, 1982). Citing as her theoretical test Coleridge's claim that "words are *living powers*, by which the things of most importance to mankind are actuated, combined, and humanized," Armstrong defines romantic language as "idealist," meaning it "discloses a concern with the relationship of subject and object and with the nature of reality. Idealist language assumes that the object is known as a category of mind. It is not that the object has no existence, but rather the status of the way in which it is known as an aspect of consciousness which is the important problem" (xii). See as well, Gerald L. Bruns, *Modern Poetry and the Idea of Language* (New Haven: Yale University Press, 1974). Bruns describes romantic views of language as generally Orphic, where the belief is that language explains and interprets the world for human knowing, and postromantic views as "hermetic," by which language tries to be independent of anything external to the literary construct. My contention is that Bellow is anomalous because more Orphic than hermetic. See also notes 9 and 10, following.

4. Compare Diane Johnson in "Point of Departure," review of *The Dean's December*, by Saul Bellow, *New York Review of Books*, 4 March 1982, 6, 8. Herself a novelist, Johnson suggests that the crucial flaw in the novel stems from Bellow's "immense" approval of his character, which leads to his taking too "little trouble to convince us of his view" (6). Precisely what "his view" means

here is indeterminate. The present study finds ample evidence to conclude that Bellow achieved a sufficient distance from many of Corde's enthusiasms to be critical of them (indeed so, in time, does Corde). Even if such authorial affection were demonstrably the danger Johnson thinks it sometimes is, the charge is particularly odd when brought against Bellow, who happens frequently both to like his characters very much and to create characters of extraordinary literary success.

5. Helen Dudar, "The Graying of Saul Bellow," review of *The Dean's December,* by Saul Bellow, *Saturday Review,* January 1982, 17.

6. Robert Towers, "A Novel of Politics, Wit and Sorrow," review of *The Dean's December,* by Saul Bellow, *New York Times Book Review* 10 January 1982, 22.

7. *Shelley's Poetry and Prose,* ed. Donald H. Reiman and Sharon B. Powers (New York: Norton, 1977), 174. According to Shelley, speech precedes, even creates, thought, making it the most godlike of Prometheus's gifts to humankind. Obviously, along with Wordsworth, Coleridge, and Blake, Shelley belongs in the "idealist" camp with respect to nineteenth-century views of language as discussed by Armstrong. See note 5 above.

8. See Daniel Majdiak, "The Romantic Self and *Henderson the Rain King,*" *Bucknell Review* 19, no. 2 (1971): 125–46; also see Michael G. Yetman, "Who Would Not Sing for Humboldt?" *ELH* 48 (Winter 1981): 935–51; and Allan Chavkin, "*Humboldt's Gift* and the Romantic Imagination," *Philological Quarterly* 62, no. 1 (Winter 1983): 1–19. Each of these essays, though focusing primarily on a single novel, demonstrates Bellow's remarkably detailed knowledge of a wide range of British romantic poetry. My own and Chavkin's articles attempt, in addition, a general assessment of Bellow's place in the postromantic traditions of both Britain and America.

9. De Man sees this tendency to equate poetic images with nature, signifier with signified, as evidence of the romantics' nostalgia to possess the ontological status of the object: to effect by the naming of a natural object a sharing of the object's permanence which the subject, because it has a beginning, knows that it cannot otherwise possess. Later nineteenth-century poets, according to de Man, take the priority of the natural object more for granted. See Paul de Man, "Intentional Structure of the Romantic Image," in *Romanticism and Consciousness,* ed. Harold Bloom (New York: Norton and Company, 1970), 65–77.

10. Bruns, in *Modern Poetry and the Idea of Language,* concludes that Mallarmé sought exactly the opposite of the romantics, namely to release "language from its bondage to the world," to establish the "word in the pristine universe of nothingness, in which impossible sphere . . . the essence of beauty is to be found" (101–2). Whether Joyce as a young man conceived of himself in precisely the same language that Stephen Dedalus uses to describe himself in *A Portrait of the Artist as a Young Man*—namely, as "a priest of eternal imagination"—is problematical. What we do know for certain is that the later Joyce did not feel the need to sacramentalize his vocation as a writer, and

hence reveals a more recognizably modernist (i.e., less romantically self-conscious, more secular) attitude to language in his later works.

11. Saul Bellow, *Humboldt's Gift* (New York: Viking, 1975), 24.

12. See Jacques Derrida, *Of Grammatology,* trans. and pref. Gayatri Chakravorty Spivak (Baltimore: Johns Hopkins University Press, 1976), 1–93.

13. *The Colossus* (London: Heinemann, 1960), 43. The poem's title is "Black Rook in Rainy Weather."

14. See Marius Bewley, *The Eccentric Design: Form in the Classic American Novel* (New York: Columbia University Press, 1959). It is difficult to disagree with Bewley's conclusion that *The Great Gatsby* both restores our hope in the historical potentialities of the American dream through the mythic (non-temporal) elements of Gatsby's character, while simultaneously exploring the implications and false seductions which the dream is subject to in a "corrupt period" (270). But see also Douglas Taylor, *"The Great Gatsby:* Style and Myth," *University of Kansas City Review* 20 (Fall 1953): 30–37, rpt. in *The Modern American Novel: Essays in Criticism,* ed. and intro. Max Westbrook (New York: Random House, 1966), 59–76. Better than Bewley, Taylor explains the unique achievement of the novel: its contradictory yet successful rendering of the integrity and incorruptibility of the romantic hero's quest and, simultaneously, through Carraway, its demonstration of the essential emptiness, even banality of the actual quest objectives Gatsby pursues. These latter—a meretricious wealth and a woman unworthy of his vision—are tragically confused by the quester with their ideal counterparts in his imagination.

15. *The Second Coming* (New York: Washington Square, 1980), 411.

16. According to at least one recent commentator, not only has traditional mimetic fiction run its enfeebled course in our time but also, during the last decade or so, the metafictionists and fabulators have exhausted the potentialities of experimental fiction. Consequently, it seems, we are already well into the epoch in which theory replaces fiction as the primary form of serious literary endeavor. See especially the chapter titled "Theory of Literature Becomes Theory as Literature," in Elizabeth W. Bruss, *Beautiful Theories: The Spectacle of Discourse in Contemporary Criticism* (Baltimore: Johns Hopkins University Press, 1982), 33–79.

17. F. Scott Fitzgerald, *The Great Gatsby* (New York: Scribners and Sons, 1953), 182.

The Religious Vision of
More Die of Heartbreak

Stephen L. Tanner

Much has been said about the manifest humanism of Bellow's novels, but the religious concerns in his fiction have received little attention—at least as concerns explicitly identified as religious. This is unfortunate because "humanism" is an abused, slippery, all-purpose term that needs qualification and definition within a specific context in order to have a clear meaning, and in Bellow's novels it is the religious concerns that qualify and define the humanism. In fact, Bellow's religious concerns are the basis for his critique of certain aspects of modern humanism.

These concerns are encompassed in his preoccupation with the transcendent, that is, with the aspects of human experience and the qualities of the human personality that lie beyond the purview of positivistic science, psychology, and rationalistic philosophy. This preoccupation has become increasingly prominent in his later novels. Mention of soul, spirit, the mystery of the human person, and knowledge of the heart rather than of the intellect has increased in tandem with pointed criticism of the narrow empiricism of modern psychology, the arrogance and dehumanizing effects of scientific materialism, the sordid emptiness of merely biological sex, and the soul-damaging consequences of contemporary money and power seeking. Through engaging narrative, humor, and rich specificity, Bellow's fiction explores a paradoxical antithesis at the heart of modern humanism. When human beings follow the path of self-affirmation to the exclusion of a respectful recognition of a transcendent reality, they ultimately succeed only in undermining their own consciousness of power and purpose. This naturalistic assertion of self-sufficiency in reality denies and exterminates the true self according to the laws of an inexorable inner dialectic. To affirm themselves and preserve their source of meaning and creative energy, human beings must affirm the transcendent as well. Bellow makes this point forcefully in his foreword to Allan Bloom's *The Closing of the American Mind:*

> But the channel [to the soul] is always there, and it is our business to keep it open, to have access to the deepest parts of ourselves—to that part of us which is conscious of a higher consciousness, by means of which, we make final judgments and put everything together. The independence of this consciousness, which has the strength to be immune to the noise of history and the distractions of our immediate surroundings, is what the life struggle is all about. The soul has to find and hold its ground against hostile forces, sometimes embodied in ideas which frequently deny its very existence and which indeed often seem to be trying to annul it altogether.[1]

This statement, published the same year as *More Die of Heartbreak*, expresses the primary theme of that novel. The preoccupation with the channel to the soul provides its active principle, and it is a religious preoccupation, if a broad definition of religion is allowed. In fact, this statement from Hume's *Dialogues Concerning Natural Religion* illuminates the method and effect of *More Die of Heartbreak*:

> I am indeed persuaded, said Philo, that the best and indeed the only method of bringing everyone to a due sense of religion is by just representations of the misery and wickedness of men. And for that purpose a talent of eloquence and strong imagery is more requisite than that of reasoning and argument. For is it necessary to prove what everyone feels within himself? It is only necessary to make us feel it, if possible, more intimately and sensibly.[2]

The comic eloquence and arresting images of this novel do indeed acquaint us intimately and sensibly with the misery and wickedness in contemporary life. And while the novel contains a good deal of reasoning and argument, this intellectualizing actually functions as part of the images. As the narrator admits, "these cognitive efforts will never get us anywhere."[3] Moreover, in this portrait of contemporary life, excessive rationalism is a principal source of the misery and wickedness. "A sense of religion" is a suitable phrase for describing the effect of this novel if emphasis on the transcendent in the human soul and on the importance of efficacious love are considered essential to the religious sense.

In *More Die of Heartbreak*, Bellow has combined a rich diversity of images and motifs to convey a religious vision which, while playfully eclectic, is best identified as a version of religious existentialism. In particular, the philosophy of Nicolas Berdyaev, whom the narrator lists as one of his beloved Russian thinkers, provides the most illuminating interpretive context for the ideas and attitudes expressed in the novel. This is not to say that Berdyaev is an exclusive source for those ideas and attitudes, for while it is true that congruent passages can be found in Berdyaev's writing to clarify what this novel says about love, sex, science, rationalism, human mystery, and more, this is largely because Berdyaev's mind is the meeting place for many minds and he embodies a tradition of religious-philosophical thinking that includes voices Bellow knew at first hand. And it must be remembered that Bellow is fascinated by writers who treat the subject of a higher consciousness, regardless of their eccentricity (e.g. Swedenborg, Blake, Emerson, Whitman, Rudolph Steiner, and Jewish mystics.) This fascination is revealed with a comic touch in the whacky gurus and metaphysical theorizers so characteristic of his fiction. Nevertheless, Berdyaev's writing remains the single most useful background source for understanding the religious-philosophical concerns of *More Die of Heartbreak*, and perhaps of his later fiction in general.

The narrator of *More Die of Heartbreak*, Kenneth Trachtenberg, is a 35-year-old assistant professor of Russian literature at a university in the Midwest's rustbelt. Having grown up in Paris, he has come to America in a spirit of quest (his name in German means to seek or strive for the mountain top) to be near his uncle, Benn Crader, a distinguished botanist who teaches at the same university. In Kenneth's estimation, Benn is a visionary, "one of those passionate natures who long to find and see what perhaps does not exist on earth" (141). The archetypal metaphor of seeing as spiritual awareness appears often in the novel. Kenneth says that Benn "sees things others don't see, and the gauge of a man is the *grade* of what he can see" (85). He indulges himself in imagining that Benn's eyes "were prototypes of the original faculty of vision, of the power of seeing itself" (234). His Aunt Lena, influenced by Swedenborg and Blake, had introduced him to "the valuable idea that modes of seeing were matters of destiny, that what is sent forth by the seer affects what is seen" (306). The old Japanese professor confirms that Benn has "a special gift of observation" evidenced by "something *visionary* about the distinctness with which plants came before him'" (105). One of Kenneth's Russian philosophers had said that human eyes fall into two categories, "the receptive and the will-emanating." The first category, which is Benn's, opens one to "an eternal *now*." "Man is what he sees" (55). Paradoxically but appropriately, Benn, despite his gift of vision, is blind to the offenses of others. He has a peculiar innocence and a special capacity of love. "Sizing up the people I knew to see which of them might be capable of love in a classic form," says Kenneth, "I decided that Uncle Benn was a front runner" (23). He has charisma, or what Kenneth calls "magics" (24). As a "plant mystic" (52) he uses plants as his arcana—what you need to know "to be fertile in a creative pursuit, to make discoveries, to prepare for the communication of a spiritual mystery" (27). Kenneth identifies this "arcane vision" as his principal subject. (28).

The link between vision and the transcendent is ageless, of course, but those familiar with American literature will most immediately be reminded of the angle of vision, innocent eye, transparent eyeball, and eternal now concepts of American Transcendentalism. Bellow's familiarity with the visionary tradition is comprehensive. For example, in *Humboldt's Gift* he explicitly alludes to the American Transcendentalists and to Rudolph Steiner; in this novel he refers to Russian and Jewish versions and gives special emphasis to Swedenborg, who is mentioned on over a dozen pages throughout the novel.

Benn's visionary gifts qualify him in Kenneth's eyes as a "Citizen of Eternity," fellow citizen (although perhaps well down the scale or even in the process of naturalization) with the great prophets and sublime artists whose achievements transcend history and culture. Leading up to his statement about the strength of higher consciousness "to be immune to the noise of history and the distractions of our immediate surroundings" in his foreword to *The Closing of the American Mind,* Bellow rejects—using his own development in Chicago as evidence—the notion that history and culture are exclusive determinants of character.[4] This is relevant to the novel because Kenneth's aspirations for citizenship in eternity are played out in the "posthistorical" world of the Midwest's rustbelt. The statement in the foreword and the novel are manifestations of the same complex of ideas and attitudes. And while those ideas and attitudes are common to nearly any view of man as a spiritual being, Berdyaev's philosophy, (e.g., the first chapter of *Truth and Revelation* treating what he calls the "existential" nature of "transcendental man"), illuminates them in a particularly useful way. Berdyaev's religious existentialism is founded on the distinction between person and individual (the soul possessing a higher consciousness as distinguished from the naturalistic biological unit) and existential and objective knowledge (knowledge growing out of actual experience, including soul experience, as distinguished from abstract or rationalistic knowledge). The primary characteristic of Berdyaev's existentialism is that it "will not accept objectifying knowledge"[5] thus "transcendental man is the inner man whose existence lies outside the bounds of objectification."[6]

Unfortunately, Benn's gifts for contemplation and unselfish love do not suit him for confronting contemporary life and particularly contemporary women. As Kenneth tells him, "The higher the range of vision, the more your control is weakened" (262). Benn is a "sex-abused" and "woman-battered man" (54–55)—"a visionary with plants, a dud with women" (306). Therefore, Kenneth has come to learn a kind of mystic wisdom from him and at the same time protect him from sexual entanglements. In this mutually dependent relationship, Kenneth believes they have a "crucial project" going: to bring to human life the visionary gifts Benn brought to plant life, "to transpose his magical powers from botany to love" (330). Much of the comedy originates in the "gap between high achievement and personal ineptitude" (18.) "The greater your achievements, the less satisfactory your personal and domestic life will be," Kenneth observes (36–37)—"the quality people are always knee-deep in the garbage of personal life" (137). At one point he asks in exasperation, "Why was it necessary for the Father of Cybernetics to have his zipper checked by his wife before he left the house?" (224). This gap between intellectual achievement and blundering practical behavior has interested Bellow for a long time. In the foreword to Bloom's book, he says he meant *Herzog* to show "how little strength higher education had to offer a troubled man" because intellectual education provides little help in the conduct of life, in confronting erotic needs, and in coping with daily domestic experience (16). In this novel, treatment of the gap gets an additional twist because tuning in to the visionary areas particularly puts one out of sync with mundane affairs. The attempt to live in a higher world of mystery, love, and soul, while at the same time trying to confront domestic, financial, technological, political, and especially sexual problems is a fertile source of comedy. Being a Citizen of Eternity does not prevent one from being a fool and may even assure it.

Treating the big issues with comedy and irony and putting his own convictions in the mouths of characters who are quirky and often preposterous has allowed Bellow over the years to insinuate his ideas and values—particularly his religious values—without having to be directly accountable for them to a critical audience that would readily attack them if they were openly asserted. His novels have secrets, as people do. They are there as a bonus for the sensitive reader or as a kind of subliminal quavering. Some who wish he would assert his values more directly have viewed his technique as overly cagey, or even cowardly, but whether that was ever true or not, it does not seem to apply to his later work, which has become progressively explicit in its concern with transcendence. A more adequate explanation for why he puts wisdom in the mouths of preposterous characters and why his seekers for the big truths are always inept in the little truths of ordinary living lies in his acute awareness that, given the nature of mortal existence, wisdom is inevitably and inextricably mixed with folly, the sublime is never distant from the ridiculous, and the most inspired seer is ineluctably alloyed with a generous amount of human klutziness. Bellow often parodies or satirizes the quest for enlightenment (Henderson is a notable instance), but it is parody or satire intended to generate balance, realism, and humility rather than to belittle and destroy. The satiric norm is discernible. In this respect, he differs markedly from contemporary writers who use satire or parody either without a norm or without making the challenging artistic effort to convey a norm. In Bellow's view, it is an error on the one hand to deny the existence of big truths, and on the other to think any human will ever express them purely and definitively, let alone incorporate them into daily behavior. It is best to treasure the fragments and intimations wherever we find them in the poignant comedy of modern life.

In leaving Paris on his "soul-making" quest (37), Kenneth rejected French intellectualism (including atheistic existentialism) and his father's talented and obsessive womanizing. Neither, he concludes, can teach him to be a Citizen of Eternity. The former, in its abstraction, is out of touch with the mystery of human personality adhering in actual experience; and the latter is "death-flavored" (69). But the novel's comic irony derives from his being himself an inveterate and quirky intellectual theorizer and a vulnerable bumbler with women. Thus, the book provides variations of two characteristic Bellow paradigms. The first is the paradoxical situation of a cerebral author creating a cerebral character who provides a cerebral critique of cerebral activity. The second is the situation of the intellectual male with a rational and decidedly misogynistic perception of female entanglements who nevertheless is an incorrigible sucker for them.

Kenneth's contradictory philosophic urges derive from two contrasting influences absorbed during his youth in Paris. One was the philosopher Alexandre Kojéve, "a relentless, merciless reasoner" (155) who occasionally took dinner in his parents' home. (Kojéve, an actual philosopher, gave an important series of lectures in Paris during the thirties on the philosophy of Hegel and has influenced French philosophy since that time.) Kenneth traces his weakness for "the big overview" back to him. The notion of a "posthistorical" era that Kenneth mentions frequently comes from Hegel by way of Kojéve (36). The second influence was his first Russian language teacher, M. Yermelov, a student of the mystical tradition who propounded the notion that each of us has an angel, "a being charged with preparing us for a higher evolution of the spirit" and instilling warmth into our souls. Yermelov warned him "against the glamour of thought, the calculating intellect and its constructions, its fabrications alien to the power of life." These influences represent highly rationalistic philosophy on the one hand and mystical wisdom of the heart on the other. Bellow, drawing upon cabalistic writing and providing a figurative dimension for Benn's botany, uses the terms Tree of Knowledge and Tree of Life to identify these opposing impulses. The terms correspond respectively with Berdyaev's objective and existential knowledge. The Tree of Knowledge is associated with the truth of striving, with calculated power concerns in the areas of money, politics, technology, and sex. The Tree of Life is linked with the truth of receptivity, with love, family bonds, and the transcendent concerns of Swedenborg, Blake, and a cluster of Russian mystic philosophers including Berdyaev (57, 143). According to Yermelov, who echoes the fundamental assertion of Berdyaev's philosophy, "knowledge divorced from life equals sickness" (57). In other words, intellect without soul— objective knowledge divorced from existential knowledge—reduces the person (transcendental man) to a mere individual (a naturalistically determined biological unit). The condition of contemporary America is symbolically epitomized by the fact that the book by the sixteenth-century mystic Haym Vital concerning the Tree of Life is buried at the site of Benn's family home now occupied by the Electronic Tower, a skyscraper built by another of Kenneth's uncles who is the very embodiment of greed and political corruption (201, 253). Both that uncle and his building are fruits of the Tree of Knowledge.

According to cabalistic tradition, the Tree of Knowledge and the Tree of Life would eventually unite (56). The need for such union is reflected in Kenneth's acknowledgement that skyscrapers, though filled with "abominable enterprises," do "express an aspiration of freedom," and, perhaps deceptively, "transmit an idea of transcendence" (294). Moreover, while recognizing the advantages of living in isolation from a time in which the Tree of Knowledge dominates (Benn's apartment is described as a "defense system" against contemporary urban society), Kenneth knows such escape is neither possible nor desirable: "When you come down into contemporary life, you can really get it in the neck. If on the other hand you decline to come down into it, you'll never understand a *thing*" (227). Benn, despite the defense system of his apartment, "omitted (or disdained) to protect himself, to a degree which was scarcely compatible with the actual conditions (or outrages) of contemporary life" (46). He "didn't ask to be excused from the trials of creaturely existence. He *conspicuously* didn't" (13). The novel, with all its criticism of contemporary life, does not advocate escape. Kenneth obviously feels that an essential mark of decency is to be ashamed of being a citizen of the twentieth century, and he says that the worst you can say of anybody is that he or she is "a genuinely modern individual" (71). Nevertheless, he has a "strong thing about being contemporary" (285). Behind Kenneth's recognition that you have to "come down into contemporary life" is Bellow's understanding that the good that emerges from a conflict of values arises not from the total abandonment or destruction of one set of values but from the building of a new value, sustained, like an arch, by the tension of the original two. But such a new value will never be achieved without what Kenneth frequently refers to as "a turning point" for humankind, which begins as a turning point in the individual and is the product of the love and "power of life" associated with the transcendental person as opposed to the naturalistic individual.

This turning point cannot be brought about by calculation and rational intellect. Kenneth quotes the poet Philip Larkin: "In everyone there sleeps a sense of life according to love" (44). This quotation and Yermelov's notion of unthawing the frozen heart function to keep before the reader the paramount importance of love and its distinctness from rational intellect. It is the "rationally wicked" who are now most wide awake and who have the coldest glaciers in their breasts. This distrust of pure intellect that informs the religious vision of this novel is characteristic of mystic thinkers in general. Kenneth chooses to single out Pascal, certain Jewish mystics and Russian thinkers (including Berdyaev), Blake, and particularly Swedenborg, who, as Emerson put it, "reprobates to weariness the danger and vice of pure intellect."[7] Emerson's phrase could be applied as well to Kenneth, and consequently to Bellow. Kenneth mistrusts intellectuals, "a poor lot of people. Brainy but ignorant of the fundamentals" (111). He links them with money and manipulation, particularly in the case of Matilda, who according to her father has "brains enough to be chief executive officer of a blue-chip corporation. With her mentality you could manage NASA . . . . Her head is like a computer bank . . . ." (142–43). Bellow has described his own intention as "the rediscovery of the magic of the world under the debris of modern ideas."[8]

Among the difficulties of living as a transcendental person in contemporary America, the novel singles out "the demon of sexuality" (23) for special emphasis, perhaps because nowhere else is the gap within the same person between intelligent achievement and irrational blundering so dramatically apparent. And perhaps also because "sexual Tylenol" has become the contemporary nostrum for "spiritual headaches" (301). Della Bedell's cry "What am I supposed to do with my sexuality?" echoes through the novel, becoming in its reverberations the anguished question of a secular age in which love has degenerated into sexual mechanics. As Kenneth observes, "Once you get into the erotic life, modern style, you are accelerated till your minutest particles fly apart" (240). Benn, though a superior person, is "unable to manage his sexual needs, or to be more accurate, his *love* longings" (278). The relationship of sex and love is a key issue in this novel. "The meaning of human love" is one of the "big issues" Kenneth grapples with (292). Once again the philosophy of Berdyaev is relevant; in fact, it is obliquely alluded to. In telling of Benn's encounter with Della Bedell, Kenneth says "talk about slavery and freedom" (85). *Slavery and Freedom* is the title of a Berdyaev book whose chapter titled "The Erotic Lure and Slavery: Sex, Personality and Freedom" is markedly congruent with Kenneth's treatment of sexuality. This is not surprising because Kenneth gives a course in the Russian Sexual Mystics (329). Not only can Berdyaev be classified in that group, but his chapter summarizes the writing of three other prominent members mentioned in the novel: Solovyev, Rozanov, and Feodorov. Berdyaev, emphasizing how pervasive sex is in human life, explains its highest manifestation in love: "Real love finds the personality and recognizes it, attaches itself to everything unchangeably individual in it and affirms it for eternity, that is the meaning of love. But the climate of the world is not favorable to real love, too often it is deadly to it"[9] (225). But at the same time that sex can be a part of real love, it also

> lends itself to terrible profanation, the whole of human nature is profaned through sex. The greatest triviality may be connected with sex. Not only the physical act of sex, but also the psychical is profaned, erotics are profaned, the words of love become intolerable, it is with difficulty that they are pronounced. Here the slavery of sex takes the form of grim triviality and superficiality. Sex is dreadful in the sphere of the routine of ordinary life. It is dreadful in the bourgeois world and is connected with the power of money over human life. The slavery of sex is connected with the slavery of money.[10]

Compare this statement with Kenneth's assertion that his father, with all his womanizing, was far from love: "The premise of his eroticism was mortality. The sex embrace was death-flavored. He translated Eternity as Death" (69). Or consider it in light of the fact that Kenneth, recognizing that "sexual relations represent love *par excellence* when they are *authentically* founded" (292) and that such love is "the very essence of the Divine Spirit and the source for humankind of the warmth of Heaven" (277), is confronted on every hand by love in its degenerate contemporary forms, for example, Matilda's attempt to use Benn to gain money and social prestige or "LOV" cynically scrawled on the belly of a rape victim.

Like Berdyaev and other Russian sexual mystics, Kenneth views modern sexuality as profane and either trivial or destructive because the transcendent element is missing. "Mere Nature is Hell, as Swedenborg wrote (I ask you to remember that Aunt Lena had left her collection of Swedenborg books to me). Insofar as sex is identified with Nature, the Euclidean logic is simple . . . . Why did Swedenborg say that *mere* Nature was hell? He meant Nature in a literal view, in a mechanistic interpretation" (89). The "literal view" is a recurring motif, linked notably with the frequent allusions to Admiral Byrd's *Alone.* It is what Berdyaev calls objectification (Kenneth, incidentally, notes Swedenborg's influence on his Russian sexual mystics [p. 97]). "To be seen literally dries out one's humanity" (89). In the terms of religious existentialism, it is to be viewed as an individual rather than as a person. And "the interest of human beings is quickly exhausted by literalness. What was deadly about Admiral Byrd's observation of his companions in the Antarctic was that it was so literal. This literalness, from a sexual standpoint, is lethal. When it becomes a matter of limbs, members and organs, Eros faces annihilation" (90). The Japanese strip show and the rape hearing are both intended to show the degradation of sex on the "literal" level: "The downtown hearing was like the strip show in Kyoto in its effect. Hard-edged sex, one might call it, abstract excitement, maddening literalness when the girls invited the public to stare at their inmost parts" (209) That exposure of the female sex organ was "as literal as it was possible to be, and the more literal it was, the more mystery there seemed to be in it" (108). That is, these scientific voyeurs, "inventors of marvelous visual instruments from electron microscopes to equipment that sent back picture of the moons of Saturn" (in contrast to the visionary gifts Kenneth is seeking in Benn), cannot espy the source of mystery underlying human sexuality. The same point is made by the courtroom scene in which the scientific forensic experts microscopically scrutinize the rape victim's panties (272–73).

The degradation of sex by literalness or objectification or denial of the transcendent—whatever term is used—is of course symptomatic of contemporary American society in general as it is depicted in this novel. Kenneth wishes to transcend the literalness of scientific materialism. "By pushing to the very borders of literalness you got into visionary areas which science wanted nothing to do with," he remarks. His quest is to escape the closed prison of "mere nature . . . a fixed world of matter and energy" and "cover the whole range of human concerns" (116). He views himself as "a mysterious creature (no exception, either, most of humankind are far outside the shallow systems of psychology)" (203). The four repetitions (in addition to the title) of the statement that more die of heartbreak than of radiation reflects the novel's forceful affirmation of human concerns transcending mere physical existence. Antarctica functions symbolically as the boundary between the literal and visionary—the "boundary of boundaries" (82) where one gets "a foretaste of eternity" (163). That is, for a visionary like Benn it represents such a boundary. In the literal view of Admiral Byrd it is a dead end that exposes the paucity of human mystery and possibility. The contrast is of course strategic and central to the main theme. The Byrd incident represents "claustrophobia of consciousness" (denial of the transcendent or higher consciousness), the abolition of which Kenneth sees as "the classic modern challenge" (33).

The narration of this novel is a remarkable achievement. It is garrulous, irrepressible, intelligent, witty, candid, tolerant, and idiosyncratically opinionated. It ranges from the erudite to the slangy, from East-West relations to the quality of frozen dinners. It gives the impression of a buzzing cocktail party where you are as likely to run into William Blake as Ronald McDonald. Bellow ingeniously merges the voices and perspectives of many characters into one rich and engaging narration. His technique in accomplishing this is original and subtle. The expression of theme by the repetition of thematic motifs, however, is original and subtle in quite a different way. The originality and subtlety derive, paradoxically, from the explicitness and repetition. Poe's "To Helen," the Charles Addams cartoon, the Hitchcock film, Byrd, Kojéve, Swedenborg, Yermelov, Trees of Life and Knowledge, the Antarctic, the life as a turning point and Citizen of Eternity concepts, the more die of heartbreak statement, the antinomy of literal versus visionary, the sleep of love, the second inner person—all these are stressed and repeated to the point where Kenneth is self-conscious and apologetic about it:

> There was quite a lot at stake here. I can't continually be spelling it out. As: the curse of human impoverishment as revealed to Admiral Byrd in Antarctica; the sleep of love in human beings as referred to by Larkin; the search for sexual enchantments as the universal nostrum; the making of one's soul as the only project genuinely worth undertaking; and my personal rejection of existentialism [the French atheistic version], which led me to emigrate and which makes me so severe in my analysis of motives. That has been indicated. (155)

Indicated indeed, explicitly and repeatedly. But the overt thematic motifs summarized so explicitly here are actually part of an artful design. Using a comic narrator, an object of satire himself, to self-consciously spell out the antitheses of literal–visionary, individual–person, objective–

existential, striving–receptivity, power of intellect–power of life, manipulation–guilelessness, shrewdness–magics, rationalism–mysticism, mere nature–the transcendent, and so on, provides a kind of distance and latitude that Bellow treasures. Hawthorne turned to what he called the romance for latitude in treating the truths of the human heart. Bellow finds his latitude to do the same thing in a narrator like Kenneth.

The truths of the human heart, as Bellow sees them, have, in addition to a transcendent element and as a kind of corollary to it, a strong tincture of the Aristotelian law of measure or moderation between extremes. This is clearly seen in the dialectical pattern of motifs. Poe's "To Helen" is played off against the Addams cartoon. The Poe motif represents the idealistic view of sexual love. Poe "had run straight into a world rolled flat as a pizza by the rational intellect" and fought back with "whiskey and poetry, dreams, puzzles, perversions." But by losing touch with reality, with existential knowledge, he ends up married to a "moronic and forever prenubile girl" (209). Benn is obsessed for a time with the Poe poem. He, too, is chafing under the harness of rational intellect and deludes himself into thinking Matilda will be a kind of Helen who will satisfy his love longings. In his disillusionment, he becomes obsessed with the Addams cartoon, which represents a cynical view that love relationships can produce only unhappiness. Somewhere between these extremes is a balanced position that properly assesses physical beauty and the parameters of human happiness, that acknowledges the complexity of human personality and resists the enticements of the abstract. Kenneth's relation with Dita approaches that position. And the ideal love represented by the Poe motif also functions as an opposite to the "literal" conception of sex that pervades the novel. The problem here of locating oneself between extremes is essentially the same as the struggle to be neither more than human nor less than human that *The Victim* treats explicitly. It is an enduring aspect of Bellow's humanism. In a similar kind of dialectical relationship are the motifs of excessive, exclusive rationalism and contemporary suspense films. The pure intellect of the former finds its antithesis in films like Hitchcock's *Psycho* in which "the viewer is affected physiologically, he pumps more adrenaline, but nothing more than physiology is affected" (261). The desirable position lies somewhere between desicating intellectualism and mindless emotionalism.

The most important antithesis pairs "claustrophobia of consciousness" (33) with "hyperactive but unfocused consciousness" (36). The former is the thing Admiral Byrd and his companions suffered from. Kenneth quotes Byrd's description of it: "The time comes when one has nothing to reveal to the other, when even his unformed thoughts can be anticipated, his pet ideas become a meaningless drool" (20). Contrasting with this is "the cauldron of modern consciousness" (93), an active bubbling of intellect without soul. One of the reasons Kenneth distrusts psychology is that he sees it as "one of the lower byproducts of modern consciousness, a terrible agitation which we prize as insight' " (51). The "Great Ideas" are like "tom-toms beating inside our heads, driving us crazy" (247). These thoughts, he says, take the place of prayer nowadays.

> And we think these thoughts are serious and we take pride in our ability to think, to elaborate ideas, so we go round and round in consciousness like this. However, they don't get us anywhere; our speculations are like a stationary bicycle. . . . These proliferating thoughts have more affinity to insomnia than to mental progress. Oscillations of the mental substance is what they are, ever-increasing jitters. (301)

In the case of these extremes of consciousness, it is not a matter of simply locating some middle point between paucity and overabundance of thought. This dialectic most clearly manifests the novel's religious vision. A balanced consciousness is dependent on the transcendent. Near the conclusion, Kenneth summarizes what the antithetical thematic motifs have been intimating:

> The secret of our being still asks to be unfolded. Only now we understand that worrying at it and ragging it is no use. The first step is to stop these oscillations of consciousness that are keeping me awake. Only, before you command the oscillations to stop, before you check out, you must maneuver yourself into a position in which metaphysical aid can approach. (330–31)

At the end, Benn is headed for the North Pole to study lichen. There is "a basic life question at the bottom of his research" because lichen, like many human hearts (according to Yermelov), are frozen through and through but revive with the slightest warming (315). Benn rejects the oscillations of consciousness. His decision "has been carefully felt through. Rather than thought out" (334). He is positioning himself for metaphysical aid.

What Kenneth or Bellow means by metaphysical aid is a matter for speculation. One thing is certain: Bellow, through eloquence and strong images, does bring us to a sense of religion, and he does it perhaps more entertainingly and provocatively than does any other current American novelist. He does it by intimation rather than assertion, by a perspective of antitheses rather than direct preaching, by a comic mixture of the profound and preposterous rather than sober polemic. It would be a mistake to demand that he express his religious vision with less in-direction, for when the artist begins to think of himself as the purveyor of values, he is tempted to become self-righteous, morally secure, and just another dogmatist competing for attention in a political world. At the same time, in a world and an age in which politics is pervasive and the humanities, in Kenneth's words, are viewed as "the nursery games of mankind, which had to be left behind when the age of science began" (247), we no longer can afford art for art's sake but must appeal to our artists to conserve that sense of a higher consciousness Bellow speaks of and to make us aware of the opening to the soul. It may be that what we want and need in these times are prophets who do not think of them-selves as prophets, seekers of spiritual truth who never are satisfied with their answers.

Notes

1. Allan Bloom, *The Closing of the American Mind* (New York: Simon and Schuster, 1987), 16–17.
2. David Hume, *Dialogues Concerning Natural Religion* (New York: Hafner, 1957), 61.
3. Saul Bellow, *More Die of Heartbreak* (New York: William Morrow, 1987), 267. Further parenthetical page references will be given in the text.
4. Bloom, 13–14.
5. Nicolas Berdyaev, *Truth and Revelation* (New York: Collier, 1962), 13.
6. Ibid., 19.
7. Ralph Waldo Emerson, *The Selected Writings of Emerson,* ed. Brooks Atkinson (New York: The Modern Library), 74.
8. Quoted by Bloom, 237–38.
9. Nicolas Berdyaev, *Slavery and Freedom* (New York: Scribners and Sons, 1944), 225.
10. Ibid., 231.

The Dean Who Came In from the Cold: Saul Bellow's America of the 1980s

Gerhard Bach

I see two epochs, as though looking through open colonnades into a garden and, beyond it, into another, completely strange one: one epoch, where I am afraid to be snatched away by life from that great cosmic presentiment, the other where I will dread to leave behind this dark hot life for cosmic soaring.
—Hugo von Hofmannsthal, 1895[1]

Just because your soul is being torn to pieces doesn't mean that you stop analyzing the phenomena.
—Charlie Citrine in *Humboldt's Gift*

Dean Albert Corde, the protagonist of *The Dean's December* (1982), is no stranger to Hofmannsthal's epochal fears, but he also refuses to stop analyzing the phenomena of the world's disposition. Traversing the first of Hofmannsthal's gardens in its late twentieth-century urbanized version, and catching a glimpse of what might well be its universal counterpart, Corde, at the end of his journey, appears to have reached a typical Bellovian moment of equilibrium where he would prefer suspension among the stars in the (albeit bone-chilling) darkness of the universe to having to return to "this dark hot life" of unresolved personal qualms, societal threats, and universal ills. There is, however, that major difference of Charlie Citrine's epigrammatical reminder: Hofmannsthal's is a fear driven by hope. He clings to a *fin de siécle* Edenic view of both this world and the other, where each holds promises of such magnitude that choosing one will inevitably result in the loss of the other. In contrast, Corde's (Bellow's) is a fear of unresolve; his unrelenting wasteland-experiences on the hither side are difficult if not impossible to align with what he feels to be a universal

A version of this essay was first published in *Studies in American Jewish Literature*, 8, no. 1 (Spring 1989): 104–114.

moral issue. While Hofmannsthal's is a fear of enforced abandonment of worlds too dear to surrender, Bellow's is the modern artist's apprehension to put his shoulder of overpowering imagination to the wheel of encroaching materialism. At the end of his "long, dark month of the soul," Corde recognizes (but still fails to express in a language fully understood by his contemporaries) what Hofmannsthal eventually also accepted, namely that the two worlds he perceives are but parts of one and the same complex and disjointed reality:

> At home he set a kitchen chair out on the porch . . . . The light was the light of warmer seasons, not of deep winter. It came up from his own harmonies as well as down from above. . . . He presently felt himself being carried over the water and into the distant colors . . . . It was like being poured out to the horizon, like a great expansion. What if death should be like this, the soul finding an exit? The porch rail was his figure for the hither side. The rest, beyond it, drew you constantly as the completion of your reality.[2]

When *Mr. Sammler's Planet* appeared in 1970, critics were quick to agree that here Bellow had finally consolidated his views on American society into a normative position and in doing so had firmly established a personal platform of traditionalism against the modernism of other contemporary writers. In Sammler's plaintive question, "Who had made shit a sacrament?", Bellow was voicing, so the argument went, his own "cultured, traditional revulsion against the scatological metaphysics" of the Mailers, Barths, and Pynchons of our time.[3] It was further suggested that Bellow, in choosing the septuagenarian Artur Sammler as the propagator of his views, had in a way envisioned his own future as a writer and public figure: "Artur Sammler . . . is unmistakably a vision of his [Bellow's] own fictive career, ignored (or worse) pensioned off by the very writing it has generated" (*FP*, 3). If, for the sake of argument, we accede to this alleged pattern of self-projection, we feel compelled to put it to the test now that Bellow has reached Sammler's age—the proverbial age beyond which all time is borrowed from God. We may assume that Bellow, in making Sammler his present,

> personally, [stands] apart from all developments. From a sense of deference, from age, from good manners, he sometimes [affirms] himself to be out of it, *hors d'usage,* not a man of the times. No force of nature, nothing paradoxical or demonic, he [has] no drive for smashing through the masks of appearances. Not "Me and the Universe." (*MSP*, 110)

Is this Bellow of the 1980s, "pensioned-off," speaking against the ingrained pattern of American optimism from the safe but lonesome position of clairvoyant age, the disillusioned observer-commentator retreating to his ivory tower (which, with Flaubert, he has long known to be surrounded by a *"marais de merde"*)?[4] Has he lost touch with what is commonly accepted as "reality," and is there no urge to smash through the "masks of appearances"? *The Dean's December* as well as his more recent comments on the American condition at large provide sufficient material to clarify Bellow's present position. From these sources a new and indigenous Bellovian perspective of our age emerges: a view of the American 1980s which forcefully addresses (masked) "realities" and (unmasked) "appearances" and brings into focus the artist's struggle to find a language appropriate for describing their origins, their enactments, and their underlying mechanisms.

In his 1963 novel *The Spy Who Came In from the Cold,* John le Carrée popularized to stock-metaphor proportion the notion of post-war Eastern Europe under Communist rule as a bone-chilling, mind-freezing experience; against this he projected the notion of a comparatively warm, protective, and liberating democratic West. A distant reading of *The Dean's December* makes the novel appear to be another variant of this metaphor, and reviewers of the book were quick to respond to it, as they were to the fact that Bellow had sharpened the contrast in using two settings against which the novel unfolds: the deadeningly super-controlled icy Bucharest and a Chicago hotly running out of control. This was allegedly a modern "Tale of Two Cities," modern insofar as Bellow not only contrasted such differences as political and social structures and their implications for the individual's range of personal freedom, but that in contrasting the two cities the author also had meant to illustrate unsettling parallels between East and West, mostly relating to states of physical and societal disintegration and, in terms of their effect on the human, destructiveness and despondency. Wedged in between these two enigmas of the twentieth century struggles the protagonist, Dean Albert Corde: trying to tie together loose but related ends (Corde / rope, string); groping to penetrate—consciously, objectively and imaginatively—obvious appearances and their underlying mechanisms (Corde / heart); seeking to dissect the central nervous system of political thought and action (Corde / nerve); striving to resolve all such issues personally and communally (Corde / emotion, harmony).

If this is it, a tale of two cities/systems oscillating between difference and likeness, and many reviewers readily agreed to this notion, then it is no surprise that as a novel *The Dean's December* was widely felt to be a wearying effort, a disappointing reading assignment, another (after *Humboldt's Gift*) saddening achievement of the Nobel laureate who, by the early eighties, was desperately expected (even by his peers in the trade) "to write one of those unclassifiable American masterpieces like 'Walden.'"[5] To counteract such criticism one might first point out that the notion of "A Tale of Two Cities" oversimplifies an extremely intricate plotline with a duplex motion—back and forth as much between the two cities of Bucharest and Chicago as between action and contemplation. Functionally, Chicago is the real center of the novel, since what Corde experiences in and about Bucharest triggers off a mechanism of retrospective clarification of Chicago-based problems waiting to be resolved. Corde's distant view of events actually propels their solution in that it provides a clear frame of reference. Secondly, the "return from the cold" metaphor in this novel is tied to several options, physical (the return from Bucharest, the return from the top of the observatory at Mount Palomar) as well as spiritual (the return from destructive as well as regenerative coldness), refracting and recombining the overt polarity of East and West into ever-new constellations. Finally, there is the question of genre. If *The Dean's December*, in the pure traditional sense of the term to which all its critics tacitly cling, is judged to be a poor novel, criticism may have to reconsider its tenets: *The Dean's December*, after all, bears ample evidence of an "elective affinity" to the form of the (epistemological) essay—externally an essay about political systems East and West and how the individual manages to survive them, internally about the survivability of culture and language in an ahistorical age systematically destroying its own bases of communication.[6]

Since the publication of *The Dean's December* in 1982, Bellow has clarified some of his notions concerning the novel, mostly in interviews which, taken together, form a running commentary on the present state of America, its cultural disorientation and tortured smug pharisaical *Selbstbild*. What Bellow has to say here assumes a somewhat paradigmatic stature in that it expresses animadversions of the writer noticeably different in content, tone, and directionality from what the former critic of American "intellectual culture" had to say in the sixties and seventies. If nothing else, Bellow's tone has become less derisive (but no less witty) and noticeably so, since the Nobel lecture, the directness with which he addresses the real needs and preoccupations of man in our urbanized, technology-worshipping and commodity-ridden world expresses as much an acceptance of the public role of spokesman as the apparent desire to bring all the authority connected with it to bear.

What Bellow has to say in *The Dean's December* about the *conditio Americana* has arrested the critics' attention to such an extent that they have been content to wrestle with the factual issues the novel raises. The main argument proposed here is that such concern with the factual (i.e. with Bellow's culture-criticism per se), neither reaches the nerve center of the novel, nor fully explains Bellow's astute concern with contemporary issues. Bellow's main concern in presenting his political and social views in para-fictional terms is, as will be shown, the manner and method by which his protagonist unearths arresting cultural phenomena, and the path by which he arrives at conclusive evidence. In other words, the *how* of procedure is of greater importance to Bellow than the *what* of end results. Thus *The Dean's December*, although it does provide definite insights into the American dilemma, first and foremost concentrates on the mental, sensual, and spiritual processes instrumental in procuring such insights. Consequently, the novel establishes two prerogatives for the protagonist to contend with: in the mental-spiritual realm the refinement of thought into crystal-clear images, and in the practical realm the search for a common language with which to express these images.

The world, in trivial pursuit of "meaning," is used to rushing to conclusions and packaging them into concepts so as to have them neatly available for discourse when the situation demands. In creating Corde, Bellow rejects this intellectual diversion and its multifarious variations as mind-boggling, life-denying. Instead, he charts Corde's course as an experiential principle: if the real realities are to become visible to the inner eye, the perceptory sense with which to experience them must be readmitted to the modern mind currently devoid of imaginative powers. How does Bellow work this principal conviction into a philosophical-fictional mold?

Albert Corde's removal from his all too familiar home base in Chicago to a different type of jungle in Bucharest is an enforced displacement. Initially he dreads the thought of leaving unfinished business behind, "raging trouble" to be resolved in his absence; and Bucharest at first appears to be a setting adequate only insofar as its deathlike atmosphere conforms with Corde's death-ridden mind. Bucharest is a prison, a death-trap:

> December brown set in at about three in the afternoon. By four it had climbed down the stucco of old walls, the gray of Communist residential blocks: brown darkness took over the pavements, and then came back again from the pavements more thickly and isolated the street lamps. These were feebly yellow in the impure melancholy winter effluence. Air-sadness, Corde called this. In the final stage of dusk, a brown sediment seemed to encircle the lamps. Then there was a livid death moment. (*DD*, 3–4.)

While his wife Minna conducts their sorrowful "business" (to which in many respects the death, cremation, and burial of Minna's mother is reduced), Corde agrees to a kind of solitary confinement in Minna's old room of adolescent days. A double prison thus surrounds him: one of inner confinement within a larger societal one. But as Corde ruminates among Minna's childhood possessions, he begins to reassemble her past; this is a life of the past new to him and emblematic of the present situation, a life whose dying embers cast a gloomy light on "air-saddened" Bucharest and on what remains of Minna's family. It is a past life, nevertheless, and irretrievable, of an old European consciousness and tradition which has been crushed just as the city of Bucharest itself has been devastated in the recent (1977) earthquake. As he observes with an outwardly subdued but keen interest how people around him manage to survive and retain their humanity, a chord is struck in Corde; and his previously dulled senses of observation, perception, feeling, and imagination rekindle. Corde quickly realizes that Bucharest, in comparison to Chicago, is "quite a string of lesser evils" (*DD*, 29) that actually the "mortifying" iciness of his prison-room has a much needed mind-cleaning effect activating his dormant senses. As he goes into hiding in Minna's underheated room, the chill puts him into a trance of pure being and thus into immediate touch with a life of thought and feeling uninhibited by concepts and conscious rearrangements of impressions. He takes his cue from the flowers in his room, cyclamens which thrive and blossom in a continual state of "perfection devoid of consciousness" (*DD*, 61). The faint pattern of their leaves, "a smaller heart shape within the heart shape of the leaf" (*DD*, 156), signifies the perfect fit of the form within the mold. At the same time it is a projection of Corde's momentary predicament: to find his own spiritual "under-pattern" (*DD*, 156) within his given mold of knowledge, this "organic, constitutional, sensory oddity in which [his] soul had a lifelong freehold" (*DD*, 294).

Such a state of suspension comes as no surprise to Bellow's readers; the question, therefore, is what makes Corde different from Bellow's previous soul-searchers. Corde himself admits that "those Rilke readings hadn't been wasted: the need for pure being, the fulfillment of the soul in art, *Weltinnenraum*" (*DD*, 134). In the same train of thought, however, he returns from what is past and admits to the pressing reality of "the jungle out there" (*DD*, 134).

As Bellow proceeds to chart Corde's processes of thought, he recurrently uses two terms to signify the two elements constituting the protagonist's mental-spiritual makeup: *sense* and *soul*. Corde discovers a truth-related "sense" in himself which compels him to seek contemplative states. This sense is arresting, since it reveals that the inner and outer variants of chaos are inseparable, reciprocally conditioning and effecting, his own sense of the way things were had a strong claim on him, and he thought that if he sacrificed that sense—its truth—he sacrificed himself. Chicago was the material habitat of this sense of his, which was, in turn, the source of his description of Chicago" (*DD*, 293). In this unrestrained commitment to experiential/felt perception and sense-activated observation of the external, Corde is unlike any of the previous Bellow protagonists: unlike Augie, who sponges up "events" and knows how to skirt commitments, whose innocence is such that consultations with the soul are unnecessary since in its formative stage it is in unison with the external; unlike Sammler, who pits himself against the world, barring his vulnerable soul in moral protection against it; even unlike Citrine, who makes it his habit to "tune out" when events put him on the defensive, Corde is not yet prepared to open his soul for the world of Cantabiles to pass through and play havoc. To these, city-creatures just like Corde, their city is the reality of steel and glass and the government machine, or the vanishing protection of the middle class, or the "contempt-center of the world" (*DD*, 46). To Corde, these realities are only shadows of the real; the center of corruption lies within ourselves. Therefore, his is a search for "everyman's *inner* inner city, . . . the slums we carry around inside us" (*DD*, 228). It is this internal wasteland of the mind and the soul where civilization must begin to purge and resurrect itself.

The recovery of the real hidden within its own shadow begins for Bellow with the discovery of "sense" buried in the self. Bellow quickly establishes that he does not bear in mind the common concept of passive sense-impressions when he uses the term. Instead, he thinks of it as a propellant, an *agens* that energizes the *power of pure perception* (pure in being exempt from hardened concepts), and the *power of imagination*. Once activated, these senses become Corde's tools with which to investigate the phenomena of the external world. His investigation, quite methodically, takes him through the stages of observation, contemplation, objectivation, and resolve. Their regenerative and creative "home base" is what Bellow (disturbingly to many) calls the soul. The real becomes real ("the truth") only when the soul has taken hold of it and cleansed it from the mind-cluttering world of ready-made concepts which suffocate the self and the real. Consequently, Corde accepts it as his moral task to "recover the world that is buried under the debris of false description of non-experience," (*DD*, 270) and so he takes it upon himself "to pass Chicago through his own soul. A mass of data, terrible, murderous. It was no easy matter to put such things through. But there was no other way for reality to happen. Reality didn't exist 'out there.' It began to be real only when the soul found its underlying truth" (*DD*, 294–295).

Americans, Bellow has long been convinced, are not comfortable with matters of the "soul," except when they can be discussed. Then the term is either deflected into a vague, impressionistic otherworldly quasi-religious or quasi-sexual context, or it is extracted from the unconscious to be measured psychoanalytically. Bellow summed up his disdain in the "Interview with Myself" (1975): "To possess your soul for a few minutes you need the help of medical technology."[7] And there is no better indicator of Bellow's indignation with the soul's marketability than the cynical joke told in "Him With His Foot in His Mouth" (1984) about the celebrity who, after announcing that she was going to write her biography, was asked whether she was going to do it on a typewriter or an adding-machine.

Bellow's use of "soul" or related terms of spiritual life can be traced back to the beginning of his career—viz. the "Spirit of Alternatives" debating with Joseph in *Dangling Man*, and Dostoevsky's influence as *spiritus rector* has been duly recorded. Essays and interviews abound with matters pertaining to the life of the soul. Initially, Bellow flirts with the cryptic: in the early sixties he claims for instance the existence of "a great and eternal living truth, at once illuminating everything," which comes forth from "the very center" of those seemingly insignificant Dostoevskian protagonists after whom Joseph (*Dangling Man*) is fashioned.[8] The dilemma of the sixties, Bellow claims, was that people looked to the arts for enchantment but their own skepticism barred them from finding it. In "Skepticism and the Depth of Life," he notes that the modern reader has become increasingly reluctant to believe in "an added dimension or quality of existence."[9] The seventies are characterized by a battle Bellow wages against the denial of inner realities, initially against the pre-emptive claims of modern scientific thought and pragmatism: "Why, since the unconscious is by definition what we do not know, should we not expect to find in it traces of the soul as well as of aggression?"[10] Then he carries the battle to his own artistic grounds in claiming that art is meant to induce us to temporarily suspend all activities and to lead us to "contemplative states, . . . sacred states of the soul" ("IM," 55). Such claims, Bellow admits, are not without conflict: what draws us to a writer at the same time makes us wary of his "premises," since the source of this attraction is "an inadmissible resource, something we all hesitate to mention though we all know it intimately—the soul" ("WTM," 8). The Nobel as backbone, Bellow begins to address the issue even more forcefully in the mid-seventies and is branded by the intellectual community, which he holds in part responsible, as anti-intellectual "moral majority." All that he claims, though, is that there is a strong gravitational force pulling mankind away from itself into a collective stupor: "the individual struggles with dehumanization for the possession of the soul."[11] America of the eighties no longer is the place (as had been the Chicago of immigrants in the early 1900s) where, for lack of a supportive tradition and culture, "Your soul made—no, burnt—its own clearing" (qtd. in "SB," 267). This forgotten need of cultivating human impulses and spiritual capacities has succumbed to external prerogatives of cultivating style rather than substances: "To have a soul, to *be* one—that today is a revolutionary defiance of received opinion."[12]

Originally, then, Bellow had posited a polarity between the inner man and the outer world, where the life of the soul needed to protect itself (in detachment or introversion) against life-destroying externals (materialism or technology). This negative dialectic changes in a process of gradual metamorphoses to a syncretic reinstatement of the real through art. If contemporary America (and for that matter, the world at large) is to be understood, its phenomena must be liberated from their suffocated, shadow-like state. Hegel's *Zeitgeist* is invoked here, that spirited force by which man defines his era (cf. Hofmannsthal's telluric and cosmic gardens); this force, Corde claims, "is in us by nature" (*DD,* 269), and it must be resurrected from what otherwise would remain an abstract *Scheinwirklichkeit,* an ersatz-world of appearances burying itself under ever new and ever noisier concepts. Whether we turn to *The Dean's December* for evidence or to Bellow's non-fictional sources, the tenor of a new form of an unrestrained moral commitment to involve the soul in the affairs of the practical world reverberates strongly: "Unless you pass [the world] through your own soul, you can't understand it," Bellow categorically declares, claiming that the vicious circle in which this process is entangled will continue to characterize our era: "We live in this alleged age of communication, which comes in the form of distracting substitutes for reality. But the reality in our day comes from art. And we live in a country that has ruled this off limits" ("KMS," 50).

What images, then, appear before the perceptive mind as America is passed through the soul? And what imaginations does the soul create in turn? Bellow sums up the social context of these questions in a recent "Foreword" to a collection of lectures by Rudolph Steiner on *The Boundaries of Natural Science:* "We cannot even begin to think of social renewal until we have considered these questions. What is reality in the civilized West? 'A world of outsides without insides,' . . . of quantities without qualities, of souls devoid of mobility and of communities which are more dead than alive."[13] The central image expressive of this apocalyptic state of "civilized" society is the modern American city in collapse. New York, and, more persistently and imminently, Chicago have served as the settings for Bellow's apocalyptic nightmares. But the city is not simply a physical reality of doom functioning as a naturalistic backdrop to the writer's message. More prominently, it reflects a state of mind. In this its reciprocal nature, the city as an internal as well as an external reality is emblematic of the *conditio humana* in an outgoing twentieth century. Its physical impact on the spiritual life of man is extensive, as it relentlessly forces brutal principles of survival but also its moods of self-destruction on the soul's defenseless impregnability. Chicago's physical and social decomposition, for instance, is paralleled only by its moral, cultural disintegration. The realities governing today's Chicago are a sharp contrast to what Bellow maintains was once, from about 1900 to 1929, an ethnically and culturally diversified, lively city in which the immigrant was free to stake his material, cultural, and spiritual ground. The "old materialistic innocense has disappeared—florid bars, good carriage horses, substantial Victorian virtues, substantial carnality. . . . The crass, dirty, sinful, vulgar, rich town of politicians, merchant princes and land speculators. . . . has vanished" ("ISB," 637). Augie's Chicago was a city of innocent vulgarity; it is now a "synthetic Chicago" ("ISB," 635), "inhabited principally by philistines" ("SB," 267), divided along racial lines by "black politicians and white city-council crooks" ("ISB," p. 638). It is taboo to address violence and crime in the context of racial issues. The public is terrified by what it reads daily in the press, but it is too stupefied to speak out. And "the more the public learns, the more its paralysis increases" ("ISB," 638). As severely as Bellow criticizes the present situation, he accepts being part of it: "Inevitably, you invest your vital substance in familiar surroundings," he admits, and thus Chicago is "one of the larger provinces" of his psychic life ("ISB," 636, 635) in much the same way as Dublin had been genesis and paralysis for Joyce. There also is a cunning flirtatiousness with the vulgar when Bellow today claims a distinct preference for Chicago's "untroubled vulgarity" ("KMS," 54) over the "bogus 'culture' " of New York or San Francisco, cities which give us nothing "except the *air* of having something" ("SB," 266). Chicago is "vulgar but it's vital and it's more American, more representative" ("TSB," 60). As he collects materials for what originally was to be a non-fiction book on "his" city, Bellow realizes that all "factual" approaches to solving its internal problems so far have failed since they have followed a technological, bureaucratic, and completely unimaginative course. Apparently no one has felt the need to address such problems in an immediate, sensitive manner. This is Dean Albert Corde's moment: with his inception Bellow addresses

> the American denial of real reality, our devices for evading it, our refusal to face what is all too obvious and palpable. The book is filled with protest against this evasion, against the techniques of illusion and the submission to taboos by means of which this is accomplished. Corde thinks that we are becoming wraiths, spooks. It seems to him that we have lost all capacity for dealing with experience—no capacity to think about it, no language for it, no words. ("SB," 270)

In *The Dean's December,* then, Bellow creates a series of images in which these realities hardened into dead concepts ("shadows," "appearances") are symbolically contracted. Some of these images gain an additional dimension in that they are parallel exemplifications, East (Bucharest) and West (Chicago), of the same basic pattern, or paired associations of the one basic idea. The differences Bellow sees in these double representations, as prominent as they may be historically and politically, fade before their impinging societal similarities. Appearances may differ, Bellow insists, but once their deceptive shadows are discarded, the reality of their likeness is clear and distinct.

Corde's rekindled senses of perception and imagination gradually focus his perceptive mind on the underlying hidden realities. This is a slow and painful process, as painful as the clarifying Bucharest coldness in which it takes place. Still in Chicago, Corde's will had on occasion slackened, and he had succumbed to that classic Bellovian retreat into the self. But then "you tire of this preoccupation with the condition of being cut off and it seems better to go out and see at first hand the big manifestations of disorder and take a fresh reading from them" (*DD,* 181). He moves to Bucharest with "all the Chicago perplexities . . . injected into his nerves" (*DD,* 21). But the task of charting present conditions is extremely exasperating and Corde must force himself to put events and experiences into the proper perspective. "Begin with the crying ugliness of the Chicago night," he admonishes himself. "Put that in the center" (*DD,* 48). This perspective uncovers a city of unrest, upheaval, destruction, corruption and compromise, built on a vast sewage system into which its shiny "Magnificent Mile" is destined to topple. Leaving the city for the airport, its appalling waste is once more impressed on Corde:

> Winter's first blizzard had struck Chicago. The cab was overheated and stank of excrement. Of dogs? of people? It was torrid, also freezing; Arctic and Sahara, mixed. Also, the driver was sloshed with eau de cologne. The ribbed rubber floor was all filth and grit. Corde said, "People have even stopped wiping themselves." He took the precaution of saying this in French, and there was something false about that—raunchy gaiety (and disgust) in a foreign language (*DD,* 20)

Cynicism is not a redeeming approach, however, and therefore it falls on dead ears; but ironically, the full impact of this event comes clear to Corde later in Bucharest where he finds himself in a similar squeeze of imprisonment between killing heat and numbing cold, a predicament which culminates in a moment of existential fear in the crematorium. Horror cancels out cynicism and enforces a clear view of the final options:

> It was a tight fit in the staircase . . . . On the first landing it was cold
> again. Corde felt cut in half by the extremes of heat and cold . . . .
> Better this cold than that heat. Corde's breast, as narrow as a ladder,
> was crowded with emotions—fire, death, suffocation, put into an icy
> hold or instead, crackling in a furnace. Your last options. They still
> appeared equally terrible. How to choose between them! (*DD*, 237)

Similar terms of imprisonment and devastation had been discerned
by Corde in the Chicago governmental machine, the dead brain center
of the city creating an environment where human needs are defined by
their marketability. Among the typical urban Americans of the Chicago
species Zaehner, Corde's former brother-in-law, is an outstanding example. He combines in his person all the despicable but socially admired
traits of that "special breed" (*DD*, 35) of the Chicago insider: "A big fellow,
he was forceful, smart, cynical, political, rich, and he had no use for those
who weren't. In the city that worked, he was one of those who gave people
the works" (*DD*, 92). The more subdued but equally dangerous version of
this "breed" is found in the educated, cultured intellectuals, such as the
black ambassador in Bucharest, the busy official perpetuating the government machine from the wings just as perfectly as, at the other end of the
spectrum, the Rumanian colonel in charge of the Bucharest hospital
machine and also the journalist Dewey Spangler, who controls the media
with his weekly "crisis-chatter" (*IM*, 55).[14] These "princely communicators"
are part of America's "cultural intelligentsia" which has been a source of
constant exasperation for Bellow; they have been bred in the universities
and apprenticed in the media, and from them issues the real danger of
self-perpetuating thought control in the form of ignorant, philistine
culture-discourse. Bellow shares with Corde the contempt for American
higher education, the breeding ground of submissiveness to "facts" depart-
mentalized into so-called sciences. And it is only by "strength, luck, and
cunning" that people emerge unharmed from "the heaving wastes of the
American educational system" (*IM*, 56). The university's perpetration of
intellectualism and the skills of discourse as substitutes for education have
supported the hardening class-structure of American society. There is no
clearer indication of this for Corde than the reaction of his own university to the murder of a black student and Corde's subsequent involvement
in the case as it goes to court. Not that he regrets the loss of his job (he
feels elated), what disturbs him is the double standard the university exposes as just another variation of America's inability or unwillingness to
solve the problems of the black underclass, which a business-pious society deems "economically redundant"; it is "locked into a culture of despair
and crime . . . . There is not culture there, it's only a wilderness, and damn

monstrous, too. We are talking about a people consigned to destruction, a doomed people. . . . We do not know how to approach this population. We haven't even conceived that reaching it may be a problem. So there's nothing but death before it" (*DD*, 228–29). In this projection of another holocaust, entire cities are being written off, blacks, Puerto Ricans, the aged: "Let them be ruined, die and eliminate themselves. There are some who seem to be willing that this should happen" (*DD*, 253–54).

The distant, Bucharest-view of Chicago reveals to Corde that in the East and West alike urban societies are being stripped of their traditions and history. To substitute for this loss and to fend off the realization of doom, the city assumes a shadow-like existence, it becomes a collection of concepts and moods. However distorted or painful the individual's limited emotional view of his city is, these emotions are taken to be the city's reality. "Thus, Cain's city built with muder, and other cities built with Mystery, or Pride, all of them emotional conditions and great centers of delusion and bondage, death" (*DD*, 316). In Corde's/Bellow's own city murder, mystery (the lost Atlantis), and pride (Babylon) are also the combined foundations, but these realities are publicly declared taboo. Chicago has vested itself with the appearance of authority, changing the American ideal into distorting and devastating concepts. Liberty, equality, and justice now are commodities for those who can afford them, i.e. they are not available to the "economically redundant" except in their negative, punitive version. The city authorities, supported by the educational establishment and the media entrap the public in a "Great Noise that destroys meaning" (*SB*, 273). Realities are suffocated in a melange of discourse and communication, and the public, unable to apprehend its own predicament, goes into a stupor. The Great Noise assumes totalitarian dimension; it deafens all resistance. This threat of Western totalitarianism convinces Corde that the task of retrieving the realities buried under the garbage of communication is a pressing moral issue. Unless it is resolved, American civilization will disappear into its self-created *marais de merde*, and society will find itself on the brink of another apocalypse.

Corde's first moment of awareness of the impending crisis comes as he stands at the top of the winding staircase in the American embassy looking down. Its banister coiling inward like a nautilus shell forces his mind to confront the center of the existential dilemma. And here, in a similar, if reversed vision to the one to come on Mount Palomar, Bellow has Corde experience his personal circumstances as the fate of twentieth-century man. What he witnesses as deformity, decline, and death is not just an exaggeration of a tense mind but the state of things at large.

> No, it wasn't only two, three, five chosen deaths being painted thickly, terribly, convulsively inside him, all over his guts, liver, heart, over all his organs, but a large picture of cities, crowds, peoples, an apocalypse, with images and details supplied by his own disposition, observation, by ideas, dreams, fantasies, his peculiar experience of life. (*DD*, 77)

Paralysis and death are the symptoms of an impending collapse. There is no surer indication of this for Corde than the Beech-findings about dangerous levels of lead poisoning threatening drastic mutations in human life. But Corde refuses to accept the mode of thought in which "hard" science presents these discoveries, their direct material causes and consequences as a cause-effect chain which nicely serves to explain everything from crime to social disintegration, directly suggesting that given a balanced diet mankind could put earth back in balance. Earlier in Bucharest, Corde involuntarily remembers Goya's painting of Saturn, the leaden, "saturnine" planet,—"the naked, squatting giant, open-mouthed, devouring" (*DD*, 71). Puzzled, he ascribes the momentary vision to his hypersensitive nerves; the apocalyptic context remains, as yet, cryptic. In the wake of Beech's discoveries, however, Corde establishes the link. "Here was an apocalypse—yet another apocalypse to set before the public. It wouldn't be easy. The public was used to doom warnings; seasoned, hell—it was marinated in them . . . . *Homo sapiens sapiens* was incapable of hearing earth's own poetry, or, now, its plea. Man would degrade himself into an inferior hominid" (*DD*, 154–55).

Again Bellow's main concern is reflected in the imagery he creates to find a language which will adequately and understandably render the powerful images which the inner eye perceives. It is well worth remembering that Corde had once before attempted to do something like this in a kind of reportorial documentary on his home city, which was published in *Harper's* and, if Spangler's judgment accounts for anything, had completely failed. Initially, Corde had suspected the reason for the failure to be a matter of style (which Spangler had been quick to deride as the "drone of poetry"); now, as the Beech-case opens up before him, he realizes that it was not the words he used that failed him but that modern society, so used to warnings of doom, prefers to cling to its emotional views and distorted concepts of reality. Reassured that the only language possible to reach the core is a language inspired by the powers of perception and imagination, the language of art, Corde decides to join the Beech-project, neither as moralist nor as prophet, but solely as an *interpres* of the findings of "hard" science.

Finally, then, Bellow's intention in making Corde team up with Beech is clear. The "Tale of Two Cities," which has unexpectedly evolved as a treatise on the disintegration of language and the death of communication, approaches its final turn. Lead poisoning becomes the contracted symbol of the apocalypse. "Hard" science has lost its power to express and explain what it finds. Beech needs Corde to put his discoveries into an ancient but forgotten and therefore new language, *ars poetica*, which refuses to give up its high moral claims. The ability to put Beech's disturbing scientific results into the reality of their social context also reveals to Corde that this haunting "inability to find the adequate attitude" (*DD*, 71) is giving way to clairvoyant states. "If there are mysterious forces around, only exaggeration can help us see them" (*DD*, 250). But this sense of (artistic) exaggeration is a rare sense, and although a people severed from its own defining basis of history and culture is likely to brand this sense with another "concept"-term, as Vlada does when she calls Corde an incorrigible "romantic" (*DD*, 250), Corde's now balanced self-assurance remains undisturbed.

The Dean's December culminates in Corde's and Minna's ascent to the center of the dome of the Mount Palomar observatory. Criticism has it that this episode reflects the standard Bellow-device of a final epistemological tableau, leaving the reader to take his options: A "Dangling Dean",[15] with "A Foot in the Stockyard and an Eye on the Stars"?[16] "A Whirling Soul" (*TT*, 126), or a "Reformer"?[17] Initially, Dean Corde had established *terra firma* as his "beat," quietly admiring his wife's ability to "bring together a needle from one end of the universe with a thread from the opposite end" (*DD*, 15). Apparently, nothing has changed towards the end. Leaving his wife to her task of closing herself in with the stars, Corde still admits her to be his "representative among those bright things so thick and close" (*DD*, 346). To deny the dean an end to his dangling would leave us an Albert Corde in the guise of an Artur Sammler, and consequently a Bellow recoiling to the noncommittal "Not me and the Universe" of the sixties. But this is not so: in accepting the challenge of the Beech-project, Corde answers affirmatively to the universe's calling; he himself has become a representative, explaining to the modern technological, science-bound(ed) mind its own secret realities. If at the outset of the novel Corde muses about the needle-thread-metaphor and admits that he has no clear concept of "what there was to be sewn" (*DD*, 15), the cleansing coldness of the universe no longer leaves a doubt about the meaning of the message to be deciphered—contemporary Americans, those "civilized barbarians," must look for the essence of the inanimate and the animate world within themselves, "down to the very blood and the crystal forms inside [their] bones." (*DD*, 345). Here Bellow takes recourse with a new image to an old idea which he had issued in passing almost twenty years before, namely that "There may be some truths which are, after all, our friends in the universe." But then Bellow has long been a lonesome voice in the epistemological wilderness to a distraught (American) civilization which, in its hystery over the countdown to the dawning of a new century apparently cannot wait to hasten away from the one it threatens to leave behind in shambles.

Notes

1. Author's translation of: *"Ich sehe zwei Epochen, wie durch offene Säulengänge in einen Garten und jenseits wieder in einen ganz fremden: eine Epoche wo ich Angst habe, durch das Leben dem grossen kosmischen Ahnen entrissen zu werden, die zweite wo mir davor grauen wird, für kosmisches Schweben das dunkle heisse Leben zu verlassen."*

2. Saul Bellow, *The Dean's December* (New York: Pocket Books, 1983), 321; further references will be cited parenthetically as *DD*. References to *Mr. Sammler's Planet* (Harmondsworth, England: Penguin, 1972), will be *MSP*.

3. Frank D. McConnell, *Four Postwar American Novelists: Bellow, Mailer, Barth and Pynchon* (Chicago: University of Chicago Press, 1977), 4. Subsequent references, abbreviated *FP*, are given parenthetically in the text.

4. Saul Bellow, "The University as Villain," *Nation* 185 (16 November 1957): 362.

5. John Updike, "Toppling Towers Seen by a Whirling Soul," *New Yorker*, 22 February 1982, 126. Subsequent references in the text are abbreviated *TT*.

6. The essay, traditionally the preferred form used to express one's perception of reality (and perhaps, artistically expand its meaning, as Emerson had done), has lost much ground in an age surrendering to the factual. Bellow's "conservationist" position is reflected in his repeated references to Montaigne, Goethe, Schopenhauer and, closer to our century, Wells, Wilde, Valéry, Mann, and Musil. For factual support compare Bellow's original plans to write a nonfiction work about Chicago (William Kennedy, "If Saul Bellow Doesn't Have a Word to Say, He Keeps His Mouth Shut," *Esquire* 97 (February 1982): 49–54. Subsequent references given as *KMS;* Michiko Kakutani, "A Talk with Saul Bellow: On His Work and Himself," *New York Times Book Review* 48 (13 December 1981), rpt. in *Dialogue* (1981): 57–60. Subsequent references are given in the text as *TSB),* and his remark about the "nonfiction novelistic style" of *The Dean's December:* "But I wasn't thinking 'novel' when I wrote the book. I was dealing with a sort of mind rather than with a literary form" (Matthew C. Roudané, "An Interview with Saul Bellow," *Contemporary Literature* 25 (1984): 265–80. Subsequent references will be given in the text as *SB*.

7. Saul Bellow, "An Interview with Myself," *New Review* 2, no. 18 (1975): 54. Subsequent references, abbreviated as *IM*, are given parenthetically in the text.

8. Saul Bellow, "Facts that Put Fancy to Flight: A Novelist-Critic Discusses the Role of Reality in the Creation of Fiction," *New York Times Book Review* 22 (February 1962): 28.

9. Saul Bellow, "Skepticism and the Depth of Life," *The Arts and the Public,* ed. James Miller and P. D. Herrings (Chicago: University of Chicago Press, 1967), 28.

10. "A World Too Much With Us," *Critical Inquiry* 2 (1975): 9. Subsequent references will be given parenthetically in the text as *WTM.*

11. "The Nobel Lecture," *American Scholar* 46 (1977): 71–77, rpt. in *Dictionary of Literary Biography—Documentary Series: An Illustrated Chronicle* 3, ed. Mary Bruccoli (Detroit: Gale Research Co., 1983), 68.

12. Rockwell Gray, Harry White, and Gerald Nemanic, "Interview with Saul Bellow," *TriQuarterly* 60 (1984): 634. Subsequent references will be given parenthetically in the text as *ISB.*

13. Saul Bellow, "Foreword" to *The Boundaries of Natural Science,* by Rudolf Steiner (Spring Valley, N.Y.: Anthroposophical Press, 1983), xii–xiii.

14. Dewey Spangler's actual forerunners in the trade are dealt with *in extenso* in *To Jerusalem and Back: A Personal Account* (New York: Viking Press, 1976), where Bellow severely chides American political journalism for playing all too willingly into the hands of reality-distorters: "Our media make crisis chatter out of news and fill our minds with anxious phantoms of the real thing—a summit in Helsinki, a treaty in Egypt, a constitutional crisis in India, a vote in the U.N., the financial collapse of New York. We can't avoid being politicized (to use a word as murky as the condition it describes) because it is necessary after all to know what is going on. Worse yet, what is going on will not let us alone. Neither the facts nor the deformations, the insidious latitudes of the media (tormenting because the underlying realities are so huge and terrible), can be screened out" (21).

15. Jonathan Wilson, "Bellow's Dangling Dean," *The Literary Review* 26 (Fall 1982): 164–75.

16. Gabriel Josipovici, "A Foot in the Stockyard and an Eye on the Stars," *Times Literary Supplement,* 2 April 1982, 371.

17. Diane Johnson, "Saul Bellow as Reformer," *Terrorists and Novelists* (New York: Alfred A. Knopf, 1982), 134–40.

18. Gordon L. Harper, "Saul Bellow," *The Paris Review Interviews,* 3d ser., ed. George Plimpton (New York: Viking, 1978), 196.

LIST OF CONTRIBUTORS

H. PORTER ABBOTT is Professor of English at the University of California, Santa Barbara. He is the author of *The Fiction of Samuel Beckett: Form and Effect* (1973), and *Diary Fiction: Writing As Action* (1984). Much of his recent work has been devoted to the subject of autobiography.

ADA AHARONI is a Professor in the General Studies Department at the Technicon in Haifa. She is the author of twelve books, the latest of which is *The Second Exodus,* a historical novel on the Egyptian Jews. She teaches modern poetry, women in literature, comparative literature, Saul Bellow, and the contemporary novel. She is also a noted Israeli poet and Executive Director of the Haifa Chapter of the Saul Bellow Society.

GERHARD BACH is Professor of American Studies at the Paedagogische Hochschule Hiedelberg, Germany. During 1985/86 he was Fulbright Senior Lecturer at West Virginia University. His publications include books and articles on modern American drama, fiction, film, and literature, educational psychology, and English as a Foreign Language methodology. He is currently working on a book on Saul Bellow's urban imagery and is a member of the Executive Board of the Saul Bellow Society.

MICHAEL O. BELLAMY is Associate Professor of English at the College of St. Thomas in St. Paul, Minnesota where he teaches American literature, and literature and psychology. He is also Director of Writing-Across-the-Curriculum.

JO BRANS taught English at Southern Methodist University 1970–1984 and has published numerous articles on American literature. She has been the recipient of the McGinnis Award for Nonfiction. Her book publications include *Mother, I Have Something to Tell You* (1987) and *Listen to the Voices* (1988). Her third book, *Take Two,* will be published in 1989 by Doubleday.

ALLAN CHAVKIN is Professor of English at Southwest Texas State University. He has published over thirty articles on nineteenth-century romanticism and twentieth-century American literature. He is currently writing a book on modern American literature and the romantic tradition while on a National Endowment for the Humanities Fellowship. He teaches courses in composition and American literature.

GLORIA L. CRONIN is Associate Professor of English at Brigham Young University, Provo, Utah. She is Associate Editor of the *Saul Bellow Journal* and of *Pacific Studies*. She is Executive Director of the Saul Bellow Society. Her *Saul Bellow: Annotated Bibliography* was published by Garland Press in 1987. Currently she teaches American Jewish literature, women's literature, contemporary American literature, and composition. She is presently collaborating with L. H. Goldman on a gender studies approach to Saul Bellow's novels.

DANIEL FUCHS is Professor of English at The College of Staten Island, City University of New York. He has been Senior Fulbright Lecturer in American literature at the University of Nantes, the University of Vienna, and recently at the John F. Kennedy Institute of American Studies at the University of Berlin. He is the author of *The Comic Spirit of Wallace Stevens* (1963) and *Saul Bellow: Vision and Revision* (1984).

SUSAN GLICKMAN is an Assistant Professor of English and Canada Research Fellow in the Department of English at the University of Toronto. She is the author of two books of poetry, *Complicity* (1983) and *The Power to Move* (1986). She is currently working on a study of the English Canadian lyric, a book of short stories, and a new book of poetry entitled "Henry Moore's Sheep."

L. H. GOLDMAN is Assistant Professor at Michigan State University's American Thought Department. She is the Editor of the *Saul Bellow Journal,* President of the Saul Bellow Society, and the author of *Saul Bellow's Moral Vision: A Critical Study of the Jewish Experience* (1983). She is presently collaborating with Gloria L. Cronin on a gender studies approach to Saul Bellow's novels.

JUDIE NEWMAN is a lecturer in the Department of English Literature at the University of Newcastle, England. She has published *Saul Bellow and History* (1984) and *John Updike* (1988), as well as many scholarly articles for British and American periodicals. Her *Nadine Gordimer* appeared in 1988.

ELLEN PIFER is an Associate Professor of English and Comparative Literature at the University of Delaware. She is the author of *Nabokov and the Novel* (1980) and the editor of *Critical Essays on John Fowles* (1986). She has published extensively on modern and contemporary fiction and is currently completing a book on Saul Bellow's novels.

MATTHEW C. ROUDANÉ is Associate Professor of English at Georgia State University where he teaches American literature. His books include *Understanding Edward Albee* (1987) and *Toward the Marrow: Who's Afraid of Virginia Woolf* (forthcoming). He is the editor of three other works: *Conversations with Arthur Miller* (1987); *Contemporary American Dramatists* (1988); and *Public Issues, Private Tensions: Contemporary American Drama* (1988). He serves on the boards of five scholarly journals and published an interview with Saul Bellow in *Contemporary Literature* (1984).

MARIANN RUSSELL is Professor of English at Sacred Heart University in Bridgeport, Connecticut. She is a specialist in modern British literature and Afro-American literature and the author of *Melvin B. Tolson's Harlem Gallery: A Literary Analysis* (1981), completed while on a National Endowment for the Humanities Fellowship.

BEN SIEGEL is Professor of English at California State Polytechnic University, Pomona. He has chaired the department and directed the Annual Conferences in Modern American Writing held at the University's Kellogg West Center for Continuing Education. His books, alone or in collaboration, include *The Puritan Heritage: America's Roots in the Bible* (1964); *Biography Past and Present: Isaac Bashevis Singer* (1969); *The Controversial Sholem Asch* (1976); and *The American Writer and the University* (1988). His critical essays deal with such writers as Saul Bellow, Bernard Malamud, Philip Roth, and Daniel Fuchs. He is now on the editorial boards of *Studies in American Literature, Contemporary Literature, Arete, Journal of Popular Culture, Journal of American Culture, Saul Bellow Journal,* and *Yiddish.*

STEPHEN L. TANNER is Professor of English at Brigham Young University, Provo, Utah where he teaches American literature. He has been a Senior Fulbright Lecturer in Brazil in 1974–76 and again in 1983, as well as in Portugal in 1979. His books include *Ken Kesey* (1983), *Paul Elmer Moore* (1987), and *Lionel Trilling* (forthcoming). He is the author of numerous articles on American literature.

MOLLY STARK WEITING is the founding President of the Saul Bellow Society. Her dissertation, "The Quest For Order: The Novels of Saul Bellow," was completed at The University of Texas at Austin in 1969.

MICHAEL G. YETMAN is an Associate Professor of English at Purdue University, where he teaches romanticism and Victorian literature. He has published on these topics in numerous scholarly journals and held a Fulbright Senior Lecturer's position at Beijing University during 1981–82. He is currently finishing a manuscript entitled "China Days" about his teaching and living experience in China.

INDEX

Esquire, 144
"Esthétique du Mal," 265
Eternal Husband, 134 note 6
Evergreen Review, 144
existentialism, 147, 288; aesthetic,
295; in American Dream, An, 224;
religious, in More Die of Heartbreak,
286–87

Fallaci, Oriana, 252
Fear and Trembling, 242
feminism, 4
Fiedler, Leslie, 4–5, 95, 101–02,
144–45, 220
Finnegans Wake, 151
Fischer, D. H., 21
Fisher King legend, 197–98
Fitzgerald, F. Scott, 139, 145, 279,
282–83 note 14
Fixer, The, 259
Flaubert, Gustav, 68, 299
Four Postwar American Novelists, 211
Fraiberg, Selma, 42
Frankenstein, 123
Fraser, James, 197
freedom, in The Dangling Man, 97;
theme of, 60
Frege, Gottlob, 281
French symbolists, 146
Freud, Sigmund, 3, 17–18, 27–50,
123–24, 150, 217; and art, 40–41;
and murder, 38; and myth, 32; as
humanist, 44
Freudianism, 194, 197; parodied in
Henderson the Rain King, 197–98
Fromm, Erich, 35, 36, 37
Fuchs, Daniel, 2, 3, 27–50
Future of an Illusion, The, 33, 38, 39

Gallow, David D., 1
Gestalt psychology and Bellow, 150
Ghiberti, Lorenzo, 13
Gide, Andre, 140
Giles Goat Boy, 211

Gilson, Étienne, 228, 232, 233, 243
Glamour, 140
Glassman, Susan, 111 note 12
Glickman, Susan, 7–8, 73, 211–25
God, Bellow's view of, 54, 223; in
Mr. Sammler's Planet, 223
Goethe, Johann Wolfgang von, 156,
311 note 6
Goldman, L. H., 2, 3, 9, 51–66
"Gonzaga Manuscripts," 135 note 6
Goshkin, Anita, 111 note 12
Gothic fiction, 194
Grail legend, 197–200
Great Gatsby, The, 282–83 note 14
Greenberg, Clement, 140
Guide of the Perplexed, 52

Hamlet, 38
Harris, Mark, 2
Hartman, David, 52
Hartman, Geoffrey, 224
Hawthorne, Nathaniel, 296
Hearst, William Randolph, 144
Heart of Darkness, 70
Hegel, Georg William Friedrich, 22,
174, 275, 290, 305
Heidegger, Martin, 62, 225 note 15
Hemingway, Ernest, 116–17, 139,
145, 196; influence on Bellow, 2,
134 note 4; parodied in Henderson
the Rain King, 194
Henderson the Rain King, 6–7, 28, 35,
48, 69–70, 71, 73, 81, 87–89, 104,
117–18, 121, 135 note 6; 175–78,
247, 261, 268, 290, 306; and The
Dean's December, 275; and Nietzsche,
192 note 6; animal motifs in,
186–90; comedy in, 260; superman
in 186–90; time in, 15–19
Heraclitus, 13
hero and anti-hero, in The Dangling
Man, 163–75
heroism, parodied in Henderson the
Rain King, 196–98

Saul Bellow in the 1980s

Production Editor: Julie L. Loehr
Design: Lynne A. Brown
Proofreader: Martha A. Bates

Text Composed by Lansing Graphics, Inc.
on a Compugraphic 8400
in New Baskerville

Printed by Thomson-Shore, Inc.
on 60# Glatfelter Springforge White text
with Rainbow Antique Royal C endsheets

Bound in Holliston Peacock 10 point
Lexotone 41005 cloth and stamped in silver